I know th[barcode: P9-CNF-707]at will remain in my repertoire for a long time. —Stacey S. ✣ As the year draws to a close, I want to thank you for your contribution to my family's well-being and pleasure this year. I cooked many (many!) recipes from your NYTimes blog and with such wonderful results. For Christmas Eve, we had the bean/farro/cabbage/squash soup—astonishing! And tonight, not expecting to be cooking, I ended up using the rest of my cabbage for the cabbage/lentil/potato stew. —Patty D. ✤ I've wanted to write to you for some time to let you know how much I love your *Recipes for Health* column on NYTimes.com. It is often the first thing I read regularly in the *Times* online. I love not only your recipes but the wonderful articles which accompany them and the terrific photos. —G.M. "Mick" T. ✤ I just want to say thank you, thank you, thank you. With a baby and cooking just for two, it's hard to make something simple but tasty . . . a lot of recipes have too many steps and the healthy ones usually just taste so-so. Yours are actually yummy! —Lee F. ✤ Just a note of appreciation for the many recipes of yours that I've captured from the NYTimes and for the cooking wisdom I've acquired from using them. If someone says, "Hey, I'm getting a bumper crop of zucchini in my garden," I say, "Let's ask Martha!" My friends and I have had many a fine meal, thanks to you, and we have all become better cooks as a result. Thanks again for sharing. —Gib A.

✦ We love your recipes and can't imagine a day without Martha!!! —Marie B. ✦ I just wanted to let you know how much I appreciate your NYTimes recipes. I haven't tried one my husband and I have not liked. Your way of cooking—lots of dried beans, vegetables, olive oil, and cheese only to set off the main dish—is precisely the way I like to cook. Thank you. —Marie H. ✦ Thank you for doing such a great job of bringing ease, health, and taste to the kitchen—your recipes are little, joyful, "That sounds amazing!" moments. —Luke P. ✦ Your *Recipes for Health* column is one of the highlights of my week! —Carol N. ✦ I regularly follow your recipes at NYTimes, and I have learned so much from them. Thank you for changing so many of our diets and minds! —Megan P. ✦ Thank you for such sophisticated, yet wholesome, healthy recipes. —Pat W. ✦ My boyfriend happens to be from Nice, France, and he has remarked many times on some of your Provençal dishes tasting just like—sometimes even better than—the ones his mother makes. You have brought much joy to the kitchen and dining table of our small California apartment! Thanks for sharing your incredible talents. ✦ I have been a vegetarian since the age of 12 and often find it difficult to track down sophisticated vegetarian recipes that go beyond tofu stir-fry or homey comfort foods. So I really appreciate your *Recipes for Health* series for its focus on using vegetables creatively and elegantly. —Rae S.

THE VERY BEST OF
RECIPES FOR HEALTH

THE VERY BEST OF
RECIPES
FOR
HEALTH

250 Recipes and More from the
Popular Feature on NYTimes.com

MARTHA ROSE SHULMAN

PHOTOGRAPHS BY ANDREW SCRIVANI

RODALE

Rodale books may be purchased for business or promotional use or for special sales. For information, please write to:

Special Markets Department, Rodale Inc., 733 Third Avenue, New York, NY 10017

Printed in the United States of America

Rodale Inc. makes every effort to use acid-free ♾, recycled paper ♻.

Recipe photo on front cover: Barley and Mushroom Salad with English Peas, page 182

Recipe photos on back cover: (*top left*) Polenta with Mushrooms, Favas, and Tomatoes, page 201; (*top right*) Grilled Eggplant Panini, page 98; and (*bottom right*) Soft Tacos with Chicken and Tomato-Corn Salsa, page 329

Book design: Christina Gaugler

Library of Congress Cataloging-in-Publication Data

Shulman, Martha Rose.
   The very best of recipes for health : 250 recipes and more from the popular feature on NYTimes.com / Martha Rose Shulman.
      p.   cm.
   Includes index.
   ISBN-13 978–1–60529–573–2 hardcover
   1. Cookery (Natural foods) 2. Nutrition. 3. Health. I. Title.
TX741.S555   2010
641.5'636—dc22   2010021608

Distributed to the trade by Macmillan

2 4 6 8 10 9 7 5 3 1 hardcover

We inspire and enable people to improve their lives and the world around them.

To my dearest and only sis, Melodie,
with devotion and love.

Contents

Introduction

A few years ago Mike Mason, the online health editor at the *New York Times*, called me to find out if I'd be interested in helping him with a recipe database. At the time he didn't know exactly what form this would take, but he thought that the nutrition section should include some sort of healthy recipe offerings. I jumped at the opportunity to provide a steady stream of simple, delicious recipes to a wide audience, and a few months later we launched my series, *Recipes for Health*.

What Is Healthy Eating?

During the months following Mike's first phone call, as I began to shape the feature, I asked myself that question over and over again. I've devoted my career to healthy eating, but in a very unscientific sort of way. My approach is intuitive rather than scientific; I'm a cook, not a nutritionist, and even when I was a strict vegetarian, I was never doctrinaire. I've always wanted my food to be accessible to a wide range of cooks and eaters, and I've worked hard to create healthy food that tastes good and isn't difficult to make. My passion for good food and conviviality, and my instinct for a balanced, healthy lifestyle have always gone hand in hand. I've never sacrificed one in favor of the other; I haven't needed to. As you cook your way through the recipes in this book, you'll see that eating well needn't be an austere experience.

Here are the broad strokes of the philosophy behind *Recipes for Health*:

Eating a variety of foods made with raw ingredients (that is, not processed)

Eating low on the food chain (not exclusively so, but most of the time)

Not eating too much

Stopping to eat meals and eating mindfully

If you cook, you're halfway there, because I firmly believe that the easiest and most pleasurable way to eat well, and certainly the most economical way, is to cook the food you eat. Produce, seasonal and locally grown without pesticides if possible, and a well-stocked pantry (I'll tell you what that consists of a little later) are the linchpins of a good diet. Helping you decide what to do with these healthful ingredients is where I come in.

Over the last two or three decades we, as a nation, have lost our connection to food that is real, as opposed to manufactured and processed, and by extension lost a connection to our kitchens, even as they've become bigger and fancier. A generation has grown up watching a lot of cooking on television, but rarely seeing a parent cook at home. The point was brought home to me recently when I overheard the following conversation after my son's baseball game:

"Where's daddy?"

"He's getting dinner."

"What are we having?"

"Panda Express."

If the overwhelmingly favorable response to *Recipes for Health* is any indication, more and more people want to stop *getting* dinner and begin *making* it. Those who continue to think that they're saving precious time by *getting* it are mistaken. I have done the math, and it takes me a lot more time to drive in traffic, park the car, order food, wait for my order, check out and drive that food home than it would take to go home and make an omelet or a simple pasta dish and a salad. The omelet or the pasta and the salad are not only healthier than any meal I could buy (not to mention cheaper), they also taste infinitely better.

I hope that the recipes in this book will inspire you to think about food in a new way. I draw most of my inspiration from Mediterranean, Mexican, and Asian cuisines, inherently healthy cuisines with big flavors, in which meat to a large extent is peripheral to vegetables, beans, and grains—the foods we should be eating more of. You may be tired of plain old steamed broccoli, but a spicy Asian stir-fry (page 257) or a lemony broccoli and chickpea salad (page 42) may rekindle your taste for that familiar vegetable. Perhaps you've seen barley or wheatberries in your whole foods store or had them served alongside a piece of meat or fish, but never thought to build a salad around them. Finding new ways to serve and enjoy these healthful ingredients is at the heart of *Recipes for Health*, and it gives me enormous pleasure.

The farmers' market movement in the United States has grown exponentially over the past decade, so it is now viable for most of my readers to find locally grown produce at least during part of the year. More and more of these fruits and vegetables are certified organic and even those that are not are grown with a minimum of chemicals in carefully tended soil. In addition to produce, you can find free-range eggs and humanely raised chickens in many farmers' markets, as well as grass-fed beef (and buffalo) and other types of meats that have been produced using sustainable, humane methods. Some markets have local fisherman selling their catch as well.

Many of the farmers who sell at farmers' markets also participate in CSA groups, which stands for Community Supported Agriculture. If you join a CSA, you subscribe to a farm—basically becoming a shareholder in that farm—and in exchange you get a box of produce every week. The produce will vary with the season, and sometimes you will get a lot of one thing, depending on what's abundant at the farm. CSA members have been especially appreciative of my columns when I've devoted five recipes in a week to a vegetable they've received in their box. You can find out more about Community Supported Agriculture at www.localharvest.org.

If you don't have access to locally grown produce, don't let that put you off produce altogether. Eating fruits and vegetables that come from far away is better than eating none at all (though I draw the line at the US border; if I can only find avocados and blueberries grown halfway around the world, I find something else to eat). Now supermarkets devote entire sections of their produce departments to organically grown fruits and vegetables, and it's truly impressive to see how the range of available organic produce has grown over the years.

Another aspect of eating healthfully concerns not just what we eat, but how much. The portions in this book are sensible, because home cooks don't feel obliged to serve up the ridiculous amounts of food that restaurants and take-out chains have decided their clients expect. And because real food, cooked by you, does not contain the quantities of added sugar, salt, and fat that the food industry incorporates into their products to make you want to keep eating (and buying), you will know when you've had enough to eat. You will feel satisfied.

Lastly, take the time to sit down to your meals. I firmly believe that stopping to enjoy food at a table, whether alone or in the company of others, has got to be good for your health. If you don't stop to eat, it's difficult to be mindful about what you're eating; the pleasure will elude you. And pleasure is what eating should be about. Cooking is just the first step.

The Well-Stocked Pantry

It really pays to stock your shelves with the staples that constitute the backbone of a healthy diet. If you have a well-stocked pantry you can make dinner, even when you haven't given much thought to what you're going to cook. With Arborio rice, garlic, an onion, extra virgin olive oil, and a can of chicken broth in the pantry and some Parmesan in the refrigerator, the red pepper that's been hanging about becomes inspiration for a risotto (page 229). If you want to use up that pepper in a faster dish and you've got eggs on hand you can make a red pepper frittata (page 243), or you can stir-fry the pepper with tofu (page 262) and serve the stir-fry with the couscous or basmati rice in your cupboard.

You can build your pantry gradually as you work your way through the recipes in these pages, or just go out one day and do a major shop. I suggest that you do a little of both. Begin to stock your shelves and refrigerator with at least some of the ingredients here, adding items as you come across them in recipes you want to try.

When I speak of pantry staples, I'm also referring to items that I keep in my refrigerator and freezer. There are certain foods that I never allow myself to run out of, including eggs and yogurt, tofu, Parmesan and feta, and at least a couple of vegetables that keep well in the refrigerator, like red peppers, romaine hearts, and carrots. My master list is on the opposite page. Make a copy, put it on your refrigerator, and replace items as they run out.

DRY GOODS (pantry/cupboard shelves):

- Canned or boxed tomatoes: 28-ounce and 14-ounce sizes, preferably chopped or crushed, in juice

- Pomì marinara sauce (the only prepared marinara sauce I like; comes in a box, imported from Italy)

- Water-packed light tuna (with or without salt, depending on your preference and medical needs)

- Canned beans: black beans, chickpeas, kidney beans, white beans; rinse before using

- Canned or bottled roasted peppers (for salads, bruschetta, pasta)

- Bottled salsa

- Pasta: several shapes and sizes

- Rice: Arborio or Carnaroli for risottos, basmati for pilafs, brown and wild rice for hearty salads and whole grain sides

- Couscous

- Other grains: barley, bulgur, farro, polenta, quinoa

- Dried beans: black beans, chickpeas, pintos, white beans; also quick-cooking types like black-eyed peas and lentils

- Flour: all-purpose and whole wheat

- Extra virgin olive oil

- Canola oil (refrigerate after opening)

- Vinegar: balsamic, red wine vinegar, sherry vinegar (I use sherry vinegar the most), white wine or champagne vinegar

- Dried mushrooms: porcini are the most aromatic; shiitake for Asian dishes

- Soy sauce

- Dijon mustard (refrigerate after opening)

- Canned chicken or vegetable broth or stock

- Imported olives (refrigerate after opening)

- Anchovies (refrigerate after opening)

- Dry white wine, such as sauvignon blanc (refrigerate after opening)

- Red wine, such as Côtes du Rhone

- Salt: fine sea salt and kosher

- Honey: one with a mild flavor, such as clover

- Sugar (you won't need much here, but you'll need a little now and again)

PRODUCE THAT DOESN'T NEED REFRIGERATION:

- Garlic

- Onions

- Potatoes

REFRIGERATOR:

- Imported Parmesan cheese (preferably a block; if you have a reliable source and you use it up quickly, you can buy it grated, but not the stuff in the green can!)

- Feta cheese

- Gruyère cheese

- Fresh ginger

- Capers
- Eggs, preferably free-range
- Plain yogurt
- Milk
- Lemons
- 1 or 2 (or more, depending on the size of your family) fresh vegetables and herbs that keep well for 5 to 7 days*: Belgian endive, broccoli, chiles, green beans, mushrooms, parsley, red and green peppers, romaine lettuce, zucchini; and/or a selection of vegetables that keep well for more than a week*, such as beets, cabbage, carrots, celery, turnips, winter squash

*Of course, the fresher the better for all produce.

FREEZER:

- Active dry yeast
- Corn tortillas
- Frozen edamame
- Frozen peas
- Homemade chicken or vegetable stock if possible
- Nuts: almonds, pine nuts, walnuts
- Phyllo dough
- Whole grain bread
- Optional: boneless, skinless chicken breasts

DRIED HERBS AND SPICES (I keep my spices in the freezer to keep them fresh. Buy whole spices and grind them as you use them for the best flavor):

- Allspice
- Bay leaf
- Caraway seeds
- Cayenne
- Cinnamon
- Cloves
- Coriander seeds
- Cumin seeds
- Fennel seeds
- Nutmeg
- Oregano
- Paprika
- Pepper, whole black peppercorns
- Red-pepper flakes
- Red chile peppers (dried)
- Rosemary
- Saffron
- Thyme
- Vanilla beans

A Note about Nutritional Analyses

Many of my readers are keen to know the nutritional content of my recipes—the calories, fat and carbohydrate content, sodium content, etc. The recipes in this book have been analyzed for their nutritional content, but I would like to caution that nutritional analyses are just approximate measures. According to nutritionist Marion Nestle, PhD, MPH, professor in the department of nutrition, food studies, and public health at New York University and author of the book *What to Eat*, nutrient contents of foods vary with growing location, soil conditions, climate, transportation, and storage, so the databases that supply the information used to create these nutritional analyses are never absolute. "I always laugh when I see calories listed as anything that doesn't end with a zero. Measurements of nutrients just aren't all that precise," Marion told me recently. Also, even though the recipes tell you how many portions they make, everyone knows that we may eat a little more or a little less of a given dish, changing the numbers so neatly provided.

A much more realistic way to approach healthful eating is simply to eat a variety of unprocessed foods. Fresh foods will provide you with a range of nutrients in varying amounts—including nutrients that we may not have even discovered yet. If calories are your concern, then focus on the size of your portions, and the number of times you eat during the day. America was not a nation of overweight people when people were accustomed to eating three home-cooked meals a day.

To me, food is not about its nutritional components, but about pleasure and sustenance. To see the food that we eat in terms of their nutrients is called "nutritionism," and I don't think that a nutritionist approach to eating leads to better health. What leads to better health is being mindful about the food you eat, eating a wide variety of unprocessed foods, taking an active part in their preparation, and not eating too much.

A Note about the Recipes

I am often asked by my readers to provide recipes that address their dietary needs and concerns, such as dishes that are gluten-free or low-calorie, and dishes that are good sources of omega-3s. For that reason, every recipe in this book features a list of the most-requested categories with those that apply to the particular dish highlighted in bold. I noted high-protein dishes for the benefit of those of you who want to eat less meat but may be concerned about getting enough protein, as well as recipes that are vegetarian or vegan (or can be made so with minor alterations). As my benchmarks for the low-calorie category, I chose 250 calories for dishes that were not being served as main dishes, and 450 calories for dishes that could be served as a main dish, including soups and salads. For the low-fat recipes, I was mainly concerned with saturated fats; recipes that have less than 3 grams of saturated fat per serving, or less than 12 grams total fat get the low-fat bullet. When it comes to protein, I looked at the relationship between the number of grams of protein in a dish and the number of grams of carbohydrates. Protein and carbohydrates have the same number of calories per gram (4), so if a dish derives more than 3.5 times more calories from carbohydrates than it does from protein, I did not give it a high-protein bullet, even if the gram count for protein is relatively high.

A Note about Sodium

For any recipe in this book, the sodium content listed in the nutritional breakdown reflects only specific quantities of salt called for in the list of ingredients and the sodium that naturally occurs in the ingredients. Additions of salt to taste will vary from cook to cook and are, therefore, not included in the analysis. Salt has been associated with hypertension and other medical conditions and should, therefore, be added to dishes mindfully and in moderation. But unless you are under doctor's orders to restrict your use of salt, you should not be afraid to season your food properly. Healthy food should not taste dull. It's important to know that most of the salt intake that is plaguing the American diet (77% to be exact) comes from processed food.

Chapter 1
BREAKFAST

The aim of this chapter is not to talk you into eating a big breakfast if you're not hungry first thing in the morning, but rather to give you some healthy morning options. Breakfast certainly can set you up, and if you're trying to figure out how to avoid those hunger pangs before lunch, a substantial breakfast is your answer. If, like me, you don't tend to have much of an appetite first thing but are looking for something to keep you from becoming too hungry halfway through the morning, the smoothies on pages 12–15 might be the perfect answer for you. If you're trying to work more whole grains into your diet, check out the steel-cut oats on page 4, or the oatmeal pancakes on page 8. If eggs are your thing, turn to Chapter 9 and choose your breakfast from those recipes. And don't forget, a perfectly soft-boiled egg with a slice of whole grain toast is pretty hard to beat and very sustaining.

Cinnamon Granola

Makes about 2½ quarts

■ **VEGETARIAN** ■ VEGAN ■ **LOW-CALORIE** ■ LOW-FAT
■ HIGH-PROTEIN ■ GLUTEN-FREE ■ HIGH IN OMEGA-3S

I used to make "gift granola" every year to send to my brothers and their families at holiday time, and of course I'd keep some for myself. Eventually those families grew up (along with the health food industry that engendered granola), and I got out of the habit. Recently though, I've begun making granola again; it only took one batch to hook my son, who takes a bag of it to school every day for a mid-morning snack. I keep the heat low in my oven and line my baking sheets with parchment, so that it doesn't stick. Make sure to stir the granola every 10 to 15 minutes, and switch the top and bottom trays each time you stir. You can halve this recipe if you want to make a smaller amount, but it goes faster than you'd think.

6 cups flaked or rolled oats

2 cups oat bran

½ cup flaxseeds, coarsely ground

½ cup coconut, flaked or shaved (optional)

¾ cup chopped almonds

¾ cup broken pecans

½–1 teaspoon freshly grated nutmeg

1 tablespoon ground cinnamon

½–¾ teaspoon salt (optional)

½ cup mild honey, such as clover

⅓ cup canola oil

1 tablespoon vanilla extract

1–2 cups raisins (optional)

1. Preheat the oven to 325°F with the racks on the middle and lower settings. Line 2 baking sheets with parchment. Toss together the oats, oat bran, flaxseeds, coconut (if using), almonds, pecans, nutmeg, cinnamon, and salt (if using) in a very large bowl. Combine the honey, oil, and vanilla extract in a saucepan or in a measuring cup. Warm over low heat or at 50 percent power in a microwave. Do not let the oil mixture come to a simmer. Pour into the oat mixture. Stir to coat evenly.

2. Spread the granola on the baking sheets. Bake for 45 minutes to 1 hour, until golden, stirring every 10 to 15 minutes and switching the position of the baking sheets. Remove from the oven. Stir in the raisins (if using). Cool on the baking sheets. Store in well-sealed jars, bags, or containers.

Per ½-cup serving: 247 calories, 8 g protein, 32 g carbohydrates, 5 g fiber, 12 g fat, 1 g sat fat, 0 mg cholesterol, 0 mg sodium

ADVANCE PREPARATION: This will keep for several weeks if stored in the freezer.

Granola Muffins

Makes 12

■ **VEGETARIAN** ■ VEGAN ■ LOW-CALORIE ■ LOW-FAT
■ HIGH-PROTEIN ■ GLUTEN-FREE ■ HIGH IN OMEGA-3S

These breakfast muffins are sort of like bran muffins, but they have a little crunch and they're not nearly as sweet and huge (not to mention caloric) as the muffins sold at your local coffee shop.

1 cup Cinnamon Granola (opposite page)

½ cup 1% milk

1 cup golden raisins

1 cup whole wheat flour

2 teaspoons baking powder

½ teaspoon baking soda

¼ teaspoon salt

2 large or extra-large eggs

½ cup buttermilk or plain low-fat yogurt

¼ cup mild honey, such as clover

¼ cup canola oil

1 teaspoon vanilla extract

1. Preheat the oven to 375°F with a rack in the middle. Oil 12 muffin cups. Combine the granola and milk in a bowl and let sit for 30 minutes. Meanwhile, cover the raisins with hot water and soak for 15 minutes. Drain and blot dry on paper towels.

2. Sift together the whole wheat flour, baking powder, baking soda, and salt.

3. Beat together the eggs, buttermilk or yogurt, honey, canola oil, and vanilla extract in a medium bowl. Quickly whisk in the flour mixture. Fold in the granola and raisins. Combine well.

4. Spoon into the muffin cups, filling each about three-quarters full. Bake for 20 to 25 minutes, until lightly browned. Cool in the tin on a rack for 10 minutes. Remove to the rack to cool completely.

Per serving: 201 calories, 5 g protein, 30 g carbohydrates, 3 g fiber, 8 g fat, 1 g sat fat, 36 mg cholesterol, 199 mg sodium

ADVANCE PREPARATION: The muffins will be good for a couple of days. Refrigerate after 2 days. They also freeze well. Microwave to thaw or set out on a counter overnight.

Steel-Cut Oatmeal with Fruit

Makes 4 servings

■ **VEGETARIAN** ■ VEGAN ■ **LOW-CALORIE** ■ **LOW-FAT**
■ HIGH-PROTEIN ■ GLUTEN-FREE ■ HIGH IN OMEGA-3S

Steel-cut oatmeal is one of my favorite hot breakfasts. It has more texture than rolled or flaked oats and really sticks to your ribs. When I included a recipe for steel-cut oatmeal in my Recipes for Health column, I received about a hundred e-mails from readers, most telling me how convenient it is to cook these oats in a slow cooker or a rice cooker, setting it up before you go to bed so that breakfast is waiting for you in the morning. Some rice cookers even have a setting for steel-cut oats. If you don't have a slow cooker or rice cooker and don't have 25 to 30 minutes to spend on making breakfast in the morning, make a batch that will last a few days; it keeps well in the refrigerator and you can reheat small portions gently on top of the stove or in the microwave. You can also freeze it in ice cube trays.

2 cups 1% milk

¼ teaspoon salt

1 cup steel-cut oats

1 teaspoon unsalted butter (optional)

¼ cup dried fruit, such as raisins, dried cranberries, chopped dried apricots

2 teaspoons maple syrup, agave syrup, honey, or packed brown sugar

Fresh fruit, such as diced apples and pears (optional)

1. Combine the milk and salt with 2 cups water in a large, heavy saucepan. Bring to a boil. Slowly add the oats, stirring constantly. Reduce the heat to low, cover, and simmer for 15 minutes, stirring occasionally with a wooden spoon. Stir in the butter (if using), dried fruit, and sweetener. Cover and simmer for 10 to 15 minutes, stirring often to prevent the cereal from sticking to the bottom of the pan, until the oats are

soft and the mixture is creamy. Serve, with fresh fruit stirred in if desired, or refrigerate or freeze and reheat as desired.

Per serving: 165 calories, 7 g protein, 29 g carbohydrates, 2.5 g fiber, 3 g fat, 1 g sat fat, 6 mg cholesterol, 213 mg sodium

ADVANCE PREPARATION: Cooked steel-cut oats will keep for 5 days in the refrigerator and can be reheated on top of the stove or in the microwave. To freeze, line ice cube trays with plastic wrap. Fill each cube with oatmeal, cover with plastic wrap, and freeze. Once frozen solid, remove the cubes from the trays and freeze in a resealable plastic bag. For each portion, thaw 3 or 4 cubes in a microwave on the Defrost setting. Add additional milk if desired.

Oat Notes

Although the brand of steel-cut oats I buy is labeled with directions for cooking in the microwave, I don't find the results satisfactory. The oatmeal doesn't have the time that it needs to swell and release its starch into the liquid, so the liquid never gets creamy and the oatmeal doesn't soften properly. A better way to save time is to soak the oats overnight. Combine the oats and salt in a bowl and pour on 2 cups boiling water. Cover if desired and leave overnight. In the morning, bring the milk to a simmer in a large saucepan. Stir in the oats and any liquid remaining in the bowl. Add the remaining ingredients and simmer for 15 minutes, stirring often, until creamy.

Muesli

Makes 4 servings

■ **VEGETARIAN** ■ **VEGAN** ■ **LOW-CALORIE** ■ **LOW-FAT**
■ HIGH-PROTEIN ■ GLUTEN-FREE ■ HIGH IN OMEGA-3S

Muesli is a Swiss breakfast of very lightly toasted oatmeal and chopped nuts, with grated apple and dried fruit added just before serving.

2 cups quick-cooking (not instant) oatmeal

½ cup chopped almonds or hulled sunflower seeds

For each serving:

¼–½ tart apple, such as Granny Smith, peeled, cored, and grated

1 tablespoon dried currants, raisins, or cranberries

Milk

½–1 teaspoon packed brown sugar or honey (optional)

*If you omit the milk and honey

1. Preheat the oven to 375°F. Stir together the oatmeal and chopped almonds or sunflower seeds in a medium bowl. Line a baking sheet with parchment and spread the muesli on top in an even layer. Bake for 8 to 10 minutes, until very lightly toasted.

2. Remove the baking sheet from the oven and transfer the muesli to a bowl. (At this point it can be stored.) To serve, add the apple and dried fruit, moisten with milk, and add brown sugar or honey (if using). Stir to combine.

Per serving (without milk): 249 calories, 10 g protein, 33 g carbohydrates, 6 g fiber, 9 g fat, 0.5 g sat fat, 0 mg cholesterol, 0 mg sodium

ADVANCE PREPARATION: The oatmeal and nuts can be toasted and will keep for several weeks in the refrigerator. Add any fresh fruit just before serving.

French Toast with Raspberries

Makes 2 servings

■ **VEGETARIAN** ■ VEGAN ■ **LOW-CALORIE** ■ LOW-FAT
■ **HIGH-PROTEIN** ■ GLUTEN-FREE ■ HIGH IN OMEGA-3S

Using whole grain bread for French toast makes a very nutritious breakfast that provides each person with an egg, some calcium-rich milk, and grains all in one tasty serving. I find that the hint of vanilla in the batter gives this French toast such a sweet flavor that I rarely bother to add syrup or other topping. Also, French toast is a great way to use up stale bread.

2 large or extra-large eggs

½ cup 1% milk

Pinch of salt

¼ teaspoon vanilla extract

Pinch of freshly grated nutmeg (optional)

1 tablespoon unsalted butter

4 slices whole grain sandwich bread

Pure maple syrup

½ cup raspberries

1. Heat a griddle or a large, heavy nonstick skillet over medium heat. Whisk the eggs in a large bowl. Whisk in the milk, salt, vanilla extract, and nutmeg (if using).

2. Add the butter to the griddle or skillet and brush it around to thoroughly coat the surface. When the butter stops foaming, dip the bread slices one at a time into the batter, turning to coat both sides. The bread should be saturated with the batter, but it shouldn't be so wet that it falls apart when you lift it from the bowl. Place the bread on the griddle or in the skillet.

3. Reduce the heat to medium-low and cook slowly until golden-brown on one side, 3 to 5 minutes. Turn and cook until golden-brown on the second side. Transfer to a plate and drizzle with syrup. Garnish with raspberries, and serve.

Per serving: 304 calories, 11 g protein, 40 g carbohydrates, 3 g fiber, 12 g fat, 6 g sat fat, 230 mg cholesterol, 229 mg sodium

ADVANCE PREPARATION: This dish is best served right away.

French Toast in France

Maple syrup isn't easy to come by in France, where they call French toast *pain perdu*—lost bread. The French top their pain perdu with fruit preserves, a drizzle of honey, or a light dusting of powdered sugar. You might also substitute a dollop of low-fat yogurt or some sliced strawberries for the syrup.

Whole Wheat Buttermilk Pancakes

Makes 14 pancakes (serves 4)

■ **VEGETARIAN** ■ VEGAN ■ LOW-CALORIE ■ **LOW-FAT**
■ HIGH-PROTEIN ■ GLUTEN-FREE ■ HIGH IN OMEGA-3S

My son would eat pancakes for breakfast every day if he could, and now that I've devised a method for making them and then freezing them in packets of 3, he can. In the morning I quickly thaw and heat the pancakes in the microwave. Breakfast couldn't be simpler. They make a substantial meal that will sustain even a grown-up until lunchtime and beyond.

2 large eggs

1½ cups buttermilk

1 teaspoon vanilla extract

3 tablespoons canola oil

1 cup whole wheat flour

½ cup unbleached all-purpose flour

2 teaspoons baking powder

1 teaspoon baking soda

1 tablespoon sugar

¼ teaspoon salt

1 cup fresh or frozen blueberries

Unsalted butter (optional)

Pure maple syrup (optional)

1. Heat a heavy nonstick or cast-iron skillet or griddle over medium heat (350°F if using an electric griddle).

2. Whisk the eggs in a medium bowl. Add the buttermilk and whisk together. Whisk in the vanilla extract and oil. Sift together the whole wheat flour, all-purpose flour, baking powder, baking soda, sugar, and salt in a medium bowl. Add to the wet ingredients and whisk together quickly. Do not overbeat. A few lumps are okay.

3. Coat the hot skillet or griddle with cooking spray. Ladle 3 to 4 tablespoons of batter per pancake onto the skillet or griddle. Place 7 or 8 blueberries on each pancake. Cook until bubbles begin to break through, 2 to 3 minutes. Turn and cook for 30 seconds to 1 minute, or until nicely browned. Transfer to a plate. Continue making pancakes until all the batter is used up.

4. Serve hot, with a small amount of butter and maple syrup.

Per pancake: 119 calories, 4 g protein, 16 g carbohydrates, 2 g fiber, 5 g fat, 1 g sat fat, 36 mg cholesterol, 265 mg sodium

ADVANCE PREPARATION: You can make these in advance and freeze them for several weeks. Either freeze on a baking sheet and transfer to freezer bags or make portions of 3 pancakes each and wrap in plastic, then transfer to freezer bags. Unwrap to thaw in the microwave.

Oatmeal Buttermilk Pancakes

Makes 14 to 15 pancakes (4 to 5 servings)

■ **VEGETARIAN** ■ VEGAN ■ LOW-CALORIE ■ **LOW-FAT**
■ HIGH-PROTEIN ■ GLUTEN-FREE ■ HIGH IN OMEGA-3S

These are denser than my ordinary whole wheat buttermilk pancakes. I like them because they're very hearty and moist. For best results, allow the batter to sit overnight or for a couple of hours before cooking.

½ cup rolled oats

⅓ cup 1% milk

2 large eggs

1½ cups buttermilk

3 tablespoons canola oil

1 teaspoon vanilla extract

1 cup whole wheat flour

½ cup unbleached all-purpose flour

2 teaspoons baking powder

1 teaspoon baking soda

1 tablespoon sugar

¼ teaspoon salt

1¼ cups frozen blueberries, quartered strawberries, raisins, or dried cranberries; or, for a splurge, 1 cup chocolate chips (optional)

Unsalted butter, optional

Pure maple syrup, optional

1. Combine the rolled oats and milk in a medium bowl and set aside.

2. Whisk the eggs in a medium bowl. Add the buttermilk and whisk together. Whisk in the oil and vanilla extract. Sift together the whole wheat flour, all-purpose flour, baking powder, baking soda, sugar, and salt in a medium bowl. Add to the wet ingredients and quickly whisk together. Do not overbeat. A few lumps are okay. Fold in the oats and milk. Let sit for 1 hour, or (preferably) cover and refrigerate overnight.

3. Heat a griddle or heavy nonstick or cast-iron skillet. If necessary, spray the hot griddle or skillet with cooking spray. Ladle 3 to 4 tablespoons of batter per pancake onto the hot griddle or skillet. Place 7 or 8 berries, raisins, cranberries, or chocolate chips on each pancake. Cook until bubbles begin to break through, 2 to 3 minutes. Turn and cook for 30 seconds to 1 minute, or until nicely browned. Transfer to a plate. Continue making pancakes until all the batter is used up.

4. Serve hot, with a small amount of butter and maple syrup.

Per serving (based on 3 per serving) (without fruit): 114 calories, 4 g protein, 14 g carbohydrates, 1 g fiber, 5 g fat, 1 g sat fat, 224 mg cholesterol, 33 mg sodium

ADVANCE PREPARATION: You can keep cooked pancakes, well wrapped, in the refrigerator for a few days, or freeze them for up to a few months.

A small amount of butter goes a long way if you combine it with the syrup in a ramekin or pitcher and heat together (use 50% power in a microwave) until the butter melts. When the syrup is warm you can use less to coat your pancakes.

Morning Couscous with Oranges and Dates

Makes 6 servings

■ **VEGETARIAN** ■ **VEGAN*** ■ **LOW-CALORIE** ■ **LOW-FAT**
■ HIGH-PROTEIN ■ GLUTEN-FREE ■ HIGH IN OMEGA-3S

This is a delicious way to enjoy couscous. If you reconstitute the couscous the night before and keep it in the refrigerator overnight, all it will need is a steam in the microwave and the addition of the dried fruits and oranges in the morning.

2–3 tablespoons packed brown sugar or honey

¼ cup chopped dried apricots

2 tablespoons dried currants or raisins

1 teaspoon orange flower water (available at Middle Eastern markets), optional

1 cup couscous

½ teaspoon ground cinnamon

¼ teaspoon salt (optional)

1 tablespoon unsalted butter (optional)

2 navel oranges

8 dates, pitted and quartered lengthwise

Pomegranate seeds

*If you omit the butter and use sugar, not honey

1. Combine the brown sugar or honey with 1½ cups water in a medium saucepan and bring to a boil over high heat. Reduce the heat to medium and boil gently until the sugar has dissolved. Stir in the chopped apricots, currants or raisins, and orange flower water (if using). Set aside for 5 minutes.

2. Place the couscous in a 2-quart bowl. Add the cinnamon and salt (if using) and stir together. Pour the hot syrup over the couscous. Mix together with a fork, spatula, or wooden spoon. Set aside for 20 minutes, stirring occasionally. At this point, if you don't plan to serve the couscous right away, cover and refrigerate.

3. Shortly before serving, steam the couscous in one of two ways: Line a sieve with a double layer of cheesecloth and dump the couscous into the sieve, then set above a pot with 1 inch of boiling water. Cover and steam for 15 minutes, making sure that the couscous is suspended well above the water. Transfer to a bowl. Add the butter (if using) and toss until the butter melts. Alternatively, place in a microwave and cover tightly with a plate. Microwave for 2 minutes. Carefully uncover, stir in the butter (if using) and cover again. Microwave for another 2 minutes. Carefully remove the plate, being careful of the steam in the bowl. The couscous should be fluffy.

4. Holding the oranges over the couscous, slice away the skin and pith with a paring knife, letting any juice drip onto the couscous. Continue to hold the orange over the couscous and cut out the sections from between the membranes.

5. Either mound the couscous onto a platter or spoon into individual serving bowls. Garnish with oranges, dates, and pomegranate seeds, and serve.

Per serving: 247 calories, 5 g protein, 59 g carbohydrates, 5 g fiber, 0.3 g fat, 0 g sat fat, 0 mg cholesterol, 5 mg sodium

ADVANCE PREPARATION: The couscous can be steamed and kept in the refrigerator for up to 5 days.

Fruit Smoothies

When I was in my 20s and a strict vegetarian, I spent a lot of time in Mexico and I lived on banana smoothies. I can still taste them today. They were all about the ripe fruit that went into them, blended with fresh milk and a small amount of sugar. Smoothies make a great, quick, nutritious breakfast. You can pack in a lot of fruit, so if you're having trouble getting your 5 servings of fruits and vegetables a day, smoothies might be your ace in the hole. Don't make smoothies ahead of time. A smoothie should be drunk right away. It will thicken up as it sits, and the flavor will lose its brightness.

Frozen Banana Smoothie

Makes one 16-ounce or two 8-ounce servings

■ **VEGETARIAN** ■ **VEGAN*** ■ **LOW-CALORIE** ■ **LOW-FAT**
■ HIGH-PROTEIN ■ **GLUTEN-FREE** ■ HIGH IN OMEGA-3S

If you make your smoothies with frozen bananas you don't need to add ice, which will water down the drink. The ripeness of the banana is important here. If the banana is more starchy than sweet, your smoothie will taste dull. Ripe bananas have no hint of green in the skin and can have a few brown spots. They should be easy to break in half after you peel them. To ensure that I always have frozen bananas at the ready, I buy extra bananas every week. When some of them become very ripe, I peel and freeze them. Bananas are a very good source of manganese, as well as potassium, fiber, and vitamin B_6. This is a simple smoothie that I never tire of.

1 large ripe banana, preferably frozen

1 cup milk, almond milk, or rice milk

1 teaspoon honey

2 or 3 ice cubes, if using an unfrozen banana

*If you use almond milk or rice milk and omit the honey

Place the banana, milk, honey, and ice cubes (if using) in a blender. Blend until smooth. Serve.

Per serving: 244 calories, 10 g protein, 49 g carbohydrates, 4 g fiber, 3 g fat, 2 g sat fat, 12 mg cholesterol, 109 mg sodium

VARIATION: BANANA-PEANUT BUTTER OR BANANA-ALMOND SMOOTHIE Add 1 tablespoon peanut butter or roasted almond butter and blend.

Freezing Bananas for Smoothies

Peel bananas, slice into big chunks, and wrap each one tightly in plastic. Place the wrapped bananas in a freezer bag and use as needed.

Banana Berry Smoothie

Makes one 16-ounce or two 8-ounce servings

■ **VEGETARIAN** ■ **VEGAN*** ■ LOW-CALORIE ■ HIGH-PROTEIN
■ **LOW-FAT** ■ **GLUTEN-FREE** ■ HIGH IN OMEGA-3S

This is a nutritious smoothie that you can make year-round with frozen fruit. Blueberries and strawberries are packed with anthocyanins, the antioxidant compounds that give them their blue and red colors, and they're a very good source of vitamin C, manganese, and fiber, both soluble and insoluble. Add the protein and calcium in the milk, and you've got a meal. Make sure your banana is ripe, and if possible, freeze it beforehand.

1 large ripe banana, preferably frozen

½ cup frozen blueberries

3 cups fresh or frozen hulled strawberries

1 cup milk, almond milk, or rice milk

1 teaspoon honey

2 or 3 ice cubes, if using an unfrozen banana

If you use almond milk or rice milk and omit the honey

Place the banana, blueberries, strawberries, milk, honey, and ice cubes (if using) in a blender. Blend until smooth. Serve right away.

Per serving: 302 calories, 10 g protein, 63 g carbohydrates 7 g fiber, 3 g fat, 2 g sat fat, 12 mg cholesterol, 110 mg sodium

Pineapple Banana Mint Smoothie

Makes one 16-ounce or two 8-ounce servings

■ **VEGETARIAN** ■ **VEGAN*** ■ LOW-CALORIE ■ **LOW-FAT**
■ HIGH-PROTEIN ■ **GLUTEN-FREE** ■ HIGH IN OMEGA-3S

This tangy, minty smoothie is one of my favorites. The pineapple will meet your daily requirement for manganese, and it's a good source of vitamins C, B₁, B₆, copper and dietary fiber. It also contains a substance called bromelain, a group of digestive enzymes that can also be instrumental in reducing inflammation and healing wounds.

1 heaping cup chopped fresh pineapple (¼ large or ½ small)

1 medium ripe banana, preferably frozen

¾ cup almond milk or rice milk

6 fresh mint leaves

1 teaspoon mild honey (optional; if the almond milk or rice milk is sweetened, you may not need the honey)

2 or 3 ice cubes, if using an unfrozen banana

If you omit the honey

Place the pineapple, banana, milk, mint, honey (if using), and ice cubes (if using) in a blender. Blend until smooth.

Per serving: 275 calories, 3 g protein, 66 g carbohydrates, 7 g fiber, 2.5 g fat, 0 g sat fat, 0 mg cholesterol, 116 mg sodium

Strawberry Smoothie

Makes one 16-ounce or two 8-ounce servings

■ **VEGETARIAN** ■ **VEGAN*** ■ LOW-CALORIE ■ **LOW-FAT**
■ HIGH-PROTEIN ■ **GLUTEN-FREE** ■ HIGH IN OMEGA-3S

This will be thick and sweet, almost like a strawberry shake if you use a frozen banana that is truly ripe. Frozen strawberries will also help to give the drink a thick texture that resembles a milkshake.

- 1 medium or large ripe banana, preferably frozen

- 1 heaping cup fresh or frozen hulled strawberries

- 1 cup milk, almond milk, or rice milk

- 1 teaspoon honey

- 1/2 teaspoon vanilla extract (optional)

- 2 or 3 ice cubes, if using an unfrozen banana

*If you use almond milk or rice milk and omit the honey

Place the banana, strawberries, milk, honey, and vanilla extract (if using) in a blender. Blend until smooth. Serve immediately.

Per serving: 286 calories, 11 g protein, 59 g carbohydrates, 7 g fiber, 3 g fat, 2 g sat fat, 12 mg cholesterol, 111 mg sodium

Mango Buttermilk Smoothie

Makes one 16-ounce or two 8-ounce servings

■ **VEGETARIAN** ■ **VEGAN*** ■ LOW-CALORIE ■ **LOW-FAT**
■ HIGH-PROTEIN ■ **GLUTEN-FREE** ■ HIGH IN OMEGA-3S

This has a tropical flavor and a beautiful pale orange color. Mangoes have such a rich character that you might be surprised to learn that they are not particularly high in calories. That's because they have a relatively high percentage of water—which is why they're so juicy when ripe. They're a good source of potassium and beta-carotene. This drink is similar to an Indian lassi.

- 1 heaping cup fresh or frozen ripe mango

- 1 cup buttermilk, almond milk, or rice milk

- 1 teaspoon honey

- 1/2 medium ripe banana, preferably frozen

- 2 or 3 ice cubes, if using an unfrozen banana

*If you use almond milk or rice milk and omit the honey

Place the mango, milk, honey, banana, and ice cubes (if using) in a blender. Blend until smooth.

Per serving: 322 calories, 10 g protein, 71 g carbohydrates, 7 g fiber, 2.4 g fat, 1.4 g sat fat, 10 mg cholesterol, 258 mg sodium

Tofu Vegetable Scramble

Makes 4 servings

■ **VEGETARIAN** ■ **VEGAN** ■ **LOW-CALORIE** ■ LOW-FAT
■ **HIGH-PROTEIN** ■ **GLUTEN-FREE** ■ HIGH IN OMEGA-3S

Scrambled silken tofu is the vegan answer to scrambled eggs. The tofu will absorb the flavors of whatever you add to the dish. The small amount of curry powder in this savory scramble adds a pale yellow hue, along with the wonderful flavor of curry, to the mix. Serve with toast, tortillas, or flat bread.

1 tablespoon extra virgin olive oil

¼ cup finely chopped scallions

1 red bell pepper, diced

8 ounces mushrooms, cleaned, trimmed, and sliced

Salt

2 garlic cloves, minced

1 teaspoon minced fresh ginger

½ teaspoon mild curry powder

1 pound medium, medium-firm, or firm silken tofu

Ground black pepper

2 tablespoons chopped fresh herbs, such as parsley, cilantro, dill, chives

1. Heat the oil in a medium or large nonstick skillet over medium heat. Add the scallions and cook, stirring, until softened, 2 to 3 minutes. Add the bell pepper and cook, stirring, until it softens, 3 to 5 minutes. Add the mushrooms and a pinch of salt and cook, stirring often, until the mushrooms are tender and moist, about 5 minutes. Add the garlic, ginger, and curry powder and cook, stirring, for 1 or 2 minutes, or until the mixture is fragrant.

2. Crumble in the tofu and increase the heat to medium-high. Stir to combine, season with salt and black pepper, and continue to cook, stirring, until the tofu firms up and is heated through. Stir in the herbs.

Per serving: 130 calories, 10 g protein, 8 g carbohydrates, 2 g fiber, 7 g fat, 1 g sat fat, 0 mg cholesterol, 85 mg sodium

ADVANCE PREPARATION: You can make this several hours before adding the tofu. Set aside at room temperature or refrigerate. Heat until sizzling before proceeding.

Tofu Apple "Cheesecake" Spread

Makes about 10 servings, as a spread

■ **VEGETARIAN** ■ **VEGAN*** ■ **LOW-CALORIE** ■ LOW-FAT
■ HIGH-PROTEIN ■ GLUTEN-FREE ■ HIGH IN OMEGA-3S

This baked nondairy spread is sweetened with applesauce, honey, and spices, and it firms up as it bakes. I like to spread it on toast in the morning, but you could also slice it and serve it as you would a cheesecake.

8 ounces soft, medium, or firm silken tofu

1 cup unsweetened applesauce

¼ cup mild honey, such as clover, or agave syrup

1 tablespoon fresh lemon juice

1 tablespoon tahini

1 teaspoon vanilla extract

1 tablespoon unbleached all-purpose flour

½ teaspoon ground cinnamon

¼ teaspoon freshly grated nutmeg

¼ teaspoon salt

*If you omit the honey and use oil for the baking dish

1. Preheat the oven to 350°F. Butter or oil a 1-quart baking dish or loaf pan.

2. Place the tofu, applesauce, honey or agave syrup, lemon juice, tahini, vanilla extract, flour, cinnamon, nutmeg, and salt in a food processor blender. Process or blend until very smooth. Scrape into the prepared baking dish. Bake for 30 to 40 minutes, or until firm and just beginning to brown.

3. Allow to cool. Refrigerate until ready to serve.

Per serving: 62 calories, 2 g protein, 12 g carbohydrates, 0.5 g fiber, 1.5 g fat, 0 g sat fat, 0 mg cholesterol, 61 mg sodium

ADVANCE PREPARATION: This will keep for a week in the refrigerator. Although it will release water into the pan, which you'll want to pour off, it will still taste good.

FOR MORE BREAKFAST IDEAS SEE THE FOLLOWING RECIPES:

Chapter 2
SAUCES AND CONDIMENTS

Good sauces and condiments broaden your dinner options the way a well-stocked pantry does. One of the first things I teach beginning cooks to make is a delicious tomato sauce, using fresh, vine-ripened tomatoes in the summer and canned tomatoes during other seasons. With this one sauce under your belt, not only will you be able to make a wide range of pastas but also make a meal out of something as simple as a thick slice of bread, transform a pot of polenta or any other grain into an appealing main dish, and embellish a halibut fillet or a chicken breast. Give a kid who won't eat vegetables a plate of spaghetti and tomato sauce, and before you know it he's eaten his vegetables.

In this chapter I've grouped together sauces, dressings, and condiments that can be used in different ways and are used in recipes throughout this book. Some, like the Pickled Broccoli Stems on page 36, stand alone. Others are basic recipes, like vinaigrette, that every cook should know how to make. I'm convinced that the main reason my son has always been an enthusiastic eater of vegetables is that I always have vinaigrette to drizzle over a serving of broccoli, green beans, or asparagus as well as salads. Those vegetables taste great on their own, but they're even better doused with a good dressing.

Many of the sauces here are made with nuts and nut oils. Scientists are learning more and more about the health benefits of nuts, and I don't know a better way to incorporate them into your diet than in the pungent nut-based romesco sauce on page 29 and the skordalia on page 30.

Why should you bother to make a marinara sauce or a salad dressing when you have so many bottled options to choose from at your grocery store? The answer is simple: These are so much better and simpler. Taste your fresh, homemade tomato sauce or marinara sauce next to the jarred variety. Can you taste the stale garlic and added sugar in the store-bought sauce? Look at a bottle of salad dressing and count the number of ingredients. Then make your own, with just vinegar, olive oil, garlic, mustard, and salt. You just saved a couple of dollars, and in a matter of minutes, you've made something that tastes incredibly fresh and so much better than the manufactured dressing in the bottle—even if that bottle has the word *all-natural* or *organic* on it.

Summer Tomato Sauce

Makes about 2½ cups (5 servings)

■ **VEGETARIAN** ■ **VEGAN** ■ **LOW-CALORIE** ■ **LOW-FAT**
■ HIGH-PROTEIN ■ **GLUTEN-FREE** ■ HIGH IN OMEGA-3S

I have a small garden shaped like a pizza slice in a sunny corner outside my duplex in Los Angeles. Every summer I grow about 10 tomato plants there, and they yield enough tomatoes for me to make and freeze sauce that lasts through the winter. I measure the sauce into small resealable plastic bags by the ½-cup portion to pull out of the freezer and thaw for quick pasta dinners. This recipe is for a quick, simple marinara sauce that will only be good if your tomatoes are ripe. If you have a food mill, you don't have to peel and seed the tomatoes; you can just quarter them and put them through the mill. Cooking time will depend on the type of tomatoes you use. Plum tomatoes like Romas and San Marzanos (also known as paste tomatoes because of their dense texture), the type I use, will cook down more quickly and produce a thicker sauce than juicier varieties.

1 tablespoon extra virgin olive oil

2–3 garlic cloves, minced or thinly sliced

3 pounds ripe tomatoes, quartered if you have a food mill; peeled, seeded, and diced if you don't (see sidebar on page 21)

⅛ teaspoon sugar

2 basil sprigs

Salt

Ground black pepper (optional)

Slivered fresh basil (optional)

1. Heat the oil in a large nonstick skillet or a 3-quart saucepan over medium heat. Add the garlic. Cook, stirring, just until fragrant, 30 seconds to 1 minute. Add the tomatoes, sugar, basil, and salt (begin with ½ teaspoon and add more later if desired). Increase the heat to medium-high, and bring to a lively simmer. Reduce the heat to medium and simmer, stirring often, until thick. Pulpy tomatoes like Romas will take 15 to 20 minutes. Juicy tomatoes will take longer to cook down. The longer you cook the sauce, the sweeter it will be. You can speed up the process by turning up the heat, but stir often so the sauce doesn't scorch. Taste and adjust the seasoning with salt and black pepper (if using). Remove from the heat. Pull out the basil sprigs with tongs.

2. If you used quartered tomatoes, let the sauce cool a bit, then pass the mixture through the small or medium blade of a food mill (the holes should be small enough to keep the seeds from going through). If you used peeled, seeded tomatoes but want a sauce with a smooth texture, pulse the sauce in a food processor. If serving right away with pasta, heat through in a saucepan and garnish with the slivered basil (if using). If serving later, add the slivered basil (if using) when you reheat the sauce. If desired, thin out the sauce with a spoonful or more of cooking water from the pasta just before tossing.

Per ½-cup serving: 76 calories, 2 g protein, 11 g carbohydrates, 3 g fiber, 3.3 g fat, 0.5 g sat fat, 0 mg cholesterol, 72 mg sodium

ADVANCE PREPARATION: Tomato sauce keeps well. You can refrigerate it for up to 3 days, and freeze it for up to 6 months. To save room in your freezer, portion the sauce into small resealable plastic bags and lay flat. Or freeze the sauce in larger bags, laying flat, and break off chunks as needed.

Basic Pantry Marinara Sauce

Makes about 1½ cups (enough for 4 pasta servings)

■ **VEGETARIAN** ■ **VEGAN** ■ **LOW-CALORIE** ■ **LOW-FAT**
■ HIGH-PROTEIN ■ **GLUTEN-FREE** ■ HIGH IN OMEGA-3S

When you can't get fresh tomatoes in season, all you need to make a really good tomato sauce with a fresh taste and no hint of the bitter processed garlic aftertaste (present in almost every purchased marinara sauce I've ever tried) are the handful of ingredients below, a nonstick skillet or medium saucepan, and about 30 minutes. A sprig of basil is nice too, but it's not a deal breaker.

1 tablespoon extra virgin olive oil

2 garlic cloves, minced or thinly sliced

1 can (28 ounces) diced tomatoes

Pinch of sugar

Salt

1–2 fresh basil sprigs (optional)

Heat the oil in a wide nonstick skillet or saucepan over medium heat. Add the garlic. Cook until just fragrant, 30 seconds to 1 minute. Add the tomatoes (with juice), sugar, salt, and basil sprigs (if using). Stir and increase the heat to medium-high. When the tomatoes begin to bubble, reduce the heat back down to medium and cook, stirring often, until thick and fragrant, 20 to 30 minutes. Remove from the heat. Taste and adjust the seasoning with salt. Pull out the basil sprigs with tongs. If you want a smooth texture, pass the sauce through the fine or medium blade of a food mill or pulse in a food processor.

Per serving: 74 calories, 2 g protein, 7 g carbohydrates, 2 g fiber, 4 g fat, 0.5 g sat fat, 0 mg cholesterol, 501 mg sodium

ADVANCE PREPARATION: Tomato sauce keeps well. You can refrigerate it for up to 3 days, and freeze it for a few months. To save room in your freezer, portion the sauce into small resealable plastic bags and lay flat. Thaw as many portions as you need at a time.

OTHER ADDITIONS: You can add flavor to marinara sauce with any of the following:

• Up to 1 teaspoon crumbled dried thyme or oregano (alone or combined). Add with the tomatoes.

• A pinch of cayenne. Add toward the end of cooking.

• ¼ teaspoon red-pepper flakes. Add with the garlic.

• ⅓ cup chopped onion. Cook in the olive oil until tender, about 5 minutes, before adding the garlic.

• ¼ cup finely chopped carrot. Cook along with the onion, as above.

• ¼ cup finely chopped celery. Cook along with the onion, as above.

TOMATO SAUCE WITH . . .

Marinara sauce isn't necessarily destined for an arranged marriage with pasta or pizza. Try it with:

• Cooked chicken breasts or baked or steamed fish fillets

• Bruschetta

• Scrambled eggs

• Omelets

• Polenta

Uncooked Tomato Sauce

Makes 1½ cups

■ **VEGETARIAN** ■ **VEGAN** ■ **LOW-CALORIE** ■ **LOW-FAT**
■ HIGH-PROTEIN ■ **GLUTEN-FREE** ■ HIGH IN OMEGA-3S

If you've just come home from the farmers' market with a basket full of ripe heirloom tomatoes, or if your garden is brimming with them, you don't even need to bother cooking them before tossing them with pasta. Make this quick tomato concassé instead and serve it with pasta, alongside fish, or spooned onto bruschetta.

1 pound ripe tomatoes, finely chopped

Salt and ground black pepper

1–2 garlic cloves, minced

1 tablespoon extra virgin olive oil

1–2 tablespoons slivered or snipped fresh basil

Combine tomatoes, salt, black pepper, garlic, oil, and basil in a large bowl. Let sit for about 15 minutes or longer to allow the flavors to emerge. Taste and adjust the seasoning with salt and pepper.

Per ½-cup serving: 70 calories, 1 g protein, 6 g carbohydrates, 2 g fiber, 5 g fat, 1 g sat fat, 0 mg cholesterol, 56 mg sodium

ADVANCE PREPARATION: This can be made several hours ahead of serving.

Note: For a more refined tomato concassé, peel the tomatoes, halve them across the equator, and seed them over a sieve set over a bowl. Press the seed pods against the sieve to extract the juice, and discard the seeds. Finely chop the tomatoes, add the juice and remaining ingredients, and proceed with the recipe. If you want to accentuate the sweetness of the tomatoes, add ½ to 1 teaspoon balsamic vinegar.

Peeling and Seeding Tomatoes

To peel tomatoes, bring a pot of water to a boil and fill a bowl with ice water. Core the tomatoes and drop into the boiling water. Wait 30 seconds, then transfer to the ice water. The skins will peel off easily.

Tomato seeds are enclosed in juicy, gelatinous sacs that contain the most intense tomato flavor. When you seed tomatoes, do not just squeeze out the seeds over the sink or you'll sacrifice much of the best-tasting part of the fruit. Place a sieve over a bowl, halve the tomatoes across the equator, and squeeze over the sieve (if using plum tomatoes, halve lengthwise and use your finger to scoop out the seed pods). Rub the seed pods against the sieve with your fingers or with a pestle so that the juice goes through and the seeds stay behind. Always add this juice to a dish along with your seeded tomatoes.

Salsa Fresca (Fresh Tomato Salsa)

Makes about 2 ¼ cups

■ **VEGETARIAN** ■ **VEGAN** ■ **LOW-CALORIE** ■ **LOW-FAT**
■ HIGH-PROTEIN ■ **GLUTEN-FREE** ■ HIGH IN OMEGA-3S

Classic Mexican salsa can be used in a number of ways. It's a great accompaniment to any Mexican dish that calls for salsa, but it also partners well with grilled fish or chicken, with steamed mussels (page 316), fried or scrambled eggs, steamed rice, and a good pot of beans (page 274).

½ small red onion, minced

1½ pounds ripe tomatoes, chopped

2–3 jalapeño or serrano chile peppers, seeded if desired and minced (wear plastic gloves when handling)

¼ cup chopped cilantro

2–3 teaspoons fresh lime juice or 1 teaspoon balsamic vinegar (optional)

Salt

1. Place the onion in a small bowl and cover with cold water. Soak for 5 minutes, then drain and rinse with cold water. Drain on paper towels.

2. Combine the onion with the tomatoes, chile peppers, cilantro, lime juice or vinegar (if using), and salt in a large bowl. Let sit for 15 to 30 minutes before serving to allow the flavors to develop. Taste and adjust the seasoning with salt.

Per ¼-cup serving: 17 calories, 1 g protein, 4 g carbohydrates, 1 g fiber, 0 g fat, 0 mg sat fat, 0 mg cholesterol, 20 mg sodium

ADVANCE PREPARATION: Salsa fresca is not a great keeper. You can make it a couple of hours before you serve it, but in time it will become watery and lose its vivid flavor. Try to use it soon after you make it.

Seeding Chile Peppers

Much of the heat of chile peppers resides in the ribs and seeds. If you don't want your salsa to be super hot, discard them. But the heat has been bred out of many chile peppers sold in the United States, so taste before seeding.

Tomato and Avocado Salsa

Makes about 2 cups

■ **VEGETARIAN** ■ **VEGAN** ■ **LOW-CALORIE** ■ LOW-FAT
■ HIGH-PROTEIN ■ **GLUTEN-FREE** ■ HIGH IN OMEGA-3S

Avocado adds body and rich texture to a fresh tomato salsa. Served with fish or chicken, this salsa is almost like a side dish or salad. It's also great on its own, with soft corn tortillas and a sprinkling of crumbled queso fresco or feta cheese.

½ small red onion, finely diced

1 pound ripe tomatoes, finely diced

1–3 serrano or jalapeño chile peppers, seeded if desired and minced (wear plastic gloves when handling)

1 ripe avocado, preferably a Hass, peeled, pitted, and finely diced

1 tablespoon extra virgin olive oil

2–3 teaspoons fresh lime juice

¼ cup chopped cilantro

Salt

1. Place the onion in a small bowl and cover with cold water. Let soak for 5 minutes, then drain and rinse with cold water. Drain on paper towels.

2. Combine the onion with the tomatoes, chile peppers, avocado, oil, lime juice, cilantro, and salt. Let sit for about 15 minutes, in or out of the refrigerator, before serving.

Soaking Raw Onions

I get many e-mails from readers asking me why I soak the onions for 5 minutes in cold water. I do this whenever I'm using raw onions in a recipe. It rinses away some of the volatile oils that cause that onion flavor to linger in your mouth for hours after you finish eating. Until I learned to do this, I could never enjoy a dish with uncooked onions in it, because the abiding flavor of the onions always overpowered my overall memory of the dish.

Per ¼-cup serving: 57 calories, 1 g protein, 4 g carbohydrates, 2 g fiber, 4.5 g fat, 1 g sat fat, 0 mg cholesterol, 23 mg sodium

ADVANCE PREPARATION: This can be made a few hours before serving, but like regular tomato salsa it will become watery over time, and the avocado will darken as well.

VARIATION: TOMATO, CORN & AVOCADO SALSA

In the summer, when corn is in season, steam 1 ear of corn for 4 to 5 minutes. When cool enough to handle, use a sharp knife to slice the kernels off the cob and toss as directed on the previous page.

Roasted or Grilled Peppers

Makes enough to serve 4 as a salad,
or 8 as a condiment or hors d'oeuvre

■ **VEGETARIAN** ■ **VEGAN** ■ LOW-CALORIE ■ **LOW-FAT**
■ HIGH-PROTEIN ■ **GLUTEN-FREE** ■ HIGH IN OMEGA-3S

Roasting sweet bell peppers makes them even sweeter, with another layer of flavor from the charred skin that is removed. There are many ways to roast them. You can do it under a broiler or over a burner flame (the method I use most often if I only have one pepper to grill), or grill them over coals. Oven-roasting is the easiest method if you're roasting more than one or two peppers. It works well with our fleshy American peppers and it yields more juice than grilling does, but you have to watch closely if you roast thin lipstick peppers or piquillo-type peppers this way—if you overcook them the flesh becomes very soft and they'll fall apart when you try to peel them. Roasted or grilled peppers may be used interchangeably. Keep them on hand to add to salads, pasta, pizza, and panini.

4 medium red, green, or yellow bell peppers

Optional flavorings:

Sea salt (fine or coarse) or kosher salt and ground black pepper

Extra virgin olive oil (2–3 tablespoons)

1–2 garlic cloves, minced or pureed

Fresh basil leaves (slivered) or fresh tarragon, thyme, or marjoram (chopped)

Roasting in the oven:

1. Preheat the oven to 400°F. Line a baking sheet with foil. Place the peppers on the foil and roast in the oven for 40 to 45 minutes, using tongs to turn the peppers every 10 minutes. The peppers are done when their skins are brown and puffed. The skin won't be black and crinkled the way it is when you grill them.

2. Transfer the peppers to a bowl. Cover the bowl with a plate or with plastic wrap, and set aside for 20 to 30 minutes, or until cool.

3. Carefully remove the skins and seeds from the peppers, holding them over the bowl so you don't lose any of the juice. Oven-roasted peppers are very soft, so you can just pull them apart into halves, taking care to hold them over a bowl to catch the juices. Cut into strips, if desired, and place in another bowl. Toss with salt and pepper (if using). Strain the juice through a sieve into the bowl with the peppers. If storing for more than a day, toss with extra virgin olive oil. Refrigerate until ready to use. If you wish, toss with the garlic and fresh herbs shortly before serving.

Roasting over a flame:

Light a gas burner and place the pepper directly over the flame. Alternatively, place the pepper on a grill rack over hot coals. When I do this on my stove I like to set the pepper on a rack, or on a grill pan— the kind that has holes—for grilling vegetables on a barbecue. As soon as one section has blackened, use tongs to turn the pepper, exposing another section to the flame. Continue to turn until the entire pepper is blackened. Place in a resealable plastic bag and close tightly, or place in a bowl and cover tightly. Allow to sit until cool, then remove the charred skin. You may need to run the pepper briefly under the faucet to rinse off the final bits of charred skin. If so, pat dry with paper towels. Cut the pepper in half and hold it over a bowl while you remove the seeds and membranes. Slice and store as above.

Roasting under the broiler:

Preheat the broiler. Cover a baking sheet with foil and place the pepper on the sheet. Grill the pepper as

Garlic and Its Green Shoots

Years ago I spent a month cooking at the Bandol winery Domaine Tempier, in the South of France, with Lulu Peyraud, the proprietor's wife. Lulu taught me much of what I know about the food of Provence, and one thing she was adamant about was removing the green shoots that begin to grow inside garlic cloves a few months after the garlic is harvested. "They are bitter and they are not digestible," she told me. I never questioned Lulu's kitchen wisdom, so I have been removing green shoots ever since. I don't really think that they make garlic indigestible, but they can be bitter, so I continue to remove them.

---

close to the flame as possible, turning every 3 minutes or so, until uniformly charred. Proceed as described on the previous page.

Per serving (peppers only/based on 4 servings): 37 calories, 1 g protein, 7 g carbohydrates, 2 g fiber, 0 g fat, 0 g sat fat, 0 mg cholesterol, 5 mg sodium

ADVANCE PREPARATION: Roasted or grilled peppers will keep in the refrigerator for about 5 days. If you fully submerge them in olive oil they'll last a couple of weeks.

Drained Yogurt

Makes 1 cup

■ **VEGETARIAN** ■ VEGAN ■ **LOW-CALORIE** ■ **LOW-FAT**
■ **HIGH-PROTEIN** ■ **GLUTEN-FREE*** ■ HIGH IN OMEGA-3S

Yogurt can be drained of much of its water content, resulting in a thick, creamy product known in the Middle East as labneh or labna. Drained yogurt is like a moist, fresh, tangy cheese (and is actually sometimes referred to as yogurt cheese), and makes a great spread or dip. In Turkey and the Middle East there are a number of dips and salad dressings that begin with drained yogurt, to which pureed garlic and chopped fresh herbs are added. It's mixed with chopped cucumbers for salads, even mixed with chopped dried apricots for a sweet and tangy dip. Serve it as a spread, as a topping for rice, or as the base for a salad dressing.

I can't emphasize enough how important it is to find plain yogurt made without gums and stabilizers, otherwise the drained yogurt won't thicken properly. Look at the ingredients listed on your container. Milk and live active cultures should be all you find. Also, I use low-fat yogurt for all of my recipes, as opposed to nonfat yogurt. I find most nonfat yogurts to be too sour and often too watery.

2 cups low-fat yogurt

*If you use yogurt with no added stabilizers

Line a sieve with a double thickness of cheesecloth or a coffee filter and set it over a bowl. Place the yogurt in the sieve and refrigerate at least 2 hours, preferably 4 hours or longer. Transfer to a covered container and refrigerate.

Per 1 tablespoon serving: 20 calories, 0.5 g fat, 5 mg cholesterol

ADVANCE PREPARATION: This will last through the sell-by date on your yogurt. It will continue to give up water in its storage container. Simply pour it off.

VARIATIONS: Mix in any of the following:

- 1–2 large garlic cloves, halved, mixed with ¼ teaspoon salt and mashed to a paste using a mortar and pestle

- 1–2 tablespoons or more finely chopped fresh mint or dill (or other fresh herbs of your choice)

- ½ cup finely chopped dried apricots

- ½ teaspoon or more ground cumin (preferably freshly ground from lightly toasted cumin seeds), curry powder, or other spices

Sicilian Almond, Basil, and Tomato Sauce

Makes 1½ cups

■ **VEGETARIAN** ■ **VEGAN** ■ **LOW-CALORIE** ■ LOW-FAT
■ HIGH-PROTEIN ■ **GLUTEN-FREE** ■ HIGH IN OMEGA-3S

There are many ways to serve this vibrant, crunchy summer sauce, which is also known as Sicilian pesto (pesto Siciliano). You can toss it with pasta, pile it onto bruschetta, or serve it as an accompaniment to grilled meat, fish, and eggplant or other vegetables.

3–6 large garlic cloves, halved

4 large fresh basil leaves

¼ cup blanched almonds (raw, not roasted) (see note)

1 pound ripe tomatoes, preferably plum, peeled, seeded, and coarsely chopped (see sidebar, page 21), juice reserved

2–4 tablespoons extra virgin olive oil

Salt

Turn on a food processor and drop in the garlic. When the garlic is chopped and adhering to the sides of the bowl, stop the processor and scrape down the sides of the bowl. Add the basil and almonds and process to a paste. Turn off the machine and add the tomatoes. Pulse until you have a well-amalgamated, chunky mixture. Then, with the machine running, slowly drizzle in the olive oil. Add some or all of the tomato juice, depending on how much juice you have and how thick you want the sauce to be. Taste and adjust the seasoning with salt.

Per ½-cup serving: 186 calories, 4 g protein, 9 g carbohydrates, 3 g fiber, 16 g fat, 2 g sat fat, 0 mg cholesterol, 11 mg sodium

ADVANCE PREPARATION: You can make this several hours before serving. If holding for more than 1 hour, refrigerate, but let it come back to room temperature before serving.

Note: *To blanch almonds (if you can't find them already blanched), bring a saucepan filled with water to a boil. Fill a bowl with ice water. Drop the almonds in the boiling water, boil for 1 minute, then transfer to the ice water. Allow to cool for a few minutes, then remove from the ice water and slip off the skins.*

Nuts and Health

A recent European study measured the results of a Mediterranean diet supplemented by nuts on a sample population at risk for heart disease. Researchers found that the group that followed this diet did significantly better than a group on a regular low-fat diet, with a substantial decrease in incidents of heart disease. Although it may be difficult for some of us to shake the "low-fat" message of the early 1990s (we still need to be aware of fats, however, because they are caloric), we do ourselves a disservice if we shun all types of fats.

Some fats, namely those from plant sources, do not have an adverse affect on health if consumed judiciously; on the contrary, foods like nuts, which have a high polyunsaturated fat content, are an excellent source of vegetable protein, fiber, magnesium, calcium, folate, and vitamins K, B_6, and E. Nutritionists now recommend that nuts be included in the government's dietary recommendations.

Nut-based sauces and dips are a delicious way to work nuts into your diet. There are many Mediterranean and Mexican recipes to choose from. They keep well in the refrigerator and can be used to accompany fish, poultry, or vegetables, as a spread or dip for pita or bruschetta, or just eaten on their own.

Green Pipián

Makes about 1 ¾ cups

■ **VEGETARIAN*** ■ **VEGAN*** ■ **LOW-CALORIE** ■ LOW-FAT
■ HIGH-PROTEIN ■ **GLUTEN-FREE** ■ HIGH IN OMEGA-3S

Green pipian is a classic Mexican pumpkin seed sauce, also known as green mole. Its flavor is complex—tangy, herbal, and spicy all at the same time. Serve it with poached or pan-cooked chicken breasts, rabbit, fish (it looks very pretty with salmon), or shrimp; with grilled vegetables or with white beans and steamed or poached vegetables. Hulled untoasted pumpkin seeds are available in many whole foods stores and in Mexican markets.

½ cup raw hulled pumpkin seeds

½ pound tomatillos, husked, rinsed, and coarsely chopped, or 2 cans (13 ounces each) tomatillos, drained (available in the Mexican food section of most supermarkets)

1 serrano chile pepper or ½ jalapeño chile pepper, stemmed and coarsely chopped (wear plastic gloves when handling)

3 romaine lettuce leaves, torn into pieces

¼ small white onion, coarsely chopped, soaked for 5 minutes in cold water, rinsed and drained

2 garlic cloves, halved

¼ cup loosely packed chopped cilantro

1½ cups Vegetable stock (page 67) or chicken stock

2 tablespoons canola oil or extra virgin olive oil

Salt

If made with Vegetable Stock

1. Heat a heavy Dutch oven or large, heavy saucepan over medium heat. Add the pumpkin seeds. Wait until you hear one pop, then stir constantly until they have all puffed and popped, and smell toasty. Don't allow them to get any darker than golden or they will taste bitter. Transfer to a bowl and cool.

2. Place the cooled pumpkin seeds in a blender. Add the tomatillos, chile pepper, lettuce, onion, garlic, cilantro, and ½ cup of the stock. Cover and blend until smooth, stopping the blender to stir if necessary.

3. Heat the oil in the Dutch oven or saucepan over medium-high heat until a drop of the pumpkin seed mixture sizzles when drizzled in. Add to the pot and cook, stirring, until the mixture darkens and thickens, 8 to 10 minutes. It will splatter, so be careful and hold the lid above the pot to shield you and your stove. Add the remaining 1 cup stock, stir together, and bring to a simmer. Reduce the heat to medium-low and simmer uncovered, stirring often, until the sauce is thick and creamy, 15 to 20 minutes. Season to taste with salt. For a silkier sauce, blend again in batches.

Per ¼-cup serving: 106 calories, 3 g protein, 6 g carbohydrates, 1 g fiber, 9 g fat, 1 g sat fat, 0 mg cholesterol, 94 mg sodium

ADVANCE PREPARATION: The sauce can be made 5 days ahead and freezes well. Whisk or blend to restore its consistency after thawing. It's easy to double this recipe and freeze a batch. For a beautiful main dish, double the recipe and place cooked chicken breasts or fish fillets in a large baking dish, cover with the sauce, and heat through in a 350°F oven. Garnish with chopped cilantro and toasted pumpkin seeds and serve with rice.

Spanish Romesco Sauce

Makes about 2 cups

■ **VEGETARIAN** ■ **VEGAN** ■ **LOW-CALORIE** ■ LOW-FAT
■ HIGH-PROTEIN ■ **GLUTEN-FREE** ■ HIGH IN OMEGA-3S

Some Catalans will tell you that their famous grilled spring onion feast, called La Calçotada, is just an excuse to eat copious amounts of romesco. The thick, pungent, nut-thickened sauce made with hazelnuts and/or almonds, roasted peppers, tomatoes, and bread goes wonderfully with cooked vegetables of all kinds, whether grilled, steamed, or blanched. I serve it just as often with grilled or oven-roasted fish.

3 medium tomatoes or 4 Roma tomatoes (about ¾ pound)

2 large garlic cloves, halved

2 ounces baguette (2 thick slices) or country-style bread, lightly toasted

½ cup toasted almonds or skinned roasted hazelnuts, or a combination

1-2 teaspoons pure ground chile powder or red-pepper flakes (red-pepper flakes are hotter)

1 large red bell pepper, about ½ pound, roasted or grilled (page 24)

1 tablespoon chopped flat-leaf parsley

1 teaspoon sweet paprika or Spanish smoked paprika (pimentón)

Salt

Ground black pepper

2 tablespoons sherry vinegar

¼-½ cup extra virgin olive oil

1. Preheat the broiler and cover a baking sheet with foil. Place the tomatoes on the baking sheet and place under the broiler as close to the heat as possible. Broil for 2 to 4 minutes, until charred on one side. Turn and broil on the other side for 2 to 4 minutes, until charred. Remove from the heat, transfer to a bowl, and allow to cool. Peel and core.

2. Turn on a food processor and drop in the garlic cloves. When the garlic is chopped and adheres to the sides of the bowl, stop the processor and scrape down the sides. Add the bread, toasted nuts, and chile powder or red-pepper flakes to the bowl and process to a paste. Scrape down the sides of the bowl. Add the roasted bell pepper, tomatoes, parsley, paprika, salt, and black pepper. Process until smooth. With the machine running, add the vinegar and olive oil in a slow stream, beginning with the ¼ cup of olive oil and thinning out as desired. Process until well amalgamated, then scrape into a bowl. Taste and adjust the seasoning with salt and chile powder or red-pepper flakes as desired. If possible, allow the sauce to stand for 1 hour at room temperature before using.

Per ¼-cup serving: 164 calories, 3 g protein, 11 g carbohydrates, 2 g fiber, 12 g fat, 1.5 g sat fat, 0 mg cholesterol, 85 mg sodium

ADVANCED PREPARATION: Romesco keeps for at least 5 days in the refrigerator; the garlic will become more pungent.

Skordalia

Makes about 1½ cups

■ **VEGETARIAN** ■ **VEGAN** ■ LOW-CALORIE ■ LOW-FAT
■ HIGH-PROTEIN ■ **GLUTEN-FREE** ■ **HIGH IN OMEGA-3S**

There are many versions of skordalia, a pungent, aioli-like puree made with lots of garlic, potatoes, and olive oil. This Balkan version contains walnuts. Serve it with cooked vegetables (traditionally it's served with cooked beets and beet greens—page 125), with warm pita, or with fish.

> ½ pound russet or Yukon gold potatoes, peeled
>
> Salt
>
> 2–4 garlic cloves, halved
>
> 1 cup walnuts, coarsely chopped
>
> ⅓ cup extra virgin olive oil
>
> 2 tablespoons walnut oil
>
> 2 tablespoons fresh lemon juice
>
> 2–4 tablespoons red wine vinegar

1. Place the potatoes in a saucepan and cover with water. Add ½ teaspoon salt and bring slowly to a boil over medium heat. Reduce the heat, cover partially, and simmer until the potatoes are tender all the way through when pierced with a skewer. Drain, return the potatoes to the pot, and cover tightly. Set aside for 5 minutes. Mash the potatoes through a potato ricer, a food mill, or in a stand mixer fitted with the paddle attachment. (Do not use a food processor. Potatoes, because of the structure of their starch cells, will turn gummy in a food processor and your result will be like library paste.)

2. Use a mortar and pestle to mash the garlic to a paste with ¼ teaspoon salt. Add the walnuts and pound together (you can also do this in a food processor). Stir the garlic-walnut mixture into the potatoes. Gradually add the olive oil and the walnut oil, stirring all the while with a fork or a pestle. Add the lemon juice, vinegar, and salt to taste. The mixture should be like loose mashed potatoes. Taste and add more lemon juice, vinegar, and/or salt as needed. Transfer to a bowl and chill until ready to serve. If the mixture stiffens up, thin out with a little olive oil or water.

Per ¼-cup serving: 306 calories, 4 g protein, 9 g carbohydrates, 2 g fiber, 30 g fat, 3 g sat fat, 0 mg cholesterol, 26 mg sodium

ADVANCE PREPARATION: Skordalia will keep for up to 3 days in the refrigerator, but it will become quite pungent and it will stiffen up. It's best to eat it soon after you make it.

Turkish Yogurt and Spinach Dip

Makes about 2 cups

■ **VEGETARIAN** ■ VEGAN ■ **LOW-CALORIE** ■ **LOW-FAT***
■ HIGH-PROTEIN ■ **GLUTEN-FREE** ■ HIGH IN OMEGA-3S

This robust Turkish mixture of green vegetables, pureed garlic, fresh herbs, and yogurt can be eaten on its own as a salad, or as a dip with pita and/or raw vegetables. The same garlicky combination of yogurt and herbs can be mixed with a number of vegetables, both cooked (cabbage, beets, carrots) and raw (cucumbers), as it is in Turkey.

Salt

1 bag (6 ounces) baby spinach or 1 bunch (12 ounces) spinach, stemmed and washed

2 large garlic cloves, halved

1 tablespoon fresh lemon juice

3 tablespoons extra virgin olive oil

2 cups Drained Yogurt (page 25) or Greek yogurt

2 tablespoons chopped fresh dill

½ cup finely chopped flat-leaf parsley

2 tablespoons chopped fresh mint, or 1 teaspoon dried mint

1 bunch scallions, chopped (optional)

Ground black pepper

If the yogurt is low-fat

1. Bring a large pot of water to a boil. Fill a bowl with ice water. When the water comes to a boil, add a generous amount of salt and the spinach, and blanch for 10 to 20 seconds. Transfer to the ice water, cool for about 1 minute, then drain and squeeze dry. Chop coarsely.

2. Place the garlic and ½ teaspoon salt in a mortar and mash to a paste with a pestle. Combine with the lemon juice and olive oil and let stand for 10 minutes. Stir in the yogurt.

3. Combine the chopped spinach, dill, parsley, and mint in a medium bowl. Stir in the yogurt mixture and the scallions (if using). Add black pepper to taste and more salt if desired.

Per ¼-cup serving: 92 calories, 5 g protein, 5 g carbohydrates, 1 g fiber, 6 g fat, 1.5 g sat fat, 3 mg cholesterol, 71 mg sodium

ADVANCE PREPARATION: You can blanch and chop the spinach up to 3 days ahead. The dip will keep for a few days in the refrigerator, but it will become more pungent and the color of the spinach and herbs will darken.

Bagged Baby Spinach

If you avoid making spinach dishes because you find the stemming and cleaning to be a tedious chore, bagged baby spinach may change your life. I've done the calculation, and when you've finished stemming a typical 12-ounce bunch of spinach, you end up with about 6 ounces, the amount that comes in that expensive bag. So if your time is valuable or you find the cleaning too tedious, use the baby spinach.

Middle Eastern Avocado Puree

Makes about 1 cup

■ **VEGETARIAN** ■ **VEGAN** ■ LOW-CALORIE ■ LOW-FAT
■ HIGH-PROTEIN ■ **GLUTEN-FREE** ■ HIGH IN OMEGA-3S

Guacamole is not the only destination for mashed avocados. This puree, which is like an avocado hummus, is based on a recipe by Ana Sortun, from her book Spice: Flavors of the Eastern Mediterranean. Unlike guacamole, which should be chunky, this sauce should be smooth. It makes a great dip for pita bread or vegetables.

2 garlic cloves, halved

Salt

2 ripe avocados, pitted and scooped out

3 tablespoons tahini

¼ cup fresh lemon juice

2 tablespoons extra virgin olive oil

1 teaspoon cumin seeds, lightly toasted and ground

1. Place the garlic and ½ teaspoon salt in a large mortar and mash to a smooth paste with a pestle. Add the avocados to the mortar, and mash together with the garlic until the mixture is smooth. Work in the tahini, lemon juice, oil, cumin, and additional salt to taste.

2. Scrape into a bowl and cover with plastic wrap, setting the wrap right on top. Refrigerate until ready to use. Stir before serving.

Per ¼-cup serving: 251 calories, 4 g protein, 10 g carbohydrates, 5 g fiber, 24 g fat, 3 g sat fat, 0 mg cholesterol, 301 mg sodium

ADVANCE PREPARATION: You can make this a few hours before serving, but it is best served on the day it's made.

Note: *If you prefer, you can make this in a food processor. Turn on the food processor and drop in the garlic. When it is chopped and adhering to the sides, stop the machine and scrape down the sides of the bowl. Add the remaining ingredients and process until smooth.*

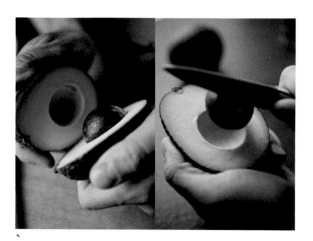

Using a Mortar and Pestle to Puree Garlic

A mortar and pestle is the perfect tool for pureeing garlic, but you have to use it the right way. Don't pound the garlic with an up-and-down wrist motion. That's too rough, and the garlic will become too pungent as you pound out the volatile oils. After gently mashing the garlic with your pestle to break it down, the motion should be more of a grinding action, circular around the inside of the bowl. The salt will help to break down the garlic and you'll have a beautiful, smooth puree that's strong-tasting but not unacceptably pungent when you finish.

Tuna Tapenade

Makes about 1¼ cups

■ VEGETARIAN ■ VEGAN ■ **LOW-CALORIE** ■ LOW-FAT
■ HIGH-PROTEIN ■ **GLUTEN-FREE** ■ HIGH IN OMEGA-3S

Many years ago, in an open-air market in a small village in the Vaucluse department of Provence, I discovered a number of tapenades made by a company called Délices du Luberon. They were traditional tapenades—made with olives, anchovies, capers, garlic, and herbs—but there were many variations. Some included almonds, others pesto, and one of my favorites combined olive oil–packed tuna with the olives. Délices du Luberon is still going strong—I bought tapenade from them just last summer at the Apt market—and so are their tapenades. This one continues to be one of my favorites. Serve it with croutons or raw vegetables, or use it as a filling for deviled eggs.

2 garlic cloves, halved

¼ pound imported black olives, pitted

1½ tablespoons capers, rinsed

4 anchovy fillets, soaked in cold water to cover for 15 minutes and drained

1 teaspoon fresh thyme leaves

1 teaspoon chopped fresh rosemary

2 tablespoons fresh lemon juice

1 teaspoon Dijon mustard

Ground black pepper

1 can (5–6 ½ ounces) olive oil–packed light tuna (not albacore) (see sidebar, page 54)

1–2 tablespoons extra virgin olive oil, as needed

Turn on a food processor and drop in the garlic. When the garlic is finely chopped and adhering to the sides of the machine, stop the machine and scrape down the sides of the bowl. Add the olives, capers, anchovy fillets, thyme, rosemary, lemon juice, mustard, and black pepper. Puree to a smooth paste. Scrape down the sides of the bowl. Add the tuna and olive oil. Process until you have a smooth

paste. Transfer to a bowl and refrigerate, covered, until ready to use.

Per ¼-cup serving: 134 calories, 9 g protein, 3 g carbohydrates, 0 g fiber, 10 g fat, 1 g sat fat, 8 mg cholesterol, 497 mg sodium

ADVANCE PREPARATION: This will keep for 3 to 4 days in the refrigerator. Place it in a bowl and if keeping for more than 1 day, cover with a film of olive oil. Cover tightly with plastic wrap and refrigerate.

Note: *When you pit the olives for this, be careful not to let any of the pits get into the bowl of olives. Check with your hands before putting the mixture into the food processor. You'll hear it if a pit gets into your food processor, then you'll have to pull out the blade and search for it, which can be a messy business. Double-check before you begin.*

VARIATION: GREEN OLIVE TAPENADE You can also make this tapenade with imported green olives, such as the picholine or lucques varieties.

A Tapenade-Filled Vegetable Platter

Tapenade makes a delicious filling for small vegetables like cherry tomatoes and baby squash. For a beautiful hors d'oeuvre platter, cut the tops off cherry tomatoes, scoop out some of the flesh and seeds with a grapefruit spoon, and spoon or pipe in some tapenade. Blanch baby pattypan squash, cut in half across the equator, scoop out seeds and fill with tapenade. It's also nice piped onto cucumber rounds.

Olive Oil Vinaigrette

Makes about ½ cup

■ **VEGETARIAN** ■ **VEGAN** ■ **LOW-CALORIE** ▪ LOW-FAT
▪ HIGH-PROTEIN ■ **GLUTEN-FREE** ▪ HIGH IN OMEGA-3S

Here's the bottom line: No bottled dressing will ever be as good as the dressing you make at home. This is the vinaigrette I eat every day. I make a triple batch once a week so that it's on hand whenever I need a vinaigrette for a salad or to brighten up vegetables. I begin with a generous pinch of salt—about ⅛ teaspoon. One of my tricks here is to marinate the garlic clove in the vinaigrette, rather than chopping it up or crushing it. That way the dressing doesn't become too pungent and will keep for longer.

2 tablespoons red wine vinegar, champagne vinegar, or sherry vinegar (sherry vinegar is my preference)

1 teaspoon balsamic vinegar (optional)

Salt, preferably coarse sea salt or fleur de sel (see sidebar, opposite page)

1 teaspoon Dijon mustard

6 tablespoons extra virgin olive oil

1 garlic clove, peeled

1. Combine the vinegars and salt in a glass measuring cup or a small bowl. Mix together until the salt dissolves Whisk in the mustard, then the olive oil.

2. Using a paring knife, slice the garlic up to the root end but not through it. Make a quarter turn and cut through the middle again, just up to but not through the root end, so that the clove stays intact but there are several exposed cut surfaces. Place the cut garlic clove in the dressing and allow to marinate for 30 minutes to an hour. Remove before serving.

Per 1-tablespoon serving: 96 calories, 0 g protein, 0 g carbohydrates, 0 g fiber, 11 g fat, 1.5 g sat fat, 0 mg cholesterol, 64 mg sodium

ADVANCE PREPARATION: This will keep for a week in the refrigerator, and if you love salads as much as I do you'll want to double or triple the recipe. You only need 1 garlic clove, however, if you do increase the recipe. The garlic continues to flavor the dressing throughout the week. You might want to remove the garlic after a day or two. I keep my dressing in a squeeze bottle, which makes it very easy to add to salads and vegetables.

VARIATION: WALNUT VINAIGRETTE Substitute 1 to 2 tablespoons walnut oil for 1 to 2 tablespoons of the olive oil. Make sure you use a fresh oil and refrigerate it after opening.

Sea Salt

I prefer to use sea salt in my vinaigrette, and with my salads in general. The French sea salt that I prefer for its fresh, sparkling flavor is hand-harvested from salt marshes in Brittany and the Camargue. The rarest and most expensive, which I never use in cooking but like to sprinkle onto foods and use in the above dressing, is fleur de sel, salt crystals that are formed on top of shallow water in salt marshes. In Brittany they are raked by women only (it being thought that men are not careful enough), as soon as the crystals sparkle.

Asian Salad Dressing

Makes about 1/2 cup

■ **VEGETARIAN** ■ **VEGAN** ■ **LOW-CALORIE** ■ LOW-FAT
■ HIGH-PROTEIN ■ **GLUTEN-FREE*** ■ HIGH IN OMEGA-3S

Use this tangy, gingery dressing with noodles, chicken salads, and grain salads that go well with Asian flavors. Feel free to spice this up with more cayenne, or by adding some Asian chili oil or minced fresh chiles.

2 tablespoons fresh lime juice

1 tablespoon seasoned rice vinegar

1 teaspoon minced fresh ginger

1 small garlic clove, minced

Salt or soy sauce

Pinch of cayenne

2 teaspoons Asian sesame oil or walnut oil

1/3 cup canola oil or peanut oil, or use half oil, half buttermilk

*If you use salt instead of the soy sauce

Whisk together the lime juice, vinegar, ginger, garlic, salt or soy sauce, cayenne, sesame or walnut oil, and canola or peanut oil and/or buttermilk in a small bowl or measuring cup. Taste and adjust the seasonings. Keep in the refrigerator.

Per 1-tablespoon serving: 96 calories, 0 g protein, 0 g carbohydrates, 0 g fiber, 11 g fat, 1 g sat fat, 0 mg cholesterol, 18 mg sodium

ADVANCE PREPARATION: This is best freshly made, but will keep for 1 or 2 days in the refrigerator.

Pickled Broccoli Stems

Makes about ³⁄₄ cup

■ **VEGETARIAN** ■ **VEGAN** ■ **LOW-CALORIE** ■ **LOW-FAT**
■ HIGH-PROTEIN ■ **GLUTEN-FREE** ■ HIGH IN OMEGA-3S

Kids and adults love these crunchy, garlicky pickles. One of my signature dishes, they are always on my coffee table for dinner guests to snack on. Why always? Because we eat a lot of broccoli, and this is the perfect destination for the stems. If you buy your broccoli with the stems attached (as opposed to the crowns only), you'll now feel like you're getting something for your money.

3 or 4 broccoli stems

¹⁄₂ teaspoon salt

1 medium garlic clove, minced or pureed

1 tablespoon sherry vinegar

2 tablespoons extra virgin olive oil

1. Peel the tough skins away from the broccoli stems and cut the stems into ¹⁄₄-inch-thick slices. Place in a medium jar and add the salt. Cover tightly and shake the jar to toss the stems with the salt. Refrigerate for several hours or overnight. The stems will lose some volume.

2. Drain the water that has accumulated in the jar. Add the garlic, vinegar, and oil and toss together. Refrigerate for several hours or overnight. Serve with toothpicks.

Per serving (based on 4 servings): 75 calories, 1 g protein, 2 carbohydrates, 1 g fiber, 7 g fat, 1 g sat fat, 0 mg cholesterol, 319 mg sodium

ADVANCE PREPARATION: These are best served within 1 day, so that the green color doesn't fade.

Chapter 3
SALADS

Salads are by nature recipes for health—or they should be. You may be shocked to find out that a serving of a typical restaurant Caesar salad can have upward of 1,200 calories, thanks to all the fried croutons and the thick, caloric dressing. But if you are in charge of what goes into your salad and, more important, your salad dressing, this won't be the case.

Since I began writing my *Recipes for Health* series, I have used salads to showcase many vegetables in season, as well as pantry staples like grains, beans, and tuna. There are salads in just about every cuisine in the world; some made with uncooked vegetables, some with cooked. Even vegetables as humble as celery, cauliflower, and carrots can be transformed into enticing salads.

Most of the salads in this chapter are light salads meant to be part of a larger meal, though I would gladly make a lunch of any of them. A few, like Mediterranean Chickpea Salad (page 41), Main Dish Tuna and Vegetable Salad (page 54), Warm Lentil Salad with Goat Cheese (page 44), and Hot and Sour Soba Salad (page 60) are substantial enough to serve as a main dish. For more salads robust enough to serve as the main event—those that highlight grains, beans, and chicken— see the list (next page).

In California, where I live and where salads reign supreme, I have achieved a certain renown for my salad making, and I've given quite a bit of thought to what defines a "good" salad. The dressing, of course, is key. It has to have enough acid but not too much. I like my salad dressings on the sharp side, but not so much that the acids overpower the oils or the ingredients in my salad. The amount of dressing you use is also important. Use enough so that you taste it with every bite, but not so much that your salad is wilted or awash in it.

Another thing that makes a salad memorable is the use of fresh herbs. The sweet, slightly anise-y flavor of fresh tarragon in my Beet and Mâche Salad with Walnuts (page 45), for example, enhances the natural sweetness in the beets, standing out but not taking over. Texture, too, is important. It's nice to have a blend of crisp and soft (lettuce, cooked beets, and goat cheese; fresh red bell peppers, chickpeas, and feta cheese). A little crunch (nuts, croutons) is often welcome. But salads shouldn't be too busy either. Decide what you want to show off—it could be as simple as a type of salad green or a grain—and then embellish it a little. And don't, please don't, overuse balsamic vinegar, which is cloying and has been much abused by cooks.

FOR MAIN-COURSE SALADS SEE ALSO:

Grated Carrot Salad

Makes 4 to 6 servings

■ **VEGETARIAN** ■ VEGAN ■ **LOW-CALORIE** ■ LOW-FAT
■ HIGH-PROTEIN ■ **GLUTEN-FREE** ■ HIGH IN OMEGA-3S

Grated carrot salads are standard fare in French cafes and charcuteries. Here I offer two versions, one with a traditional creamy vinaigrette and one with a hint of curry. They keep well and if you have one or both on hand I can guarantee you'll be eating carrots every day. I'll go weeks without making it, then when I get around to it I wonder how I could have forgotten how much I like these.

1 tablespoon fresh lemon juice

1 tablespoon sherry vinegar or white wine vinegar

1 teaspoon Dijon mustard

Salt and ground black pepper

2 tablespoons extra virgin olive oil or canola oil

2 tablespoons canola oil

2 tablespoons buttermilk

1 pound carrots, grated

1/4 cup finely chopped flat-leaf parsley

Whisk together the lemon juice, vinegar, mustard, salt, and black pepper, in a small bowl. Whisk in the oil and buttermilk. Toss with the carrots and parsley in a large bowl. Taste and adjust the seasoning with salt. Refrigerate if not eating right away. (I recommend making this 30 minutes to 1 hour ahead, then tossing again. Some liquid may accumulate in the bottom of the bowl, but I just stir it back into the salad because it's tasty.)

Per serving (based on 4 servings): 168 calories, 1 g protein, 10 g carbohydrates, 3 g fiber, 14 g fat, 2 g sat fat, 0 mg cholesterol, 140 mg sodium

ADVANCE PREPARATION: Grated carrot salads (without parsley) hold well for 1 or 2 days in the refrigerator. Add the parsley shortly before serving.

VARIATION: CURRY-LACED GRATED CARROT SALAD Use a total of 2 tablespoons lemon juice and omit the vinegar. Add 1 teaspoon curry powder and 1/2 teaspoon ground cumin (preferably from lightly toasted cumin seeds, freshly ground) to the dressing.

Moroccan Cooked Carrot Salad

Makes 4 servings

■ **VEGETARIAN** ■ **VEGAN*** ■ **LOW-CALORIE** ■ LOW-FAT
■ HIGH-PROTEIN ■ **GLUTEN-FREE** ■ HIGH IN OMEGA-3S

There are many versions of this comforting cooked carrot salad throughout the Middle East and North Africa. This one, seasoned with lemon juice, cumin, garlic, and olive oil, is always a crowd pleaser.

1 pound carrots, thinly sliced

3–4 tablespoons extra virgin olive oil

2 large garlic cloves, minced, or crushed to a paste with 1/4 teaspoon salt in a mortar and pestle

1 teaspoon cumin seeds, lightly toasted and ground

1/2 teaspoon ground black pepper

Salt

2–3 tablespoons fresh lemon juice

1/4 cup chopped flat-leaf parsley

Imported oil-cured black olives, for garnish

2 hard-cooked eggs, cut in wedges (optional)

*If you omit the hard-cooked eggs

1. Place the carrots in a steamer basket over 1 inch of boiling water. Cover and steam for 5 to 8 minutes, or until tender. Remove from the heat, rinse with cold water, and drain on paper towels.

2. Heat 2 tablespoons of the olive oil in a large, heavy skillet and add the garlic and cumin. Cook, stirring,

for about 30 seconds, until the garlic smells fragrant. Stir in the carrots, the pepper, and salt to taste. Stir together for a few minutes, until the carrots are nicely seasoned. Remove from the heat and stir in the lemon juice, remaining 1 to 2 tablespoons olive oil, and the parsley. Taste and adjust the salt and lemon juice as desired. Transfer to a platter, and decorate with olives and hard-cooked eggs (if using). Serve at room temperature.

Per serving: 149 calories, 1 g protein, 13 g carbohydrates, 4 g fiber, 11 g fat, 2 g sat fat, 0 mg cholesterol, 118 mg sodium

ADVANCE PREPARATION: You can make this several hours before serving. The dish, without the lemon juice and parsley, will keep for a couple of days in the refrigerator. Reheat gently on top of the stove and add the lemon juice and parsley.

Marinated Carrots with Fresh Mint

Makes 4 to 8 servings

■ **VEGETARIAN** ■ **VEGAN** ■ **LOW-CALORIE** ■ LOW-FAT
■ HIGH-PROTEIN ■ **GLUTEN-FREE** ■ HIGH IN OMEGA-3S

This is a great thing to do with carrots when they've been around in the refrigerator a little too long. Even better when they're sturdy and sweet. I like to serve them as hors d'oeuvres and pack them in my son's lunchbox.

1 pound carrots, quartered lengthwise and cut into 2- or 3-inch lengths

Coarse sea salt

2 tablespoons sherry vinegar

2 tablespoons extra virgin olive oil

1 tablespoon slivered fresh mint

Place the carrots in a steamer basket set over boiling water. Cover and steam for 5 to 6 minutes, or until just tender. Rinse under cold water and toss with a pinch of salt, the vinegar, and olive oil. Marinate for 15 minutes, then toss with the mint. Serve at room temperature, or refrigerate and serve chilled.

Per serving (based on 4 servings): 111 calories, 1 g protein, 11 g carbohydrates, 3 g fiber, 7 g fat, 1 g sat fat, 0 mg cholesterol, 109 mg sodium

ADVANCE PREPARATION: These keep well in the refrigerator for a week.

Mediterranean Chickpea Salad

Makes 4 main-course servings, 6 side-dish servings

■ **VEGETARIAN** ■ VEGAN ■ **LOW-CALORIE** ■ LOW-FAT
■ **HIGH-PROTEIN** ■ **GLUTEN-FREE** ■ HIGH IN OMEGA-3S

A substantial dish like this one is never far from hand if you have canned chickpeas. Make sure to rinse them well. Don't hesitate to make this salad in winter as well, without the tomatoes. If you're using dried chickpeas that you cooked, try serving this warm. Warm or cold, it's quickly assembled.

For the salad:

2 cans (15 ounces each) chickpeas, rinsed and drained, or 4 cups cooked chickpeas

¼ cup chopped flat-leaf parsley, or a combination of parsley and other herbs, such as chives, tarragon, marjoram, basil, and mint

1 small red bell pepper, chopped

2 medium tomatoes, diced

½ small red onion, sliced, soaked in cold water for 5 minutes, drained, rinsed, and dried on paper towels (optional)

6 kalamata olives, pitted and quartered lengthwise

½ cup (2 ounces) crumbled feta cheese

For the dressing:

1 tablespoon fresh lemon juice

1 tablespoon red wine vinegar, champagne vinegar, or sherry vinegar

1 small garlic clove, minced or pureed

¼ teaspoon cumin seeds, lightly toasted and crushed or coarsely ground

Salt and ground black pepper

¼ cup extra virgin olive oil

2 tablespoons plain low-fat yogurt

1. To make the salad: Toss together the chickpeas, herbs, bell pepper, tomatoes, onion (if using), olives, and feta cheese.

2. To make the dressing: Whisk together the lemon juice, vinegar, garlic, cumin, salt, black pepper, olive oil, and yogurt. Toss with the chickpeas.

> **Per serving (based on 4 servings):** 355 calories, 12 g protein, 29 g carbohydrates, 8 g fiber, 22 g fat, 5 g sat fat, 17 mg cholesterol, 524 mg sodium

ADVANCE PREPARATION: The salad can be assembled several hours before you wish to serve it. Keep in the refrigerator. Leftovers will still taste good the next day.

The Canned Beans in My Pantry

Canned beans are like instant health food, an excellent source of protein and fiber and a very good source of calcium, iron, folate, and potassium. When the broth from a pot of home-cooked beans isn't essential to a recipe, I always turn to canned. So I try to always have on hand one can each of chickpeas, cannelini, and black beans. Just make sure to rinse the beans well before you use them.

Warm Chickpea and Broccoli Salad

Makes 4 main-course servings, 6 side-dish servings

■ **VEGETARIAN** ■ VEGAN ■ LOW-CALORIE ■ LOW-FAT
■ **HIGH-PROTEIN** ■ **GLUTEN-FREE** ■ HIGH IN OMEGA-3S

I developed this salad one week when I was working with broccoli, one of those vegetables that I cook all the time but don't use in too many recipes—I usually just steam it and drizzle on some vinaigrette. I got to thinking, it's so good with vinaigrette, how about using it in a salad? It goes well with chickpeas. Red pepper and onion add color and crunch, and I like the way the dressing lodges in the florets. But don't dress the salad too early, because the bright green florets will eventually fade to a drab olive color because of the acid in the dressing.

½ pound (1 heaping cup) dried chickpeas, soaked for 6 hours or overnight in 1 quart water

1 bay leaf

Salt

½ small red onion, sliced

8 ounces broccoli crowns, broken into florets

2 tablespoons fresh lemon juice

½ teaspoon Dijon mustard

1 small garlic clove, minced

Ground black pepper

6 tablespoons extra virgin olive oil (or ¼ cup olive oil and 2 tablespoons buttermilk, for a low-fat dressing)

1 small red bell pepper, cut into 2-inch strips

¼ cup chopped flat-leaf parsley, or a combination of parsley and dill

2 ounces Parmesan, shaved (about ½ cup)

1. Drain the chickpeas and place in a large saucepan with enough water to cover by 2 inches. Add the bay leaf and bring to a boil. Reduce the heat, cover, and simmer for 1 hour. Add 1 teaspoon salt or more to taste. Continue to simmer 30 minutes to 1 hour, or until the chickpeas are tender.

2. Meanwhile, place the onion in a bowl and cover with cold water. Soak for 5 minutes, then drain and rinse. Dry on paper towels.

3. Place the broccoli in a steamer basket and steam over boiling water for 5 minutes. Drain, rinse with cold water to stop the cooking, and set aside.

4. Combine the lemon juice, mustard, garlic, salt, and black pepper. Whisk in oil (or the oil and buttermilk). Set aside.

5. When the chickpeas are tender, drain and discard the bay leaf. Toss the chickpeas with the onion, broccoli, bell pepper, and dressing. Add the herbs and Parmesan. Toss again, and serve warm.

Per serving (based on 4 servings): 482 calories, 19 g protein, 41 g carbohydrates, 12 g fiber, 29 g fat, 5 g sat fat, 12 mg cholesterol, 336 sodium

ADVANCE PREPARATION: You can cook the chickpeas 3 to 4 days ahead and refrigerate. Reheat and proceed with the recipe.

Seasoning Dried Beans

A reader recently e-mailed me to ask why his dried chickpeas always tasted dull compared to canned chickpeas. "I soak them and cook them for 1½ to 2 hours, yet they never taste vivid like canned beans." I wrote him back and asked if he were adding salt to the dried beans when he cooked them, and a few days later received a response thanking me profusely for solving the problem. Unless you have salt restrictions in your diet, it is essential to season dried beans with salt when you cook them, or they will taste dull. My rule of thumb is to add 1 teaspoon salt per quart of water. And no, the salt will not toughen the skins of the beans.

Warm Lentil Salad with Goat Cheese

Makes 4 to 6 main-course servings, 8 side-dish servings

■ **VEGETARIAN** ■ VEGAN ■ **LOW-CALORIE** ■ LOW-FAT
■ **HIGH-PROTEIN** ■ **GLUTEN-FREE** ■ HIGH IN OMEGA-3S

Serve this warm, comforting salad as a main course or as a side or starter. Use French green Le Puy lentils or black beluga lentils, both of which are smaller and firmer than brown lentils but have the same type of earthy flavor. They stay intact when you cook them, whereas brown lentils tend to fall apart. That's not so important if you're making lentil soup, but it does make a difference if you're making a salad.

For the salad:

1 pound (about 2¼ cups) French green or beluga lentils, rinsed and picked over

1 medium onion, halved

2 large garlic cloves, smashed but left whole

1 bay leaf

Salt

For the dressing:

¼ cup sherry vinegar or red wine vinegar

1 garlic clove, minced

2 teaspoons Dijon mustard

¼ cup extra virgin olive oil

Salt and ground black pepper

¼ cup minced flat-leaf parsley, or a mixture of parsley and chives

1 log (4 or 5 ounces) fresh goat cheese, cut into rounds

1. To make the salad: Combine the lentils, onion, garlic, and bay leaf in a large saucepan or soup pot. Add enough water to cover by 1½ inches. Bring to a simmer, add ¾ teaspoon salt, cover, and continue to simmer for 30 minutes, or until the lentils are tender all the way through but still intact. Set a sieve over a bowl and drain the lentils. Discard the onion, bay leaf, and garlic. Return the liquid to the pot and bring to a boil. Cook for 10 to 15 minutes, or until reduced to ½ cup. Taste and adjust the seasoning with salt.

2. Preheat the oven to 350°F.

3. To make the dressing: Whisk together the vinegar, garlic, mustard, oil, and reduced cooking liquid from the lentils. Season to taste with salt and black pepper. Stir in the parsley or parsley and chives and toss with the lentils.

4. Place the lentils in a baking dish and top with the rounds of goat cheese. Heat through for 15 minutes, or until the goat cheese has softened, and serve.

Per serving (based on 4 servings): 585 calories, 29 g protein, 66 g carbohydrates, 16 g fiber, 25 g fat, 8 g sat fat, 22 mg cholesterol, 294 mg sodium

ADVANCE PREPARATION: The lentils can be made and tossed with the dressing up to 3 days ahead. Do not add the parsley until just before warming the salad. Warm the mixture on top of the stove, stir in the parsley, then top with the goat cheese and warm in the oven as directed.

Beet and Mâche Salad with Walnuts

Makes 4 servings

■ **VEGETARIAN** ■ VEGAN ■ **LOW-CALORIE** ■ LOW-FAT
■ HIGH-PROTEIN ■ **GLUTEN-FREE** ■ HIGH IN OMEGA-3S

Mâche is a small, delicate, dark leafy green, also known by its English name, lamb's lettuce. It's now widely available. This is a classic French salad. I add a small amount of goat cheese or feta cheese to mine for a tart contrast to the sweetness of the beets.

For the salad:

4 medium beets (see note)

1 package (5 ounces) mâche, rinsed and dried (about 4 cups)

2 tablespoons broken walnuts, preferably from shelled fresh walnuts

½ cup (2 ounces) crumbled mild goat cheese or feta cheese

2 teaspoons minced fresh tarragon

1 teaspoon minced chives

For the dressing:

1 tablespoon sherry vinegar

1 teaspoon balsamic vinegar

Sea salt, kosher salt, or fleur de sel

½–1 teaspoon Dijon mustard

1 very small garlic clove, finely minced or put through a press

3 tablespoons extra virgin olive oil

1 tablespoon walnut oil

Ground black pepper

1. To make the salad: Preheat the oven to 425°F. Cut the greens away from the beets, reserving them for another use and leaving about ¼ inch of stems. Scrub the beets and place in a baking dish. Add ¼ inch water to the dish and cover tightly with foil or a lid. Place in the oven and roast for 40 minutes. Remove from the oven and allow to cool until you can handle them. Cut away the stem ends and slip off the skins. Cut into wedges or slice into half-moons. Combine with the mâche, walnuts, cheese, tarragon, and chives in a large bowl.

2. To make the dressing: Combine the sherry vinegar, balsamic vinegar, salt, mustard, and garlic in a small bowl and whisk until well mixed. Whisk in the olive oil and walnut oil. Add black pepper to taste.

3. Toss the salad with the dressing and serve.

Per serving: 246 calories, 6 g protein, 10 g carbohydrates, 3 g fiber, 21 g fat, 5 g sat fat, 11 mg cholesterol, 192 mg sodium

ADVANCE PREPARATION: The roasted beets will keep for 5 days in the refrigerator. You can make the dressing several hours ahead of serving.

Note: If you can find only small beets, use 5 or 6 and roast them for 30 minutes. If you can only find large, use 3 and roast them for 45 to 50 minutes.

VARIATION: Substitute 4 Belgian endives, sliced, for the mâche.

Kosher Salt

If I don't use sea salt or fleur de sel in a recipe, I usually use kosher salt. Chefs like kosher salt because the crystals are bigger than those in regular salt, so you need less of it to season food. Food seasoned with kosher salt isn't as salty as food seasoned with the same volume of free-flowing table or fine sea salt.

Mediterranean Beet and Yogurt Salad

Makes 4 servings

■ **VEGETARIAN** ■ VEGAN ■ **LOW-CALORIE** ■ LOW-FAT
■ HIGH-PROTEIN ■ **GLUTEN-FREE** ■ HIGH IN OMEGA-3S

Different versions of this pungent, pretty salad are popular from Turkey to North Africa. Red beets are used throughout the Mediterranean, but you could use any type. If you mix the yogurt into the beets, your salad will be pink. I prefer to spoon it over the top.

4 medium beets (see note, page 45)

2 tablespoons extra virgin olive oil

1½ tablespoons sherry vinegar, white wine vinegar, or cider vinegar

1 teaspoon sugar

Salt and ground black pepper

1 garlic clove, halved

½ cup plain low-fat Greek yogurt or drained plain low-fat yogurt

2 tablespoons minced fresh dill

1. Preheat the oven to 425°F. Cut the greens away from the beets, leaving about ¼ inch of stems. Scrub the beets and place in a baking dish. Add ¼ inch water to the dish and cover tightly with foil or a lid. Place in the oven and cook 40 minutes. Remove from the oven and allow to cool until you can handle them. Cut away the stem ends and slip off the skins. Cut into wedges or slice into half-moons.

2. Stir together the oil, vinegar, sugar, and salt and black pepper to taste. Toss with the warm beets. Allow to marinate for 2 to 3 hours at room temperature or in the refrigerator.

3. Place the garlic and ⅛ teaspoon salt in a mortar and mash to a paste with a pestle. Stir into the yogurt. The mixture should taste sharp. If you wish, mash another garlic clove and add to the yogurt. Stir in half of the dill. Add salt and black pepper to taste. Drain the beets. Stir some of the marinade into the yogurt (to taste). Toss with the beets, or arrange the beets on a platter and drizzle the yogurt over the top. Sprinkle on the remaining dill, and serve.

Per serving: 78 calories, 4 g protein, 15 g carbohydrates, 2 g fiber, 1 g fat, 0.5 g sat fat, 1 mg cholesterol, 109 mg sodium

ADVANCE PREPARATION: The beets can be prepared and marinated 4 to 5 days ahead.

Mediterranean Cucumber and Yogurt Salad

Makes 4 to 6 servings

■ **VEGETARIAN** ■ VEGAN ■ **LOW-CALORIE** ■ **LOW-FAT**
■ **HIGH-PROTEIN** ■ **GLUTEN-FREE** ■ HIGH IN OMEGA-3S

Called cacik (pronounced jah-JIK) in Turkey, tarator in the Balkans, tzatziki in Greece, each version of this salad is a variation on a theme: yogurt, cucumbers, garlic, fresh herbs. The yogurt is thick, and pungent with mashed garlic; the cucumbers either finely chopped or grated, then salted and allowed to wilt. Walnuts enrich the Balkan version, which is also considered a soup, as is cacik. India has its version too, raita, the cooling mixture that accompanies hot curries (though the Indian version does not have garlic in it). Whatever the cuisine, it's one of my favorite combinations, one I never forgo when I see it on a menu.

1 European cucumber or 3 Persian cucumbers, finely chopped or grated

Salt

2 cups drained plain low-fat yogurt (page 25)

2–3 garlic cloves, halved, mashed to a paste with ⅛ teaspoon salt with a mortar and pestle

2 tablespoons chopped fresh mint

Ground black pepper

2 tablespoons extra virgin olive oil (optional)

Sprig of mint (optional garnish)

1. Toss the cucumber with a generous amount of salt. Leave to wilt in a colander set in the sink for 20 minutes. Rinse and drain on paper towels.

2. Whisk together the yogurt, garlic, mint, salt, black pepper, and oil (if using). Stir in the cucumbers. Adjust the seasonings and serve.

Note: *To serve as a soup, place a couple of ice cubes in*

each of 4 bowls. If you wish, thin out the cucumber-yogurt mixture with a little water. Spoon into the bowls.

Per serving (based on 4 servings): 75 calories, 9 g protein, 6 g carbohydrates, 1 g fiber, 2 g fat, 1.5 g sat fat, 5 mg cholesterol, 69 mg sodium

ADVANCE PREPARATION: Don't make this too far ahead, as the cucumber will continue to release water into the salad, and the flavors and the color will fade.

VARIATIONS:

• Substitute dill for the mint.

• Stir ¼ to ½ cup finely chopped walnuts in with the other ingredients and substitute 1 tablespoon walnut oil for 1 tablespoon of the olive oil.

• Add 1 tablespoon fresh lemon juice or white wine vinegar.

Summer Salad
with Feta Cheese

Makes 4 to 6 servings

■ **VEGETARIAN** ■ VEGAN ■ **LOW-CALORIE** ■ LOW-FAT
■ HIGH-PROTEIN ■ **GLUTEN-FREE** ■ HIGH IN OMEGA-3S

During the summer, when tomato production in my garden is in full swing, I tend to make this modified Greek salad almost nightly. You can add other vegetables—romaine lettuce hearts, broken up or cut into wide strips; bell peppers, sliced into rings; red onion, sliced (soak in cold water for 5 minutes, then rinse and drain if you don't want the strong taste of raw onion to linger in your mouth). Basil or parsley can stand in for or accompany the mint. Don't bother making the salad if your tomatoes aren't local and in season.

> 1 pound ripe tomatoes, cut into wedges (if large, halve the wedges crosswise), or 1 pint cherry tomatoes, halved
>
> ½ European cucumber or 1 Persian or Japanese cucumber, halved lengthwise, seeded if desired, then sliced into half-moons about ⅓ inch thick.
>
> Sea salt or fleur de sel (see sidebar, page 35) and ground black pepper
>
> 2 tablespoons red wine vinegar or sherry vinegar
>
> ¼ cup extra virgin olive oil
>
> ½ cup (2 ounces) crumbled feta cheese
>
> 1–2 tablespoons chopped fresh mint, or ¾ teaspoon dried oregano

Toss together the tomatoes, cucumber, salt, pepper, vinegar, and oil. Add the cheese and herbs, and toss again. Taste, adjust the seasonings, and serve.

Per serving (based on 4 servings): 200 calories, 4 g protein, 6 g carbohydrates, 2 g fiber, 18 g fat, 5 g sat fat, 17 mg cholesterol, 246 mg sodium

ADVANCE PREPARATION: You can assemble the salad hours before adding the salt and black pepper, vinegar, and olive oil. If you salt the salad too long before serving, it will become watery as the salt draws out the juices from the vegetables.

VARIATIONS: Add any or all of the ingredients below:

- ½ small red onion, sliced, soaked in cold water for 5 minutes, then rinsed and drained on paper towels
- 12–18 imported Greek black olives, such as kalamatas or amphissas, pitted
- 1 small green, yellow, or red bell pepper, sliced
- 1 heart of romaine lettuce, cut into 2-inch pieces
- Torn or chopped fresh basil
- Chopped flat-leaf parsley

Roasted Pepper and Tomato Salad

Makes 4 servings

■ **VEGETARIAN** ■ VEGAN ■ **LOW-CALORIE** ■ LOW-FAT
■ HIGH-PROTEIN ■ **GLUTEN-FREE** ■ HIGH IN OMEGA-3S

When tomatoes and bell peppers sit side by side at the farmers' market in late August and through September, I make lots of dishes using both of them, including this salad, as well as Pipérade (page 248) and Spanish Romesco Sauce (page 29). If you're looking for a recipe that will help you increase your intake of lycopene and vitamin C, look no further.

1½ pounds red or red and yellow bell peppers, roasted (page 24)

1 tablespoon plus 1 teaspoon sherry vinegar

1 small garlic clove, minced

¼ cup extra virgin olive oil

Salt and ground black pepper

1 tablespoon slivered fresh basil or chopped flat-leaf parsley, or a combination

The heart of 1 head of leaf lettuce or romaine, washed and dried

1 pound ripe tomatoes, cut into wedges

½ cup (2 ounces) crumbled goat cheese, blue cheese, or feta cheese (optional)

1. Cut the bell peppers into ½-inch-wide strips. Mix together the vinegar, garlic, oil, and salt and black pepper to taste. Toss 2 tablespoons of the vinegar mixture with the bell peppers. Add half of the basil and/or parsley to the peppers. Toss again.

2. Tear the lettuce into bite-size pieces. Toss with the tomatoes and the remaining dressing and fresh herbs. Line a platter or a wide bowl with the lettuce and tomatoes. Top with the bell peppers. Sprinkle on the cheese (if using). Serve at room temperature or slightly chilled.

Per serving: 207 calories, 3 g protein, 16 g carbohydrates, 5 g fiber, 15 g fat, 2 g sat fat, 0 mg cholesterol, 51 mg sodium

ADVANCE PREPARATION: Roasted or grilled bell peppers will keep in the refrigerator about 5 days. If you fully submerge them in olive oil, they'll last a couple of weeks.

Zucchini and Avocado Salsa Salad

Makes 6 servings

■ **VEGETARIAN** ■ **VEGAN** ■ **LOW-CALORIE** ■ LOW-FAT
■ HIGH-PROTEIN ■ **GLUTEN-FREE** ■ HIGH IN OMEGA-3S

I like to eat this salsa salad with rice. The salt in the salad draws a lot of juice from the tomatoes and zucchini, and when you spoon the mixture over the rice the juice penetrates it like a sauce. Whenever you make a dish with uncooked zucchini, be sure to slice or dice very fine, so that the zucchini can absorb the dressing or seasonings.

1 medium zucchini, diced very small

Salt

1 pound ripe tomatoes, finely chopped

1–2 jalapeño or serrano chile peppers, seeded if desired and finely chopped (wear plastic gloves when handling)

¼–½ cup chopped cilantro

1 Hass avocado, ripe but not too soft, cut into tiny dice

3 tablespoons fresh lemon or lime juice

3 tablespoons extra virgin olive oil

Boston lettuce or romaine lettuce leaves or 3 cups steamed white rice, for serving

1. Sprinkle the zucchini with salt and drain in a colander for 15 minutes. Rinse if the zucchini tastes very salty, and drain on paper towels.

2. Combine the tomatoes, chile peppers, and cilantro in an attractive bowl. Combine the zucchini, avocado, and lemon or lime juice in another bowl. Taste and add salt if desired. Add to the tomatoes and toss together gently with the oil. Taste and adjust the seasonings. Serve on lettuce leaves as a salad, or serve over rice.

Per serving: 124 calories, 2 g protein, 7 g carbohydrates, 3 g fiber, 11 g fat, 2 g sat fat, 0 mg cholesterol, 34 mg sodium

ADVANCE PREPARATION: You can assemble this several hours ahead. It will even keep for a day in the refrigerator, but it will become watery—not a bad thing if you are serving it over rice, with the juices poured over.

Fine Dicing Zucchini

To cut the zucchini into a tiny dice, first slice them, very thin, lengthwise. Stack several slices and cut them into a fine dice.

Cold Steamed Eggplant with Sesame Soy Dressing

Makes 6 servings

■ **VEGETARIAN** ■ **VEGAN** ■ **LOW-CALORIE** ■ **LOW-FAT**
■ HIGH-PROTEIN ■ GLUTEN-FREE ■ HIGH IN OMEGA-3S

Steamed eggplant has a delicate, silky texture. For the best flavor, dress the eggplant while still hot, then refrigerate and serve the salad cold. If you want to add more spice to this salad, include the minced serrano chile. I don't peel the eggplant. It's prettier that way, and some of the most valuable nutrients in eggplant are in the deep purple skin.

2 pounds eggplant, preferably Japanese eggplants

1 tablespoon soy sauce

1 tablespoon fresh lime juice

1 tablespoon seasoned rice vinegar

1 small garlic clove, minced

1–2 teaspoons minced fresh ginger

Pinch of cayenne or red-pepper flakes

1 tablespoon Asian sesame oil or walnut oil

2 tablespoons extra virgin olive oil

1 small serrano chile pepper, seeded if desired and minced (wear plastic gloves when handling), optional

Salt and ground black pepper

1 tablespoon chopped fresh chives or cilantro

1 bag (6 ounces) baby arugula, washed and dried, for serving

1 small red bell pepper, thinly sliced (optional)

1. If using Japanese eggplant, halve lengthwise, then cut into pieces that will fit into your steamer. If using large globe eggplants, quarter lengthwise then across. Place in a steamer basket set over boiling water and steam for 10 to 15 minutes, or until thoroughly tender and you can cut through with the tip of a knife with no resistance. You will probably have to do this in 2 batches.

2. Meanwhile, make the dressing: Whisk together the soy sauce, lime juice, vinegar, garlic, ginger, cayenne or red-pepper flakes, sesame or walnut oil, and olive oil. Set aside.

3. When the eggplant is tender, use tongs to remove it from the steamer and transfer to a cutting board. Allow to cool for 5 minutes, then cut into 1-inch-wide slices. Season with salt and black pepper. While still warm, toss the eggplant with the dressing and the chile pepper (if using). Refrigerate for 1 hour or longer.

4. Remove the eggplant from the refrigerator. Gently toss with the chives or cilantro. Arrange the arugula on a platter and top with the eggplant. Garnish with the bell pepper, if desired.

Per serving: 109 calories, 3 g protein, 10 g carbohydrates, 6 g fiber, 7.5 g fat, 1 g sat fat, 0 mg cholesterol, 254 mg sodium

ADVANCE PREPARATION: You can make this through Step 3 several hours ahead of serving.

Baby Salad Greens with Sweet Potato Croutons and Stilton

Makes 4 servings

■ **VEGETARIAN** ■ VEGAN ■ **LOW-CALORIE** ■ LOW-FAT
■ HIGH-PROTEIN ■ **GLUTEN-FREE** ■ HIGH IN OMEGA-3S

During the fall and winter I buy sweet potatoes regularly. I usually roast them, but sometimes I use this vitamin-rich vegetable in salads. They contrast beautifully here with a pungent blue cheese like Stilton. Other cheeses I like for this salad are goat cheese and feta.

For the dressing:

¼ cup buttermilk

2 tablespoons extra virgin olive oil

1 tablespoon fresh lime juice

1 teaspoon balsamic vinegar

½ teaspoon Dijon mustard

1 small garlic clove, minced

Salt and ground black pepper

For the salad:

1 large sweet potato (10 to 12 ounces), peeled and cut into ½-inch dice

1 tablespoon extra virgin olive oil

1 bag (6 ounces) baby salad greens

½ cup (2 ounces) crumbled Stilton or other blue cheese

1 tablespoon chopped fresh herbs, such as tarragon, parsley, chervil, chives, or a combination

1. To make the dressing: Whisk together the buttermilk, olive oil, lime juice, vinegar, mustard, garlic, and salt and black pepper to taste in a small bowl.

2. To make the salad: Place the sweet potatoes in a steamer basket set over boiling water. Cover and steam for 5 minutes, until just tender. Remove from the heat and drain on paper towels.

3. Heat the olive oil in a medium, nonstick skillet over medium-high heat. Add the sweet potatoes and cook, shaking the pan and moving the pieces around often, for 10 minutes, or until evenly browned on all sides. Remove from the heat; drain on paper towels.

4. Place the salad greens in a salad bowl and top with the cheese. Toss with the dressing. Sprinkle on the herbs and sweet potato croutons and serve.

Per serving: 212 calories, 6 g protein, 13 g carbohydrates, 2 g fiber, 16 g fat, 5 g sat fat, 13 mg cholesterol, 331 mg sodium

ADVANCE PREPARATION: You can steam the sweet potatoes and make the dressing several hours ahead.

Main Dish Tuna and Vegetable Salad

Makes 4 to 6 main-course servings

■ VEGETARIAN ■ VEGAN ■ LOW-CALORIE ■ LOW-FAT
■ HIGH-PROTEIN ■ GLUTEN-FREE ■ HIGH IN OMEGA-3S

Think beyond the Provençal version of this salad, Salade Niçoise, a summer salad that includes tomatoes, cucumbers, and green peppers. A tuna, potato, and vegetable salad is a winner year-round, with some adjustments. If tomatoes are out of season, shred a carrot; if green beans don't look good, use broccoli. And always include lots of minced fresh herbs. You can substitute 2 tablespoons of yogurt for some of the olive oil for a lower-fat dressing.

For the vinaigrette:

2 tablespoons good quality red or white wine vinegar or sherry vinegar

1 tablespoon fresh lemon juice

1 garlic clove, small or large, finely minced or mashed to a paste with a mortar and pestle

1 teaspoon Dijon mustard

Salt and ground black pepper

½ cup extra virgin olive oil (or 6 tablespoons oil plus 2 tablespoons plain low-fat yogurt)

For the salad:

1 pound medium Yukon gold or fingerling potatoes, cut into ¾-inch dice

Salt and ground black pepper

1 can (5–6½ ounces) water-packed light tuna (not albacore), drained

6 ounces green beans, halved if long

1 small red or green bell pepper, thinly sliced or diced

1 small cucumber (preferably Persian), halved lengthwise and sliced into half-moons

3–4 tomatoes, cut into wedges, shredded or shaved using a vegetable peeler

2–4 tablespoons chopped fresh herbs, such as parsley, basil, tarragon, chives, or marjoram

1 small head of Boston lettuce or romaine heart, or 4–5 cups mixed baby salad greens

A handful of imported black olives

2 hard-cooked eggs, preferably free-range, peeled and cut into wedges

1. To make the vinaigrette: Mix together the vinegar, lemon juice, garlic, mustard, and salt and pepper with a fork or a small whisk. Whisk in the oil or oil and yogurt.

2. To make the salad: Steam the potatoes above 1 inch of simmering water for 10 to 15 minutes, or until tender. Transfer to a large salad bowl and season with salt and pepper. Add the tuna. While the potatoes are hot, toss with ¼ cup of the dressing.

3. Fill a bowl with ice water. Bring a pot of water to a boil. When the water comes to a boil, add a generous amount of salt and the green beans. Cook for 4 to

Canned Tuna

Tuna is a superb source of protein, B vitamins, and the trace mineral selenium, and the water-packed version is an excellent source of omega-3s. Unfortunately, albacore tuna is also high in methylmercury, and for this reason it's not recommended for pregnant women, women who might become pregnant, nursing mothers, or young children. Light chunk tuna is a better bet. The FDA recommends that people in these groups eat no more than 6 ounces of albacore tuna a week, and no more than 12 ounces of light tuna. (Some nutritionists advise pregnant and nursing mothers to avoid tuna entirely.) Of course, the cans that used to weigh 6 ounces now weigh 5 ounces, so you shouldn't have trouble staying within these parameters.

How to Make Hard-Cooked Eggs

I like the yolks of my hard-cooked eggs to remain ever so slightly soft in the middle, and I look for free-range eggs with very yellow yolks. Place the eggs in a saucepan, cover with cold water, and bring to a boil. Cover the pot tightly and turn off the heat. Let the eggs stand in the hot water for 10 minutes for a dark, very slightly soft yolk, or 12 minutes for a thoroughly hard-boiled yolk. Meanwhile, fill a bowl with ice water. Drain and chill the eggs in the ice bath for several minutes, then peel or store.

5 minutes, or until just tender. Transfer to the ice water, cool, and drain. Dry on paper towels. If using broccoli, steam for 4 to 5 minutes, refresh in the ice water, then drain and dry on paper towels. Add the cooked vegetables to the salad bowl. Add the bell pepper, cucumber, and half of the herbs. Toss together with another ¼ cup of the dressing.

4. Add half of the tomatoes, the remaining herbs, and the salad greens to the salad bowl. Toss with the remaining dressing. Alternatively, toss the salad greens and remaining herbs with the remaining dressing. Pile onto a platter or into a wide salad bowl. Top with the potato mixture. Garnish with the rest of the tomatoes, olives, and eggs.

> **Per serving (based on 4 servings):** 488 calories, 18 g protein, 32 g carbohydrates, 5 g fiber, 32 g fat, 5 g sat fat, 117 mg cholesterol, 286 mg sodium

ADVANCE PREPARATION: The dressing and all the vegetables can be prepared several hours before assembling the salad. The potatoes can be cooked and tossed with the tuna and dressing several hours ahead as well.

VARIATION: WINTER MAIN DISH TUNA AND VEGETABLE SALAD Substitute broccoli florets for the green beans and 1 large carrot for the tomatoes. Steam the broccoli for 4 to 5 minutes and either grate the carrot or save with a vegetable peeler.

Warm Potato Salad with Goat Cheese

Makes 6 servings

■ **VEGETARIAN** ▢ VEGAN ■ **LOW-CALORIE** ▢ LOW-FAT
▢ HIGH-PROTEIN ■ **GLUTEN-FREE** ▢ HIGH IN OMEGA-3S

Everybody loves this creamy salad. What's not to like about warm potatoes infused with soft goat cheese and a tangy vinaigrette? You can use Yukon golds, fingerlings, or red bliss potatoes. The goat cheese melts into the dressing when you toss it with the hot potatoes.

For the dressing:

2 tablespoons white wine vinegar or sherry vinegar

1 teaspoon Dijon mustard

1 small or medium garlic clove, minced or pureed with a mortar and pestle

Salt and ground black pepper

⅓ cup extra virgin olive oil (or ¼ cup low-fat yogurt or buttermilk and 2 tablespoons extra virgin olive oil, for a low-fat dressing)

For the salad:

1½ pounds Yukon gold or red bliss potatoes or a combination, scrubbed and cut into ¾-inch dice, or fingerlings, scrubbed and sliced ¾ inch thick

Salt and ground black pepper

2–4 tablespoons finely chopped red onion, soaked for 5 minutes in cold water, drained, rinsed, and dried on paper towels

2 tablespoons chopped flat-leaf parsley

½ cup (2 ounces) crumbled soft goat cheese

2–3 fresh sage leaves, thinly slivered (optional)

1. To make the dressing: Whisk together the vinegar, mustard, garlic, and salt and black pepper. Whisk in the oil (or the yogurt and oil). Taste and adjust the seasonings. Set aside.

2. To make the salad: Steam the potatoes above 1 inch of boiling water for 10 to 12 minutes, or until tender but not mushy. Remove from the heat. While hot, toss the potatoes in a bowl with salt and pepper, the onion, parsley, goat cheese, and dressing. Sprinkle in the sage (if using) and serve.

Per serving: 238 calories, 5 g protein, 19 g carbohydrates, 2 g fiber, 16 g fat, 4 g sat fat, 9 mg cholesterol, 137 mg sodium

ADVANCE PREPARATION: You can make the dressing several hours before making the salad.

Broccoli and Endive Salad with Goat Cheese and Red Peppers

Makes 6 servings

■ **VEGETARIAN** ■ VEGAN ■ **LOW-CALORIE** ■ LOW-FAT
■ HIGH-PROTEIN ■ **GLUTEN-FREE** ■ HIGH IN OMEGA-3S

Another twist on the broccoli-in-a-salad theme, this one plays bitter against sweet with the endive and the sweet roasted peppers. It's a beautiful salad that makes a very nice dinner party first course. I blanch the broccoli here rather than steam it because it's brighter when blanched. But be very careful not to blanch it for more than 2½ minutes, or it will be mushy. If you prefer, you can steam it for 4 to 5 minutes.

For the dressing:

2 tablespoons sherry vinegar or champagne vinegar

1 teaspoon balsamic vinegar

Salt

1 small garlic clove, minced or pureed with a mortar and pestle

1 teaspoon Dijon mustard

6 tablespoons extra virgin olive oil (or ¼ cup extra virgin olive oil and 2 tablespoons buttermilk, for a lower fat dressing)

For the salad:

12 ounces broccoli crowns (2 good-size crowns)

Salt

1 red bell pepper, roasted or grilled (page 24), cut into strips

1 tablespoon lightly toasted pine nuts

¾ cup (3 ounces) crumbled goat cheese

6 Belgian endives, leaves separated

2–4 tablespoons chopped fresh herbs, such as a mix of parsley, basil, tarragon, chives, or marjoram

1. To make the dressing: Mix together the vinegars, salt, garlic, and mustard in a small bowl. Whisk in the oil (or buttermilk and oil). Set aside.

2. To make the salad: Bring a saucepan of water to a boil. Fill a bowl with ice water. When the water comes to a boil, salt generously and add the broccoli. Cook for 2½ minutes. Transfer to the ice water, let cool for a few minutes, and drain. Dry on paper towels. Toss in a bowl with the roasted pepper, pine nuts, goat cheese, and half of the dressing.

3. Toss together the endives, herbs, and remaining dressing in a wide salad bowl. Top with the broccoli mixture, and serve.

Per serving: 221 calories, 6 g protein, 7 g carbohydrates, 4 g fiber, 20 g fat, 5 g sat fat, 11 mg cholesterol, 135 mg sodium

ADVANCE PREPARATION: You can make the dressing and blanch the broccoli several hours ahead. Do not toss the broccoli with the dressing until you're ready to serve the salad, or the color will fade and the flavor will change.

Toasting Pine Nuts

Pine nuts are oily, and once they begin to toast they can burn quickly if you don't watch carefully. Heat them in a dry skillet over medium-high heat. Once they begin to smell toasty, shake the pan constantly. Remove them from the pan as soon as they begin to color. Look for pine nuts from the Mediterranean or domestic pine nuts.

Japanese Spinach with Sesame Dressing

Makes 4 small servings

■ **VEGETARIAN** ■ **VEGAN** ■ **LOW-CALORIE** ■ **LOW-FAT**
■ HIGH-PROTEIN ■ GLUTEN-FREE ■ HIGH IN OMEGA-3S

Cold spinach bathed in a nutty sesame dressing is my all-time favorite Japanese appetizer. Recipes vary, with some calling for rice wine vinegar, others for dashi, and most much sweeter than mine. This one isn't as authentic as the Japanese recipes I've seen, because it doesn't call for as much sugar. If you are on a low-sodium diet, reduce the amount of soy sauce by half or more. If you are on a no-sodium diet, use lemon juice instead of soy sauce. A grooved Japanese mortar and pestle, called a suribachi, is the perfect implement for crushing but not pulverizing the sesame seeds, but you can also use a regular mortar and pestle or a spice mill.

Salt

2 bags (6 ounces each) baby spinach or 1½ pounds bunch spinach, stemmed and washed

3 tablespoons sesame seeds, preferably toasted

1 tablespoon plus 1 teaspoon low-sodium soy sauce

2 teaspoons sugar

1 tablespoon sake

½ teaspoon Asian sesame oil

1. Bring a large pot of water to a boil. Fill a bowl with ice water. When the water comes to a boil, salt generously and add the spinach. Blanch the spinach for 10 to 20 seconds. Transfer to the ice water using a deep-fry skimmer. Drain and gently squeeze out the water. Chop coarsely.

2. If your sesame seeds have not been toasted, heat a dry skillet over medium heat and add the sesame seeds. Shake the pan and stir constantly, and as soon as the seeds turn golden and smell nutty, transfer to a suribachi, mortar and pestle, or a spice mill. Allow to cool. Grind the seeds just until crushed.

3. Combine the soy sauce and sugar in a small bowl. Stir until the sugar has dissolved. Add the sake and 1 tablespoon water, then stir in the crushed sesame seeds. If the mixture is pasty, thin out with 1 or 2 more tablespoons of water. Toss with the spinach until the spinach is coated with the dressing. Be careful not to bruise the spinach leaves. Divide into 4 small bunches and place in the middle of 4 small plates or bowls. Drizzle on a few drops of sesame oil. Serve at room temperature.

Per serving: 95 calories, 4 g protein, 13 g carbohydrates, 5 g fiber, 4 g fat, 0.5 g sat fat, 0 mg cholesterol, 328 mg sodium

ADVANCE PREPARATION: You can blanch the spinach up to 1 day ahead. The dish can be assembled and refrigerated several hours before serving.

Spinach Salad with Seared Shiitake Mushrooms

Makes 4 to 6 servings

■ **VEGETARIAN** ▢ VEGAN ■ **LOW-CALORIE** ▢ LOW-FAT
▢ HIGH-PROTEIN ■ **GLUTEN-FREE** ▢ HIGH IN OMEGA-3S

Spinach and mushroom salad is a classic, but seared shiitakes make this version a little different. You shouldn't have much trouble finding shiitake mushrooms; they're sold in my supermarket along with cremini and button mushrooms. When you pan-cook them over high heat, as you do here, their flavor intensifies.

For the dressing:

1 tablespoon red or white wine vinegar or sherry vinegar

1 tablespoon fresh lemon juice

1 small garlic clove, finely minced or mashed to a paste with a mortar and pestle

1 teaspoon Dijon mustard

Salt and ground black pepper

⅓ cup extra virgin olive oil (or ¼ cup low-fat yogurt or buttermilk and 2 tablespoons extra virgin olive oil, for a low-fat dressing)

For the salad:

1 package (6 ounces) baby spinach, rinsed and dried

1–2 tablespoons pine nuts or broken walnut pieces, lightly toasted

1 celery rib, preferably from the inner heart of the celery, thinly sliced

¼ cup (1 ounce) crumbled goat cheese, feta cheese, or blue cheese, or 1 ounce Parmesan, shaved (about ¼ cup)

1 teaspoon canola oil

6 large or 8 smaller fresh shiitake mushrooms, stemmed and sliced

Salt and ground black pepper

1. To make the dressing: Combine the vinegar, lemon juice, garlic, mustard, and salt and pepper in a small bowl or a glass measuring cup. Mix together with a fork or a small whisk. Whisk in the olive oil (or yogurt or buttermilk and olive oil). Set aside.

2. To make the salad: Combine the spinach, nuts, celery, and cheese in a salad bowl.

3. Heat a skillet over medium-high heat. Add the canola oil. When very hot, add the mushrooms. Shake the skillet once, then let the mushrooms cook without moving them around until they begin to sweat and soften (watch closely). After 1 or 2 minutes, when the mushrooms have begun to sear and release moisture, stir. Cook for about 5 minutes, season to taste with salt and black pepper, and remove from the heat. Add to the spinach mixture and toss with the dressing. Serve at once.

Per serving (based on 4 servings): 257 calories, 4 g protein, 9 g carbohydrates, 3 g fiber, 24 g fat, 5 g sat fat, 7 mg cholesterol, 225 mg sodium

ADVANCE PREPARATION: All the ingredients can be prepped and the salad dressing made several hours before you cook the mushrooms and dress the salad.

Mushroom and Fresh Herb Salad

Makes 4 servings

■ **VEGETARIAN** ■ VEGAN ■ **LOW-CALORIE** ■ LOW-FAT
■ HIGH-PROTEIN ■ **GLUTEN-FREE** ■ HIGH IN OMEGA-3S

I first tasted a salad made from nothing but fresh herbs at L'Arpège restaurant in Paris. It was a revelation. But this wonderful idea has been kicking around outside of 3-star restaurants for centuries. Herb salads are eaten throughout the Middle East, and in Georgia, Armenia, and Iran. Use a selection of sweet- and sharp-tasting herbs, such as tarragon, chervil, parsley, wild arugula, and dill, and slice the mushrooms as thin as you can. You can also serve this salad on top of bruschetta.

8 ounces large firm white or cremini mushrooms, trimmed and very thinly sliced

2 tablespoons fresh lemon juice

2 cups fresh herb leaves, such as tarragon, chervil, dill, chives, wild arugula, and parsley (see sidebar), coarsely chopped (1 cup chopped herbs)

1 ounce Parmesan, shaved (about ¼ cup)

1 teaspoon balsamic vinegar

Salt and ground black pepper

¼ cup extra virgin olive oil

1. Toss the mushrooms with 1 tablespoon of the lemon juice in a salad bowl. Add the herbs and Parmesan.

2. Combine the remaining 1 tablespoon lemon juice and the vinegar. Add the salt and black pepper, and whisk in the olive oil. Toss with the mushrooms, herbs, and Parmesan, and serve.

Per serving: 194 calories, 5 g protein, 6 g carbohydrates, 0 g fiber, 17 g fat, 3 g sat fat, 5 mg cholesterol, 165 mg sodium

ADVANCE PREPARATION: You can prepare all the ingredients a few hours before, but serve the salad right after you assemble it. The herbs will wilt quickly once tossed.

Chopping a Lot of Parsley and Other Fresh Herbs

The easiest way to chop a lot of parsley, if it doesn't require a very fine mince, is to do it with a scissors. Place the cleaned herb leaves in a glass measuring cup or a wide glass or jar (such as a jelly jar) and chop by cutting with scissors, pointing the scissors tip straight down in the measuring cup.

Hot and Sour Soba Salad

Makes 6 servings

■ **VEGETARIAN** ■ **VEGAN*** ■ LOW-CALORIE ■ LOW-FAT
■ HIGH-PROTEIN ■ GLUTEN-FREE ■ HIGH IN OMEGA-3S

I find any combination of noodles and hot and sour dressing addictive, and none more so than these earthy buckwheat noodles. You can make a meal of this salad if you add a little protein to the mix in the form of tofu, shredded chicken, or shrimp.

For the dressing:

1–2 tablespoons peanut butter

1 tablespoon soy sauce

2 tablespoons white wine vinegar or seasoned rice wine vinegar

1–2 teaspoons hot chili oil

Pinch of cayenne

1 large garlic clove, minced

2 teaspoons minced fresh ginger

Salt and ground black pepper

1 tablespoon Asian sesame oil

2 tablespoons canola oil

½ cup Vegetable Stock (page 67) or chicken stock

For the salad:

Salt

½ pound soba noodles

1 cup diced or julienned cucumber (peeled if the cucumber has been waxed)

¼ cup chopped cilantro

¼ cup coarsely chopped walnuts

Lettuce, baby spinach, radicchio, or arugula for serving (optional)

*If made with Vegetable Stock

1. To make the dressing: Heat the peanut butter for 10 to 20 seconds in a microwave to make it easier to mix. Combine with the soy sauce, vinegar, chili oil, cayenne, garlic, ginger, salt, and black pepper, and whisk together. Whisk in the sesame oil, canola oil, and stock. Set aside.

2. To make the salad: Bring a large pot of water to a boil. Add salt if desired and the noodles. When the water returns to a boil and bubbles up, add a cup of cold water to the pot. Allow the water to come back to a boil and add another cup of cold water. Allow the water to come back to a boil and add another cup of water. When the water comes to a boil for the last time, the noodles should be cooked through.

Drain and toss immediately with the dressing (whisk the dressing again first).

Add the cucumber, cilantro, and walnuts and toss together. Taste and adjust the seasonings. Serve over a bed of salad greens if desired.

Per serving: 269 calories, 8 g protein, 34 g carbohydrates, 2 g fiber, 14 g fat, 2 g sat fat, 1 mg cholesterol, 586 mg sodium

ADVANCE PREPARATION: You can cook the noodles up to 3 days ahead. Toss them with 2 teaspoons canola oil and refrigerate. The noodles may also be cooked several hours ahead, tossed with the dressing, and held at room temperature. Toss with the cucumber, cilantro, and walnuts shortly before serving.

VARIATIONS: Add any of these to the mix:

• 4 to 8 ounces poached, shredded chicken breast (page 322)

• 4 to 6 ounces cooked shrimp

• 4 to 8 ounces uncooked or pan-fried cubed tofu (page 254)

Rice Noodle Salad

Makes 4 main-course servings, 6 side-dish servings

■ **VEGETARIAN*** ■ **VEGAN*** ■ **LOW-CALORIE** ■ **LOW-FAT**
■ HIGH-PROTEIN ■ **GLUTEN-FREE**** ■ HIGH IN OMEGA-3S

Also known as rice sticks, Southeast Asian rice flour noodles are delicate and versatile, and especially welcome to those who cannot eat wheat. Available in Asian grocery stores, the noodles require a 20-minute soak in warm water to soften, then usually 1 to 1½ minutes of cooking in boiling water (though I've found that if I keep noodles around for too long, more than a year, they may take 3 to 5 minutes to cook). You can also use Chinese cellophane noodles (made from bean starch) for this Thai salad. It makes a satisfying lunch, or it can be served as a starter or side dish.

For the dressing:

¼ cup fresh lime juice

2 tablespoons Thai fish sauce or 1 tablespoon soy sauce

1 teaspoon sugar

2–3 teaspoons finely minced ginger

½ teaspoon red-pepper flakes or a pinch of cayenne

2 tablespoons Asian sesame oil

2 tablespoons canola oil

For the salad:

3 ounces dried rice noodles or cellophane noodles

½ small Napa cabbage or 1 romaine heart

3 scallions, thinly sliced on the diagonal (optional)

1 cup coarsely chopped cilantro

1 medium carrot, grated or cut into fine julienne

Lettuce leaves, for the bowl or platter

*If you omit the fish sauce

**If you omit the soy sauce

1. To make the dressing: Mix together the lime juice, fish sauce or soy sauce, sugar, ginger, red-pepper flakes or cayenne, sesame oil, and canola oil. Taste and adjust the seasonings.

2. To make the salad: Place the rice or cellophane noodles in a large bowl and cover with warm water. Soak for 20 minutes and drain. Bring a large pot of water to a boil and add the noodles. Cook for 1½ minutes, or until tender. Drain well. Cut coarsely into approximately 4-inch lengths using scissors. Toss with all but 2 tablespoons of the dressing.

3. If using Napa cabbage, cut the halved cabbage in half again, cut out the core, then slice crosswise into thin strips. If using romaine, halve lengthwise, then slice crosswise into thin strips. Toss with the noodles, scallions (if using), cilantro, and carrot.

4. Line a platter or bowl with lettuce leaves and pile on the salad. Spoon on the remaining dressing, and serve.

Per serving (based on 4 servings): 219 calories, 2 g protein, 23 g carbohydrates, 2 g fiber, 14 g fat, 2 g sat fat, 0 mg cholesterol, 711 mg sodium

ADVANCE PREPARATION: You can prepare this through Step 2 up to 1 day ahead and refrigerate. The assembled salad through Step 3 will hold for a couple of hours, making it a good choice for a buffet.

Chapter 4
SOUPS

If you are looking for ways to shift the focus of your meals away from meat and incorporate more vegetables into your diet, soups are a good place to start. There are probably more soups than any other type of dish in the *Recipes for Health* archives, because no matter what type of produce from the farmers' market I'm writing about, or which grains, beans, or other pantry staples I'm featuring, there is always a simple and hearty potage to show them off.

I didn't grow up in a soup-eating family. There was the occasional Campbell's chicken noodle soup or tomato soup with saltine crackers for lunch, but I cannot remember one dinner in my childhood that revolved around soup. When I began to cook for myself, however, I discovered how convenient—and inexpensive—it is to combine beans and/or grains and vegetables in one pot, and how delicious and filling a meal a well-seasoned soup can be. When I decided to make a career of cooking, I opened a "Supper Club"—weekly 3-course dinners for 30 paying guests in my home. The meals were vegetarian, and they always began with a soup, which I would make in a huge canning pot. On cold winter days I would sell soup to street vendors and shoppers on The Drag on Guadalupe Street across from the University of Texas campus, and I taught many a soup class in my vegetarian cooking classes.

I learned even more about soups when I lived in France for 12 years, where soup and bread (sometimes but not always with salad) are often served as the evening meal, especially when the main meal of the day has been a substantial lunch.

The most important thing I learned was that French home cooks do not fret over their soups. They come home from work and make them quickly. A chef will tell you that you need stock for a good soup, but home cooks know that water, vegetables, and aromatics are all that you need to make a comforting dinner like Potato "Bouillabaisse" (page 76), Creamy Cabbage Soup with Gruyère (page 80), or Provençal Greens Soup (page 72).

Some of the soups here that include beans require more simmering time, but no more work. Hearty, filling soups such as North African Bean and Squash Soup (page 84) may look like long recipes when you eye the ingredients list, but in fact, the instructions are simple: Soften the aromatics in oil, simmer the beans, add more vegetables, and let the soup cook unattended until everything is tender and fragrant. The Italian word *minestrone* means "big soup," and even those soups that don't have their origins in Italy are big enough to convince the staunchest meat-and-potatoes kind of guy that a soup can make a meal.

Vegetable Stock

Makes about 7 cups

■ **VEGETARIAN** ■ **VEGAN** ■ **LOW-CALORIE** ■ **LOW-FAT**
■ HIGH-PROTEIN ■ **GLUTEN-FREE** ■ HIGH IN OMEGA-3S

I don't make vegetable stock as a matter of course, but when I want to give my vegetarian soups or a risotto a little more flavor, I'll make a very simple one, like this. I prefer it to commercial vegetable stocks, which to my palate taste acrid. Hang on to vegetable trimmings—parsley stems, carrot tops, mushroom stems, the outer leaves of leeks and their dark green ends—and use them for homemade vegetable stock instead of letting them go to waste. If you're making a one-vegetable soup, like the corn soup on page 85, then it really makes a difference if you make a stock with the trimmings (in this case, the corncobs).

1 onion, quartered

1 garlic head, halved crosswise

4 carrots, sliced

1–2 celery ribs, sliced

1 leek, sliced

Bouquet garni made with a few flat-leaf parsley sprigs, 1–2 thyme sprigs, and a bay leaf (see below)

Vegetable trimmings such as chard ribs (sliced), parsley stems, leek greens (cleaned and sliced), mushroom stems, scallion trimmings, carrot tops, turnip peels

6 peppercorns

Salt

Combine the onion, garlic, carrots, celery, leek, bouquet garni, vegetable trimmings, peppercorns, and salt in a large soup pot. Add 2 quarts water and bring to a boil over high heat. Reduce the heat and cover partially. Simmer gently for 30 to 45 minutes. Strain through a sieve lined with cheesecloth. Use within 1 day, or freeze in small containers.

Per 1-cup serving: 20 calories, 0 g protein, 5 g carbohydrates, 0 g fiber, 0 g fat, 0 g sat fat, 0 mg cholesterol, 330 mg sodium

ADVANCE PREPARATION: This is best if used when freshly made, though it can be frozen.

Bouquet Garni

This French cooking term refers to a bundle of flavorings added to soups and stews and discarded at the end of cooking. A bouquet garni usually consists of sprigs of parsley and thyme and a bay leaf, tied together with kitchen string. Other herbs like sage or cilantro can also be used, depending on the recipe. You can include spices like peppercorns and tie the ingredients into a piece of cheesecloth. I often add a Parmesan rind to my bouquet garni, particularly for hearty minestrones. The Parmesan adds a rich, almost meaty dimension to the broth, so hang on to the rinds when you buy your hunks of Parmesan. Keep them in the refrigerator until you need them for a soup.

Garlic Broth

Makes about 7 cups

■ **VEGETARIAN** ■ **VEGAN** ■ **LOW-CALORIE** ■ **LOW-FAT**
■ HIGH-PROTEIN ■ **GLUTEN-FREE** ■ HIGH IN OMEGA-3S

Whole cloves of garlic, uncut and simmered gently for 1 hour with aromatics, yield a mild, sweet-tasting, comforting broth that makes an ideal vegetarian stand-in for chicken broth. According to nutritionist Jonny Bowden, garlic needs to be crushed, sliced, or chopped in order for its compounds to be released. For this broth, I just crush the cloves lightly by leaning on them with the flat side of my knife. The less crushed they are, the milder the broth will taste.

2 garlic heads, separated into cloves, unpeeled

1 tablespoon extra virgin olive oil

Bouquet garni made with a bay leaf, a fresh sage leaf, and a couple of sprigs each of thyme and flat-leaf parsley (see bottom of page 67)

Salt

1. Bring a medium saucepan of water to a boil over high heat. Fill a bowl with ice water. Drop the garlic into the boiling water. Blanch for 30 seconds, then transfer to the ice water. Allow to cool for a few minutes, then drain and remove the skins. They'll be loose and easy to remove. Lightly crush the cloves by leaning on them with the flat side of a chef's knife.

2. Place the garlic in a large saucepan with the oil, bouquet garni, salt, and 2 quarts water. Bring to a gentle boil over medium-high heat. Reduce the heat, cover, and simmer for 1 hour. Strain, discarding the solids. Taste and adjust the seasoning with salt.

ADVANCE PREPARATION: This can be made a day ahead and freezes well. It's at its best, however, the day it's made.

Roasted Tomato Soup

Makes 4 servings

■ **VEGETARIAN** ■ **VEGAN** ■ **LOW-CALORIE** ■ **LOW-FAT**
■ HIGH-PROTEIN ■ GLUTEN-FREE ■ HIGH IN OMEGA-3S

Roasting tomatoes intensifies their flavor, concentrating the sugars to give them a caramelized dimension. When you make this with vine-ripened tomatoes that are sweet to begin with, you'll have a soup with an unimaginable depth of flavor. This recipe is inspired by one that I learned to make with Mark Peel, chef-owner of Campanile in Los Angeles.

4 pounds ripe tomatoes

2 tablespoons extra virgin olive oil

1 small onion, chopped

2 large garlic cloves, minced

¼ teaspoon sugar

2 ounces country bread (1 thick slice), lightly toasted

2 sprigs each of basil, flat-leaf parsley, and thyme

Salt and ground black pepper

2 cups water or Garlic Broth (opposite page)

Fleur de sel (optional)

Slivered fresh basil leaves (optional)

Garlic croutons (page 326), optional

1. Preheat the broiler. Line 1 or 2 baking sheets with foil. Place the whole, uncut tomatoes on the foil. Place under the broiler at the highest rack setting (about 2 to 3 inches from the heat). Cook the tomatoes, turning with tongs when charred on one side. (This could take anywhere from 2 to 6 minutes, depending on your broiler, so watch carefully.) Char on the other side. Remove from the heat. Tip the tomatoes and any juice on the baking sheet into a large bowl. When the tomatoes are cool enough to handle, peel, core, and chop coarsely.

2. Heat the oil in a large, heavy soup pot or Dutch oven over medium heat. Add the onion. Cook, stirring, until tender, about 5 minutes. Add the garlic. Cook, stirring, for 1 minute, or until the garlic is fragrant. Stir in the tomatoes and their juices, sugar, bread, basil, parsley, thyme, and salt. Cook, stirring often, until the tomatoes have cooked down and the mixture is thick and beginning to adhere to the bottom of the pot, about 20 minutes. Adjust the seasoning with salt and black pepper. Remove from the heat.

3. Blend the soup using an immersion blender, or in batches in a food processor or blender (do not close the blender tightly; place a towel over the blender lid to prevent hot soup from splashing out) until smooth. Strain the soup through a medium sieve into a bowl, pressing the soup through with the bottom of a ladle, a rubber spatula, or a pestle. Rinse the blender or food processor with the water or broth and add to the puree (or just add to the puree if you used an immersion blender).

4. Return the strained soup to the pot and bring to a simmer. Simmer, stirring often, for 15 minutes, or until thick and fragrant. Taste and adjust the seasoning with salt. Serve. If desired, garnish with a sprinkling of fleur de sel, slivered basil, and a few garlic croutons.

Per serving: 193 calories, 5 g protein, 27 g carbohydrates, 6 g fiber, 8 g fat, 1 g sat fat, 0 mg cholesterol, 153 mg sodium

ADVANCE PREPARATION: The soup will hold well for several hours. You can roast the tomatoes a day ahead and refrigerate.

Winter Tomato and Celery Soup with Rice

Makes 4 to 6 servings

■ **VEGETARIAN** ■ **VEGAN*** ■ **LOW-CALORIE** ■ **LOW-FAT**
■ HIGH-PROTEIN ■ **GLUTEN-FREE** ■ HIGH IN OMEGA-3S

Every so often I focus my attention on celery recipes. That's because, like most cooks, I'm often faced with the remains of a bunch lingering in my refrigerator after I've used the one rib that I needed for a dish. This flavorful winter soup, which is simpler than a minestrone yet satisfying in the same way, is a great way to use it up.

2 tablespoons extra virgin olive oil

1 medium onion, chopped

1 medium carrot, diced

4 celery ribs, diced

4 garlic cloves, minced

Salt

1 can (28 ounces) diced tomatoes

Pinch of sugar

2 tablespoons tomato paste

Bouquet garni made with 2 sprigs each of thyme and flat-leaf parsley, a bay leaf, and a Parmesan rind (page 67)

1 teaspoon dried oregano

½ cup rice, preferably Arborio or Carnarolli

Ground black pepper

¼ cup chopped flat-leaf parsley

Very thinly sliced celery, from the inner heart (optional)

Freshly grated Parmesan

*If you omit the Parmesan

1. Heat the oil in a large, heavy soup pot or Dutch oven over medium heat. Add the onion, carrot, and celery. Cook, stirring often, until the onion is tender, about 5 minutes. Add the garlic and ½ teaspoon salt. Stir together until fragrant, about 1 minute. Add the tomatoes with their juices and the sugar. Bring to a simmer and cook, stirring often, for about 10 minutes, or until the tomatoes have cooked down somewhat and are fragrant.

2. Add 1½ quarts water, the tomato paste, bouquet garni, oregano, and salt to taste. Bring to a boil over high heat. Reduce the heat, cover, and simmer for 30 minutes. Taste and adjust the seasonings. Stir in the rice, cover, and simmer for 15 to 20 minutes, or until the rice is tender.

Adjust the seasonings with salt and ground black pepper. Remove the bouquet garni. Stir in the parsley and serve, garnishing each bowl with thinly sliced celery heart if you want some crunch, and passing the Parmesan at the table.

Per serving (based on 4 servings): 249 calories, 8 g protein, 37 g carbohydrates, 5 g fiber, 9 g fat, 2 g sat fat, 4 mg cholesterol, 553 mg sodium

ADVANCE PREPARATION: You can make this up to 1 day ahead, but the rice will continue to soften and absorb liquid. If you do make it ahead, don't add the rice until you reheat the soup, then simmer until it's cooked.

Adding Salt When Softening Aromatics

When I cook aromatics in oil and want to prevent them from browning, I add a little salt (usually ¼ to ½ teaspoon). This causes the vegetables to sweat, and the water they release will keep them from browning.

Hearty Vegetarian Borscht

Makes 6 to 8 servings

■ **VEGETARIAN** ■ VEGAN ■ **LOW-CALORIE** ■ **LOW-FAT**
■ HIGH-PROTEIN ■ **GLUTEN-FREE** ■ HIGH IN OMEGA-3S

Borscht can be very heavy when it's made with beef stock and meat bones. I make a porcini mushroom broth for mine, so that it has an intense, savory flavor, without all the fat. This borscht is all about vegetables.

1 ounce (about 1 cup) dried porcini mushrooms

1 bunch beets (4 medium or 3 large), the beets peeled and diced, the greens stemmed, washed, and coarsely chopped

2 garlic cloves, thinly sliced

Salt

1 teaspoon sugar

1 tablespoon sherry vinegar or champagne vinegar

1 tablespoon canola oil

1 medium onion, chopped

½ pound turnips, peeled and diced

½ pound carrots, diced

2 cups shredded green or red cabbage

¼ pound white or cremini mushrooms, trimmed and sliced

Bouquet garni made with a bay leaf, 10 flat-leaf parsley stems, 6 black peppercorns, and 3 allspice berries, all tied in a piece of cheesecloth (see page 67)

Ground black pepper

2–3 teaspoons fresh lemon juice

¼ cup chopped flat-leaf parsley

1 cup low-fat plain Greek yogurt or Drained Yogurt (page 25)

1. Place the mushrooms in a large bowl and pour on 1 quart of boiling water. Let rest for 30 minutes, then

strain through a cheesecloth-lined sieve set over a bowl. Press the mushrooms over the sieve to extract any remaining flavorful liquid. Set the cooking liquid aside. Rinse the mushrooms thoroughly in several changes of water to remove any grit, and chop.

2. While the mushrooms are soaking, combine the beets, garlic, and 5 cups water in a saucepan and bring to a boil over high heat. Add salt (about 1 teaspoon) and the sugar, reduce the heat, and simmer uncovered for 30 minutes. Stir in the vinegar.

3. Meanwhile, heat the oil in a large, heavy soup pot or Dutch oven over medium heat. Add the onion. Cook, stirring, until just tender, 3 to 5 minutes. Add the turnips, carrots, cabbage, white or cremini mushrooms, porcini mushrooms, reserved mushroom soaking liquid, 2 cups water, the bouquet garni, and salt to taste. Bring to a boil. Reduce the heat, cover, and simmer for 40 minutes.

Stir in the beets, beet broth, and the chopped beet greens. Simmer for 10 minutes. Stir in the lemon juice. Taste and adjust seasonings with salt and pepper. Remove the bouquet garni. Heat the soup through, stir in the parsley, and serve, garnishing each bowl with a generous spoonful of yogurt.

Per serving (based on 6 servings): 132 calories, 7 g protein, 20 g carbohydrates, 5 g fiber, 3.5 g fat, 1 g sat fat, 2 mg cholesterol, 139 mg sodium

ADVANCE PREPARATION: You can make this soup a few days ahead; it gets better overnight. Don't add the parsley until serving.

Working with Beets

The best tool to use for peeling raw beets is a vegetable (or potato) peeler. If you mind having your hands stained with beet juice, hold the beet in a paper towel while you peel. The paper towel trick will also work if you are peeling cooked beets. (Beet juice will wash off pretty easily with soap and water though.)

Provençal Greens Soup

Makes 4 servings

■ **VEGETARIAN** ■ VEGAN ■ **LOW-CALORIE** ■ LOW-FAT
■ HIGH-PROTEIN ■ GLUTEN-FREE ■ HIGH IN OMEGA-3S

In Provence this simple, nutritious soup is made with the kind of greens that you might forage on an afternoon's walk, such as nettles, watercress, and dandelion greens. If you are using cultivated greens and want to settle on one type, I recommend Swiss chard. The soup is a typical French garlic soup, the type of quick, satisfying meal you could make if you have greens on hand, with little forethought.

2 tablespoons extra virgin olive oil

2 leeks, halved lengthwise, sliced crosswise, rinsed well and drained on paper towels

4 garlic cloves, sliced

Salt

6 cups chopped greens (leaves only), such as Swiss chard, dandelion greens, watercress, or beet greens

1½ quarts water, Vegetable Stock (page 67), or Garlic Broth (page 68)

Ground black pepper

2 large eggs

4 thick slices country bread, toasted and rubbed with a cut garlic clove

Grated Parmesan (optional)

1. Heat 1 tablespoon of the oil in a large, heavy soup pot over medium heat. Add the leeks. Cook, stirring, until tender, 3 to 5 minutes. Add the garlic and a generous pinch of salt. Cook, stirring, until the garlic is fragrant, about 1 minute. Add the greens and stir until they begin to wilt. Add the water (or stock or broth) and salt to taste. Bring to a simmer. Reduce the heat and simmer, partially covered, for 15 to 20 minutes, or until the greens are very tender and the broth sweet. Add black pepper, taste, and adjust the seasoning.

2. Beat the eggs in a bowl. Making sure that it is not boiling, whisk a ladle of the hot soup into the beaten eggs. Remove the soup from the heat, and stir the tempered eggs into the soup. Brush the bread slices with the remaining 1 tablespoon oil. If desired, cut the garlic toast into cubes. Place a slice (or a handful of cubes) in each bowl. Ladle in the soup, sprinkle on some Parmesan if desired, and serve.

Per serving: 212 calories, 7 g protein, 24 g carbohydrates, 2 g fiber, 10.5 g fat, 2 g sat fat, 106 mg cholesterol, 385 mg sodium

ADVANCE PREPARATION: You can make the soup several hours ahead, but add the eggs just before serving.

Potato and Parsley Soup

Makes 6 servings

■ **VEGETARIAN*** ■ VEGAN ■ **LOW-CALORIE** ■ **LOW-FAT**
■ HIGH-PROTEIN ■ **GLUTEN-FREE** ■ HIGH IN OMEGA-3S

My French friend Christine Picasso made this simple, beautiful soup one snowy night years ago in Provence. It typifies the way a French cook can put together a nutritious, comforting dinner in no time. Christine's rule is to never spend more than 30 minutes making a meal, and she consistently turns out wonderful food that we love to linger over.

1 tablespoon extra virgin olive oil

1 medium onion, chopped

2 leeks, white and light-green parts only, chopped

5 garlic cloves, sliced

Salt

1½ pounds Yukon gold or russet potatoes, peeled and diced

6 cups water, Garlic Broth (page 68), or chicken stock

Leaves from 1 large bunch flat-leaf parsley, washed, plus additional for garnish

1–1½ cups 1% milk

Ground black pepper

If made with water or Garlic Broth

1. Heat the oil in a large, heavy soup pot or Dutch oven over medium heat. Add the onion. Cook, stirring, until tender, about 5 minutes. Add the leeks, garlic, and ½ teaspoon salt. Stir together for about 2 minutes, or until the leeks begin to soften and the mixture is fragrant. Add the potatoes, water (or broth or stock), and salt to taste. Bring to a boil. Reduce the heat, cover, and simmer for 45 minutes, or until the potatoes are falling apart. Stir in the parsley and remove from the heat.

2. Puree the soup using an immersion blender or in batches in a blender (remove the inner lid and cover the top with a towel to avoid hot splashes). Strain through a medium sieve, pressing the soup through with the bottom of a ladle or with a pestle, and return to the pot. Thin out as desired with milk, and heat through over medium heat. Add black pepper, taste and adjust the salt, and serve, garnishing each bowl with parsley leaves.

Per serving: 244 calories, 6 g protein, 46 g carbohydrates, 4 g fiber, 3 g fat, 1 g sat fat, 2 mg cholesterol, 97 mg sodium

ADVANCE PREPARATION: You can make this several hours before serving.

VARIATION: Substitute 1 bunch watercress, thick stems removed, for the parsley.

Pureed Red Pepper and Potato Soup

Makes 6 to 8 servings

■ **VEGETARIAN*** ■ **VEGAN*** ■ **LOW-CALORIE** ■ **LOW-FAT**
■ HIGH-PROTEIN ■ GLUTEN-FREE ■ HIGH IN OMEGA-3S

There was a time, about 20 years ago, when pureed red peppers were all the rage. They were so overused by restaurants that eventually they fell out of fashion. But there was a reason that red pepper puree was so popular, and that's because of its intense rich flavor. This beautiful orange soup is a reminder of that. Make sure to strain it after you puree it, a quick step that spares you the more involved process of peeling the peppers.

2 tablespoons extra virgin olive oil, plus a drizzle for serving

1 medium onion, chopped

1 large carrot, chopped

Salt

4 large garlic cloves, minced

1 tablespoon tomato paste

2 pounds (4 large) red bell peppers, cut into large squares

2 teaspoons sweet paprika

1 pound russet potatoes (about 2 medium), peeled and diced

2 quarts Garlic Broth (page 68), Vegetable Stock (page 67), or chicken stock

Bouquet garni made with a bay leaf and a couple of sprigs each of thyme and flat-leaf parsley (page 67)

Ground black pepper

Garlic croutons (page 326), optional

Slivered basil leaves or chopped fresh thyme leaves (optional)

If made with Vegetable Stock or Garlic Broth

1. Heat the oil in a large, heavy soup pot over medium heat. Add the onion and carrot. Cook, stirring often, until the onion begins to soften, 2 to 3 minutes. Add a generous pinch of salt. Continue to cook, stirring often, until tender, about 5 minutes. Stir in the garlic and the tomato paste. Stir for 1 or 2 minutes, until the garlic is fragrant and the tomato paste has darkened. Add the bell peppers, paprika, and another generous pinch of salt. Cook, stirring often, until the peppers begin to soften, about 5 minutes.

2. Add the potatoes, broth or stock, and bouquet garni. Bring to a simmer. Add salt to taste. Cover and simmer over low heat for 1 hour. Remove the bouquet garni.

3. Blend the soup until smooth in a blender or food processor (working in $1^1/_2$-cup batches and covering the blender or food processor with a kitchen towel to prevent the hot soup from splashing). Strain the soup through a medium sieve, pushing the soup through the sieve with a spatula or the bottom of a ladle, and return to the pot. Heat through over medium heat, adjust the seasoning with salt and black pepper, and serve. Garnish with garlic croutons and basil or thyme, if desired. Drizzle a few drops of the oil over each serving.

Per serving (based on 6 servings): 173 calories, 3 g protein, 29 g carbohydrates, 4 g fiber, 5 g fat, 1 g sat fat, 0 mg cholesterol, 502 mg sodium

ADVANCE PREPARATION: The soup can be made a day ahead and gently reheated.

Potato "Bouillabaisse"

Makes 4 servings

■ **VEGETARIAN*** ■ VEGAN ■ **LOW-CALORIE** ■ LOW-FAT
■ **HIGH-PROTEIN** ■ GLUTEN-FREE ■ HIGH IN OMEGA-3S

This is known as a poor man's bouillabaisse because it is made sans fish, but saffron adds a touch of luxury to any dish. It infuses the broth and lends its beautiful hue to the potatoes. A poached egg adds protein and richness.

2 tablespoons extra virgin olive oil

1 large onion, halved and thinly sliced

2 leeks, white and light-green parts only, halved lengthwise, sliced crosswise, and rinsed well

3-4 large garlic cloves, minced or sliced

1 pound ripe tomatoes, peeled, seeded, and chopped, or 1 can (14 ounces) diced tomatoes

Salt

Bouquet garni made with 1 cleaned leek green, 1 bay leaf, 1 thin slice of orange zest, and a couple of sprigs each of flat-leaf parsley and thyme (page 67)

1½ quarts water, Garlic Broth (page 68), Vegetable Stock (page 67), or chicken stock

1¼ pounds waxy potatoes or Yukon golds, scrubbed and sliced

Generous pinch of saffron threads

1 thin strip orange zest

Ground black pepper

2 tablespoons chopped flat-leaf parsley

4 large eggs

4-8 thin slices country bread or baguette, toasted and rubbed with a cut clove of garlic (optional)

*If made with Vegetable Stock, water, or Garlic Broth

1. Heat the oil in a large, heavy soup pot or Dutch oven over medium heat. Add the onion and leeks. Cook, stirring, until tender, about 5 minutes. Add the garlic and stir together for about 1 minute, or until fragrant.

Add the tomatoes, ½ teaspoon salt, and bouquet garni. Cook, stirring from time to time, for 10 minutes, until the tomatoes have cooked down and are fragrant. Add the water (or broth or stock) and potatoes. Bring to a boil. Add the saffron, orange zest, and salt to taste. Reduce the heat. Cover and simmer for 20 to 25 minutes, or until the potatoes are tender. Taste and adjust the seasoning with salt and black pepper. Remove the bouquet garni and stir in the parsley.

2. Carefully break the eggs into a bowl. Making sure that the soup is at a bare simmer, slide the eggs into the soup. Cover (you can turn off the heat at this point) and let stand for 5 minutes, or until the eggs are set. Ladle the soup into wide soup bowls, with an egg for each portion. Garnish with the garlic toasts, if desired, and serve.

Per serving: 300 calories, 11 g protein, 38 g carbohydrates, 5 g fiber, 13 g fat, 3 g sat fat, 212 mg cholesterol, 143 mg sodium

ADVANCE PREPARATION: The soup can be made through Step 1 a day ahead and refrigerated. Return to a simmer and proceed with the recipe

Mushroom and Dried Porcini Soup

Makes 4 servings

■ **VEGETARIAN*** ■ **VEGAN**** ■ **LOW-CALORIE** ■ **LOW-FAT**
■ HIGH-PROTEIN ■ GLUTEN-FREE ■ HIGH IN OMEGA-3S

With virtually no fat, this soup has a tonic quality, which makes it not only a great starter or light supper, but also a delicious and effective between-meals pick-me-up. For such a simple potage, it has very intense flavor.

1 ounce (about 1 cup) dried porcini mushrooms

4 ounces fresh white mushrooms or fresh shiitakes

1 quart Vegetable Stock (page 67) or chicken stock

2 large garlic cloves, thinly sliced

1 can (14 ounces) whole tomatoes, drained and chopped

Salt and ground black pepper

Fresh lemon juice

4–8 thin slices baguette, toasted and rubbed with a cut garlic clove (optional)

2 tablespoons freshly grated Parmesan (optional)

1 tablespoon chopped fresh chives

*If made with Vegetable Stock

**If you omit the Parmesan

1. Place the porcinis in a heatproof bowl or glass measuring cup and cover with 2 cups of boiling water. Let soak for 30 minutes. Meanwhile, wipe the fresh white mushrooms (removing and sandy ends), break off the stems, and set them aside. If using shiitakes, discard the stems. Set the caps aside in a separate bowl.

2. Drain the porcinis through a cheesecloth-lined sieve set over a bowl. Squeeze the cloth over the sieve to extract as much flavorful liquid as possible. Set aside the soaking liquid. Rinse the mushrooms in several changes of water to remove any grit. Measure the soaking liquid and add enough water to make 2 cups.

3. Combine the soaking liquid, stock, porcini mushrooms, fresh mushroom stems, garlic, tomatoes, and 1 teaspoon salt in a soup pot or a large saucepan. Bring to a simmer over medium-high heat. Cover and simmer over very low heat for 1 hour. Strain the soup through a sieve. Discard the solids and return the soup to the saucepan. Add salt and black pepper to taste.

4. Slice the fresh mushroom caps paper-thin and toss with just a few drops lemon juice. Add to the soup pot. Heat through for 5 minutes.

5. If garnishing with the garlic toasts, top them with the Parmesan and place in a hot oven or toaster oven until the Parmesan has melted. Ladle the soup into bowls. Garnish each serving with chives and 1 or 2 cheese toasts, if desired.

Per serving: 77 calories, 4 g protein, 14 g carbohydrates, 2 g fiber, 0 g fat, 0 g sat fat, 0 mg cholesterol, 567 mg sodium

ADVANCE PREPARATION: You can make this through Step 3 a day ahead, and the flavor will be more intense. Refrigerate overnight. Return to the heat, bring to a simmer, taste, adjust the seasonings, and continue with Step 4.

Rich Garlic Soup with Spinach and Pasta Shells

Makes 6 servings

■ **VEGETARIAN** ■ VEGAN ■ **LOW-CALORIE** ■ LOW-FAT
■ **HIGH-PROTEIN** ■ GLUTEN-FREE ■ HIGH IN OMEGA-3S

Garlic soup in its simplest form (without the spinach) is one of my fallback meals, a comforting dinner I can count on because I always have the makings. It's easy and requires very little planning. This one is a meal in a bowl with a generous egg yolk enrichment and lots of iron-rich spinach.

- 2 garlic heads, separated into cloves, unpeeled

- 1 tablespoon olive oil

- Bouquet garni made with a bay leaf, a couple of sprigs each of thyme and parsley, and a fresh sage leaf (page 67)

- Salt

- ½ cup small macaroni shells

- 6 slices (½ inch thick) country bread, toasted and rubbed with a cut garlic clove

- ½ cup (2 ounces) grated Gruyère cheese

- 1 bag (6 ounces) baby spinach

- 4 large or extra-large egg yolks

1. Bring a medium saucepan of water to a boil over high heat. Fill a bowl with ice water. Drop the garlic cloves into the boiling water. Blanch for 30 seconds, then transfer to the ice water. Allow to cool for a few minutes, then drain and remove the skins. They'll be loose and easy to remove. Lightly crush the cloves by leaning on them with the flat side of a chef's knife.

2. Place the garlic in a large saucepan with the oil, bouquet garni, 2 quarts water, and salt. Bring to a gentle boil. Reduce the heat, cover, and simmer for 1 hour. Strain through a sieve and return the broth to the saucepan. Taste and adjust the salt, and return to a simmer.

3. Add the macaroni shells to the broth and simmer until cooked al dente, about 5 minutes.

4. If desired, cut the garlic toast into cubes. Place a slice or a handful of cubes in each of 6 soup bowls and top with a heaping tablespoon of cheese.

5. Add the spinach to the simmering broth and stir for 30 seconds to 1 minute, until all the spinach is wilted. Beat the egg yolks in a bowl. Remove the soup from the heat and whisk a ladleful of the hot garlic broth into the egg yolks (the broth should not be boiling). Stir the tempered egg yolks back into the soup. Do not allow the soup to boil. Stir for 1 minute, then taste and adjust the seasonings. Ladle the soup over the cheese-topped toasts and serve.

Per serving: 230 calories, 9 g protein, 25 g carbohydrates, 3 g fiber, 11 g fat, 3 g sat fat, 151 mg cholesterol, 365 mg sodium

ADVANCE PREPARATION: You can make the garlic broth through Step 2 a day ahead and refrigerate.

Creamy Cabbage Soup with Gruyère

Makes 6 servings

■ **VEGETARIAN*** ■ VEGAN ■ LOW-CALORIE ■ LOW-FAT
■ HIGH-PROTEIN ■ GLUTEN-FREE ■ HIGH IN OMEGA-3S

It's possible to make a soup creamy without adding cream. When I make vegetable purees, a potato does the trick, and while this soup isn't a puree, the grated potato still plays a thickening role. The Parmesan rind that simmers along with the vegetables infuses the soup without adding additional cheese, and that too makes the soup taste richer than it actually is.

1 tablespoon extra virgin olive oil

1 medium onion, chopped

1 russet potato, peeled and grated

³⁄₄ pound cabbage (about ¹⁄₂ medium head), cored and shredded

Salt

5 cups water, Vegetable Stock (page 67), or chicken stock

1 Parmesan rind

Ground black pepper

2 cups 1% milk

1 cup (4 ounces) grated Gruyère cheese

6 thick slices (¹⁄₂ inch) French or country bread, toasted and cut into small squares

Minced fresh chives

*If made with Vegetable Stock or water

1. Heat the oil in a large, heavy soup pot over medium heat. Add the onion and cook, stirring, until tender, about 5 minutes. Add the potato, cabbage, and a generous pinch of salt. Stir together for 1 minute, taking care that the potatoes don't stick to the pot. Add the water or stock, Parmesan rind, and salt and black pepper to taste. Bring to a simmer.

Cover and simmer over low heat for 30 minutes, or until the vegetables are tender. Remove the Parmesan rind with tongs and discard.

2. Add the milk to the soup. Stir to combine well and heat through without boiling. Stir the Gruyère into the soup a handful at a time. Continue to stir until the cheese has melted. Taste and adjust the seasonings. Serve, garnishing each bowl with a handful of croutons and a sprinkling of chives.

Per serving: 267 calories, 14 g protein, 33 g carbohydrates, 3 g fiber, 10 g fat, 4 g sat fat, 24 mg cholesterol, 349 mg sodium

ADVANCE PREPARATION: The soup can be made a few hours ahead and reheated. Be careful not to let it boil.

Pureed White Bean and Winter Squash Soup

Makes 6 servings

■ **VEGETARIAN** ■ **VEGAN** ■ LOW-CALORIE ■ **LOW-FAT**
■ **HIGH-PROTEIN** ■ GLUTEN-FREE ■ HIGH IN OMEGA-3S

Ever since I made my first pureed white bean soup, a Julia Child recipe in From Julia Child's Kitchen *that was enriched at the end—and I do mean enriched—with a mixture of cream, butter, egg yolks, lemon juice, and herbs, I've been hooked. But bean soups don't need cream, egg yolks, or butter to taste rich. This one combines white beans with winter squash, resulting in a pale orange puree with a sweet, comforting flavor.*

1 pound dried white beans (such as navy beans, small white beans, or cannellini beans), rinsed, picked over, and soaked for 6 hours or overnight in 2 quarts water

2 tablespoons extra virgin olive oil, plus additional, if desired, for drizzling

1 medium onion, chopped

4 garlic cloves, minced

Salt

Bouquet garni made with a bay leaf, a couple of sprigs each of thyme and parsley, and 2 sage leaves (page 67)

2 leeks, white part only, well washed and chopped

1 pound winter squash, peeled, seeded, and diced

Ground black pepper

Slivered fresh sage leaves

Garlic croutons (see page 326)

1. Drain the soaked beans. Heat 1 tablespoon of the oil in a large, heavy soup pot over medium heat. Add the onion. Cook gently until tender, about 5 minutes. Add 2 of the garlic cloves and $\frac{1}{2}$ teaspoon salt. Stir together for about 30 seconds, then add the drained beans and $2\frac{1}{2}$ quarts water. Bring to a gentle boil and skim off any foam. Add the bouquet garni, reduce the heat, cover, and simmer for 1 hour.

2. Meanwhile, heat the remaining 1 tablespoon oil in a wide, heavy skillet over medium heat. Add the leeks and a generous pinch of salt. Cook gently, stirring, until tender, about 3 minutes. Add the remaining 2 cloves garlic and the squash. Cook, stirring, until the garlic is fragrant and the squash is coated with oil and just beginning to soften, about 3 minutes. Remove from the heat and stir into the beans. Add salt to taste and continue to simmer for 30 minutes to 1 hour, until the beans and vegetables are thoroughly tender and falling apart. Taste and adjust the seasoning with salt. Remove the bouquet garni and discard.

3. Puree the soup using an immersion blender or a food mill fitted with the fine or medium plate. Return to the pot, heat through, taste and adjust the seasonings with salt and black pepper. Serve, garnishing each bowl with sage, croutons, and a drizzle of oil, if desired.

Per serving: 340 calories, 16 g protein, 58 g carbohydrates, 20 g fiber, 6 g fat, 1 g sat fat, 0 mg cholesterol, 46 mg sodium

ADVANCE PREPARATION: You can make this up to 1 or 2 days ahead and reheat. It will thicken. If desired, thin out with water or stock.

Pureeing a Hot Soup

When you puree a hot soup in a blender, you must work in small batches and be careful not to put the cover on tightly. If you puree the hot soup with the lid on tight, the hot liquid will create a vacuum, causing the lid to blow off and hot liquid to splash out. I puree in $1\frac{1}{2}$-cup batches and I don't cover the blender with a lid at all, but instead pull a dish towel down tightly over the top to prevent hot splashes. You could also remove the lid's center plug if your blender cover has one. Either way, start with the blender on low and increase the speed once some of the steam has been released.

Red Lentil Soup

Makes 6 servings

■ **VEGETARIAN*** ■ **VEGAN** ■ LOW-CALORIE ■ **LOW-FAT**
■ **HIGH-PROTEIN** ■ **GLUTEN-FREE** ■ HIGH IN OMEGA-3S

When I was developing this soup, I served it two ways: as a rustic, thick lentil and tomato soup, and as a puree. My son liked it better as a thick lentil soup, and I preferred the texture of the puree. The bottom line is that they're both very good; the pureed version is more refined. Red lentils are a beautiful orange color when dry, but they become yellow when they cook. You can find them in Middle Eastern and Indian markets.

2 tablespoons canola oil or peanut oil

1 medium or large onion, chopped

4 garlic cloves, minced

Salt

2 teaspoons cumin seeds, lightly toasted and ground (see sidebar)

2 teaspoons coriander seeds, lightly toasted and ground (see sidebar)

2 teaspoons hot curry powder

1 can (28 ounces) diced tomatoes

1 pound red lentils, rinsed and picked over

2 quarts water, Vegetable Stock (page 67), or chicken stock

¼ teaspoon ground black pepper

Cayenne (optional)

1 tablespoon fresh lime juice (more to taste)

Drained Yogurt (page 25)

Chopped cilantro

If made with Vegetable Stock or water

1. Heat the oil in a large, heavy soup pot over medium heat. Add the onion. Cook, stirring, until tender, about 5 minutes. Add the garlic, a generous pinch of salt, cumin, coriander, and curry powder. Stir together for about 1 minute, until the garlic is fragrant. Stir in the tomatoes (with juice). Bring to a simmer and cook, stirring often, for 10 minutes, or until the tomatoes have cooked down slightly. Add salt to taste.

2. Stir in the lentils and water or stock. Bring to a boil. Reduce the heat, cover, and simmer for 30 minutes. Add salt to taste and continue to simmer for 15 to 30 minutes, or until the lentils have fallen apart and thickened the soup. Using the back of a spoon, mash the lentils against the side of the pot to further thicken the soup. Add the black pepper, taste, and add cayenne if you want more spice. Taste and adjust the salt. Stir in the lime juice.

3. If you wish, puree with an immersion blender or in batches in a blender, holding a towel over the lid to prevent hot soup from splashing out, and return to the pot. Heat through and serve. Garnish each serving with a dollop of yogurt and a generous sprinkling of cilantro.

Per serving: 359 calories, 23 g protein, 55 g carbohydrates, 14 g fiber, 7 g fat, 0 g sat fat, 0 mg cholesterol, 251 mg sodium

ADVANCE PREPARATION: You can make this a day ahead. It will keep for 3 or 4 days in the refrigerator.

Toasting Spices

You will get a lot more flavor out of your spices if you use whole spices and grind them yourself. Spices that have been ground lose flavor very quickly. My recipes often direct you to lightly toast the spices first, which yields a richer flavor. To toast spices, place in a small skillet over medium heat and heat them, shaking the pan so they'll move around and toast evenly until fragrant, about 5 minutes. There should be a faint popcorn aroma coming from the skillet. Remove from the heat immediately and transfer to a spice mill or a mortar and pestle. Allow to cool slightly, then grind.

North African Bean and Squash Soup

Makes 4 to 6 servings

■ **VEGETARIAN** ■ **VEGAN** ■ **LOW-CALORIE** ■ **LOW-FAT**
■ **HIGH-PROTEIN** ■ GLUTEN-FREE ■ HIGH IN OMEGA-3S

Beans and winter squash can be paired in many ways. This thick, hearty Algerian soup is spicy and complex (but not complicated). The traditional recipe sometimes includes an assortment of beans and a spherical type of couscous called muhammas, *for which I sometimes substitute vermicelli. You can find* muhammas *in Middle Eastern markets. Algerians would also add a mutton shank to the soup, but I love the pure vegetal, earthy flavors of this lighter version.*

1 cup dried chickpeas, rinsed, picked over, and
 soaked for 6 hours or overnight in 1 quart water

1 bunch cilantro

1 small dried red chile pepper, such as a Japanese
 chile pepper

2 tablespoons extra virgin olive oil, plus additional
 for drizzling

1 large onion, chopped

2 medium carrots, diced

Salt

4 plump garlic cloves, minced

1 tablespoon sweet paprika

1 teaspoon ground turmeric

1 can (28 ounces) diced tomatoes

½ pound winter squash, peeled, seeded, and diced

1-2 teaspoons harissa or ⅛-¼ teaspoon cayenne

Ground black pepper

½ cup vermicelli or muhammas (also sold as
 Israeli couscous)

2 tablespoons chopped fresh mint

Lemon wedges (optional)

1. Drain the chickpeas and set aside. Tie half of the cilantro sprigs into a bundle with the dried red chile pepper. Chop the rest of the cilantro, and set aside.

2. Heat the oil in a large bean pot or Dutch oven over medium heat. Add the onion and carrots. Cook, stirring, until tender, about 5 minutes. Add ½ teaspoon salt, the garlic, paprika, and turmeric. Stir together for about 1 minute, or until fragrant. Add the tomatoes (with juice). Cook, stirring often, for 10 minutes, or until the tomatoes have cooked down and the mixture is fragrant.

3. Add the chickpeas and 1½ quarts water. Bring to a boil. Add the bundle of cilantro. Reduce the heat, cover, and simmer for 1 hour. Add the squash, harissa or cayenne, and salt and pepper to taste. Continue to simmer for 1 hour.

4. Add the vermicelli or muhammas. Simmer until tender, about 5 minutes. Remove the cilantro bundle with tongs and discard. Stir in the reserved cilantro and the mint. Taste and adjust the seasoning with salt. Serve with lemon wedges, if desired.

Per serving (based on 4 servings): 352 calories, 14 g protein, 56 g carbohydrates, 13 g fiber, 10 g fat, 1 g sat fat, 0 mg cholesterol, 386 mg sodium

ADVANCE PREPARATION: This gets better overnight, but don't add the pasta (or *muhammas*), chopped cilantro, or mint until shortly before serving. You may need to thin it out with water. The soup will keep for 3 to 4 days in the refrigerator.

VARIATION: In spring and summer, substitute ½ pound diced zucchini for the winter squash. Simmer the zucchini for no longer than 30 minutes.

Fragrant Puree
of Corn Soup

Makes 4 servings

■ **VEGETARIAN** ■ **VEGAN** ■ **LOW-CALORIE** ■ **LOW-FAT**
■ HIGH-PROTEIN ■ **GLUTEN-FREE** ■ HIGH IN OMEGA-3S

This soup is all about corn, intensely so. If your corn isn't sweet, then the soup will be dull, so it's worth testing the corn before you begin to make sure it's good. Use the corncobs for the stock and the kernels for the soup. The soup should be velvety smooth—don't skip the straining step.

For the stock:

4 large or 5 medium ears of corn

1 small onion, quartered

$\frac{1}{2}$ pound carrots, sliced

1 garlic clove, smashed but left whole

Salt

For the soup:

1 tablespoon canola oil

1 small or $\frac{1}{2}$ medium sweet onion, chopped

Salt

1. To make the stock: Cut the kernels from the corncobs and set aside. Combine the corncobs, onion, carrots, and garlic in a large soup pot. Add 2 quarts water and bring to a boil over high heat. Season with a small amount of salt (you will be reducing this broth, so don't salt fully at this point). Reduce the heat, cover, and simmer for 1 hour. Strain through a sieve set over a bowl and discard the solids. Return the broth to the pot. Bring to a boil and reduce to 5 cups. (The circumference of the pot will determine how long this will take. It will be faster in a wide pot.) Taste and adjust the seasonings.

2. To make the soup: Heat the oil in a heavy soup pot over medium heat. Add the onion and salt. Cook, stirring, until tender, about 5 minutes. Add all but $\frac{3}{4}$ cup of the corn kernels. Cook gently for about 3 minutes, stirring, then add the stock. Bring to a simmer. Cover and simmer over low heat for 30 minutes.

3. Steam the reserved corn kernels over boiling water for 4 minutes. Set aside.

4. Transfer the soup to a blender in 1- to $1\frac{1}{2}$-cup batches, taking care not to cover the top tightly with a lid (cover with a towel to avoid hot splashes). Blend the soup until smooth. Strain the soup through a medium sieve, pressing with the bottom of a ladle or with a spatula, and return to the pot. Heat through, taste, and adjust the seasonings. Place a generous spoonful of the reserved corn in each bowl, ladle in the soup, and serve.

Per serving: 150 calories, 5 g protein, 24 g carbohydrates, 3 g fiber, 6.6 g fat, 0 g sat fat, 0 mg cholesterol, 37 mg sodium

ADVANCE PREPARATION: You can prepare the soup several hours before you serve. Heat through gently on top of the stove.

Cutting Kernels from an Ear of Corn

Stand the ear of corn upright on a large cutting board or in the center of a wide bowl. Position your knife between the kernels and the cob and with a sawing motion, cut straight down to the bottom of the ear. The kernels will fall off in a strip. Turn the ear and repeat the motion until all the kernels are removed.

Barley Soup with Mushrooms and Kale

Makes 6 to 8 servings

■ **VEGETARIAN*** ■ **VEGAN**** ■ **LOW-CALORIE** ■ **LOW-FAT**
■ HIGH-PROTEIN ■ GLUTEN-FREE ■ HIGH IN OMEGA-3S

Barley and mushroom soup is a classic Central European dish. I've added kale to the mix, and my stock is a mushroom stock rather than the traditional meat stock. You're getting a hearty meal in a bowl here, though a simple green salad would be welcome afterward.

1/2 ounce (about 1/2 cup) dried porcini mushrooms

1–2 tablespoons extra virgin olive oil

1 large onion, chopped

1/2 pound cremini mushrooms, cleaned, trimmed, and sliced thick

2 large garlic cloves, minced

Salt

3/4 cup whole or pearl barley

1 1/2 quarts water, Vegetable Stock (page 67), or chicken stock

Bouquet garni made with a few sprigs each of thyme and parsley, a bay leaf, and a Parmesan rind (page 67)

8–10 ounces kale (regular or cavolo nero), stemmed and washed thoroughly

Ground black pepper

*If made with Vegetable Stock or water

**If made with Vegetable Stock and you omit the Parmesan rind

1. Place the porcini mushrooms in a heatproof bowl or glass measuring cup and pour on 2 cups boiling water. Let set for 30 minutes. Set a sieve over a bowl and line it with cheesecloth. Lift the mushrooms from the water and squeeze over the sieve. Rinse in several changes of water, squeeze out the water, and set aside. Strain the soaking liquid through the cheesecloth-lined sieve. Add water as necessary to make 2 cups. Set aside.

2. Heat the oil in a large, heavy soup pot or Dutch oven over medium heat. Add the onion. Cook, stirring often, until just about tender, about 5 minutes. Add the cremini mushrooms. Cook, stirring, until the mushrooms are beginning to soften, about 3 minutes. Add the garlic and 1/2 teaspoon salt. Continue to cook for about 5 minutes, or until the mixture is juicy and fragrant. Add the porcini mushrooms, barley, mushroom soaking liquid, water or stock, bouquet garni, and salt to taste. Bring to a boil. Reduce the heat, cover, and simmer for 45 minutes. Meanwhile, stack the kale leaves in bunches and cut crosswise into slivers.

3. Add the slivered kale to the soup and simmer for 15 to 20 minutes. The barley should be tender and the broth aromatic. The kale should be very tender. Remove the bouquet garni. Taste and adjust the seasonings with salt and a generous amount of black pepper, and serve.

Per serving (based on 6 servings): 156 calories, 6 g protein, 28 g carbohydrates, 6 g fiber, 3 g fat, 0.5 g sat fat, 0 mg cholesterol, 54 mg sodium

ADVANCE PREPARATION: The soup will keep for about 3 days in the refrigerator, but the barley will swell and absorb the liquid, so you will need to add more water or stock to the pot when you reheat (or if it's really thick, you could serve it as a pilaf).

Veracruzana Black Bean Soup with Spinach or Lamb's Quarters

Makes 6 servings

■ **VEGETARIAN** ■ **VEGAN*** ■ **LOW-CALORIE** ■ **LOW-FAT**
■ **HIGH-PROTEIN** ■ **GLUTEN-FREE** ■ HIGH IN OMEGA-3S

Beans and greens make a natural marriage in many culinary cultures. Both foods have always been an important and inexpensive source of nourishment. They also happen to taste very good together. In Mexico a wide range of greens (quelites) *are eaten in soups, stews, and tortilla-based dishes. This soup is inspired by a black bean soup made in the highlands of Veracruz, with a local green called* xonequi *that is somewhat like lamb's quarters (a close relative of spinach). Make it a day ahead and it will taste even better.*

2 tablespoons canola oil

1 medium onion, chopped

4 large garlic cloves, minced

2 teaspoons cumin seeds, lightly toasted and ground

12 ounces dried black beans, rinsed and picked over, soaked in 2 quarts water for 6 hours or overnight, liquid reserved

2 chipotle chiles in adobo sauce, seeded and finely chopped

½ cup chopped cilantro

Salt

12 ounces (two 6-ounce bags or 2 bunches) spinach or lamb's quarters

Queso fresco

Corn tortillas

*If you omit the queso fresco

1. Heat the oil in a large, heavy soup pot or Dutch oven over medium heat. Add the onion. Cook, stirring, until it begins to soften, about 3 minutes. Add two of the garlic cloves and the cumin. Cook, stirring, until fragrant, about 1 minute. Add the beans and soaking liquid. Add water as needed to cover by 2 inches and bring to a boil. Reduce the heat to low. Skim off any foam that rises. Cover and simmer for 1 hour.

2. Add the chiles, ¼ cup of the cilantro, salt to taste, and the remaining two cloves garlic. Continue to simmer for 1 hour, until the beans are quite soft and the broth is thick and fragrant. Taste and adjust the seasonings with salt. Let set overnight in the refrigerator for the best flavor.

3. Partially puree the soup using an immersion blender. Alternatively, puree 2 cups of the beans with a small amount of broth in a blender or a food processor, and stir back into the soup. Bring to a simmer. Add the spinach or lamb's quarters, a handful at a time. Simmer for 3 to 5 minutes, or until tender. Stir in the remaining ¼ cup cilantro. Taste and adjust the seasonings. Garnish each bowl with a sprinkle of queso fresco. Serve with warm corn tortillas.

Per serving: 269 calories, 13 g protein, 44 g carbohydrates, 8 g fiber, 5 g fat, 0 g sat fat, 0 mg cholesterol, 116 mg sodium

ADVANCE PREPARATION: The cooked beans will keep 3 to 4 days in the refrigerator and freeze well.

Lentil Soup with Lots of Cilantro

Makes 4 servings

■ **VEGETARIAN** ■ **VEGAN*** ■ **LOW-CALORIE** ■ **LOW-FAT**
■ **HIGH-PROTEIN** ■ **GLUTEN-FREE** ■ HIGH IN OMEGA-3S

Fresh cilantro is used widely in the Middle East, where this soup has its origins, and in North Africa. It's a great seasoning for lentils, and there's no shortage of it here.

1 tablespoon extra virgin olive oil

2 garlic cloves, minced

1¼ teaspoons cumin seeds, lightly toasted and ground

Pinch of cayenne

½ pound (1 heaping cup) brown lentils, rinsed and picked over

1 small onion, halved

1 bay leaf

Salt and ground black pepper

1 cup chopped cilantro (from 1 large bunch)

Plain low-fat yogurt (optional)

*If you omit the yogurt

1. Heat the oil in a large, heavy soup pot over medium heat. Add the garlic. Stir until fragrant, about 1 minute. Stir in the cumin and cayenne. Stir together briefly, then add the lentils, onion, bay leaf, 1½ quarts water, and salt to taste. Bring to a boil, reduce the heat, and simmer for 40 minutes, or until the lentils are tender and the broth aromatic. Add the black pepper and taste, then adjust the seasoning with salt. Discard the onion and bay leaf.

2. Coarsely puree the soup using an immersion blender or a food mill. Alternatively, puree half of the soup in a blender, 1½ cups at time, covering the top of the blender with a towel to avoid hot splashes, and stir back into the soup. Heat through.

3. Stir the cilantro into the soup just before serving. Taste, adjust the seasonings, and serve, garnishing each bowl with a dollop of yogurt.

Per serving: 242 calories, 15 g protein, 37 g carbohydrates, 17 g fiber, 4 g fat, 0.5 g sat fat, 0 mg cholesterol, 54 mg sodium

ADVANCE PREPARATION: The soup can be made through Step 2 up to a day ahead of time. You may need to thin it out with a little water. Add the cilantro just before serving.

FOR MORE RECIPES COMBINING BEANS AND GREENS SEE:

Chickpeas with Baby Spinach (page 283)

Couscous with Black-Eyed Peas and Greens (page 289)

Red Chard, Potato, and White Bean Ragout (page 286)

Stewed Lentils with Cabbage (page 295)

Miso Soup with Tofu and Vegetables

Makes 2 servings

■ **VEGETARIAN** ■ **VEGAN** ■ **LOW-CALORIE** ■ **LOW-FAT**
■ **HIGH-PROTEIN** ▪ GLUTEN-FREE ▪ HIGH IN OMEGA-3S

Miso soup is a mainstay in Japan, widely eaten for breakfast and as a start to a meal in a culinary culture with a salty rather than sweet palate. This is much like the classic miso soup you get in Japanese restaurants, with some added vegetables. Miso is a highly nutritious fermented bean and grain paste; you can find it in Japanese markets and whole-foods stores. Its high sodium content makes it unsuitable for those who must watch their salt intake.

2 cups kombu dashi (see sidebar) or water

2 tablespoons dark miso paste

1 small carrot, cut into matchsticks or very thinly sliced

4 medium or 2 large white or cremini mushrooms, cleaned, trimmed, and very thinly sliced

6 ounces firm tofu, regular or silken, cut into ¼-inch dice

1 scallion, white and light-green parts only, thinly sliced

½ cup chopped watercress or baby spinach

2 teaspoons snipped chives

1. Heat the dashi or water in a saucepan over medium heat until warm but not boiling. Place the miso in a bowl and ladle in about ½ cup of the warm dashi or water. Mix with a fork or whisk until the miso is well blended. Set aside.

2. Bring the remaining dashi or water to a simmer (not a boil). Add the reserved miso mixture. Mix together but do not allow to boil. Add the carrot, mushrooms, tofu, scallion, and watercress or spinach. Bring to a simmer and remove from the heat. Garnish each serving with the chives.

Per serving: 100 calories, 9 g protein, 9 g carbohydrates, 1 g fiber, 3 g fat, 0 g sat fat, 10 mg cholesterol, 801 mg sodium

ADVANCE PREPARATION: Everything can be prepared hours in advance, but make the soup at the last minute.

Kombu Dashi (Stock)

Kombu dashi is a very mild stock, made simply by soaking sea kelp—kombu—in warm water for 6 to 8 hours. It's the easiest stock you'll ever make. Kombu, a sea vegetable, is an excellent source of iodine and vitamin K, and a good source of folate, magnesium, riboflavin, and pantothenic acid, iron, and calcium. To make kombu stock, soak 2 ounces kombu (wiped clean with a damp paper towel) in 2 quarts warm water for 6 to 8 hours. Remove the kombu from the water. Season the broth as desired.

Hot Yogurt Soup with Barley and Cilantro

Makes 4 to 6 servings

■ **VEGETARIAN*** ■ VEGAN ■ **LOW-CALORIE** ■ **LOW-FAT**
■ **HIGH-PROTEIN** ■ GLUTEN-FREE ■ HIGH IN OMEGA-3S

In the Middle East, yogurt is used in hot dishes as well as cold. Stirring in a little cornstarch stabilizes the yogurt so that it doesn't curdle when it cooks. This simple soup is both comforting and light, even with the barley. It makes a satisfying meal at any time of year.

1 tablespoon extra virgin olive oil

1 medium onion, finely chopped

2 garlic cloves, minced

½ cup pearl or whole barley, rinsed

3 cups Vegetable Stock (page 67) or chicken stock

Salt

1 tablespoon cornstarch blended with 2 tablespoons water

3 cups plain low-fat yogurt

Ground black pepper

½ cup chopped cilantro

Fresh lemon juice (optional)

Lemon, sliced paper-thin

*If made with Vegetable Stock

1. Heat the oil in a large, heavy soup pot over medium heat. Add the onion. Cook, stirring, until the onion is tender and beginning to color, about 10 minutes. Add the garlic and barley and stir together until the garlic smells fragrant, about 30 seconds. Add the stock and salt to taste, and bring to a boil. Reduce the heat to low, cover, and simmer 40 minutes, or until the barley is tender.

2. Stir the cornstarch mixture into the yogurt. Remove the soup from the heat and stir in the yogurt mixture. Return the soup to low heat and bring to a bare simmer, stirring. Do not boil. Add salt to taste and a generous amount of black pepper. Stir in the cilantro. Season with lemon juice (or squeeze a few drops over each bowl), if desired. Serve hot or warm, garnished with lemon slices.

Per serving (based on 4 servings): 246 calories, 10 g protein, 42 g carbohydrates, 7 g fiber, 5 g fat, 2 g sat fat, 8 mg cholesterol, 401 mg sodium

ADVANCE PREPARATION: The soup can be made a day ahead (though it's best freshly made), but don't stir in the cilantro or the lemon juice until just before serving, and be sure to reheat gently.

Chilled Zucchini-Yogurt Soup with Fresh Mint

Makes 4 to 6 servings

■ **VEGETARIAN** ■ VEGAN ■ **LOW-CALORIE** ■ **LOW-FAT**
■ **HIGH-PROTEIN** ■ **GLUTEN-FREE** ■ HIGH IN OMEGA-3S

I learned to make this unbelievably easy zucchini soup from my French friend, Sabine Boulongne. It's a summer soup, very refreshing because of the mint and yogurt, and a good example of how easy it can be to put together a nutritious and satisfying dinner with little effort. You can chill it by placing the bowl of soup into a larger bowl filled with ice and water. And make sure to strain the soup for the best texture.

2 pounds zucchini, sliced

Salt

3 cups plain low-fat yogurt

3 tablespoons finely chopped mint

Ground black pepper

2 tablespoons fresh lemon juice

1 garlic clove, mashed to a paste with a mortar and
    pestle (optional)

For garnish:

1 small zucchini, sliced paper-thin

Salt

4 mint leaves, thinly slivered

1. Place 2 cups water in the bottom of a saucepan fitted with a steamer basket. Bring to a boil over high heat. Place the zucchini in the steamer basket, cover the pot, and steam for 15 minutes. Remove from the heat and allow to cool for about 5 minutes. Do not drain the steaming water.

2. Place half of the zucchini in a food processor. Add ³/₄ teaspoon salt and puree until smooth. Add half of the steaming water and pulse until smooth. Scrape into a bowl, and repeat with the remaining zucchini and steaming water, and another ³/₄ teaspoon salt. Scrape into the bowl with the first batch. Whisk in the yogurt, mint, black pepper, lemon juice, and garlic (if using). Taste and adjust the seasoning with salt. Refrigerate until chilled.

3. Toss the paper-thin slices of zucchini with a generous pinch of salt. Place in a sieve set over a bowl or in the sink. Let rest for 15 minutes. (The zucchini will soften.) Rinse and pat dry.

4. Strain the cold soup through a medium sieve into a bowl. Use a rubber spatula to press the soup against the sieve and to scrape the outside of the sieve, to extract maximum flavor and to get as much soup through as you can. Ladle the soup into bowls. Garnish with several slices of the sliced zucchini and a sprinkle of the mint, and serve.

Per serving (based on 4 servings): 129 calories, 10 g protein, 22 g carbohydrates, 5 g fiber, 2 g fat, 1 g sat fat, 8 mg cholesterol, 172 mg sodium

ADVANCE PREPARATION: This is best served on the day it's made (but that doesn't prevent me from enjoying leftovers for lunch the next day, especially if the soup is made without the optional garlic).

Chilled Yogurt or Buttermilk Soup with Toasted Barley

Makes 6 servings

■ **VEGETARIAN** ■ VEGAN ■ **LOW-CALORIE** ■ **LOW-FAT**
■ **HIGH-PROTEIN** ■ GLUTEN-FREE ■ HIGH IN OMEGA-3S

In this chilled soup, the barley is toasted before simmering in water. Then it's added to yogurt or buttermilk, along with cucumber, tomatoes, celery, and seasonings. It's perfect when you're hungry on a hot summer day, because it will fill you up but it won't weigh you down. Make sure your yogurt has no gums or stabilizers in it, or the soup won't have an appealing texture.

⅓ cup pearl barley

Salt

1 cup finely diced cucumber

1 quart plain low-fat yogurt (free of gums and stabilizers) or buttermilk, or a combination of the two

2 ripe but firm tomatoes, cut into small dice

1 celery rib, cut into small dice

1 garlic clove, finely minced or mashed to a paste with a little salt in a mortar and pestle

2 tablespoons fresh lemon juice

2 tablespoons snipped fresh chives

2 teaspoons cumin seeds, lightly toasted and ground

Ground black pepper (optional)

2 tablespoons slivered fresh mint leaves

1. Heat a heavy saucepan over medium-high heat. Add the barley. Stir or shake in the pan until the barley begins to smell toasty, about 5 minutes. Add 2 cups water and ½ teaspoon salt (or more to taste) and bring to a boil. Reduce the heat and simmer until tender, about 45 minutes. Remove from the heat, drain, and set aside.

2. While the barley is cooking, place the cucumber in a bowl and sprinkle with salt. Toss and transfer to a sieve set over the bowl. Allow to drain for 30 minutes. Rinse well and drain on paper towels.

3. Combine the barley, cucumber, yogurt or buttermilk, tomatoes, celery, garlic, lemon juice, chives, and cumin in a large bowl. Season to taste with salt and black pepper (if using). Chill for 1 hour or longer. Garnish each serving with the mint.

Per serving: 135 calories, 9 g protein, 24 g carbohydrates, 5 g fiber, 2 g fat, 1 g sat fat, 7 mg cholesterol, 134 mg sodium

ADVANCE PREPARATION: You can make this several hours before serving.

Avocado Gazpacho

Makes 4 servings

■ **VEGETARIAN** ■ **VEGAN*** ■ **LOW-CALORIE** ■ LOW-FAT
■ HIGH-PROTEIN ■ **GLUTEN-FREE**** ■ HIGH IN OMEGA-3S

These days chefs in Spain are being fanciful with their gazpachos. This has the tangy flavor of traditional gazpacho Andaluz, with a creamy texture.

1 ripe Hass avocado, about 6–7 ounces (fairly large), peeled, pitted, and quartered

1½ pounds ripe tomatoes, peeled

2–4 garlic cloves

2 heaping tablespoons coarsely chopped red or white onion, soaked for 5 minutes in cold water, drained and rinsed

2 tablespoons extra virgin olive oil

1–2 tablespoons sherry vinegar or wine vinegar

½–1 teaspoon sweet paprika

Salt

Garnishes (optional):

½ cup finely chopped cucumber

½ cup finely chopped tomato

¼ cup chopped fresh basil or flat-leaf parsley, or whole fresh basil or parsley leaves

½ cup finely chopped green bell pepper

½ cup small croutons

1 hard-cooked egg, finely chopped

**If you omit the croutons and egg

**If you omit the croutons

1. Combine the avocado, tomatoes, garlic, onion, oil, vinegar, paprika, and salt and black pepper in a blender and blend until smooth. Taste and adjust the seasonings with salt. Pour into a bowl or pitcher, thin out as desired with ice water, cover, and chill for several hours.

2. Just before serving, arrange the garnishes (if using) in small bowls on a platter. Serve the soup in bowls and pass the garnishes.

Per serving: 155 calories, 2 g protein, 11 g carbohydrates, 4 g fiber, 13 g fat, 2 g sat fat, 0 mg cholesterol, 48 mg sodium

ADVANCE PREPARATION: This will keep for a day in the refrigerator.

Salmorejo

Makes 4 servings

■ **VEGETARIAN** ■ **VEGAN*** ■ **LOW-CALORIE** ■ **LOW-FAT**
■ HIGH-PROTEIN ■ GLUTEN-FREE ■ HIGH IN OMEGA-3S

Salmorejo is a thicker first cousin of gazpacho Andaluz, a simple mixture of tomatoes, bread, and olive oil. Its success depends entirely on the quality of your tomatoes and oil. Traditionally, the soup is served with ibérico or serrano ham, but I also like to garnish mine with diced cucumber or green pepper. Salmorejo also makes a great sauce for grilled fish.

> 2½ pounds ripe tomatoes, peeled
>
> 5 ounces stale French baguette, crust removed, sliced
>
> 2 garlic cloves, halved
>
> 2 tablespoons extra virgin olive oil
>
> 1–2 tablespoons sherry vinegar
>
> Salt
>
> ¼ cup diced serrano ham, cucumber, or green bell pepper

*If you omit the serrano ham

1. Combine the tomatoes, baguette, garlic, oil, vinegar, and salt in a bowl and toss together. Cover and set aside for 1 hour.

2. Transfer to a blender. Blend at high speed until homogenized. Chill for several hours. Garnish each bowl with 1 tablespoon of ham, cucumber, or bell pepper, and serve.

> **Per serving:** 288 calories, 8 g protein, 38 g carbohydrates, 6 g fiber, 12 g fat, 2 g sat fat, 8 mg cholesterol, 268 mg sodium

ADVANCE PREPARATION: This will keep for a day in the refrigerator.

Clear Summer Borscht

Makes 6 servings

■ **VEGETARIAN** ■ **VEGAN*** ■ **LOW-CALORIE** ■ **LOW-FAT**
■ HIGH-PROTEIN ■ **GLUTEN-FREE** ■ HIGH IN OMEGA-3S

This light, glistening, lemony summer soup, served cold, is infused with garlic and is utterly refreshing, even thirst-quenching. If you enrich the borscht with yogurt, the color will be dark pink. If you don't, it will be a clear, dark red.

> 2 pounds beets (8 medium, usually 2 bunches), peeled, halved, and sliced into thin half-moons
>
> 2 teaspoons salt
>
> 6 tablespoons fresh lemon juice (from 2–3 lemons)
>
> 1 tablespoon sugar
>
> 2 large garlic cloves, halved lengthwise
>
> ¾ cup plain low-fat yogurt (optional)
>
> 1 small cucumber, peeled and finely diced
>
> Chopped fresh dill or chives

*If you omit the yogurt

1. Combine the beets, 7 cups water, and 1 teaspoon of the salt in a soup pot and bring to a simmer over medium-high heat. Cover and simmer for 30 minutes. Add the lemon juice, remaining 1 teaspoon salt, and the sugar. Continue to simmer, uncovered, for 20 minutes. Remove from the heat and add the garlic. Allow to cool, then cover and refrigerate until chilled. Season to taste and discard the garlic cloves.

2. Place 2 tablespoons of yogurt (if using) into the center of each soup bowl. Ladle in the soup. Garnish with cucumber and dill or chives.

> **Per serving:** 63 calories, 2 g protein, 15 g carbohydrates, 3 g fiber, 0 g fat, 0 g sat fat, 0 mg cholesterol, 861 mg sodium

ADVANCE PREPARATION: This soup can be made a day ahead and will be good for 2 to 3 days.

Chapter 5
PANINI, BRUSCHETTA, AND PIZZA

Keep a loaf of wholesome bread, a few vegetables, and some cheese on hand, and you'll always have the makings for grilled Italian sandwiches (panini) or open-face bruschetta. They make quick, simple lunches and suppers, and they also go well with the soups and salads in the previous two chapters.

Panini and bruschetta, like pasta and pizza, invite all sorts of fillings and toppings, from pantry staples to vegetables from the farmers' market to leftovers, like that half-bowl of thick vegetable soup or ratatouille left over from last night's dinner—not enough for a real portion but too good to throw out. Open a can of beans and a can of tuna, toss them together with herbs, extra virgin olive oil, and vinegar, and pile the mixture onto lightly toasted bread for a tuna and beans bruschetta, my idea of beans on toast (page 103); or scramble up some eggs with asparagus (page 100). When I have mushrooms that are beginning to shrivel or a lone red pepper that's seen better days, I'll cook them up and pile them onto or between slices of toasted bread. Any vegetable side dish, in fact, can become the focus of a meal when it becomes the topping for a bruschetta or a filling for a panini.

Seek out whole grain breads. Whole grains, even when ground, retain their fiber and nutrients from the germ and the bran. You'll find, also, that whole grain breads have a nuttier, more satisfying flavor than white bread.

Grilled Eggplant Panini

Makes 1 serving

■ **VEGETARIAN** ■ VEGAN ■ **LOW-CALORIE** ■ LOW-FAT
■ **HIGH-PROTEIN** ■ GLUTEN-FREE ■ HIGH IN OMEGA-3S

Grilling eggplant slices on a panini grill is worth the price of the grill. They're ready in 2 to 3 minutes, they require very little oil, and if you don't use them for this sandwich you can top them with tomato sauce, chop them up, and toss them with pasta or rice, or drizzle them with vinaigrette and sprinkle with feta cheese and fresh herbs, such as mint, parsley, basil, or marjoram.

2-4 eggplant slices (½ inch thick) (depending on the size of the eggplant)

Salt

Extra virgin olive oil

1 tablespoon pesto (optional)

½ roasted red bell pepper (page 24) or 2-3 slices tomato

Ground black pepper

2 tablespoons (1 ounce) grated cheese, such as mozzarella, fontina, Gruyère, Parmesan, or a combination

2 thick slices whole grain country bread

1. Sprinkle the eggplant with salt and let sit for 15 minutes. Pat dry with a paper towel and brush lightly with the oil.

2. Preheat a panini grill. Arrange the eggplant in an even layer. Grill for 3 minutes, or until cooked through and nicely marked by the grill. Remove from the heat.

3. Spread a little pesto, if desired, on one slice of bread. Top with eggplant slices, then with bell pepper or tomato. Sprinkle with the black pepper. Top with the cheese and the second slice of bread. Brush both the outside top and bottom surfaces of the sandwich with some oil. Grill for 5 minutes, or until it's nicely toasted and the cheese has melted. Cut into halves or thirds, depending on the size of the bread. Serve hot.

Per serving: 424 calories, 18 g protein, 44 g carbohydrates, 15 g fiber, 21 g fat, 7 g sat fat, 33 mg cholesterol, 599 mg sodium

ADVANCE PREPARATION: The eggplant can be grilled and the panini assembled several hours before it is grilled.

VARIATIONS:

• Add sliced red onion and chopped fresh basil.

• Spoon a little vinaigrette over the tomatoes.

• Sprinkle the eggplant slices with a pinch of red-pepper flakes.

Spinach and Red Bell Pepper Panini

Makes 4 servings

■ **VEGETARIAN** ■ VEGAN ■ **LOW-CALORIE** ■ LOW-FAT
■ **HIGH-PROTEIN** ■ GLUTEN-FREE ■ HIGH IN OMEGA-3S

If you're looking for something different to do with the bagged spinach that you usually use for salads, look no farther than these beautiful panini. The roasted red bell peppers contribute lots of flavor and color. If you don't have bell peppers already roasted on hand, you can roast them on the panini grill. Just quarter length-wise, brush with olive oil, and pop in the panini press for 2 to 4 minutes.

The red bell peppers contribute a great set of nutrients to this dish—those antioxidant-rich carotenoids found in red vegetables and fruits, as well as vitamins C and B_6.

Salt

2 bags (6 ounces each) baby spinach or 1 bunch
   fresh spinach, stemmed and washed

3 tablespoons extra virgin olive oil

2 garlic cloves, minced

Ground black pepper

8 slices whole grain country bread

1 large or 2 smaller roasted red bell peppers
   (page 24), sliced

1 cup (4 ounces) grated mozzarella, Gruyère, or
   fontina cheese

1. Bring a large pot of generously salted water to a boil over high heat. Fill a bowl with ice water. Add the spinach to the boiling water and blanch for 10 to 20 seconds. Transfer to the ice water. Cool for a few minutes, then drain and squeeze out the excess water. Chop coarsely.

2. Heat 1 tablespoon of the oil in a large, heavy skillet over medium heat. Add the garlic. Cook, stirring, until the garlic is fragrant, about 30 seconds. Stir in the spinach. Toss together to coat with the oil, and season to taste with the salt and black pepper. Remove from the heat.

3. Preheat a panini grill. Top 4 of the bread slices with the spinach. Top the spinach with strips of roasted bell pepper, then with cheese. Top with the remaining bread slices and press together. Brush the outside top and bottom surfaces of the sandwich with the remaining 2 tablespoons oil. Place in the panini grill and grill for 5 minutes, or until the cheese has melted and the bread is toasty. Halve the panini and serve hot.

Per serving: 362 calories, 16 g protein, 35 g carbohydrates, 9 g fiber, 18 g fat, 3 g sat fat, 0 mg cholesterol, 512 mg sodium

ADVANCE PREPARATION: You can prepare the spinach through Step 2 several hours or even a day ahead of assembling the panini.

Panini with Artichokes, Spinach, and Peppers

Makes 4 servings

■ **VEGETARIAN** ■ VEGAN ■ **LOW-CALORIE** ■ LOW-FAT
■ **HIGH-PROTEIN** ■ GLUTEN-FREE ■ HIGH IN OMEGA-3S

You can make this quickly if you use frozen artichoke hearts.

3 tablespoons olive oil

2 garlic cloves, minced

1½ cups sliced cooked artichoke hearts

1 teaspoon fresh thyme leaves

12 ounces baby spinach, blanched (page 99) and coarsely chopped

Kosher salt and ground black pepper

1 large or 2 small roasted red bell peppers (page 24), cut in strips

1 cup (4 ounces) grated Gruyère

8 slices whole grain country bread

1. Heat 1 tablespoon of the oil in a large, heavy skillet over medium heat and add the garlic. Cook, stirring, until the garlic is fragrant, about 30 seconds, then stir in the artichoke hearts. Stir for a few minutes, until the artichoke hearts are beginning to color, and add the thyme leaves, spinach, and salt and pepper.

2. Preheat a panini grill. Brush 4 bread slices with oil and place oiled side down on your work surface. Top each slice with the artichoke mixture, peppers, and cheese. Top with the remaining bread and brush the tops with olive oil. Grill for 4 to 5 minutes, until the cheese has melted and the bread is toasty. Slice in half and serve hot.

Per serving: 390 calories, 17 g protein, 40 g carbohydrates, 12 g fiber, 19 g fat, 6 g sat fat, 22 mg cholesterol, 600 mg sodium

ADVANCE PREPARATION: You can prepare the artichoke filling through Step 2 a day ahead.

Bruschetta with Scrambled Eggs and Asparagus

Makes 4 servings

■ **VEGETARIAN** ■ VEGAN ■ **LOW-CALORIE** ■ LOW-FAT
■ **HIGH-PROTEIN** ■ GLUTEN-FREE ■ HIGH IN OMEGA-3S

I eat scrambled eggs a lot more often for dinner than I do for breakfast. This dish makes a beautiful, light supper, and it's easy to throw together. To get really creamy scrambled eggs, cook them slowly over low heat.

½ pound asparagus, trimmed

4–8 thick slices whole grain country bread

1 garlic clove, halved

1 tablespoon extra virgin olive oil

6 large or extra-large eggs

1 tablespoon 1% milk

Salt and ground black pepper

1 tablespoon unsalted butter

1 tablespoon snipped fresh chives

1. Steam the asparagus above 1 inch of boiling water or until tender, 5 to 8 minutes. Remove from the heat, rinse briefly with cold water, drain, and cut crosswise and on the diagonal into ½-inch-thick pieces.

2. Toast the bread, rub with the cut clove of garlic, and brush with the oil. Set aside on plates or on a platter.

3. Beat together the eggs, milk, salt, and black pepper. Melt the butter in a nonstick skillet over low heat. Add the eggs and cook slowly, stirring with a silicone spatula, until the eggs are just set but still creamy. Stir in the asparagus and chives. Spoon onto the bruschetta and serve.

Per serving: 247 calories, 14 g protein, 15 g carbohydrates, 3 g fiber, 15 g fat, 5 g sat fat, 324 mg cholesterol, 254 mg sodium

ADVANCE PREPARATION: Steamed asparagus will keep for 3 or 4 days in the refrigerator.

Bruschetta with White Bean Puree

Makes 4 servings

■ **VEGETARIAN** ■ **VEGAN** ■ LOW-CALORIE ■ **LOW-FAT**
■ **HIGH-PROTEIN** ■ GLUTEN-FREE ■ HIGH IN OMEGA-3S

This recipe will give you more white bean puree than you'll need for the bruschetta. The savory, hummus-like mixture makes a great high-protein, high-fiber dip or spread, so you'll be glad to have plenty left over. You can use canned white beans for this, though they won't taste as good. Substitute milk for the bean broth and omit the garlic.

1 cup dried white beans, rinsed and picked over, soaked for 6 hours or overnight in 1 quart water

1 medium onion, halved

4 garlic cloves

1 bay leaf

Salt

3 tablespoons extra virgin olive oil

2 tablespoons fresh lemon juice

Ground black pepper

4–8 thick slices country bread, preferably whole grain

1 tablespoon chopped fresh sage, rosemary, or parsley

1. Drain the beans and transfer to a large, heavy saucepan. Add the onion, 2 of the garlic cloves, the bay leaf, and 1 quart water. Bring to a boil over high heat. Reduce the heat, cover, and simmer for 1 hour. Add salt to taste and simmer for 30 minutes to 1 hour, or until the beans are thoroughly tender. Drain through a sieve set over a bowl. Set aside the cooking liquid. Discard the onion and bay leaf.

2. Mash 1 of the raw garlic cloves with ¼ teaspoon salt with a mortar and pestle.

3. Place the beans and the mashed garlic in a food processor and puree. With the machine running, add 2 tablespoons of the bean broth, 2 tablespoons of the oil, and the lemon juice. Stop the machine, taste and adjust the seasoning with salt and black pepper. Add more of the bean broth as needed for a creamier consistency. The mixture should have the same consistency as moist hummus.

4. Lightly toast the bread. Halve the remaining garlic clove and rub the toast, then brush with the remaining 1 tablespoon oil. Top with the white beans, sprinkle with the herbs, and serve.

Per serving: 362 calories, 16 g protein, 49 g carbohydrates, 16 g fiber, 12 g fat, 2 g sat fat, 0 mg cholesterol, 177 mg sodium

ADVANCE PREPARATION: The white bean puree will keep for 5 days in the refrigerator. It will become thicker with time. Thin out as desired with milk.

Bruschetta with Tuna, Arugula, and Beans

Makes 4 servings

■ VEGETARIAN ■ VEGAN ■ LOW-CALORIE ■ **LOW-FAT**
■ **HIGH-PROTEIN** ■ GLUTEN-FREE ■ **HIGH IN OMEGA-3S**

This is a little like a chopped Salade Niçoise on a piece of toast. You can use fresh or canned tuna. If you have a some seared fresh tuna left over from a meal, the bruschetta would be a good destination for it.

1 cup (about 2 ounces) tightly packed, coarsely chopped arugula

1 can (5–6½ ounces) water-packed or olive oil–packed light tuna, drained

1 can (15 ounces) white beans, rinsed and drained

1 tablespoon sherry or red wine vinegar

Salt and ground black pepper

3 tablespoons extra virgin olive oil

2 garlic cloves, 1 minced, 1 halved

4–8 thick slices whole grain country bread

1. Combine the arugula, tuna, and beans in a large bowl. Whisk together the vinegar, salt, black pepper, oil, and minced garlic in a small bowl. Toss with the salad.

2. Toast the bread and rub with the cut clove of garlic. Top with the salad. Press down on the salad with a fork so that it doesn't all fall off the bread, and serve.

Per serving: 259 calories, 15 g protein, 25 g carbohydrates, 6 g fiber, 13 g fat, 2 g sat fat, 12 mg cholesterol, 550 mg sodium

ADVANCE PREPARATION: You can combine all the ingredients for the topping (except for the arugula) hours or even a day ahead. When you're ready to serve, add the arugula, toss, and make the toasts.

Bruschetta with Mushroom Topping

Makes 4 servings

■ **VEGETARIAN** ■ **VEGAN*** ■ **LOW-CALORIE** ■ **LOW-FAT**
■ HIGH-PROTEIN ■ GLUTEN-FREE ■ HIGH IN OMEGA-3S

The savory mushroom sauté that tops this bruschetta is good with lots of dishes. It can be tossed with pasta or served as a side dish with grains, meat, or fish. Use any type of mushroom you prefer.

1 pound white, cremini, or wild mushrooms,
   or a combination, rinsed briefly and wiped dry

2 tablespoons extra virgin olive oil

½ small or medium onion, finely chopped

3 garlic cloves, 2 minced, 1 halved

Salt

3 ripe tomatoes, peeled, seeded, and diced, or
   1 can (14 ounces) chopped tomatoes, drained

Ground black pepper

2 tablespoons minced flat-leaf parsley

4–8 thick slices whole grain country bread

Grated or shaved Parmesan or Gruyère
   (optional)

*If you omit the cheese

1. Trim the mushroom stems (discard stems if using shiitakes) and cut into thick slices. (If using wild mushrooms, chop coarsely.) Heat 1 tablespoon of the oil in a large, heavy nonstick skillet over medium heat. Add the onion. Cook, stirring, until tender and beginning to color, 5 to 8 minutes. Add the mushrooms, minced garlic, and a generous pinch of salt. Cook, stirring, until the mushrooms begin to soften and sweat. Stir in the tomatoes and ½ cup water. Add salt to taste and bring to a simmer. Reduce the heat, cover, and simmer for 30 minutes. Stir occasionally. Stir in the black pepper and parsley. Taste and adjust the seasonings. Remove from the heat.

2. Lightly toast the bread and rub with the cut garlic. Brush with the remaining 1 tablespoon oil. Warm the mushrooms and spoon over the bruschetta. Top with the Parmesan or Gruyère, if desired, and serve.

Per serving: 180 calories, 7 g protein, 20 g carbohydrates, 3 g fiber, 9 g fat, 1 g sat fat, 0 mg cholesterol, 159 mg sodium

ADVANCE PREPARATION: You can cook the mushrooms several hours ahead and reheat. If they dry out, add a little water to the pan when you reheat.

Bruschetta with Roasted Bell Peppers and Goat Cheese

Makes 4 servings

■ **VEGETARIAN** ■ VEGAN ■ **LOW-CALORIE** ■ LOW-FAT
■ **HIGH-PROTEIN** ■ GLUTEN-FREE ■ HIGH IN OMEGA-3S

I keep jarred roasted bell peppers in my pantry so that I can make impromptu meals like these comforting bruschetta. But for the best flavor, roast the peppers yourself (page 24). Oven-roasted peppers are the sweetest.

4 large red bell peppers

Salt and ground black pepper

2 tablespoons extra virgin olive oil

1–2 garlic cloves, halved

4–8 thick slices whole grain country bread

3 ounces goat cheese, crumbled or thinly sliced

Slivered fresh basil leaves

1. Roast the bell peppers in a 400°F oven as directed on page 24 and allow to cool in a covered bowl. Carefully remove the skins and seeds from the peppers and discard, holding the peppers over the bowl so you don't lose any of the liquid. Cut into strips, place in another bowl, and toss with salt, black pepper, and 1 tablespoon of the oil. Strain the juice from the peppers through a sieve into the bowl. If desired, mince or puree one of the garlic cloves and add to the peppers.

2. Preheat the oven to 350°F. Toast the bread. Rub with the cut clove of garlic and brush with the

remaining 1 tablespoon oil. Place the bruschetta on a baking sheet. Spoon on the peppers and top with the goat cheese. Warm in the oven until the cheese has softened, about 8 minutes. Garnish with the basil and serve.

Per serving: 198 calories, 10 g protein, 23 g carbohydrates, 5 g fiber, 8 g fat, 5 g sat fat, 17 mg cholesterol, 262 mg sodium

ADVANCE PREPARATION: Roasted or grilled bell peppers will keep in the refrigerator for about 5 days. If you cover them with olive oil, they'll last for a couple of weeks.

In the fat-phobic days of the 1990s, when any fat was a bad fat, we eschewed avocados because, like nuts and olives, they have a very high fat content. Now we know that the fats in avocados are, for the most part, healthy monounsaturated fats, particularly oleic acid (the primary fat in olive oil). I don't think twice about eating avocado just about every day, especially in spring and summer when they are at their best. As part of a quick lunch, I'll eat them with cottage cheese, in a quesadilla, or on a sandwich (my father told me they used to call avocados poor man's butter when he was a child, though now they would more aptly be described as rich man's butter), and this nutrient-dense food sustains me until dinner.

In addition to their high oleic acid content, avocados are a good source of dietary fiber and vitamins K, C, and B_6, as well as folate, copper, and potassium (half of a medium avocado has more potassium than a medium banana). Studies have indicated that the fats in avocados help with the absorption of carotenoids in other vegetables—another good reason to include them in salads and salsas.

Tofu and Avocado Sandwich

Makes 1

■ **VEGETARIAN** ■ **VEGAN** ■ **LOW-CALORIE** ■ **LOW-FAT** ■ **HIGH-PROTEIN** ■ GLUTEN-FREE ■ HIGH IN OMEGA-3S

I don't know if this really qualifies as a recipe, but it definitely has a place in this chapter. It's my son's favorite at-home lunch, and the open-face version is one of my all-time favorites, too. It's an at-home lunch because it doesn't travel well in a lunchbox; the soy sauce dissipates into the tofu, and the bread can get soggy over time. I like to make this on mixed-grains sandwich bread. It can also be served open-faced.

2 slices whole grain bread

Dijon mustard

2–3 ounces firm tofu, sliced

Soy sauce

⅓ large or ½ small avocado, sliced

Salt (optional)

Tomato (when in season), sliced

Spread some mustard on 1 slice of bread. Pat the tofu dry with paper towels. Arrange on top of the mustard-covered bread in 1 layer. Drizzle soy sauce over the tofu and spread it around with a knife so that all the tofu is seasoned. Top with slices of the avocado (if the avocado is very soft, spread the avocado over the top slice of bread). If you wish, season the avocado with a little salt and top with slices of tomato. Top with the other slice of bread and press down. Halve the sandwich and serve.

Per serving: 315 calories, 14 g protein, 33 g carbohydrates, 9 g fiber, 15 g fat, 2 g sat fat, 0 mg cholesterol, 787 mg sodium

Pizzas

Pizza is many things to many people, but one thing that doesn't come to mind is healthy. That's because the average pizza-chain pizza isn't healthy; those huge pies have thick, doughy crusts, and even before the extras (pepperoni, sausage, etc.) are added, they're weighted down with cheese. But go into a pizzeria in Rome or Naples, and you'll find a dizzying array of pizzas that really are good for you. Their crusts are thin, they're sold by the reasonably sized slice, and many are topped with seasonal vegetables. In summer you'll find tomatoes and roasted peppers, squash and eggplant; in winter, spring, and fall you might find mushrooms, caramelized onion, or fennel. Italian pizzas are not without cheese and meat, but never more than a few ounces of one or the other or each. Think of these pizzas as edible vegetable platters.

Food Processor Whole Wheat Pizza Dough

Makes two 12- to 14-inch crusts

■ **VEGETARIAN** ■ **VEGAN** ■ LOW-CALORIE ■ **LOW-FAT**
■ HIGH-PROTEIN ■ GLUTEN-FREE ■ HIGH IN OMEGA-3S

Whole wheat pizza crust has a nutty flavor and real nutritional value. Since the crust is what pizza is primarily about, this is a good thing. But a crust made with too much whole wheat flour can be heavy, dry, and tough. I've found that this formula, which has a balance of whole wheat and all-purpose flour, makes a crust that is both delightful to eat, and full of whole grain nutrients like dietary fiber, manganese, and magnesium.

2 teaspoons active dry yeast

½ teaspoon sugar

1 tablespoon extra virgin olive oil, plus additional for brushing the pizza crusts

1¼ cups stone-ground whole wheat flour

1½ cups unbleached all-purpose flour, plus additional for kneading, if necessary

1¼ teaspoons salt

Semolina or cornmeal, for the pan

Olive oil

1. Combine the yeast and 1 cup warm water in a 2-cup glass measuring cup. Add the sugar and stir together. Let sit for 2 to 3 minutes, or until the water is cloudy. Stir in the olive oil.

2. Combine the whole wheat flour, all-purpose flour, and salt in a food processor fitted with the steel blade. Pulse once or twice, then, with the machine running, pour in the yeast mixture. Process until the dough forms a ball on the blades. Remove from the processor (the dough will be a little tacky; flour or moisten your hands so it won't stick) and knead on a lightly floured surface for a couple of minutes, adding flour as necessary for a smooth dough. Shape into a ball and pinch the dough together on the bottom.

3. Transfer the dough to a clean, lightly oiled bowl, rounded side down first, then rounded side up. Cover the bowl tightly with plastic wrap. Leave it in a warm spot to rise for 1 to 1½ hours. When it is ready, the dough will stretch as it is gently pulled.

4. Divide the dough into 2 equal balls. Put the balls on a lightly oiled tray or platter, cover with plastic wrap brushed or sprayed with vegetable oil or with

a damp towel, and leave them to rest for 15 to 20 minutes. At this point, the dough balls can be placed in a wide bowl, covered with plastic wrap, and refrigerated for up to 3 days. Or you can wrap them loosely in lightly oiled plastic wrap and refrigerate them in a resealable plastic bag. You will need to allow them to come to room temperature and punch them down again when you are ready to roll out the pizzas.

5. Preheat the oven to 450°F. Place a pizza stone if you have one on the middle rack of the oven. Roll or press out one of the balls of dough to a 12- to 14-inch circle. Keep the other ball covered, or refrigerate in a plastic bag if not using right away. Lightly oil a pizza pan and dust with semolina or cornmeal. Place the dough on the pizza pan and use your fingers to form a slightly thicker raised rim around the edge of the circle. Brush everything but the rim with a little olive oil, then top the pizza with the toppings of your choice.

6. Place the pizza pan on the stone. Bake as directed.

Per ⅓ crust: 247 calories, 7 g protein, 42 g carbohydrates, 4 g fiber, 5 g fat, 1 g sat fat, 0 mg cholesterol, 485 mg sodium

ADVANCE PREPARATION: The pizza dough can be refrigerated after the first rise for up to 3 days (see Step 4). The rolled out dough can be frozen. Transfer directly from the freezer to the oven.

Pizza with Mushrooms, Goat Cheese, Arugula, and Walnuts

Makes one 12- to 14-inch pizza, about 3 servings

■ **VEGETARIAN** ■ VEGAN ■ LOW-CALORIE ■ LOW-FAT
■ HIGH-PROTEIN ■ GLUTEN-FREE ■ HIGH IN OMEGA-3S

Eating this is like eating a salad and a pizza at the same time. There's a wonderful assortment of textures here: the crisp pizza crust, the creamy goat cheese, crunchy walnuts, and the arugula.

Semolina or cornmeal, for the pan

½ recipe Whole Wheat Pizza Dough (page 108)

2 tablespoons extra virgin olive oil

8 ounces mushrooms, trimmed, cleaned, and sliced

Salt and ground black pepper

1 cup (4 ounces) crumbled goat cheese

3 tablespoons chopped walnuts

1 teaspoon fresh thyme leaves

About 1 heaping cup arugula leaves

1 teaspoon walnut oil

¼ teaspoon balsamic vinegar

1. Preheat the oven to 450°F, preferably with a pizza stone in it. Lightly oil a 12- to 14-inch pizza pan and dust with semolina or cornmeal. Roll out the dough to fit the pan. Place on the pan and use your fingers to form a slightly thicker raised rim around the edge of the circle.

2. Heat 1 tablespoon of the oil in a large, heavy skillet over medium-high heat. Add the mushrooms. Cook, stirring, until the mushrooms are tender and moist, about 4 to 5 minutes. Season with salt and black pepper and remove from the heat.

3. Crumble the goat cheese into a bowl, add the walnuts, and lightly toss together.

4. Brush the dough with 2 teaspoons of the remaining oil and top with the mushrooms. Sprinkle on the thyme, and place in the oven. Bake for 10 minutes. Remove from the oven, sprinkle with the goat cheese and walnuts, and return to the oven for 5 to 10 minutes, or until the crust is nicely browned and the cheese has softened.

5. Toss the arugula with the remaining 1 teaspoon olive oil, the walnut oil, and vinegar. Scatter it over the pizza and serve.

Per serving: 549 calories, 19 g protein, 48 g carbohydrates, 6 g fiber, 32 g fat, 10 g sat fat, 30 mg cholesterol, 734 mg sodium

ADVANCE PREPARATION: The dough can be refrigerated for up to 3 days.

Making Pizza without Pans

You can bake the pizza directly on the hot pizza stone if you have a baker's peel, a wooden paddle with a handle used to slide pizzas and breads into hot ovens. Dust the baker's peel generously with semolina and place the pizza on the peel. When you are ready to bake the pizza, slide the pizza from the peel onto the stone, placing the peel over the stone and jerking it toward you with a quick movement of your wrist and arm, so that the pizza slides off onto the stone.

Pizza with Spring Onions and Fennel

Makes one 12- to 14-inch pizza, about 3 servings

■ **VEGETARIAN** ▪ VEGAN ▪ LOW-CALORIE ▪ LOW-FAT
▪ HIGH-PROTEIN ▪ GLUTEN-FREE ▪ HIGH IN OMEGA-3S

Fennel and spring onions, cooked gently until they begin to cara-melize, make a sweet topping for a pizza.

Semolina or cornmeal, for the pan

2 tablespoons extra virgin olive oil

1 medium sweet spring onion, chopped (about 1 cup)

Salt

1 large or 2 medium fennel bulbs, trimmed (1¼ pounds trimmed bulbs), tough outer layers removed, cored, and chopped

2 garlic cloves, minced

Ground black pepper

2 tablespoons minced fennel fronds

½ recipe Whole Wheat Pizza Dough (page 108)

¼–½ cup (1-2 ounces) grated Parmesan

1. Preheat the oven to 450°F, preferably with a pizza stone in it. Lightly oil a 12- to 14-inch pizza pan and dust with semolina or cornmeal. Heat 1 tablespoon of the oil in a large, heavy skillet over medium heat. Add the onion and ½ teaspoon salt. Cook, stirring often, until the onion is tender, about 5 minutes. Add the chopped fennel and garlic and stir together. Cook, stirring often, until the fennel begins to soften, about 5 minutes. Reduce the heat to low, cover, and cook gently, stirring often, until the fennel is very tender and sweet and just beginning to color, about 15 minutes. Season to taste with salt and pepper. Stir in the chopped fennel fronds and remove from the heat.

2. Roll or press out the pizza dough, line the pan and use your fingers to form a slightly thicker raised rim around the edge of the circle. Brush all but the rim of the pizza crust with the remaining 1 tablespoon oil and sprinkle on the Parmesan. Spread the fennel mixture over the crust in an even layer. Place on top of the pizza stone and bake for 15 to 20 minutes, or until the edges of the crust are brown and the topping is beginning to brown. Remove from the heat. Serve hot, warm, or at room temperature.

Per serving: 411 calories, 11 g protein, 55 g carbohydrates, 9 g fiber, 17 g fat, 3 g sat fat, 6 mg cholesterol, 115 mg sodium

ADVANCE PREPARATION: The fennel topping can be made a day ahead of time and held in the refrigerator. The dough can be made up to 3 days ahead and held in the refrigerator.

Fennel is a good source of vitamin C and a very good source of fiber, folate, and potassium. It contains many phytonutrients, including the flavonoids rutin and quercetin, and a compound called anethole, the main component of its anise-y flavor, which may have anti-inflammatory properties.

Pizza Margherita

Makes one 12- to 14-inch pizza, about 3 servings

■ **VEGETARIAN** ■ VEGAN ■ LOW-CALORIE ■ LOW-FAT
■ HIGH-PROTEIN ■ GLUTEN-FREE ■ HIGH IN OMEGA-3S

This classic pizza—a small amount of mozzarella and a lot of fresh, sliced tomatoes—has given birth to other related pies in my kitchen. Sometimes I substitute goat cheese for the mozzarella, sometimes feta. The important element here is the ripe, in-season tomatoes.

Semolina or cornmeal, for the pan

½ recipe Whole Wheat Pizza Dough (page 108)

2 tablespoons Garlic Olive Oil (recipe follows)

½ cup (2 ounces) shredded mozzarella, or crumbled goat cheese or feta

1½–2 pounds ripe tomatoes, sliced about ¼ inch thick (I like to use a mix of mostly red with some yellow and green tomatoes)

Salt and ground black pepper

Several fresh basil leaves, torn into small pieces

1. Preheat the oven to 450°F, preferably with a pizza stone in it. Lightly oil a 12- to 14-inch pizza pan or a baking sheet and dust with semolina or cornmeal. Roll or press out the pizza dough, line the pan and use your fingers to form a slightly thicker raised rim around the edge of the circle.

2. Gently brush the crust with 1 tablespoon of the Garlic Olive Oil. Sprinkle the cheese over the surface and top with the tomato slices, overlapping them slightly. Season with salt and black pepper.

3. Place the pizza pan in the oven. Bake until the edges begin to brown, 15 to 20 minutes. Remove from the heat and drizzle the remaining 1 tablespoon Garlic Olive Oil over the tomatoes. Sprinkle on the basil and serve. Or allow to cool, then sprinkle on the basil and serve.

Per serving: 424 calories, 13 g protein, 52 g carbohydrates, 7 g fiber, 19 g fat, 4 g sat fat, 15 mg cholesterol, 662 mg sodium

ADVANCE PREPARATION: The dough can be made up to 3 days ahead and held in the refrigerator. The pizza can be served at room temperature.

Garlic Olive Oil

½ cup extra virgin olive oil

3 garlic cloves, minced

Combine the oil and garlic in a small, heavy saucepan and place over medium-low heat. Insert a thermometer. When the oil reaches 140°F, remove from the heat and allow to cool. Strain. Refrigerate the oil and use as directed.

Pizza with Roasted Peppers and Mozzarella

Makes one 12- to 14-inch pizza, about 3 servings

■ **VEGETARIAN** ■ VEGAN ■ LOW-CALORIE ■ LOW-FAT
■ HIGH-PROTEIN ■ GLUTEN-FREE ■ HIGH IN OMEGA-3S

If you can't get your kids to eat peppers in a salad, you might try this pizza. There's no tomato sauce, but it's still red.

Semolina or cornmeal, for the pan

2 large red bell peppers, roasted (page 24)

Salt and ground black pepper

1–2 garlic cloves, minced

2 tablespoons extra virgin olive oil

½ recipe Whole Wheat Pizza Dough (page 108)

1 large green bell pepper, seeded and sliced into rings

4 ounces mozzarella, thinly sliced

1 ounce Parmesan, shaved (about ¼ cup)

2 tablespoons slivered fresh basil

1. Preheat the oven to 450°F, preferably with a baking stone in it. Lightly oil a 12- to 14-inch pizza pan and dust with semolina or cornmeal.

2. Peel the roasted red bell peppers, remove the seeds and membranes (holding the peppers over a bowl to catch the juices), and thinly slice. Toss in the bowl with the juices, salt and black pepper to taste, the garlic, and 1 tablespoon of the oil.

3. Roll out the dough, line the pizza pan and use your fingers to form a slightly thicker raised rim around the edge of the circle. Brush all but the rim of the dough with the remaining 1 tablespoon oil.

Arrange the green bell pepper rings over the dough. Place in the oven for 10 minutes. Remove from the oven and top with slices of mozzarella, placing the cheese inside and between the pepper rings. Distribute the roasted peppers over the surface of the pizza and drizzle on the juice remaining in the bowl. Return to the oven for 5 to 10 minutes, or until the crust is nicely browned and the cheese has melted. Remove from the oven, scatter the Parmesan and the basil over the top, and serve.

Per serving: 531 calories, 20 g protein, 54 g carbohydrates, 7 g fiber, 26 g fat, 9 g sat fat, 37 mg cholesterol, 937 mg sodium

ADVANCE PREPARATION: The peppers can be roasted a day ahead. The dough can be made up to 3 days ahead and held in the refrigerator.

Pizza with Green Garlic, Potatoes, and Herbs

Makes one 12- to 14-inch pizza, about 3 servings

■ **VEGETARIAN** ■ VEGAN ■ LOW-CALORIE ■ LOW-FAT
■ HIGH-PROTEIN ■ GLUTEN-FREE ■ HIGH IN OMEGA-3S

A pizza topped with potatoes may sound strange—in fact, I once received a rather angry e-mail from a reader accusing me of fabricating it—but I have seen this pizza in Roman pizzerias, where it is much loved. Make it in the spring and early summer, while you can get that luscious, juicy green garlic at the farmers' market (see page 222).

> Salt
>
> 1 bulb green garlic, sliced, or if the bulb has formed cloves, 4 cloves, thinly sliced
>
> ½ pound small red potatoes or other waxy potatoes, scrubbed
>
> Semolina or cornmeal, for the pan
>
> ½ recipe Whole Wheat Pizza Dough (page 108)
>
> 2 tablespoons extra virgin olive oil
>
> ¼ cup (1 ounce) grated Parmesan
>
> Ground black pepper
>
> 1 tablespoon chopped fresh rosemary or 1 teaspoon crumbled dried rosemary, or 2 teaspoons dried oregano

1. Bring a pot of water to a boil over high heat, add salt to taste, and drop in the garlic. Blanch for 30 seconds, transfer to a bowl of cold water using a slotted spoon, then drain and dry on paper towels.

2. Add the potatoes to the pot and bring to a gentle boil. Reduce the heat to medium-low, cover partially, and simmer the potatoes until just tender when pierced with a knife, 10 to 15 minutes, depending on the size of the potatoes. Drain and rinse under cold water. When cool enough to handle, slice about ¼ inch thick.

3. Preheat the oven to 450°F, preferably with a baking stone in it. Lightly oil a 12- to 14-inch pizza pan and dust with semolina or cornmeal. Roll or press out the pizza dough, line the pan and use your fingers to form a slightly thicker raised rim around the edge of the circle. Brush all but the rim of the crust with 1 tablespoon of the oil and sprinkle on the Parmesan. Top with the sliced potatoes and sliced garlic. Season generously with salt and black pepper, and sprinkle on the rosemary or oregano. Drizzle on the remaining 2 tablespoons olive oil. Bake until the crust is browned and crisp, about 15 minutes. Serve hot or at room temperature.

Per serving: 446 calories, 13 g protein, 58 g carbohydrates, 6 g fiber, 18 g fat, 4 g sat fat, 8 mg cholesterol, 683 mg sodium

ADVANCE PREPARATION: The cooked potatoes and blanched garlic will keep for 1 to 2 days in the refrigerator. The dough can be made up to 3 days ahead and held in the refrigerator.

Pizza Marinara with Tuna and Capers

Makes one 12- to 14-inch pizza, about 3 servings

■ VEGETARIAN ■ VEGAN ■ LOW-CALORIE ■ LOW-FAT
■ HIGH-PROTEIN ■ GLUTEN-FREE ■ **HIGH IN OMEGA-3S**

This pizza tastes like Southern Italy to me, though it is also popular along the Mediterranean coast of France. The hot red-pepper flakes are especially nice, but don't overdo it. Just a light sprinkle will give the pizza a little heat.

> Semolina or cornmeal, for the pan
>
> 1 can (14 ounces) whole tomatoes, finely chopped and drained in a sieve for 1 hour, or ¾ cup Summer Tomato Sauce (page 19)

2 garlic cloves, minced (1 if using Summer Tomato Sauce, which is already seasoned)

Salt

1 can (5–6 ½ ounces) olive oil-packed light (not albacore) tuna (see sidebar on page 54)

½ recipe Whole Wheat Pizza Dough (page 108)

1 teaspoon thyme leaves, chopped

1 teaspoon minced fresh rosemary

Red-pepper flakes

1 tablespoon capers, rinsed

½ red bell pepper, cut into thin strips

1 tablespoon extra virgin olive oil

1. Preheat the oven to 450°F, preferably with a baking stone in it. Lightly oil a 12- to 14-inch pizza pan and dust with semolina or cornmeal.

2. If using drained canned tomatoes, season with half of the garlic and salt to taste.

3. Break up the tuna in a bowl with a fork and add the remaining garlic and half of the thyme and rosemary.

4. Roll or press out the pizza dough, line the pan and use your fingers to form a slightly thicker raised rim around the edge of the circle. Spread the tomatoes or tomato sauce over the dough. Distribute the tuna over the tomato sauce. Sprinkle on the remaining thyme and rosemary, the red-pepper flakes, capers, and bell pepper. Drizzle on the olive oil.

5. Place the pizza pan on the stone in the hot oven. Bake for 15 to 20 minutes, or until the crust is brown and crisp. Serve hot or at room temperature.

Per serving: 420 calories, 14 g protein, 50 g carbohydrates, 6 g fiber, 15 g fat, 2 g sat fat, 20 mg cholesterol, 1,099 mg sodium

ADVANCE PREPARATION: The dough can be made up to 3 days ahead and held in the refrigerator. The tomato sauce will keep for 3 to 4 days in the refrigerator and freezes well.

Pissaladière (Provençal Onion Pizza)

Makes one 12- to 14-inch pizza/ 3 servings

■ VEGETARIAN ■ VEGAN ■ LOW-CALORIE ■ LOW-FAT
■ HIGH-PROTEIN ■ GLUTEN-FREE ■ HIGH IN OMEGA-3S

This is a signature Provençal dish from Nice and its environs, a pizza spread with a thick, sweet layer of onions that have been cooked slowly until they caramelize, and garnished with olives and anchovies.

3 tablespoons extra virgin olive oil

2 pounds sweet onions, finely chopped

3 garlic cloves, minced

2 teaspoons fresh thyme leaves, or 1 teaspoon dried thyme

½ bay leaf

Salt and ground black pepper

1 tablespoon capers, drained, rinsed, and mashed in a mortar and pestle or finely chopped

Semolina or cornmeal

½ recipe Whole Wheat Pizza Dough (page 108)

12 anchovy fillets, soaked in water for 5 minutes, drained, rinsed, and dried on paper towels

12 Niçoise olives

1. Heat 2 tablespoons of the olive oil in a large, heavy nonstick skillet over medium heat. Add the onions and cook, stirring, for 3 minutes, or until they begin to sizzle and soften. Add the garlic, thyme, bay leaf, a generous pinch of salt, and some black pepper. Stir everything together, turn the heat to low, cover, and cook slowly for 45 minutes, stirring often. The onions should melt down to a golden brown puree. If they begin to stick, add a few tablespoons of water. Stir in the capers, taste, and adjust the seasonings. If there is still liquid in the pan, cook over medium heat, uncovered, until it evaporates.

2. Preheat the oven to 450°F, preferably with a pizza stone in it. Lightly oil a 12- to 14-inch pizza pan and dust with semolina or cornmeal. Roll out the pizza dough and line the pan. Brush the remaining 1 table-spoon oil over the bottom but not the rim of the crust. Spread the onions over the crust in an even layer. Cut the anchovies in half and decorate the top of the pizza with them, making twelve small X's. Place an olive in the middle of each X. Place on the pizza stone and bake for 15 to 20 minutes, or until the edges of the crust are brown and the onions are beginning to brown. Serve hot, warm, or room temperature.

Per serving: 568 calories, 15 g protein, 72 g carbohydrates, 25 g total fat, 4 g saturated fat, 14 mg cholesterol, 7 g fiber, 1,660 mg sodium

ADVANCE PREPARATION: The onion topping can be made a day ahead of time and held in the refrigerator. The dough can be made several days ahead and held in the refrigerator, or it can be frozen.

Chapter 6
SIMPLE VEGETABLES

Although this entire book is filled with vegetable and grain recipes, in this chapter I've grouped the dishes that you are most likely to serve along with other dishes or as starters. That said, I could certainly make a meal of the artichoke ragout on page 121.

Every healthy cuisine in the world is healthy because it revolves around produce, usually served in conjunction with staple grains. As scientists have isolated more and more nutrients over the last century, we've begun to understand a bit more about why vegetables are so important for health. But we have to be careful not to lose sight of why we should eat them in the first place: because they make good eating. The farmers' market movement in this country has afforded us unprecedented access to seasonal produce, grown without chemicals. I think that the produce I find every Wednesday at the Santa Monica Farmers' Market in Los Angeles rivals what I see at the most beautiful markets in the South of France. Since every culinary culture treats them differently, the variety of vegetable dishes you can make is infinite.

In recent decades scientists have isolated an increasing number of phytochemicals (from the Greek word *phyto*, meaning plant), and they are believed to be beneficial to health. But nutrition is not an exact science, and for each nutrient that has been discovered in a lab there are probably many more undiscovered ones that contribute to a plant's overall beneficence. I've included overviews in this chapter of what, so far, nutritionists have discovered about the specific produce items I discuss.

Phytochemicals

Scientists think that these chemical compounds produced by plants may be among the reasons that increased consumption of plant-based foods is beneficial to our health. Many different compounds have been identified and many health claims attributed to them, though there is little proof that any of these compounds is effective when isolated (into supplements, for example) from the food in which nature has packaged it. Some appear to act as antioxidants, protecting our cells against oxidative damage. When cells break down, they become more susceptible to certain types of cancer, so anything that protects against this kind of damage may be protecting the body against cancers and other diseases related to aging. Some phytochemicals stimulate enzymes, while others interfere with DNA replication and could therefore play a role in cancer prevention. Some phytochemicals appear to have antibacterial powers, while others have the ability to bind physically to cell walls and prevent the adhesion of pathogens. Here are some of the types of phytochemicals that we've been hearing about, and the roles that they are believed to play.

- **Carotenoids:** Yellow, orange, and red pigments synthesized by plants. They include alpha-carotene, beta-carotene, beta-cryptoxanthin, lutein, zeaxanthin, and lycopene. All are being studied for their antioxidant properties.

- **Chlorophyll** and **Chlorophyllin:** Natural, fat-soluble chlorophylls found in plants. They may be effective in blocking the carcinogenic effects of certain toxins.

- **Curcumin:** The compound that gives turmeric its yellow color. Curcumin is being studied for its anti-inflammatory activity. It may be effective in the prevention of some inflammatory diseases, such as certain gastrointestinal cancers and Alzheimer's disease.

- **Flavonoids:** This is a large family of polyphenolic compounds that can be broken down into subclasses. They appear to play a roll in cell-signaling pathways. Some of the subclasses in the flavonoid family include:

  - **Anthocyanidins:** Found in red, blue, and purple berries; red and purple grapes; red wine; eggplant; and purple cabbage

  - **Flavanols:** Found in tea, chocolate, grapes, berries, apples, and red wine

  - **Flavanones:** Found in citrus fruits and juices

  - **Flavonols:** Found in yellow onions, scallions, kale, broccoli, apples, berries, tea, and many other foods (not to be confused with flavanols, above)

  - **Flavones:** Found in parsley, thyme, celery, hot chile peppers

  - **Isoflavones:** Found in soybeans, soy foods, legumes

- **Organosulfur Compounds:** From garlic. Thought to have potential to prevent and treat certain diseases.

- **Indole-3-Carbinol** and **Isothiocyanates** such as **Sulforaphane:** These chemicals are derived from the breakdown of compounds found in cruciferous vegetables (cabbage, kale, broccoli, etc.) and are being studied to determine their role in preventing certain cancers.

- **Lignans:** These polyphenols found in seeds (flaxseeds are the richest source), whole grains, legumes, fruits, and vegetables are being studied for their possible role in the prevention of hormone-related cancers, osteoporosis, and cardiovascular diseases.

Artichokes

Every Mediterranean cuisine appreciates artichokes. I don't know how people figured out how to eat them in the first place, but I'm glad they did. They're a wonderful food to eat, and very low in calories. They require a little work, but it's time well spent.

What Nutritionists Know about Artichokes

Whenever I taste bitter overtones in a vegetable, I suspect that this means there are beneficial ingredients hidden within. If your acupuncturist has ever prescribed Chinese herbs for an ailment, you'll know what I'm talking about. Although cooked artichokes don't taste strongly bitter, there is definitely a bitter note to their background flavor (taste the water after you've steamed them; that's *really* bitter. Or pour yourself a shot of Cynar, an Italian liqueur made from artichokes that is regarded as a digestive).

In this case, at least, it turns out I'm right. Artichokes are a rich source of a flavonoid complex called silymarin, a powerful antioxidant that is the active ingredient in milk thistle (artichokes are the flower buds of a kind of thistle). Silymarin has long been used for the treatment of liver, gallbladder, and digestive disorders, and is present in many skin-care products. It protects the liver from toxins, promotes the growth of new cells, and helps with the digestion and metabolism of fats. Artichokes are also a good source of magnesium, potassium, and fiber. They contain some folate, and the carotenoids lutein and zeaxanthin, which have been shown to be beneficial for your eyes.

Steamed Artichokes with Vinaigrette Dipping Sauce

Makes 2 to 4 servings

■ **VEGETARIAN** ▪ VEGAN ■ **LOW-CALORIE** ■ **LOW-FAT**
▪ HIGH-PROTEIN ■ **GLUTEN-FREE** ▪ HIGH IN OMEGA-3S

Some people think that eating an artichoke is a lot of work. I think it's fun, and I enjoy the leisurely pace of working away at one. I sometimes make a meal of a large globe artichoke, the kind that can be as big as a small grapefruit. I steam it, make up one or two dipping sauces, and work away at it until I get to the heart. Then I scrape away the chokes and eat the prize at the middle. This is the simplest way to prepare artichokes—hardly any trimming involved. The time is spent in the eating.

2 large or 4 medium artichokes

1 lemon, halved

Dipping sauce (see page 120)

1. Lay an artichoke on its side on a cutting board. Cut off the top one-fourth of the artichoke using a large, sharp knife. Rub the cut surfaces with the lemon. Cut off the stem so the artichoke will stand upright, and rub the bottom with the lemon. Pull off the tough bottom leaves, called bracts. Using scissors, cut away the thorny end of each remaining bract. Rub the cut edges with the lemon.

2. Bring 2 inches of water to a boil in a steamer or pasta pot over high heat. Place the artichokes in the steamer basket or directly in the water. Reduce the heat, cover, and simmer for 45 minutes, or until a leaf pulls away easily, with no resistance. Remove from the heat. Serve hot or at room temperature, with a sauce for dipping the leaves. When you reach the papery leaves that cover the choke at the middle, cut them away, along with the hairy choke, and discard. Slice up the heart and enjoy.

Per serving (based on 2 servings): 33 calories, 2 g protein, 9 g carbohydrates, 3 g fiber, 0 g fat, 0 g sat fat, 0 mg cholesterol, 70 mg sodium

Yogurt/Mayonnaise Vinaigrette

Makes ¾ cup

Per 1 tablespoon: 76 calories, 0 g protein, 0.5 g carbohydrates, 0 g fiber, 8 g fat, 1 g sat fat, 1 mg cholesterol, 60 mg sodium

VARIATION: Substitute 1 tablespoon fresh lemon juice for 1 tablespoon of the vinegar.

■ **VEGETARIAN** ■ VEGAN ■ **LOW-CALORIE** ■ LOW-FAT
■ HIGH-PROTEIN ■ GLUTEN-FREE ■ HIGH IN OMEGA-3S

Traditionally, steamed artichokes are served with drawn butter, hollandaise, or with a mayonnaise. I use a vinaigrette-based sauce, thickened with just a little bit of mayonnaise and yogurt.

2 tablespoons white wine vinegar or sherry vinegar

Sea salt or kosher salt

1 teaspoon Dijon mustard

1 small garlic clove. minced or pureed in a mortar and pestle

2 tablespoons Best Foods or Hellmann's mayonnaise (or use a soy-based mayonnaise)

2 tablespoons plain low-fat yogurt (or use soy yogurt)

⅓ cup extra virgin olive oil

Ground black pepper

Whisk together the vinegar, salt, mustard, and garlic. Whisk in the mayonnaise, yogurt, and oil. and Blend well. Taste, adjust the salt, and add the black pepper. Use as a dip for artichokes or other vegetables.

How to Trim Small Artichokes

Fill a bowl with water and add the juice of one-half lemon. Cut the stems off the artichokes, and using a sharp knife, cut off the tops: about ½ inch from the top for baby artichokes, 1 inch for larger artichokes. Rub the cut parts with the other half of the lemon. Break off the tough outer leaves until you get to the lighter, tender green leaves near the middle. Using a paring knife, trim away the woody bottoms of the leaves, the "shoulders" at the bottom of the artichokes, above the stem. Cut small baby artichokes in half, large artichokes into quarters, and cut away the chokes if the artichokes are mature. Immediately place in the bowl of acidulated water.

Artichoke, Mushroom, and Potato Ragout

Makes 4 to 6 servings

■ **VEGETARIAN** ■ **VEGAN** ■ LOW-CALORIE ■ **LOW-FAT**
■ HIGH-PROTEIN ■ **GLUTEN-FREE** ■ HIGH IN OMEGA-3S

When artichokes begin to show up at my farmers' market in the spring, but it's still cool outside and summer vegetables won't be around for a few months, I make this robust Provençal ragout with mushrooms and potatoes. The porcini mushrooms contribute a rich, almost meaty dimension to the dish.

1 ounce (about 1 cup) dried porcini mushrooms

12 baby or 6 medium or large artichokes

2 tablespoons extra virgin olive oil

1 large onion, thinly sliced

4–5 large garlic cloves, sliced

1 tablespoon tomato paste

1 pound small potatoes, scrubbed and quartered

½ cup dry white wine, such as sauvignon blanc or pinot grigio

1 bay leaf

1 generous thyme sprig

Salt and ground black pepper

1 teaspoon fresh lemon juice

¼ cup chopped flat-leaf parsley

1. Place the dried porcini in a large heatproof bowl or glass measuring cup. Pour 2 cups of boiling water over the mushrooms. Set aside for 30 minutes.

2. Meanwhile, prepare the artichokes following the instructions on the opposite page.

3. Place a sieve lined with cheesecloth or paper towels over a bowl. Drain the mushrooms. Squeeze the mushrooms over the sieve to extract as much liquid as possible, then rinse in several changes of water to rid them of grit. Set aside. Add enough water to the strained soaking liquid to measure 3 cups.

4. Heat the oil in a large, heavy nonstick skillet or Dutch oven over medium heat. Add the onion and cook, stirring, until tender, about 5 minutes. Stir in the garlic and mushrooms and cook, stirring, until fragrant, about 1 minute. Add the tomato paste and cook, stirring, until the paste darkens and begins to caramelize, 3 to 5 minutes.

5. Drain the artichokes. Add the artichokes and potatoes to the pot. Stir together for 1 minute, then stir in the wine. Bring to a boil and cook until most of the liquid is gone, then add the soaking liquid from the mushrooms, the bay leaf, thyme, salt, and black pepper. Bring to a simmer and reduce the heat. Cover and simmer for 40 minutes, or until the potatoes and artichokes are tender. Uncover, increase the heat and reduce the liquid in the pan to thicken.

Remove from the heat. Discard the bay leaf. Taste and adjust the seasonings with salt and pepper. Stir in the lemon juice and parsley. Serve hot.

Per serving (based on 4 servings): 264 calories, 8 g protein, 39 g carbohydrates, 8 g fiber, 7 g fat, 1 g sat fat, 0 mg cholesterol, 158 mg sodium

ADVANCE PREPARATION: The dish can be made 1 or 2 days ahead and reheated.

FOR MORE ARTICHOKE RECIPES SEE:

Artichoke Heart Frittata (page 247)

Baby Artichoke Risotto (page 223)

Panini with Artichokes, Spinach, and Peppers (page 100)

Asparagus

There's a lot you can do with asparagus, besides just eating it steamed and unadorned or—if you've got nice fat stalks—roasted (see recipe on opposite page). Delicate thin stalks go wonderfully with eggs, either stirred into scrambled eggs or tossed with finely chopped hard-cooked eggs and a vinaigrette. I love to toss it with pasta and use it in soups.

When you shop for asparagus, examine the flowers—the tips—carefully. They are the first part of the stalk to deteriorate, and if the asparagus is bunched too tightly and allowed to become wet (as too often happens in supermarkets, where they continually mist the vegetables), they will spoil quickly. They get really nasty too, so make sure you don't ruin your dinner by inadvertently including a mushy flower or two. If you do find a spoiled end in your bunch, just snap it off and discard, and wash all of the asparagus thoroughly. The rest of the stalk will taste fine.

Before cooking asparagus, remove the tough stem end, which will snap off when you bend the stalk. Save these and simmer to make a delicious broth. Indian and Chinese medicine recommends the stalks for their diuretic properties and for strengthening the reproductive system.

What Nutritionists Know about Asparagus

The tender, edible part of this lovely plant is an excellent source of vitamin K, folate, vitamin C, beta-carotene, and a very good source of a number of other nutrients, including tryptophan, vitamins B_1, B_2, B_6, and niacin (B_3), manganese, dietary fiber, phosphorus, and potassium. All this comes in a very low-calorie package: There are about 40 calories in a cup of cooked asparagus.

Roasted Asparagus

Makes 4 to 6 servings

■ **VEGETARIAN** ■ **VEGAN** ■ **LOW-CALORIE** ■ **LOW-FAT**
■ HIGH-PROTEIN ■ **GLUTEN-FREE** ■ HIGH IN OMEGA-3S

When you roast asparagus like this, it becomes positively juicy. I thought that 1 pound would be enough for 4 people, but the thick stalks—the best kind to use—are especially irresistible, so err on the side of extravagance and polish off the leftovers, if you have them, for lunch the next day.

2 pounds thick asparagus, trimmed

2 teaspoons extra virgin olive oil

Salt and ground black pepper

1 teaspoon fresh thyme leaves (optional)

Fresh lemon juice (optional)

1. Preheat the oven to 400°F. Oil a baking sheet or a baking dish large enough for the asparagus to fit in 1 layer. Arrange the asparagus in the dish and toss with the oil, salt, and black pepper. Place in the oven

and roast for 10 to 15 minutes, or until they begin to shrivel and color lightly.

2. Remove from the heat. Toss with the thyme and season with the lemon juice, if desired.

> **Per serving (based on 4 servings):** 42 calories, 1 g protein, 2 g carbohydrates, 1 g fiber, 4 g fat, 0.5 g sat fat, 0 mg cholesterol, 583 mg sodium

ADVANCE PREPARATION: If you want to serve this hot, there's nothing to do in advance. You can, however, serve it at room temperature. Don't add the lemon juice until just before serving.

Asparagus alla Parmigiana

Makes 4 to 6 servings

■ **VEGETARIAN** ■ VEGAN ■ LOW-CALORIE ■ **LOW-FAT**
■ HIGH-PROTEIN ■ **GLUTEN-FREE** ■ HIGH IN OMEGA-3S

If you travel in Italy during the springtime, you'll find asparagus prepared this way in menus all over the country. It couldn't be simpler. In its authentic version it would include lots of butter, but I prefer this olive oil version.

2 pounds asparagus, trimmed

Salt and ground black pepper

1/2 cup (2 ounces) grated Parmesan

1-2 tablespoons extra virgin olive oil

1. Place the asparagus in a steamer basket over boiling water. Cover and cook for 5 minutes. Rinse with cold water to stop the cooking and drain on a kitchen towel.

2. Preheat the oven to 425°F with the rack in the upper third of the oven. Butter or oil a rectangular or oval baking dish. Lay the asparagus in the dish in overlapping rows, with the tips in the second row

overlapping the bottoms in the first row, so that all of the asparagus tips are exposed. As you place the asparagus in the dish, sprinkle each row with salt, black pepper, and some of the Parmesan. Drizzle the olive oil over all.

3. Bake the asparagus for 15 minutes, or until sizzling and the cheese is lightly colored. Let rest for about 5 minutes before serving.

> **Per serving (based on 4 servings):** 138 calories, 10 g protein, 9 g carbohydrates, 8 g fat, 3 g sat fat, 12 mg cholesterol, 5 g fiber, 258 mg sodium

ADVANCE PREPARATION: You can steam the asparagus and assemble the casserole several hours before baking. You could also steam the asparagus a day ahead. Proceed with Step 2 just before baking.

FOR MORE ASPARAGUS RECIPES SEE:

Asparagus and Herb Frittata (page 240)

Asparagus and Parmesan Omelet (page 238)

Bruschetta with Scrambled Eggs and Asparagus (page 100)

Risotto with Asparagus, Fresh Fava Beans, and Saffron (page 224)

Wild Rice and Brown Rice Salad with Walnut Vinaigrette and Asparagus (page 178)

Beets

When I wrote my first *Recipes for Health* column on beets for NYTimes.com, the editor gave it the headline "Beets: The New Spinach." The headline got a lot of attention, the column was widely read and e-mailed, and hopefully many readers started cooking this delicious, beautiful, and highly nutritious vegetable.

Canned beets deserve the disdain they've always been met with, but unless your beets come out of a can, it's hard not to like this vegetable. Chefs know this, which is why you find beet dishes on many restaurant menus. They're easy to find in supermarkets and farmers' markets, available and good year-round (though their season is June through October, when they are at their most tender). In addition to red beets, look for beautiful golden beets and pink-and-white striated Chioggia beets. They can be used interchangeably, unless the red color is important to the dish. Look for unblemished bulbs with sturdy, unwilted greens. Whatever type of beets you buy, always buy them with the greens attached, so you get 2 vegetables for the price of 1. In fact, you can often get beet greens for free at the farmers' market, because some misguided people ask the vendors to chop off the tops when they buy their beets. When you get them home, cut off the greens and store them and the beets separately.

What Nutritionists Know about Beets

Beets and their greens are high in folate, manganese, and potassium. The greens add a whole set of nutrients to the picture, most notably beta-carotene, vitamin C, iron, and calcium.

Sautéed Beet Greens with Garlic and Olive Oil

Makes 2 to 4 servings

■ **VEGETARIAN** ■ **VEGAN** ■ **LOW-CALORIE** ■ **LOW-FAT**
■ HIGH-PROTEIN ■ **GLUTEN-FREE** ■ HIGH IN OMEGA-3S

When I get back from the market, I often blanch these greens right away (Step 1). They are great on their own, served as a side dish, or added to pasta, an omelet or risotto, or a gratin or quiche. Use this technique for virtually any leafy green, such as chard, kale, or mustard greens.

> 1 pound beet greens (2 large or 3 small bunches)
>
> Salt
>
> 1–2 tablespoons extra virgin olive oil
>
> 1–2 garlic cloves, minced
>
> ¼ teaspoon red-pepper flakes (optional)
>
> Ground black pepper

1. Bring a large pot of water to a boil over high heat. Meanwhile, stem the greens and wash the leaves in 2 rinses of water. Fill a bowl with ice water. When the water comes to a boil, salt generously and add the greens. Blanch for 2 minutes, or until tender. Transfer immediately to the ice water, cool for a moment, then drain and gather the leaves in a bunch between your hands and press out the water. Chop coarsely.

2. Heat the oil in a large, heavy nonstick skillet over medium heat. Add the garlic and red-pepper flakes (if using). Cook, stirring, until the garlic is fragrant and translucent, 30 to 60 seconds. Stir in the greens. Cook, stirring, for 2 minutes, or until the greens are nicely seasoned with the garlic and oil. Season with salt and black pepper, remove from the heat, and serve.

Per serving (based on 2 servings): 115 calories, 5 g protein, 10 g carbohydrates, 8 g fiber, 7 g fat, 1 g sat fat, 0 mg cholesterol, 585 mg sodium

ADVANCE PREPARATION: The blanched greens will keep in the refrigerator for about 3 days.

> Note: *Some people enjoy a few drops of lemon juice with their cooked greens, so you might want to pass a plate of lemon wedges. The acid dulls the color of the greens, which is why it's best to add the lemon juice when you serve the greens and not before.*

Roasted Beets

Makes 4 servings

■ **VEGETARIAN** ■ **VEGAN** ■ **LOW-CALORIE** ■ **LOW-FAT**
■ HIGH-PROTEIN ■ **GLUTEN-FREE** ■ HIGH IN OMEGA-3S

Roasting beets is the easiest and most flavorful way to cook them. They're great on their own or simply dressed with a vinaigrette. Keep them on hand in the refrigerator. When you roast beets, the skins slip right off, so this may change your beet-cooking life if that task has always prevented you from working with them. I find that roasted beets keep longer if I leave them in their skins until I need them.

> 1 bunch beets, small, medium, or large

Preheat the oven to 425°F. Cut the greens away from the beets, leaving about ¼ inch of stems. Scrub the beets and place in a baking dish or lidded ovenproof casserole. Add ¼ inch of water to the dish. Cover tightly. Roast the beets for 30 to 40 minutes for small beets (3 ounces or less), 40 to 45 minutes for medium beets (4 to 6 ounces), and 50 to 60 minutes for large beets (8 ounces), or until easily penetrated with the tip of a knife or a skewer. Remove from the oven and allow to cool in the covered baking dish.

Per serving: 44 calories, 2 g protein, 10 g carbohydrates, 0 g total fat, 0 g saturated fat, 0 mg cholesterol, 3 g fiber, 80 mg sodium

ADVANCE PREPARATION: Roasted beets in their skins will keep for 5 days in a covered bowl in the refrigerator. Before serving, cut away the ends and slip off the skins.

FOR MORE BEET RECIPES SEE:

Beet and Mâche Salad with Walnuts (page 45)

Clear Summer Borscht (page 96)

Farro Salad with Beets, Beet Greens, and Feta (page 195)

Hearty Vegetarian Borscht (page 71)

Mediterranean Beet and Yogurt Salad (page 46)

Pink Risotto with Beet Greens and Roasted Beets (page 231)

Cabbage

When I explain that healthy eating does not have to be expensive, cabbage is my best argument. This vegetable has been emblematic of peasant food forever, practically everywhere on the globe. Whereas in some cultures it is admittedly too often boiled to death, others serve it stir-fried, make tasty cabbage soups or cabbage pies, sweet and sour sautés and gratins, and tangy salads that are much tastier showcases for its versatility.

The family of vegetables that cabbage belongs to is referred to as both the Cruciferae family and the Brassica family (both are correct). Other relatives include kale, broccoli, collards, and Brussels sprouts. The sulfur compounds in cruciferous vegetables are the source of many of their nutritional attributes, but also the source of bad smells if they are overcooked. When cabbage is cooked properly, however, it develops a sweet flavor and fragrant aroma that is far from the funky one that I for one will always associate with my Russian-immigrant grandparents' apartment.

What Nutritionists Know about Cabbage

Many nutritionists consider the cruciferous family of vegetables to which cabbage belongs the most beneficial family of vegetables; nutritionist and author Jonny Bowden calls cabbage "the most important [vegetable] in the world from the point of view of nutritional benefits and cancer-fighting ability." Cabbage possesses phytochemicals such as sulforaphane, which protects the body against free radicals, and indoles, which help metabolize estrogens. It's also an excellent source of vitamins K and C, and a very good source of dietary fiber, vitamin B_6, folate, manganese, and omega-3 fatty acids.

Italian Sweet and Sour Cabbage

Makes 4 to 6 servings

■ **VEGETARIAN** ■ VEGAN ■ **LOW-CALORIE** ■ **LOW-FAT**
■ HIGH-PROTEIN ■ **GLUTEN-FREE** ■ HIGH IN OMEGA-3S

We might associate cabbage more with Central European cuisine than with that of the Mediterranean, yet it has played a major role there since the Middle Ages, when it was probably the most widely eaten vegetable. Cabbage lends itself to sweet and sour preparations; the trick is to cook the cabbage long enough to bring out its sweetness but not so long that it becomes mushy and sulfuric. Serve this with rice.

1 tablespoon extra virgin olive oil

1 small onion, thinly sliced

1 cabbage, quartered, cored, and thinly sliced

Salt

3 large tomatoes, peeled, seeded, and chopped, or 1 can (14 ounces) diced tomatoes

2 tablespoons red or white wine vinegar

1 tablespoon mild honey

Ground black pepper

Heat the oil in a large nonstick skillet over medium heat. Add the onion. Cook, stirring, until tender, about 5 minutes. Add the cabbage and a generous pinch of salt and cook, stirring, until it begins to wilt, about 5 minutes. Add the tomatoes (with juice), vinegar, and honey. Stir together and cook uncovered, stirring often, for 20 minutes, or until the cabbage is tender and fragrant. Taste and adjust the seasonings with salt and black pepper. Serve hot or warm.

Per serving (based on 4 servings): 136 calories, 4 g protein, 25 g carbohydrates, 8 g fiber, 4 g fat, 1 g sat fat, 0 mg cholesterol, 85 mg sodium

ADVANCE PREPARATION: This will keep for about 3 to 4 days in the refrigerator and is even better the day after it's made.

Seared Red Cabbage Wedges

Makes 6 servings

■ **VEGETARIAN** ■ **VEGAN** ■ **LOW-CALORIE** ■ **LOW-FAT**
■ HIGH-PROTEIN ■ **GLUTEN-FREE** ■ HIGH IN OMEGA-3S

In addition to all the great nutrients that regular cabbage brings you, red cabbage is a rich source of anthocyanins, those healthy phytochemicals—found in red, purple, and blue fruits and vegetables—that may have powerful antioxidant and anti-inflammatory properties. This recipe is incredibly easy. Don't be afraid to use high heat, and to allow the cabbage to color in the pan before turning it. The seared flavor of the cabbage is almost addictive.

1 small head red cabbage

2–3 tablespoons extra virgin olive oil

Salt and ground black pepper

1. Cut the cabbage into wedges ¾ to 1 inch thick at the thickest point, leaving the core intact so the wedges stay together.

2. Heat the oil over medium-high heat in a heavy cast iron or nonstick skillet. When it is very hot, place as many cabbage wedges as will fit in the pan in one layer in the pan. Cook for 3 to 5 minutes, until golden brown on one side. Using tongs or a spatula, turn over and cook on the other side for 5 minutes, until nicely browned and crispy on the edges and the cabbage is tender. Season generously with salt and black pepper. Serve hot.

Per serving: 71 calories, 1 g protein, 7 g carbohydrates, 2 g fiber, 5 g fat, 1 g sat fat, 0 mg cholesterol, 50 mg sodium

ADVANCE PREPARATION: Make this just before serving for the best results.

Braised Red Cabbage with Apples

Makes 6 to 8 servings

■ **VEGETARIAN** ■ **VEGAN** ■ **LOW-CALORIE** ■ **LOW-FAT**
■ HIGH-PROTEIN ■ **GLUTEN-FREE** ■ HIGH IN OMEGA-3S

I never tire of this classic purple cabbage dish. The cabbage cooks for a long time and ends up very tender and sweet. I like to serve the cabbage with bulgur, or as a side dish with just about anything. You can halve the quantities in this recipe if you don't want to make such a large amount, but it will keep well.

1 large head (2–2½ pounds) red cabbage

2 tablespoons canola oil

1 small onion, thinly sliced

5–6 tablespoons balsamic vinegar

2 tart apples, such as Braeburn or Granny Smith, peeled and sliced

¼ teaspoon ground allspice

Salt and ground black pepper to taste

1. Quarter, core, and shred the cabbage crosswise. Place the cabbage in a bowl and cover with cold water while you prepare the remaining ingredients.

2. Heat the oil over medium heat in a large skillet or Dutch oven and add the onion. Cook, stirring, for 3 minutes, or until just about tender. Add 2 tablespoons of the vinegar and cook, stirring, for 3 minutes, or until the mixture is golden. Add the apples and stir for 2 to 3 minutes.

3. Drain the cabbage and add to the skillet. Toss to coat thoroughly. Sprinkle with the allspice, 2 tablespoons of the vinegar, and salt to taste, and toss well. Cover and cook over low heat for 1 hour, stirring from time to time. Add black pepper, taste, and adjust the salt. Taste again and add 1 or 2 more tablespoons vinegar if needed.

Per serving (based on 6 servings): 132 calories, 3 g protein, 22 g carbohydrates, 5 g fiber, 5 g fat, 0 g sat fat, 0 mg cholesterol, 79 mg sodium

ADVANCE PREPARATION: This tastes even better the day after you make it and will keep for 3 or 4 days in the refrigerator. Reheat gently.

FOR MORE CABBAGE RECIPES SEE:

Creamy Cabbage Soup with Gruyère (page 80)

Hearty Vegetarian Borscht (page 71)

Provençal Kale and Cabbage Gratin (page 271)

Stewed Lentils with Cabbage (page 295)

Sweet and Sour Cabbage with Tofu and Grains (page 260)

Carrots

How often do you plan dinner around carrots? It's worth thinking about in the depths of winter, when your choice of fresh vegetables, especially colorful ones, can be limited. Farmer friends of mine have told me that their stored winter carrots are even sweeter than their tender spring carrots. Some farmers' markets offer an array of heirloom carrot varieties, including purple and yellow ones. The colors are beautiful, but I find that the familiar orange carrots have the best texture. Purple and yellow carrots tend to be starchy and not as sweet.

What Nutritionists Know about Carrots

The nutrients that make this vegetable such a healthy choice are called carotenoids, which convert to vitamin A in the liver and form protective antioxidant compounds. That carrots are good for the eyes is no old wives' tale; the alpha- and beta-carotene that convert to vitamin A help in the formation of a purple pigment in the retina called rhodopsin, which the eye needs in order to see in dim light. Carrots are also a good source of two other carotenoids that are believed to have antioxidant properties, lutein and zeaxanthin, which help protect the eyes against macular degeneration and cataracts. In addition to being an excellent source of carotenoids, carrots are a very good source of vitamins C and K, dietary fiber, and potassium.

Roasted Carrots and Parsnips with Rosemary and Garlic

Makes 4 servings

■ **VEGETARIAN** ■ **VEGAN** ■ **LOW-CALORIE** ■ **LOW-FAT**
■ HIGH-PROTEIN ■ **GLUTEN-FREE** ■ HIGH IN OMEGA-3S

Parsnips are carrots' sweeter cousins, with a rich, nutty flavor. Because the core can be woody, I always remove it; this can be a tedious task but it's worth it. Roasting will intensify the sweetness of both of these vegetables, and that will be set off by the savory rosemary flavor that infuses the mixture.

1 pound carrots

$^3/_4$ pound parsnips

4 large garlic cloves, smashed but left whole

Salt and ground black pepper

3–4 rosemary sprigs

2 tablespoons extra virgin olive oil

1. Preheat the oven to 425°F. Oil a baking sheet or a baking dish large enough to fit all the vegetables in a single layer. Cut the carrots and parsnips into 3-inch lengths. Quarter the fat lengths and halve the thin ends so that the pieces are about the same size. Cut away the cores from the parsnips. Place the carrots and parsnips in a large bowl. Add the garlic, salt, black pepper, rosemary, and oil. Toss until all the vegetables are coated with oil.

2. Arrange in an even layer in the baking sheet or dish. Cover with foil and place in the oven for 30 minutes. Reduce the heat to 375°F and uncover the vegetables. Stir gently, and continue to roast until lightly browned and tender, 20 to 30 minutes. Remove from the heat, and serve.

Per serving: 179 calories, 2 g protein, 27 g carbohydrates, 7 g fiber, 8 g fat, 1 g sat fat, 0 mg cholesterol, 124 mg sodium

ADVANCE PREPARATION: The vegetables can hold for a few hours once roasted; cover and reheat in the oven at 350°F.

FOR MORE CARROT RECIPES SEE:

Grated Carrot Salad (page 39)

Marinated Carrots with Fresh Mint (page 40)

Moroccan Cooked Carrot Salad (page 39)

Risotto with Spring Carrots and Leeks (page 228)

Spicy Tunisian Carrot Frittata (page 244)

Cauliflower

Cauliflower is one of the most versatile of vegetables, but you might not think of it as such. It can seem pretty drab if it's served plain (though I like it that way too), and like its Brassica family cousins cabbage and broccoli, it's downright unappetizing if overcooked. But from the Mediterranean to India, cauliflower shines in salads and pastas, gratins and soups, curries and risottos, and North African stews (tagines) that are served with couscous. It's at its best from December through March, when produce markets may look pretty spare if you live in a northern climate. In addition to the familiar white cauliflower most of us grew up with, now we're seeing gorgeous purple, pale orange, and light-green cauliflowers in farmers' markets and many supermarkets as well. They all taste the same, and you can use them interchangeably. If you have trouble getting your kids to eat dishes with cooked cauliflower, try serving the florets raw, with Russian dressing for dipping. Even some vegetable-averse kids seem to like it this way.

What Nutritionists Know about Cauliflower

Like other cruciferous vegetables, cauliflower is a source of abundant phytonutrients and enzymes with antioxidant properties that help the liver neutralize potentially toxic substances that can damage the body's cells. It's an excellent source of vitamins C and K, folate, and dietary fiber, and a very good source of vitamins B$_5$ (pantothenic acid) and B$_6$ (pyridoxine), tryptophan, and manganese.

Spicy South Indian Cauliflower

Makes 4 to 6 servings

■ **VEGETARIAN** ■ **VEGAN** ■ **LOW-CALORIE** ■ **LOW-FAT**
■ HIGH-PROTEIN ■ **GLUTEN-FREE** ■ HIGH IN OMEGA-3S

Cauliflower lends itself well to curries, and the combination of cauliflower and turmeric, an essential spice in curries, has an added health benefit, as turmeric has its own antioxidant properties. Serve this chile pepper–laced stir-fry with rice or other grains, and with flat Indian bread. It's inspired by a dish I always order at one of my favorite restaurants in Los Angeles, Bombay Café.

1 large head (1¾–2 pounds) cauliflower, broken into florets

2 tablespoons canola or peanut oil

1 piece (1 inch) ginger, peeled, sliced, and thinly slivered or minced

1 teaspoon cumin seeds, lightly toasted and crushed

1–2 serrano chile peppers, seeded if desired and minced (wear plastic gloves when handling)

1 cup chopped fresh or canned tomatoes

2 teaspoons coriander seeds, lightly toasted and ground

½ teaspoon turmeric

¼ teaspoon cayenne

Salt

¼ cup chopped cilantro

1 lime, cut into wedges

1. Place the cauliflower in a steamer basket set over 1 inch of boiling water. Cover and steam for 1 minute. Lift the lid and allow steam to escape for 15 seconds, then cover and steam for 5 minutes, or until the cauliflower is just tender. Remove from the heat

and refresh with cold water. Quarter the larger florets and set all of the cauliflower aside.

2. Heat the oil in a large, heavy nonstick skillet or wok over medium heat. Add the ginger, cumin, and chile peppers. Cook for 1 minute. Add the cauliflower and cook for 2 to 3 minutes. Stir in the tomatoes, coriander, turmeric, cayenne, and $1/2$ teaspoon salt. Cook, stirring, for 5 minutes, or until the tomatoes have cooked down and the mixture is fragrant. Taste and adjust the seasoning with salt. Add the cilantro and stir for 30 seconds. Serve, passing lime wedges for squeezing.

Per serving (based on 4 servings): 140 calories, 5 g protein, 17 g carbohydrates, 7 g fiber, 8 g fat, 1 g sat fat, 0 mg cholesterol, 202 mg sodium

ADVANCE PREPARATION: Although this is best served right away, I enjoy the leftovers mixed with rice for a couple of days, and I have made it a few hours ahead of time and reheated on top of the stove. In this case, stir in the cilantro just before serving.

Roasted Cauliflower

Makes 4 to 6 servings

■ **VEGETARIAN** ■ **VEGAN** ■ **LOW-CALORIE** ■ **LOW-FAT**
■ HIGH-PROTEIN ■ **GLUTEN-FREE** ■ HIGH IN OMEGA-3S

Roasting cauliflower adds a dimension to its flavor. As it caramelizes in the hot oven, sweet flavors emerge. Make sure, though, to blanch the cauliflower first, or it will be hard, its flavors locked in. You can serve this plain, on its own, or toss it with pasta and tomato sauce.

Salt

1 large cauliflower, broken into florets

2 tablespoons extra virgin olive oil

1. Preheat the oven to 400°F. Oil a baking sheet or a large baking dish. Meanwhile, bring a large pot of water to a boil over high heat. Salt generously and add the cauliflower. Blanch for 2 minutes and transfer to a bowl of cold water. Drain the cauliflower and blot dry.

2. Toss the cauliflower with the oil and salt to taste in a large bowl. Transfer to the baking sheet or baking dish, making sure to scrape out all of the oil from the bowl with a rubber spatula. Place in the oven and roast for 30 minutes, stirring occasionally, until the cauliflower is tender and lightly browned. Serve hot.

Per serving (based on 4 servings): 116 calories, 4 g protein, 11 g carbohydrates, 5 g fiber, 7 g fat, 1 g sat fat, 0 mg cholesterol, 99 mg sodium

ADVANCE PREPARATION: The blanched cauliflower will keep for a few days in the refrigerator.

Cauliflower Gratin with Goat Cheese Topping

Makes 6 side-dish servings

■ **VEGETARIAN** ■ VEGAN ■ LOW-CALORIE ■ LOW-FAT
■ **HIGH-PROTEIN** ■ GLUTEN-FREE ■ HIGH IN OMEGA-3S

Of all the many gratins that I make, this is the easiest to throw together. It works as a vegetarian main dish, as part of a selection of vegetables, or as a side. The goat cheese, garlic, olive oil, and thyme give the dish Provençal overtones.

1 large or 2 smaller cauliflowers (about 2 pounds), broken into florets

Salt and ground black pepper

3 tablespoons extra virgin olive oil

1 teaspoon chopped fresh thyme or $1/2$ teaspoon dried thyme

1 large garlic clove, halved

6 ounces fresh goat cheese

5 tablespoons 1% milk

3 tablespoons plain, dry bread crumbs

1. Preheat the oven to 450°F. Oil a 2-quart gratin dish with olive oil.

2. Place the cauliflower in a steamer basket over 1 inch of boiling water. Cover and steam for 1 minute. Lift the lid and allow steam to escape for 15 seconds, then cover and steam for 6 to 8 minutes, or until the cauliflower is tender. Remove from the heat and refresh with cold water. Drain on paper towels, then transfer to the gratin dish.

3. Season the cauliflower generously with salt and black pepper. Toss with 2 tablespoons of the oil and half of the thyme. Arrange in an even layer in the gratin dish.

4. Place the garlic and ¼ teaspoon salt in a mortar and mash to a paste with a pestle. Combine with the goat cheese and milk in a food processor and blend until smooth. Add black pepper to taste and the remaining thyme, and pulse until smooth. Spread this mixture over the cauliflower in an even layer.

5. Just before baking, sprinkle on the bread crumbs and drizzle on the remaining 1 tablespoon oil. Bake for 15 to 20 minutes, or until the top is lightly browned and the dish is sizzling. Serve at once.

Per serving: 198 calories, 9 g protein, 12 g carbohydrates, 4 g fiber, 13 g fat, 5 g sat fat, 14 mg cholesterol, 209 mg sodium

ADVANCE PREPARATION: You can make this through Step 3 hours in advance. Cover with plastic wrap and refrigerate if holding for more than 2 hours.

Marinated Cauliflower with Fennel and Coriander Seeds

Makes 4 to 6 servings

■ **VEGETARIAN** ■ **VEGAN** ■ **LOW-CALORIE** ■ **LOW-FAT**
■ HIGH-PROTEIN ■ **GLUTEN-FREE** ■ HIGH IN OMEGA-3S

This is a popular way to prepare vegetables in France, where the method is called à la Grecque—though I've never had anything like it in Greece. It's a great way to keep this highly nutritious vegetable on hand and ready to eat.

1 medium head cauliflower, broken into florets

½ cup dry white wine, such as sauvignon blanc or pinot grigio

¼ cup fresh lemon juice

¼ cup extra virgin olive oil

2 tablespoons white wine vinegar or champagne vinegar

2 teaspoons coriander seeds

2 teaspoons fennel seeds

1 teaspoon whole black peppercorns

1 bay leaf

Salt

1. Place the cauliflower in a steamer basket over boiling water. Cover and cook for 5 minutes. Rinse under cold water.

2. Combine 2 cups water, the wine, lemon juice, olive oil, vinegar, coriander seeds, fennel seeds, peppercorns, and bay leaf in a large, heavy soup pot or Dutch oven. Bring to a boil over high heat, reduce the heat to medium, and boil gently for 5 minutes. Add the cauliflower, reduce to a simmer, and simmer for 7 minutes. Using tongs, remove the cauliflower from the pan and place in a bowl. It's fine if some of the spices from the pot come with the cauliflower to the bowl (the coriander seeds are especially nice).

3. Bring the liquid in the pot back to a boil and allow it to reduce by half its volume. Add salt to taste. Place a strainer over the bowl with the cauliflower and strain in the reduced liquid. If you wish, before throwing out the contents of the strainer, toss a teaspoon of the seeds into the bowl with the cauliflower. Serve at room temperature or chilled.

Per serving (based on 4 servings): 192 calories, 3 g protein, 10 g carbohydrates, 4 g fiber, 14 g fat, 2 g sat fat, 0 mg cholesterol, 81 mg sodium

ADVANCE PREPARATION: This is an excellent keeper. You can make it up to 5 days before you serve it.

FOR MORE CAULIFLOWER RECIPES SEE:

Barley Orzotto with Cauliflower and Red Wine (page 180)

Couscous with Beans and Cauliflower (page 287)

Fusilli with Cauliflower, Tomato Sauce, and Olives (page 215)

Celery

Celery is one of those vegetables that sits around in the refrigerator after you buy a bunch for the one rib you need to make a soup or stew, or as Thanksgiving approaches, stuffing. If you don't have kids who will eat celery ribs filled with peanut butter, what do you do with the rest of the bunch? It will keep for weeks, but I bet you've thrown out a lot of drooping ribs of celery. That's too bad, because there are plenty of things to do with this vegetable, especially the tender inner ribs that you didn't get to—the heart—which are the best part. I've become enamored of celery in salads. Sliced very thin, it adds a crunchy herbal dimension that you may not have known was missing.

What Nutritionists Know about Celery

Celery has long been used in Chinese medicine to help control high blood pressure. It contains phytochemicals called phthalides that reduce stress hormones and work to relax the muscle walls in arteries, increasing bloodflow. The vegetable is a source of vitamins K and C, and a very good source of potassium, folate, dietary fiber, molybdenum, manganese, and vitamin B_6.

Braised Hearts of Celery Vinaigrette

Makes 6 servings

■ **VEGETARIAN*** ■ **VEGAN*** ■ **LOW-CALORIE** ■ **LOW-FAT**
■ HIGH-PROTEIN ■ **GLUTEN-FREE** ■ HIGH IN OMEGA-3S

Braised celery has a much milder flavor than raw celery, and needs a robust, lemony sauce. I was introduced to braised celery hearts in France, where it is standard fare in cafés and traiteurs (where food is prepared to go), and I've always loved it. It's a great starter or side dish, and it keeps for a few days in the refrigerator.

Salt

3 celery hearts (the lighter, inner ribs), halved lengthwise, ends trimmed

2 tablespoons extra virgin olive oil

$1/2$ medium onion, sliced

4 garlic cloves, sliced

1 cup Vegetable Stock (page 67) or chicken stock

2 tablespoons fresh lemon juice

$1/4$ cup dry white wine, such as sauvignon blanc

Ground black pepper

1 large lemon, sliced

1 tablespoon finely chopped flat-leaf parsley

*If made with Vegetable Stock

1. Preheat the oven to 400°F. Bring a large pot of water to a boil over high heat. Salt generously and drop in the celery. Boil until partially cooked, about 3 minutes. Drain, pat dry, and lay the hearts side by side, cut side up, in a baking dish.

2. Heat 1 tablespoon of the oil in a medium skillet over medium heat. Add the onion and $1/2$ teaspoon salt. Cook, stirring, until the onion softens, about 5 minutes. Add the garlic. Stir together for 1 minute, or until fragrant. Add the stock, lemon juice, and wine. Bring to a boil and remove from the heat. Pour over the celery. Season the celery with salt and pepper and arrange the lemon slices on top. Cover tightly with foil and place in the oven. Braise for

40 minutes, or until the celery is thoroughly tender but still holds its shape. Remove from the heat and allow the celery to cool in the liquid.

3. Remove the celery from the pot with tongs. Cut the halved bunches in half lengthwise again. Transfer to a platter or a wide serving dish. Pour the liquid into a saucepan and bring to a boil over high heat. Reduce by about half and pour over the celery. Drizzle on the remaining 1 tablespoon oil, grind on some black pepper, and sprinkle on the parsley. Serve warm or at room temperature, or chill and serve cold. Spoon the liquid from the platter over each portion.

Per serving: 68 calories, 0.5 g protein, 5 g carbohydrates, 1 g fiber, 5 g fat, 1 g sat fat, 0 mg cholesterol, 97 mg sodium

ADVANCE PREPARATION: You can make this a day ahead and keep it in the refrigerator, covered.

FOR MORE CELERY RECIPES SEE:

White Beans with Celery (page 291)

Winter Tomato and Celery Soup with Rice (page 70)

Swiss Chard

Of all the greens I cook with, chard is the most versatile; it's sturdier than spinach, yet has a more delicate flavor than other robust greens like kale or turnip greens.

Chard comes in different colors. The leaves are always dark green, but red chard has red veins and stalks and yellow chard has yellow veins and stalks while those of regular chard are white. Some farmers grow all three together and sell it as "rainbow chard." Chard stalks of all colors are edible—the wide ones are best—and add texture and flavor to the dishes they're cooked into.

What Nutritionists Know about Swiss Chard

Most of chard's nutrients are in the greens. It's a superb source of calcium and potassium, vitamin C, and beta-carotene, as well as the carotenoids lutein and zeaxanthin, which are proving to be of great value in protecting the eyes against vision problems.

Swiss Chard with Pine Nuts and Currants

Makes 4 servings

■ **VEGETARIAN** ■ **VEGAN** ■ **LOW-CALORIE** ■ **LOW-FAT**
■ HIGH-PROTEIN ■ **GLUTEN-FREE** ■ HIGH IN OMEGA-3S

Tall cone-bearing pine trees are found along the Mediterranean coast; consequently, pine nuts are a common ingredient in regional cuisines. You will find versions of this dish from Spain to Turkey, made as often with spinach as with Swiss chard. I prefer to use chard, because the chard stands up better to the cooking but still has a delicate flavor.

3 tablespoons dried currants, raisins, or golden raisins

Salt

2 pounds Swiss chard, stemmed and washed in several changes of water, stems diced and set aside

2 tablespoons extra virgin olive oil

3 tablespoons pine nuts

1–2 garlic cloves, minced

Ground black pepper

1. Place the currants in a bowl and pour on hot water to cover. Soak for 10 minutes and drain.

2. Fill a bowl with ice water. Bring a large pot of water to a boil over high heat. Salt generously and add the chard leaves. Cook for 1 to 2 minutes, or until just tender. Transfer to the bowl of ice water and let set for a few minutes. Drain and squeeze out as much water as you can. Chop coarsely.

3. Heat the oil in a large, heavy nonstick skillet over medium heat. Add the chard stems and cook for 3 to 5 minutes, or until tender. Add the pine nuts and cook, stirring, until they begin to color, 2 to 3 minutes. Add the garlic and cook, stirring, just until the garlic begins to be fragrant, 30 seconds to 1 minute. Add the chopped greens and drained currants or raisins. Toss together until they are well coated with oil and heated through, 2 to 3 minutes. Season to taste with salt and black pepper, and serve, or allow to cool and serve at room temperature.

Per serving: 166 calories, 5 g protein, 15 g carbohydrates, 4 g fiber, 12 g fat, 1 g sat fat, 0 mg cholesterol, 520 mg sodium

ADVANCE PREPARATION: The blanched greens will keep in a covered bowl in the refrigerator for about 3 to 4 days.

2 large bunches rainbow chard

2 tablespoons canola oil

Salt

2 garlic cloves, minced

2–3 teaspoons minced fresh ginger

Soy sauce (optional)

*If you omit the soy sauce

1. Bring 1 inch of water to a boil in a steamer. Meanwhile, strip the leaves from the stems of Swiss chard. Wash the leaves and stalks in several rinses of water. If the stems are wide, trim the ends and cut in ¼-inch dice. If they are skinny, discard.

2. Place the leaves in the steamer basket, cover, and steam for 3 to 5 minutes, or until the leaves have wilted (do this in batches if it's easier). Remove from the steamer, rinse with cold water, squeeze out the excess water, and coarsely chop.

3. Heat the oil over medium-high heat in a large, heavy nonstick skillet. Add the chard stems and cook, stirring, for 3 minutes, or until crisp-tender. Add a generous pinch of salt, the garlic, and ginger and cook, stirring, for 30 seconds to 1 minute, or until the garlic and ginger are fragrant and just beginning to color. Stir in the chard leaves and stir for a couple of minutes. Season with salt or, if desired, soy sauce. Serve hot.

Per serving: 85 calories, 2 g protein, 5 g carbohydrates, 2 g fiber, 7 g fat, 1 g sat fat, 0 mg cholesterol, 278 mg sodium

ADVANCE PREPARATION: The steamed chard leaves will keep in the refrigerator for about 3 days.

Rainbow Chard with Garlic and Ginger

Makes 4 servings

■ **VEGETARIAN** ■ **VEGAN** ■ **LOW-CALORIE** ■ **LOW-FAT**
■ HIGH-PROTEIN ■ **GLUTEN-FREE*** ■ HIGH IN OMEGA-3S

Farmers often bunch red, green, and yellow chard together and sell the bunches as rainbow chard. I usually blanch the greens or steam them, then cook them with garlic and red-pepper flakes or with garlic and ginger. If the stems are wide, dice them up and cook them along with the leaves.

Swiss Chard with White Beans and Rice

Makes 4 servings

■ **VEGETARIAN** ■ **VEGAN*** ■ **LOW-CALORIE** ■ **LOW-FAT**
■ **HIGH-PROTEIN** ■ **GLUTEN-FREE** ■ HIGH IN OMEGA-3S

This brothy dish isn't quite brothy enough to qualify as a soup; it's more like a comforting stew. If you wish to use another type of bean, such as pintos or borlottis, that would work too.

¾ pound Swiss chard (1 small bunch)

2 tablespoons extra virgin olive oil

1 onion, chopped

2–4 garlic cloves, minced

½ pound (1 heaping cup) dried white beans,
    soaked for 6 hours or overnight in 1 quart water

1 bay leaf

1 Parmesan rind (optional but recommended)

Salt

1 cup Arborio or Carnaroli rice

Ground black pepper

2–3 teaspoons fresh lemon juice (optional)

*If you omit the Parmesan rind

1. Strip the leaves from the stems of Swiss chard. Wash the leaves and stems in several rinses of water. Dice the stems if they're wide (discard if they're skinny) and set aside. Stack the leaves and cut in wide ribbons or coarsely chop. Set the stems and leaves aside separately.

2. Heat the oil in a Dutch oven over medium heat. Add the onion and chard stems. Cook, stirring often, for 5 minutes, or until the onion softens. Add half the garlic, stir together for 30 seconds to 1 minute, or until fragrant. Add the beans and 2 quarts water.

Tie the bay leaf and Parmesan rind (if using) together with a kitchen string to make retrieval easier. Add to the pot. Bring to a gentle boil, reduce the heat, and simmer for 1 hour. Add the remaining garlic and salt to taste, and simmer for 30 minutes to 1 hour longer, until the beans are tender.

3. Add the rice and black pepper and simmer for 15 minutes, or until the rice is tender. Stir in the chard leaves and simmer for 5 to 10 minutes, or until tender but still bright. The mixture should be soupy but thick. Season to taste with salt and black pepper. Squeeze on some lemon juice if desired, and serve in wide soup bowls.

Per serving: 452 calories, 19 g protein, 77 g carbohydrates, 13 g fiber, 8 g fat, 1 g sat fat, 0 mg cholesterol, 228 mg sodium

ADVANCE PREPARATION: You can make this through Step 2 up to 3 days ahead. Bring to a simmer and proceed with Step 3.

FOR MORE CHARD RECIPES SEE:

Couscous with Black-Eyed Peas and Greens (page 289)

Frittata with Greens (page 242)

Pasta with Swiss Chard and Tomato Sauce (page 214)

Provençal Greens Soup (page 72)

Red Chard, Potato, and White Bean Ragout (page 286)

Stir-Fried Tofu and Greens (page 264)

Swiss Chard and Red Bell Pepper Gratin (page 268)

Tofu and Rainbow Chard Hotpot (page 265)

Corn

Corn is a grain that we treat like a vegetable when we eat it fresh, on or off the cob. In the Connecticut summer meals of my youth, corn was on the table every night. "It's a short season," my father would say, as we passed the platter around for the fourth time. Two dozen ears were never too many for our family of six. My mother would steam the ears in a huge canner and heap them onto a big kitchen towel on a platter, then wrap the towel around to keep them warm. There would also be a big platter of ripe beefsteak tomatoes, and meat of some kind. But that would hardly be noticed in the presence of sweet corn on the cob.

Steaming is the easiest way to cook corn on the cob. Whether on or off the cob, cook it soon after you buy it, and for no more than 4 to 5 minutes.

What Nutritionists Know about Corn

Corn is a good source of several nutrients, including thiamine (vitamin B_1), pantothenic acid (vitamin B_5), folate, dietary fiber, vitamin C, phosphorus, and manganese. A cup of corn supplies 19 percent of the recommended daily dose of folate, and about a quarter of the daily value for thiamine.

Grilled Corn on the Cob with Chipotle Mayonnaise

Makes 6 to 12 servings

■ **VEGETARIAN** ■ VEGAN ■ **LOW-CALORIE** ■ LOW-FAT
■ HIGH-PROTEIN ■ **GLUTEN-FREE** ■ HIGH IN OMEGA-3S

The spicy dip that I serve with grilled corn (as well as with steamed or boiled corn) is sort of like a Mexican aioli: pungent with garlic, smoky and spicy with chipotle chiles in adobo sauce. You can also serve it as a dip with vegetables or chips, or use it as a flavorful spread for sandwiches and panini. The recipe makes more than you'll need for 6 ears of corn, so you'll have enough if you're having a crowd for a barbecue.

6–12 ears corn

2 large garlic cloves, halved

1/4 teaspoon salt

1 large or 2 small chipotle chiles in adobo sauce, seeded

1 teaspoon adobo sauce from the canned chipotles

1/4 cup mayonnaise, preferably Hellmann's or Best Foods

1/2 cup plain low-fat Greek-style yogurt

1. Preheat a grill to medium-hot or prepare a medium-hot charcoal fire. Remove the outer leaves of the corn husks, leaving 2 layers. Gently pull down the remaining leaves, pull off the silk, and fold the leaves back up, covering the corn. For each ear, cut 2 pieces of butcher's string about 6 inches long. Tie the cobs at the top and midway down with the wet string. Place in a bowl or a sink filled with cold water and soak for 15 to 30 minutes.

2. Meanwhile, mash the garlic and salt to a smooth paste with a mortar and pestle. Add the chiles and mash together with the garlic. Stir in the adobo sauce, mayonnaise, and yogurt. Mix together well.

3. When the coals of your grill are medium-hot, remove the corn from the water and pat dry. Place the corn on the grill rack and grill until the corn is uniformly charred, turning the ears often, 10 to 20 minutes, depending on the heat of your grill. Remove from the grill and, holding the ears with a kitchen towel, cut away the strings and remove the leaves. Wrap the corn in a kitchen towel to keep warm.

4. Serve with the chipotle dip. Place a generous spoonful on a plate and roll the corn in it, or spread it on the corn with a knife.

Per 1-ear serving (based on 6 ears): 161 calories, 4 g protein, 18 g carbohydrates, 2 g fiber, 9 g fat, 1 g sat fat, 4 mg cholesterol, 359 mg sodium

ADVANCE PREPARATION: You can prepare the corn for grilling hours ahead. The dip will keep for a day in the refrigerator.

Pan-Cooked Corn with Cilantro

Makes 4 to 6 servings

■ **VEGETARIAN** ■ **VEGAN** ■ **LOW-CALORIE** ■ **LOW-FAT**
■ HIGH-PROTEIN ■ **GLUTEN-FREE** ■ HIGH IN OMEGA-3S

When sweet corn had a shorter season I would rarely serve it any way other than on the cob. Now that sweet corn is at the farmers' market for several months, beginning in the late spring and extending through September, I cook it both on the cob and off. Here it's brightened with cilantro; one vibrant herb adds complexity to a simple preparation.

2 tablespoons extra virgin olive oil

1 small onion, preferably a white or red spring onion, finely chopped

Kernels from 6 ears of corn

Salt and ground black pepper

2 tablespoons chopped cilantro

1. Heat the oil in a heavy skillet over medium heat. Add the onion and cook, stirring, for 5 minutes, or until tender. Add the corn and stir for 1 minute. Add $\frac{1}{4}$ cup water and increase the heat to high.

2. When the water comes to a boil, season the corn mixture with salt and black pepper and cook, stirring often, for 4 to 5 minutes, or until the water has just about evaporated. Stir in the cilantro. Taste and adjust the seasonings with salt and black pepper. Serve hot.

Per serving: 205 calories, 6 g protein, 29 g carbohydrates, 3 g fiber, 11 g fat, 1 g sat fat, 0 mg cholesterol, 37 mg sodium

ADVANCE PREPARATION: You should serve this right away once it's cooked, but you can prepare the ingredients several hours before you begin to cook.

Succotash with Fava Beans or Edamame

Makes 6 servings

■ **VEGETARIAN** ■ **VEGAN** ■ **LOW-CALORIE** ■ **LOW-FAT**
■ HIGH-PROTEIN ■ **GLUTEN-FREE** ■ HIGH IN OMEGA-3S

If you begin to get corn on the cob at your farmers' markets before the fava beans are finished for the season, and if you have the patience to skin the favas (they are worth the time), then try this succotash with favas. Edamame, which are perfectly good frozen, are equally pretty, and they're delicious too.

1½ cups shelled fava beans or 1 cup fresh shelled or thawed frozen edamame

Salt

6 ears of corn, husked

2 tablespoons extra virgin olive oil

1 small onion, preferably a white or red spring onion, finely chopped

2 garlic cloves, minced

1 medium bell pepper, finely diced

Salt and ground black pepper

1 tablespoon minced fresh tarragon

1. If using fava beans, bring a large pot of water to a boil. Fill a bowl with ice water. Salt the boiling water generously and add the favas. Boil small favas for 1 minute, larger favas for 2 minutes and use a skimmer or slotted spoon to transfer them to the ice water. Allow to cool in the water, then drain and slip off the skins, using your thumbnail to open them up at the spot where the bean was attached to the pod. Set aside. (If using edamame, set aside in a bowl.)

2. Bring the water back to a boil and add the corn. Blanch for 2 minutes and transfer to a bowl of cold water. Drain well and cut the kernels off the cobs.

3. Heat the oil in a large skillet over medium heat and add the onion. Cook, stirring, for 5 minutes, or until tender. Add a generous pinch of salt, the garlic, and bell pepper. Cook, stirring, for 3 minutes, or until the pepper is just tender. Stir in the corn kernels and cook, stirring, for 2 to 3 minutes, or until tender. Stir in the favas or edamame and season to taste with salt and black pepper. Add the tarragon and heat through, stirring. Serve hot.

Per serving: 271 calories, 14 g protein, 42 g carbohydrates, 12 g fiber, 8 g fat, 1 g sat fat, 0 mg cholesterol, 55 mg sodium

ADVANCE PREPARATION: You can make the dish through Step 2 several hours ahead. The final pan-cooking of the vegetables should be done shortly before serving.

FOR MORE CORN RECIPES SEE:

Corn and Vegetable Gratin with Cumin (page 272)

Corn Risotto with Sage (page 233)

Fragrant Puree of Corn Soup (page 85)

Soft Tacos with Chicken and Tomato-Corn Salsa (page 328)

Summer Succotash with Black Beans (page 163)

Eggplant

People have strong feelings about eggplant; they love it or they hate it, citing bitterness or the heaviness of eggplant dishes. I'd always salted eggplant before cooking to purge it of its bitter juices until my friend and colleague Russ Parsons explained that's an old wives' tale. According to Parsons, salting does improve eggplant's texture if it's going to be fried, but that's the only reason to purge it. Which brings me to another point: Frying isn't the only way to go about cooking eggplant. That's a good thing, because eggplant will soak up every ounce of fat you give it and more. This is why so many eggplant dishes are heavy.

I get around frying eggplant in an overabundance of oil, even in dishes where it's sautéed, by roasting it first. Then I cut it up and cook it again with the other ingredients in the dish. It's a great method, as long as you don't need neat, firm slices. Roasted eggplant has a deep, complex flavor. Eggplant is also terrific grilled—one of my favorite methods for grilling it is in a panini grill. This is very efficient if your recipe doesn't call for lots and lots of eggplant. You can also steam eggplant (see the delicious salad on page 52).

What Nutritionists Know about Eggplant

Resist the temptation to peel away the skin. That beautiful purple skin contains eggplant's most valuable nutrient, a substance, called nasunin, that is a powerful antioxidant. Nasunin is in the same family of antioxidant flavonoids, called anthocyanins, that are present in other fruits and vegetables with red, blue, and purple hues (berries, beets, red cabbage). So choose the purple varieties when you shop, and leave the skin on.

Roasted Eggplant

Roasting is the first step in many of my eggplant recipes. Large globe eggplants take 20 to 25 minutes, depending on how plump they are. Small, narrow eggplants like Japanese eggplants take about 15 minutes. The roasted eggplant is fragrant and delicate; if you need it to hold its shape in the recipe, roast just until you see the skin beginning to wrinkle.

1. Preheat the oven to 450°F. Cut the stem end off the eggplant, and halve lengthwise. Score large eggplants down the middle with the tip of a knife, being careful not to cut through the skin. Japanese eggplants and other small eggplants needn't be scored.

2. Cover a baking sheet with foil and brush the foil with extra virgin olive oil. Place the eggplant on the foil, cut side down. Place in the oven and roast large, fat eggplants for 20 to 25 minutes (depending on the size), and small, narrow Japanese eggplants (and other varieties) for 15 minutes, or until the skin has begun to shrivel, the edges and cut surface are browned, and the eggplant has softened but it hasn't collapsed.

3. Remove from the oven and use a spatula to detach from the foil if the eggplant is sticking (don't worry if a thin surface of browned eggplant stays behind). Place the eggplant halves cut side down on a rack set over a baking sheet, or in a colander in the sink. Allow to cool and drain for 15 to 30 minutes.

ADVANCE PREPARATION: You can roast eggplant several hours before you wish to use it in a recipe.

Caponata

Makes 6 to 8 servings

■ **VEGETARIAN** ■ **VEGAN** ■ **LOW-CALORIE** ■ **LOW-FAT**
■ HIGH-PROTEIN ■ **GLUTEN-FREE** ■ HIGH IN OMEGA-3S

Caponata is a Sicilian sweet-and-sour version of ratatouille. Because eggplant absorbs flavors like a sponge, it's particularly good in such a pungent dish. Like most eggplant dishes, this gets better overnight. It's meant to be served at room temperature, and I like it cold as well. It makes a great topping for bruschetta. The red bell peppers are optional here; when I included them in the recipe in my column I received an angry email from an Italian reader who said that red bell peppers would never be included in a caponata because of their strong flavor. I think they make it look pretty and I don't find the flavor too strong.

1½ pounds eggplant (1 very large or 2 medium), roasted (page 143) and cooled

2 tablespoons extra virgin olive oil

1 medium onion, chopped

2 celery ribs, from the heart, diced

3 large garlic cloves, minced

2 red bell peppers, diced (optional)

Salt

1 pound ripe, in-season tomatoes, preferably paste tomatoes such as Romas, peeled, seeded, and finely chopped, or 1 can (14 ounces) crushed tomatoes

Pinch plus 2 tablespoons sugar

3 heaping tablespoons capers, rinsed

3 tablespoons coarsely chopped pitted green olives

3 tablespoons red or white wine vinegar or sherry vinegar

Ground black pepper

1. Chop the roasted eggplant coarsely.

2. Heat 1 tablespoon of the oil in a large, heavy nonstick skillet over medium heat. Add the onion and celery. Cook, stirring, until the onion softens, about 5 minutes. Add the garlic. Cook for 1 minute, or until the garlic begins to be fragrant. Add the peppers (if using) and ½ teaspoon salt. Cook, stirring, until just about tender, about 8 minutes. Add the remaining 1 tablespoon oil and the eggplant. Cook, stirring, for 5 minutes, or until the vegetables are tender. The eggplant will fall apart, which is fine. Season to taste.

3. Add the tomatoes (with juice) to the pan with ½ teaspoon salt and a pinch of sugar. Cook, stirring and scraping the bottom of the pan often, for 5 to 10 minutes, or until the tomatoes have cooked down somewhat and are fragrant. Add the capers, olives, remaining 2 tablespoons sugar, and the vinegar. Reduce the heat to medium-low and cook, stirring often, for 20 to 30 minutes, or until the vegetables are thoroughly tender and the mixture is quite thick, sweet, and fragrant. Season to taste with salt and black pepper and remove from the heat. Allow to cool to room temperature. If possible, cover and chill overnight. Serve at room temperature.

Per serving (based on 6 servings): 130 calories, 3 g protein, 20 g carbohydrates, 8 g fiber, 5 g fat, 1 g sat fat, 0 mg cholesterol, 171 mg sodium

ADVANCE PREPARATION: Caponata will keep for 3 to 5 days in the refrigerator.

Eggplant and Tomato Confit

Makes 6 servings

■ **VEGETARIAN*** ■ **VEGAN*** ■ **LOW-CALORIE** ■ **LOW-FAT**
■ HIGH-PROTEIN ■ **GLUTEN-FREE** ■ HIGH IN OMEGA-3S

Eggplant and tomatoes star in many Provençal dishes. In this thick, concentrated combination, the vegetables are cooked together for a very long time (as opposed to the way they're prepared in ratatouille, another popular Provençal dish that features these vegetables), until they meld into a confit. The authentic dish includes a couple of finely chopped anchovies, which season the dish as it simmers. They're optional here, but worth including for a deep, rich flavor; their presence is not overwhelming.

> 2 pounds (2 large or 3 medium) eggplant, roasted (page 143) and cooled
>
> 2 tablespoons extra virgin olive oil
>
> 2 medium onions, finely chopped
>
> 3–4 large garlic cloves, minced
>
> 3 pounds ripe tomatoes, peeled, seeded, and chopped, or 2 cans (28 ounces each) diced or pureed tomatoes
>
> ⅛ teaspoon sugar
>
> 2 anchovy fillets, soaked for 5 minutes in water, rinsed and finely chopped (optional)
>
> 1 teaspoon chopped fresh thyme leaves or ½ teaspoon dried thyme
>
> 1 basil sprig plus 1 tablespoon slivered fresh basil leaves
>
> Salt and ground black pepper

*If you omit the anchovy fillets

1. Cut the eggplant into 1-inch dice.

2. Heat the oil in a large, heavy nonstick skillet over medium heat. Add the onions. Cook, stirring, until they soften, about 5 minutes. Add the garlic and cook, stirring, for 1 minute, or until the garlic is

fragrant. Stir in the tomatoes (and juice), eggplant, sugar, anchovies (if using), thyme, basil sprig (not the slivered basil), salt, and black pepper. Stir together and bring to a simmer.

3. Reduce the heat to very low, cover, and cook, stirring occasionally, for 1 to 1½ hours, or until the mixture has cooked down to a thick, fragrant mixture. Remove and discard the basil sprig. Taste and adjust the seasonings. Sprinkle the slivered basil over the top. Serve hot or at room temperature as a starter, side dish, or topping for polenta, rice, bruschetta, or pasta.

Per serving: 114 calories, 4 g protein, 23 g carbohydrates, 10g fiber, 6 g fat, 1 g sat fat, 0 mg cholesterol, 41 mg sodium

ADVANCE PREPARATION: This keeps for 4 to 5 days in the refrigerator. You can use leftovers to fill an omelet or a sandwich.

FOR MORE EGGPLANT RECIPES SEE:

Cold Steamed Eggplant with Sesame Soy Dressing (page 52)

Grilled Eggplant Panini (page 98)

Steamed Jasmine Rice with Grilled Eggplant Salad (page 177)

Stir-Fried Tofu and Eggplant with Asian Basil (page 263)

Kale

Kale is in the same Brassica family of vegetables as cabbage (the Italian for black kale, the most popular Italian variety, is *cavolo nero*, which translated literally means "black cabbage")—and like all members of this family it's packed with health-promoting sulfur compounds. Because the leaves are so sturdy, kale stands up to longer cooking than other leafy greens such as Swiss chard, spinach, and beet greens. Whereas those greens suffer from overcooking, stewed kale has a sweet flavor.

Supermarkets generally stock curly kale, the variety with the sturdy silvery-green, ruffled leaves. At farmers' markets you'll find several varieties, including the dark green cavolo nero; red Russian kale, which has purplish leaves and red veins; and the plum-red Redbor kale. They can be used interchangeably unless otherwise specified.

What Nutritionists Know about Kale

Of all fruits and vegetables, kale has been found to have the greatest antioxidant capacity, at least according to nutritionist Jonny Bowden. It's an excellent source of manganese and vitamins K and C, and a very good source of dietary fiber, tryptophan, calcium, copper, vitamin B_6, iron, and potassium. Kale is loaded with beta-carotene and the carotenoids lutein and zeaxanthin.

Kale can be simmered for a long time, as in the recipe on page 148, or it can be blanched and then quickly pan-cooked in olive oil as it is here. Long-simmered kale yields a sweet, nourishing "pot liquor," which you will definitely want to sop up with thick slices of country bread or simply sip with a spoon. Kale loses its bright color as it simmers, and the flavor of the stewed kale is stronger than the quicker pan-cooked kale, but the overall effect is sweet and comforting. The pan-cooked kale is brighter, both in color and flavor; but the same amount of kale will yield about half as much, because it loses a lot of volume when it's blanched. The simmered kale, on the other hand, first collapses in the pan, then swells as it cooks.

2. Heat the oil in a large, heavy nonstick skillet over medium heat. Add the garlic and cook, stirring, until the garlic is fragrant, 30 to 60 seconds. Add the kale. Stir for 2 to 3 minutes, or until the kale is nicely seasoned with the garlic and oil. Add salt and black pepper to taste. Remove from the heat, and serve.

Per serving: 130 calories, 5 g protein, 15 g carbohydrates, 3 g fiber, 8 g fat, 1 g sat fat, 0 mg cholesterol, 98 mg sodium

ADVANCE PREPARATION: The blanched greens will keep in the refrigerator for about 3 days.

Blanched and Pan-Cooked Kale with Garlic and Olive Oil

Make 4 servings

■ **VEGETARIAN** ■ **VEGAN** ■ **LOW-CALORIE** ■ **LOW-FAT**
■ HIGH-PROTEIN ■ **GLUTEN-FREE** ■ HIGH IN OMEGA-3S

2 large bunches kale (about 1¼ pounds total)

Salt

2 tablespoons extra virgin olive oil

2 garlic cloves, minced

Ground black pepper

1. Bring a large pot of water to a boil over high heat. Stem the kale and wash the leaves in 2 rinses of water. Fill a bowl with ice water. When the water comes to a boil, salt generously and add the kale. Blanch for 4 minutes, or until the kale is tender but still bright green. Transfer immediately to the ice water, then drain and squeeze out the water. Chop coarsely or cut into strips.

Simmered Kale

Make 4 servings

■ **VEGETARIAN** ■ • **VEGAN** ■ **LOW-CALORIE** ■ **LOW-FAT**
■ HIGH-PROTEIN ■ **GLUTEN-FREE** ■ HIGH IN OMEGA-3S

Many of the vitamins in the kale leach into the pot liquor, so make sure to include it with the kale. The recipe is based on Judy Rogers' Boiled Kale, Four Ways from The Zuni Café Cookbook. *Serve this on thick slices of toasted bread rubbed with garlic. It's nice topped with a poached egg, and it's good with rice.*

- 2 tablespoons extra virgin olive oil
- 1 small onion, chopped
- 2 garlic cloves, sliced
- Salt
- 10–12 ounces kale, stemmed, washed thoroughly, cut crosswise into $1/4$-inch-wide ribbons
- Ground black pepper

1. Heat the oil in a large, heavy soup pot or Dutch oven over medium-low heat. Add the onion. Cook, stirring, until the onion begins to soften, about 3 minutes. Add the garlic and a generous pinch of salt. Cook, stirring, until fragrant, 30 seconds to 1 minute.

2. Add the kale, a handful at a time. Cook, stirring, until the kale wilts, then add another handful until all the kale has been added and has wilted. Add water (3 to 4 cups), to cover the kale by about $1/2$ inch, and salt to taste. Bring to a simmer. Cover and simmer for 30 minutes, stirring occasionally. The kale should be tender but not mushy and the liquid in the pan, sweet. Taste and adjust the seasonings.

Per serving: 105 calories, 3 g protein, 9 g carbohydrates, 2 g fiber, 8 g fat, 1 g sat fat, 0 mg cholesterol, 68 mg sodium

ADVANCE PREPARATION: This can be made a day ahead and reheated. The flavor will become stronger.

FOR MORE KALE RECIPES SEE:

Barley Soup with Mushrooms and Kale (page 86)

Buckwheat Pasta with Kale (page 219)

Mashed Potatoes with Kale (page 155)

Provençal Kale and Cabbage Gratin (page 271)

Stir-Fried Tofu and Greens (page 264)

Mushrooms

Mushrooms are the most versatile of vegetables. Wild mushrooms are luxurious and meaty, but I would never hesitate to substitute with a less expensive and more common white button mushroom or cremini. Cultivated mushrooms are pleasing to eat raw or cooked. They are destined for salads. But when they begin to dry out and wrinkle, I cook them to add to pastas, omelets, or risottos, or I serve them as a side dish.

What Nutritionists Know about Mushrooms

Mushrooms are an excellent source of B vitamins and many minerals, particularly selenium, copper, potassium, phosphorous, zinc, and manganese—but they also contain a powerful phytochemical called L-ergothioneine that appears to act as an antioxidant. They contain more protein than most vegetables, and their meaty texture makes them a perfect choice for vegetarians. Shiitake, maitake, oyster, and king oyster mushrooms contain the highest amount of L-ergothioneine, but creminis, portobellos, and white button mushrooms are also good sources.

Pan-Cooked Mushrooms

Makes 4 servings

■ **VEGETARIAN** ■ **VEGAN** ■ **LOW-CALORIE** ■ **LOW-FAT**
■ HIGH-PROTEIN ■ **GLUTEN-FREE** ■ HIGH IN OMEGA-3S

If you find that you've bought a box of mushrooms and several days later they're still lingering in your refrigerator, cook them up. They may be too shriveled for a salad, but they'll reconstitute when you cook them in olive oil. Mushrooms are sponge-like, which is why it's a good idea to cook them with flavorful ingredients like shallots, garlic, herbs, and wine. You can use all cultivated mushrooms here, or use a mixture of cultivated and wild mushrooms. Serve pan-cooked mushrooms on their own as a side dish or as a sort of sauce with fish, meat, or grains; toss them with pasta; use them as an omelet filling; or pile them onto a thick slice of lightly toasted bread rubbed with garlic.

2 pounds white or cremini mushrooms, or a mixture of white or cremini mushrooms and wild mushrooms (such as oyster mushrooms, maitakes, or chanterelles), rinsed briefly and wiped clean

2 tablespoons extra virgin olive oil

2 shallots, minced

2 garlic cloves, minced

1–2 teaspoons chopped fresh thyme or rosemary (or a combination)

Salt and ground black pepper

1/4 cup dry white wine, such as sauvignon blanc

2 tablespoons chopped flat-leaf parsley

1. Trim off the ends of the mushroom stems and cut the caps into thick slices. Heat a large, heavy skillet over medium-high heat. Add 1 tablespoon of the oil. When the oil is hot (you can feel the heat when you hold your hand above the pan), add the mushrooms and cook, stirring or tossing in the pan, for about 3 minutes, or until they begin to soften and sweat. Add the remaining 1 tablespoon oil and reduce the heat to medium.

2. Add the shallots, garlic, and thyme or rosemary. Stir together, add salt and black pepper to taste, and cook, stirring often, for 1 to 2 minutes, or until the shallots and garlic have softened and the mixture is fragrant. Add the wine and cook, stirring often and scraping the bottom of the pan, until the wine has evaporated. Taste and adjust the seasonings. Remove from the heat and stir in the parsley.

Per serving: 137 calories, 5 g protein, 11 g carbohydrates, 0 g fiber, 7 g fat, 1 g sat fat, 0 mg cholesterol, 53 mg sodium

ADVANCE PREPARATION: You can make this dish several hours ahead and reheat. If it dries out, add a little water, stock, or wine to the pan when you reheat.

Soft Tacos with Mushrooms, Onion, and Chipotle Chile

Makes 4 servings

■ **VEGETARIAN** ■ VEGAN ■ **LOW-CALORIE** ■ **LOW-FAT**
■ **HIGH-PROTEIN** ■ **GLUTEN-FREE** ■ HIGH IN OMEGA-3S

*Mushrooms make a robust filling for vegetarian tacos and quesa-
dillas. Hot, smoky chipotle chiles complement the earthy flavor of
the mushrooms. You can use creminis, white button, or oyster
mushrooms for these spicy tacos.*

1 tablespoon extra virgin olive oil

1 small onion, thinly sliced

1 pound cremini, white button, or oyster
    mushrooms, cleaned, stems trimmed, and sliced

Salt

1–2 garlic cloves, minced

1 chipotle chile in adobo sauce, seeded and
    chopped

2 tablespoons minced cilantro or flat-leaf parsley

8 corn tortillas

½–¾ cup (2–3 ounces) crumbled queso fresco or
    feta cheese

Fresh or bottled salsa (optional)

1. Heat the oil in a large nonstick skillet over medium
heat. Add the onion. Cook, stirring often, until tender, about 5 minutes. Add the mushrooms. Increase
the heat to medium-high. Cook, stirring, until the
mushrooms begin to soften and sweat, 2 to 3 minutes. Reduce the heat to medium and add ½ teaspoon salt, the garlic, and chile. Continue to cook
until the mushroom liquid has evaporated from the
pan, 5 to 10 minutes. Stir in the cilantro or parsley.
Taste and adjust the seasonings.

2. Heat the tortillas: You can wrap the tortillas in
foil and heat through in a 350°F oven for 10 to 15 minutes, or heat 1 at a time in a dry skillet over medium-
high heat until flexible, or heat in a microwave.
Place 2 tortillas on each plate. Top each tortilla with
a spoonful of mushrooms and a sprinkling of cheese.
Fold the filled tortillas in half and serve, passing the
salsa (if using) separately in a bowl.

Per serving: 251 calories, 10 g protein, 36 g carbohydrates,
4 g fiber, 8 g fat, 2 g sat fat, 9 mg cholesterol, 133 mg sodium

ADVANCE PREPARATION: The mushroom filling
will keep for up to 3 days in a covered bowl in the
refrigerator. It's best to reheat and stir in the cilantro
or parsley just before serving.

FOR MORE MUSHROOM RECIPES SEE:

Artichoke, Mushroom, and Potato Ragout (page 121)

**Barley and Mushroom Salad with English Peas
(page 182)**

Barley Soup with Mushrooms and Kale (page 86)

Bruschetta with Mushroom Topping (page 104)

Fettuccine with Pan-Cooked Mushrooms (page 214)

Mushroom and Dried Porcini Soup (page 76)

Mushroom and Fresh Herb Salad (page 60)

**Oven-Steamed Salmon with Pan-Cooked Mushrooms
(page 308)**

**Pasta with Dried Mushrooms and Tomato Sauce
(page 212)**

**Pizza with Mushrooms, Goat Cheese, Arugula, and
Walnuts (page 110)**

**Polenta Gratin with Mushrooms and Tomatoes
(page 203)**

**Polenta with Mushrooms, Favas, and Tomatoes
(page 201)**

**Spinach Salad with Seared Shiitake Mushrooms
(page 58)**

Bell Peppers

Bell peppers are available in supermarkets year-round, but they're at their best in late summer and early fall, when peppers in red and orange, yellow and purple, every shade of green, and every shape are piled high at farmers' markets. I especially like an intensely sweet tapered red variety called lipstick peppers, which are much like Spanish piquillo peppers.

Peppers offer the cook endless possibilities. Roast them and they become a household staple (page 24) to keep on hand at all times for snacks, salads, and quick toppings for sandwiches and bruschetta. Fry or stew them and stir them into scrambled eggs and frittatas, risottos, pastas, and pilafs. Uncooked, they make a great, healthy, crunchy/juicy snack, a vegetable that kids will eat. And on top of all that, they're beautiful!

What Nutritionists Know about Bell Peppers

Peppers are very low in calories (1 cup of sliced raw red bell pepper has about 25) and red peppers in particular are an excellent source of vitamins C and B$_6$, and a very good source of potassium and vitamin K. By weight, red bell peppers have three times as much vitamin C as citrus fruit. They also contain lycopene, the antioxidant-rich carotenoid found in tomatoes and other red fruits and vegetables.

Stewed Peppers with Tomatoes, Onions, and Garlic

Makes 6 servings

■ **VEGETARIAN** ■ **VEGAN** ■ **LOW-CALORIE** ■ **LOW-FAT**
■ HIGH-PROTEIN ■ **GLUTEN-FREE** ■ HIGH IN OMEGA-3S

There are variations of this dish throughout the Mediterranean. The Basque pipérade, made with slender, slightly piquant peppers called piments d'espelette and stirred into scrambled eggs along with Bayonne ham, has some heat; whereas Italian peperonata is sweet through and through. A North African version, chakchouka, spiced with fiery harissa and tabil (a spice blend made with caraway and coriander, cayenne, and garlic) is usually served with eggs poached right on top of the stew (page 249). Serve as a side dish, as a topping for pizza, pasta, polenta, rice, or bruschetta, as a filling for an omelet, or stir into scrambled eggs.

2 tablespoons extra virgin olive oil

1 medium onion, chopped

2 large garlic cloves, minced

3 large red bell peppers (about 1½ pounds), or a combination of red and yellow bell peppers, thinly sliced or chopped

Salt

1 can (14 ounces) diced tomatoes, drained of some but not all of its juice, or 1½ cups peeled, chopped fresh tomatoes

1 teaspoon fresh thyme leaves or ½ teaspoon dried thyme

Ground black pepper

1. Heat the oil in a large nonstick skillet or heavy casserole over medium heat. Add the onion. Cook, stirring, until tender, about 5 minutes. Add the garlic and bell peppers. Cook, stirring often, for 5 minutes, until the peppers are beginning to soften. Add

$^{1}/_{2}$ teaspoon of salt. Cook for 5 minutes, or until the peppers are tender.

2. Add the tomatoes and thyme. Season to taste with salt and black pepper. Simmer, stirring occasionally, until the tomatoes have cooked down somewhat, about 10 minutes. Cover, reduce the heat, and simmer over low heat for 15 to 20 minutes or longer, stirring occasionally, until the mixture is thick and fragrant. Taste and adjust the seasonings.

Per serving: 86 calories, 2 g protein, 10 g carbohydrates, 3 g fiber, 5 g fat, 1 g sat fat, 0 mg cholesterol, 117 mg sodium

ADVANCE PREPARATION: The stewed peppers will keep for about 5 days in the refrigerator.

Warm Grilled Peppers with Yogurt Topping

Makes 4 servings

■ **VEGETARIAN** ■ VEGAN ■ **LOW-CALORIE** ■ **LOW-FAT**
■ HIGH-PROTEIN ■ **GLUTEN-FREE** ■ HIGH IN OMEGA-3S

Hot foods are often served with cooling yogurt toppings in Turkey, where this dish originates. We can't get the slightly hot, light-green çarliston peppers that are typically used in Turkey, but you could use Anaheims, or a mix of bell peppers and Anaheims.

2 pounds mixed Anaheim and bell peppers (red, yellow, or green)

½ cup Drained Yogurt (page 25)

2 tablespoons fresh lemon juice (optional)

2–4 garlic cloves, mashed to a paste with a generous pinch of salt in a mortar and pestle

2 teaspoons chopped fresh dill or mint

Salt and ground black pepper

1. Grill the peppers following the directions on page 24 until blackened. Remove from the heat and place in a bowl. Cover the bowl and allow the peppers to sit for 15 minutes. Skin the peppers, cut in half, and remove the seeds and membranes. Cut larger bell peppers lengthwise into quarters. Place on a platter.

2. Mix together the drained yogurt, lemon juice, garlic, dill or mint, and salt and black pepper to taste. Spoon over the warm peppers and serve.

Per serving: 112 calories, 7 g protein, 23 g carbohydrates, 5 g fiber, 1 g fat, 0 g sat fat, 0 mg cholesterol, 62 mg sodium

ADVANCE PREPARATION: Roasted peppers will keep for 5 days in the refrigerator. They will continue to release liquid, which they can marinate in. Pour it off and warm the peppers before serving.

FOR MORE PEPPER RECIPES SEE:

Baked Orzo with Tomatoes, Roasted Pepper, and Zucchini (page 217)

Broccoli and Endive Salad with Goat Cheese and Red Peppers (page 56)

Bruschetta with Roasted Bell Peppers and Goat Cheese (page 106)

Frittata with Red Peppers and Peas (page 243)

North African Chakchouka (page 249)

Panini with Artichokes, Spinach, and Peppers (page 100)

Pipérade (page 248)

Pizza with Roasted Peppers and Mozzarella (page 113)

Pureed Red Pepper and Potato Soup (page 74)

Rainbow Tofu (Stir-Fried Tofu and Peppers) (page 262)

Red Bell Pepper Risotto with Saffron (page 229)

Roasted or Grilled Peppers (page 24)

Roasted Pepper and Tomato Salad (page 49)

Sautéed Summer Squash with Red Bell Pepper (page 162)

Spinach and Red Bell Pepper Panini (page 99)

Swiss Chard and Red Bell Pepper Gratin (page 268)

Potatoes

During the height of the low-carb craze, potatoes fell out of fashion. That's too bad, because potatoes are a wholesome and sustaining food, one of the world's most widely eaten vegetables. These tubers have nourished entire populations well for centuries, and I don't mean in the form of french fries. If your diet is varied and you eat an abundance of vegetables, there's no reason to leave out potatoes.

Instead of adding lots of saturated fat to my baked potatoes in the form of butter and/or sour cream, I moisten them with a healthy dollop of plain yogurt (okay, sometimes a little bit of butter too). Because most of the fiber and potassium is located in the skin of the potato, and most of the vitamin C is in the flesh closest to the skin, it's important to include the skin whenever possible (the colcannon that follows notwithstanding). But this is also where pesticide residues reside, so seek out organic potatoes. They're easy to find in farmers' markets, and fun to shop for too; the only difficulty will be deciding which of the many varieties displayed to choose. One rule of thumb—the more color in the potato flesh, the more nutrients there will be.

What Nutritionists Know about Potatoes

Potatoes are high in B vitamins and vitamin C, potassium, and fiber, with some protein and lots of complex carbohydrates. A plain, 7-ounce baked potato eaten with the skin contains half of the Daily Values of vitamins C and B_6 recommended for adults, with only 220 calories and zero grams of fat. They are high on the glycemic index, particularly starchy varieties like russets, which is significant if you suffer from diabetes or insulin resistance.

Waxy and Starchy Potatoes

There are three types of potatoes: high-starch (mealy or floury), low-starch (waxy or boiling), and medium-starch. The high-starch varieties include russets (Idahos) and, not surprisingly, are considerably higher on the glycemic index than waxy (low-starch) potatoes—or even medium-starch potatoes (Yukon golds are medium-starch). High-starch potatoes are the best potatoes for mashing, baking, and frying. They're good for gratins because of their ability to absorb liquids, and for thickening soups, because they fall apart easily. But if you need to avoid high-glycemic foods, waxy varieties are a better choice. Common waxy varieties and types include red potatoes (such as Red Bliss and Red Pontiac), fingerlings, creamers, and white boiling potatoes.

Mashed Potatoes with Kale (Colcannon)

Makes 4 to 6 servings

■ **VEGETARIAN** ■ VEGAN ■ LOW-CALORIE ■ LOW-FAT
■ HIGH-PROTEIN ■ **GLUTEN-FREE** ■ HIGH IN OMEGA-3S

Colcannon is one of the great signature dishes of Ireland. The most common version pairs cabbage with potatoes, but the dish can also be made with kale, and that's the version I usually make. You can substitute extra virgin olive oil for the butter (in which case it will be more Mediterranean than Irish).

2 pounds russet potatoes, scrubbed and peeled if desired, or partially peeled

Salt

1 pound (1 large bunch) kale, either curly green or cavolo nero, ribs removed, leaves washed

1¼ cups 1% milk

2 heaping tablespoons chopped scallions (about 3 scallions)

Ground black pepper

2 tablespoons unsalted butter or extra virgin olive oil

1. Cover the potatoes with water in a saucepan. Add ½ teaspoon salt and bring to a boil over high heat. Reduce the heat to medium, cover partially, and cook until tender all the way through when pierced with a knife, 30 to 45 minutes. Drain off the water and return the potatoes to the pan. Cover tightly and steam over very low heat for 2 to 3 minutes. Remove from the heat and, while still hot, mash with a potato masher or a fork, pass through a food mill, or beat in a stand mixer fitted with the paddle.

2. While the potatoes are cooking, bring a large pot of water to a boil over high heat. Fill a bowl with ice water. When the water comes to a boil, salt generously and add the kale. Cook the kale for 4 to 6 minutes (after the water returns to the boil), or until the leaves are tender but still bright green. Transfer to the ice water, allow to cool for a couple of minutes, then drain and squeeze out excess water. Chop fine (you can use a food processor).

3. Toward the end of the potato cooking time, combine the milk and scallions in a saucepan and bring to a simmer. Remove from the heat and let steep for a few minutes. Stir the chopped kale into the hot mashed potatoes and beat in the milk-scallion mixture and butter or oil. The mixture should be fluffy. Add salt and black pepper to taste. Serve right away, or keep warm in a double boiler. (Set the bowl in a

saucepan filled one-third of the way with water. Make sure the water doesn't touch the bottom of the bowl. Bring the water to a simmer. Stir the potato and kale mixture occasionally.)

Per serving (based on 4 servings): 320 calories, 11 g protein, 56 g carbohydrates, 5 g fiber, 7.5 g fat, 4 g sat fat, 19 mg cholesterol, 131 mg sodium

ADVANCE PREPARATION: You can make this several hours before serving and reheat in a double boiler.

Potato and Leek Gratin with Cumin

Makes 6 to 8 side-dish servings

■ **VEGETARIAN** ■ VEGAN ■ LOW-CALORIE ■ LOW-FAT ■ HIGH-PROTEIN ■ **GLUTEN-FREE** ■ HIGH IN OMEGA-3S

There are healthier ways to approach this dish than the traditional rich mixture of potatoes and cream. In fact, there are many. You don't need cream to achieve what I think is the best thing about a potato gratin, which is the way the sliced potatoes soak up flavors as they bake, and the way the gratin crisps around the edges. Serve this as a vegetarian main dish, as a side, or as part of a selection of vegetable dishes.

1 garlic clove, halved

1 tablespoon extra virgin olive oil

1 pound leeks, white and light-green parts only, halved lengthwise, sliced crosswise, and well washed

Salt and ground black pepper

1 teaspoon cumin seeds, lightly toasted and crushed

2 pounds russet potatoes or Yukon golds, peeled if using russets, scrubbed if using Yukon golds, and sliced 1/4 inch thick

3/4 cup (3 ounces) grated Gruyère cheese

2 1/3 cups 1% milk

1. Preheat the oven to 375°F. Rub the inside of a 2-quart gratin dish or baking dish with the cut side of the garlic clove. Brush the dish lightly with some oil.

2. Heat the 1 tablespoon olive oil in a large, heavy nonstick skillet over medium heat. Add the leeks. Cook, stirring often, until tender, about 5 minutes. Add 1/2 teaspoon salt and black pepper to taste. Stir in the cumin. Stir together for 30 seconds and remove from the heat.

3. Place the potatoes in a large bowl and season generously with salt and black pepper. Add the leek mixture and half of the cheese, and toss together. Arrange in the baking dish in an even layer. Pour in the milk. Set the baking dish on a baking sheet and place in the oven.

4. Bake the gratin for 45 minutes, checking after 30 minutes and pressing the potatoes down into the milk with the back of a spoon if necessary. Remove from the oven. Gently press the potatoes down into the liquid. Sprinkle the remaining cheese over the top and bake for another 30 to 45 minutes, or until nicely browned. Cool for 10 to 15 minutes before serving.

Per serving (based on 6 servings): 215 calories, 9 g protein, 32 g carbohydrates, 3 g fiber, 6 g fat, 3 g sat fat, 15 mg cholesterol, 103 mg sodium

ADVANCE PREPARATION: The gratin can be made up to a day ahead and reheated in a 325°F to 350°F oven before serving.

Provençal Summer Potato and Tomato Gratin

Makes 4 to 6 servings

■ **VEGETARIAN** ■ VEGAN ■ LOW-CALORIE ■ LOW-FAT
■ HIGH-PROTEIN ■ **GLUTEN-FREE** ■ HIGH IN OMEGA-3S

Tomatoes and a small amount of water provide plenty of simmering juice for the potatoes in this savory gratin. You can use pretty much any type of potato here. I know this because I've made it with odds and ends that had been sitting around in my pantry for a little too long. They included a russet, a few Yukon golds, and some fingerlings.

2 garlic cloves, halved

2½ pounds ripe tomatoes, peeled and sliced

1 tablespoon extra virgin olive oil

2 teaspoons fresh thyme leaves, or 1 teaspoon dried thyme

Salt and ground black pepper

2 pounds potatoes, peeled if desired or scrubbed, sliced about ¼ inch thick

1–2 rosemary sprigs

½ cup tightly packed grated Gruyère cheese (2 ounces)

1. Preheat the oven to 400°F. Rub a 3-quart gratin dish or baking dish with one of the garlic halves. Brush the baking dish with some oil. Mince the remaining garlic and toss with the tomatoes and the 1 tablespoon oil. Add the thyme. Season to taste with salt and black pepper.

2. Make 1 layer of half of the potato slices, slightly overlapping, and season generously with salt and black pepper. Layer half of the tomatoes over the potatoes. Place the rosemary on top. Repeat the layers with the remaining potatoes and tomatoes. Be sure to season each layer generously with salt and black pepper. Pour any juices left in the tomato bowl over the vegetables.

3. Bring 1 cup water to a boil over high heat and carefully pour into the baking dish. Bake for 45 minutes, checking after 30 minutes and pressing the potatoes down into the liquid with the back of a spoon. Remove from the oven. Press the potatoes down into the liquid, sprinkle on the cheese, and bake for another 30 to 45 minutes, until most of the liquid has been absorbed by the potatoes and the gratin is lightly browned. Serve hot or warm.

Per serving (based on 4 servings): 310 calories, 11 g protein, 52 g carbohydrates, 7 g fiber, 8 g fat, 3 g sat fat, 0 mg cholesterol, 96 mg sodium

ADVANCE PREPARATION: The gratin can be assembled several hours before you bake it, and it doesn't have to be served hot, so you can bake it 1 or 2 hours ahead and serve it warm.

FOR MORE POTATO RECIPES SEE:

Artichoke, Mushroom, and Potato Ragout (page 121)

Pizza with Green Garlic, Potato, and Herbs (page 114)

Potato "Bouillabaisse" (page 76)

Potato and Parsley Soup (page 74)

Pureed Red Pepper and Potato Soup (page 74)

Red Chard, Potato, and White Bean Ragout (page 286)

Skordalia (page 30)

Warm Potato Salad with Goat Cheese (page 55)

Spinach

Spinach is available year-round, in bunches and bags. Those ubiquitous bags of baby spinach have transformed this nutrient-dense vegetable into a convenience food in my kitchen. I used to spend hours stemming and washing spinach, and it was so disheartening, after all that work, to get so little cooked spinach out of that 12-ounce bunch. So I did an experiment: I bought a bunch that weighed about ¾ pound, stemmed it, and then weighed the leaves. They weighed 6 ounces, exactly what you get in a bag of baby spinach, which requires no stemming and just a quick rinse.

There are, to be sure, environmental and economical concerns connected with baby spinach in a bag. If you are reluctant to use bagged spinach, know that an 11- or 12-ounce bunch and a 6-ounce bag are interchangeable. After removing the leaves from the stems, make sure to wash bunch spinach thoroughly in at least 2 changes of water. Whatever type of spinach you buy, it's one of the most nutritious vegetables you can eat, and considerably more delicate than other leafy greens. Because of this it's easy to overcook it, and overcooked spinach is drab and unappealing, Popeye notwithstanding. So follow the instructions carefully, blanching for no more than 30 seconds.

What Nutritionists Know about Spinach

Spinach is filled with flavonoids that act as antioxidants, and its plentiful supplies of vitamin K (1,000 percent of the Daily Value in 1 cup of cooked spinach) contribute to bone health. The list of nutrients that come in large quantities in a serving of spinach is a long one, including iron, vitamin C, manganese, folate, magnesium, calcium, potassium, vitamins B_2 and B_6, tryptophan, and dietary fiber. All this, with no prep time and 10 to 20 seconds of cooking, make bagged baby spinach hard to beat.

Spinach with Sweet Spices and Pungent Yogurt

Makes 3 servings

■ **VEGETARIAN** ■ VEGAN ■ **LOW-CALORIE** ■ **LOW-FAT**
■ HIGH-PROTEIN ■ **GLUTEN-FREE** ■ HIGH IN OMEGA-3S

Here's a wonderful way to eat your spinach. The subtle spices and the contrast of the cool yogurt and the hot spinach are what I love best about it. This is very nice served with Arabic bread.

1 whole clove or ⅛ teaspoon ground cloves

2 allspice berries or ⅛ teaspoon ground allspice

½ teaspoon coriander seeds or cumin seeds

⅛ teaspoon ground cinnamon

1 garlic clove, halved

Salt

1 cup Drained Yogurt (page 25)

1 tablespoon extra virgin olive oil

1 tablespoon pine nuts

1 bag (12 ounces) or 2 bags (6 ounces each) baby spinach, washed, or 2 bunches, stemmed and washed

Ground black pepper

1. Heat a small dry skillet over medium heat. Add the clove, allspice, and coriander or cumin. Heat, shaking the pan, until the spices begin to smell toasty, about 3 minutes. (Watch very closely if the spices are already ground to avoid burning them.) Transfer to a bowl and allow to cool for a few minutes, then grind in a spice mill. Add the cinnamon, and set aside.

2. Mash the garlic with ¼ teaspoon salt to a paste with a mortar and pestle. Combine with the yogurt and set aside.

3. If using baby spinach, place in a bowl and pour on boiling water to cover. Let sit for 2 minutes, then drain, rinse with cold water, squeeze out excess water, and chop coarsely. If using bunch spinach, bring a large pot of water to a boil and fill a bowl with ice water. When the water comes to a boil, salt generously and add the spinach. Blanch for 10 to 20 seconds and transfer to the ice water. Drain and squeeze out the excess water.

4. Heat the oil in a large, heavy skillet over medium heat. Add the pine nuts. Cook, stirring, until they begin to color, 2 to 3 minutes. Remove from the skillet with a slotted spoon and set aside. Add the spices to the skillet. Once they begin to sizzle, cook, stirring, for about 30 seconds, then add the spinach, pine nuts, and salt and black pepper to taste. Cook, stirring, until the spinach is heated through and coated with the oil and spices, 2 to 3 minutes. Transfer to a serving dish and spoon the yogurt over the top.

Per serving: 154 calories, 9 g protein, 16 g carbohydrates, 6 g fiber, 8 g fat, 2 g sat fat, 3 mg cholesterol, 250 mg sodium

ADVANCE PREPARATION: The spinach can be blanched up to 3 days ahead and kept in the refrigerator.

Simple Wilted Spinach with Lemon Juice

Makes 3 to 4 servings

■ **VEGETARIAN** ■ **VEGAN** ■ **LOW-CALORIE** ■ **LOW-FAT**
■ HIGH-PROTEIN ■ **GLUTEN-FREE** ■ HIGH IN OMEGA-3S

This is my favorite thing to do with spinach: wilt it, douse it with a little lemon juice, and eat it right away. The ascorbic acid in the lemon juice facilitates the absorption of the rich iron stores that spinach has to offer.

1½ pounds bunch spinach, stemmed and washed thoroughly, or 2 bags (12 ounces each) baby spinach, rinsed but not dried

Salt and ground black pepper

½ lemon

Heat a large nonstick skillet over high heat and add the wet spinach leaves in batches. As each batch begins to collapse, add another, until all the spinach has been added to the pan. When all of the spinach has wilted, season with salt and black pepper and stir for 1 to 2 minutes. It should be tender but not at all mushy, and a rich dark green color. Remove from the heat, squeeze on a small amount of lemon juice, and serve.

Per serving (based on 3 servings): 55 calories, 7 g protein, 9 g carbohydrates, 1 g total fat, 0 g saturated fat, 0 mg cholesterol, 5 g fiber, 228 mg sodium

ADVANCE PREPARATION: You can keep the cooked spinach in the refrigerator for 3 or 4 days. Don't add lemon juice until you serve it.

Spinach with Cumin, Aleppo Pepper, and Pine Nuts

Makes 4 servings

■ **VEGETARIAN** ■ **VEGAN*** ■ **LOW-CALORIE** ■ **LOW-FAT**
■ HIGH-PROTEIN ■ **GLUTEN-FREE** ■ HIGH IN OMEGA-3S

In Turkey this dish would be served as part of a mezze, a collection of appetizers. I like to serve the spinach as a side dish. The garlicky yogurt topping, typical of Turkish cuisine, is optional here.

For the topping (optional):

½ cup Drained Yogurt (page 25)

2 garlic cloves, mashed to a paste with a generous pinch of salt in a mortar and pestle

Fresh lemon juice

For the spinach:

2 tablespoons extra virgin olive oil

1 small red onion, finely chopped

1 tablespoon pine nuts

1½ teaspoons cumin seeds, lightly toasted and crushed or ground

1 teaspoon Aleppo pepper

½ teaspoon sugar

2 bags (12 ounces each) baby spinach, rinsed

Salt and ground black pepper

*If you omit the yogurt topping

1. To make the topping (if using): Stir together the drained yogurt, garlic paste, and lemon juice to taste. Taste and add more salt if needed.

2. To make the spinach: Heat the olive oil in a large, heavy skillet over medium heat. Add the onion and cook, stirring, for 3 minutes, or until it begins to soften. Add the pine nuts, cumin, Aleppo pepper, and sugar. Cook, stirring, for 3 minutes, or until the onion is tender and the pine nuts have begun to color. Add the spinach, in batches if necessary, and cook, stirring, until it wilts. Season to taste with salt and black pepper, remove from the heat and serve hot with a spoonful of the yogurt topping. if desired.

Per serving: 160 calories, 5 g protein, 21 g carbohydrates, 9 g fiber, 9 g fat, 1 g sat fat, 0 mg cholesterol, 309 mg sodium

ADVANCE PREPARATION: You can make this recipe several hours ahead and reheat the spinach gently on top of the stove.

FOR MORE SPINACH RECIPES SEE:

Buckwheat Crêpes with Spinach and Egg (page 251)

Chickpeas with Baby Spinach (page 283)

Frittata with Greens (page 242)

Japanese Spinach with Sesame Dressing (page 57)

Miso Soup with Tofu and Vegetables (page 90)

Panini with Artichokes, Spinach, and Peppers (page 100)

Rich Garlic Soup with Spinach and Pasta Shells (page 78)

Spinach and Fresh Herb Frittata with Walnuts and Yogurt (page 246)

Spinach and Red Bell Pepper Panini (page 99)

Spinach Salad with Seared Shiitake Mushrooms (page 58)

Spinach, Tofu, and Sesame Stir-Fry (page 257)

Turkish Yogurt and Spinach Dip (page 31)

Veracruzana Black Bean Soup with Spinach or Lamb's Quarters (page 88)

Summer Squash

Summer squash to many means zucchini, the best known variety here in the States, and the one we can get at any time of year in the supermarket. But there are many other varieties of summer squash. Some are round and dense; others are flat with a scalloped edge. Some are long, others are shorter and bulbous at one end. Colors vary from dark green, to striated lighter green, to pale green, to yellow. Yellow squash comes in several shapes and sizes, including a curvy crookneck variety and a long yellow zucchini variety. Each type varies in density and texture, and although cooking times may vary, they can be used interchangeably in most recipes.

What Nutritionists Know about Summer Squash

Summer squash is an excellent low-calorie food, with only 19 calories per cup of raw squash. The reason it's so low-calorie is that water comprises about 95 percent of its weight. For this reason it's not exactly a nutritional powerhouse, but it is nonetheless a very good source of manganese and vitamin C, and a good source of folate, dietary fiber, potassium, and copper.

Sautéed Summer Squash with Red Bell Pepper

Makes 6 to 8 servings

■ **VEGETARIAN** ■ **VEGAN** ■ **LOW-CALORIE** ■ **LOW-FAT**
■ HIGH-PROTEIN ■ **GLUTEN-FREE** ■ HIGH IN OMEGA-3S

You can begin a variety of summer squash dishes with this easy sauté. It's a first step for the Summer Squash Gratin on page 267, and it makes a great filling for a taco (see especially the succotash variation, on opposite page) and a colorful frittata. Toss it with pasta, serve it with rice or other grains, or just serve it on its own as a side dish. The succotash variation makes a more substantial dish.

2 tablespoons extra virgin olive oil

½ medium onion, chopped

2 large garlic cloves, minced

1½ pounds summer squash, cut into ¼-inch dice

1 small red bell pepper, diced

Salt and ground black pepper

2 tablespoons chopped flat-leaf parsley

Heat the oil in a large, heavy skillet over medium heat. Add the onion. Cook, stirring often, until tender, 5 to 8 minutes. Add the garlic, squash, bell pepper, and salt to taste. Increase the heat to medium-high and cook, stirring, until the squash is translucent and the bell pepper tender, about 10 minutes (see note). Add black pepper and taste and adjust the salt. Stir in the parsley and remove from the heat.

Per serving (based on 6 servings): 70 calories, 2 g protein, 6 g carbohydrates, 2 g fiber, 5 g fat, 1 g sat fat, 0 mg cholesterol, 28 mg sodium

ADVANCE PREPARATION: You can make this a few hours before you serve it. reheat it gently before serving. If you're using it as a filling for another dish, it will hold for 3 days in the refrigerator. The squash may throw off some juice in the refrigerator; just stir the dish well and use it, juice and all.

Note: *Some types of squash cook faster than others. Zucchini cooks more quickly than pattypan, for example.*

VARIATION: HERBED SUMMER SQUASH WITH CHEESE Substitute 1 tablespoon chopped or slivered fresh mint, or 2 teaspoons chopped fresh marjoram, for the parsley. Sprinkle with feta cheese or Parmesan.

VARIATION: SUMMER SUCCOTASH WITH BLACK BEANS Add the kernels from 2 ears of corn and 1 to 1½ cups cooked black beans (if using canned beans, rinse them first) or shelled edamame 5 minutes after adding the squash. Proceed with the recipe. This makes a great filling for tacos (sprinkle with queso fresco or feta cheese).

Zucchini "Pasta"

Makes 4 servings

■ **VEGETARIAN** ■ **VEGAN*** ■ **LOW-CALORIE** ■ **LOW-FAT**
■ HIGH-PROTEIN ■ **GLUTEN-FREE** ■ HIGH IN OMEGA-3S

If you don't eat wheat, or you're on a low-carbohydrate diet and miss pasta, this can stand in for fettuccine. Be very careful not to overcook it; it will be al dente *after just a few minutes of cooking, after which it will quickly fall apart. When cooked just right, it's silky and wonderful. You can eat it as is, or toss it with a fresh tomato sauce (page 19). Use a vegetable peeler or a mandoline to make the thin zucchini strips. This is easy to do with a peeler, which is what I use, and it goes more quickly than you might think.*

> 2 pounds yellow or green zucchini, or a combination
>
> 2 tablespoons extra virgin olive oil
>
> ½ teaspoon salt
>
> Ground black pepper
>
> ¾ cup fresh tomato sauce (page 19), optional
>
> 1 ounce Parmesan, shaved (optional)

*If you omit the Parmesan

1. Cut the zucchini into lengthwise ribbons using a vegetable peeler. Peel off several ribbons from 1 side, then turn the zucchini and peel off more ribbons. Continue to turn and peel off ribbons until you get to the seeds at the core of the zucchini. Discard the core. You can also do this on a mandoline, adjusted to a very thin slice.

2. Cook the zucchini strips in 2 batches. Heat 1 tablespoon of the oil in a large nonstick skillet over medium-high heat. When it's hot, add the zucchini and salt. Cook, tossing and stirring the zucchini, for 2 to 3 minutes only, just until softened and beginning to be translucent. Adjust the salt and add black pepper to taste. Transfer to a serving dish. Repeat with the remaining 1 tablespoon of oil and zucchini. Serve, topping with the tomato sauce and Parmesan if desired.

Per serving: 99 calories, 3 g protein, 8 g carbohydrates, 3 g fiber, 7 g fat, 1 g sat fat, 0 mg cholesterol, 313 mg sodium

ADVANCE PREPARATION: This is best served right away, but you can enjoy leftovers, which I like to eat cold, doused with lemon juice and a drop of olive oil.

FOR MORE SUMMER SQUASH RECIPES SEE:

Baked Orzo with Tomatoes, Roasted Pepper, and Zucchini (page 217)

Chilled Zucchini-Yogurt Soup with Fresh Mint (page 92)

Summer Squash Gratin (page 267)

Summer Squash Risotto (page 230)

Zucchini and Avocado Salsa Salad (page 50)

Winter Squash

Even though summer heat in Southern California persists through October, which can be the hottest month here, I always know it's fall when I begin to see hard winter squashes in the farmers' markets. Local farmers raise butternuts of all sizes and kabochas (the large, dark green pumpkin-shaped squashes), hubbards, deep-orange Cinderella pumpkins (*Rouge Vif d'Étampes*), delicatas, and spaghetti squash.

Large, hard winter squashes with gnarled skins like kabochas can be a bit daunting to work with. They're so thick and hard that you might wonder where to begin. I usually roast these rough- and thick-skinned squashes before I try to tackle peeling them: Halve or quarter the squash, scrape away the seeds and fibrous membranes, put the pieces on an oiled, foil-lined baking sheet, then roast at 375°F or 400°F until they are soft enough to pierce with the tip of a knife. Then you can peel them easily and proceed with a given recipe. Butternut squashes, though equally hard, have a smooth skin that you can peel away with a vegetable peeler, though you can also roast them before you cut them up.

What Nutritionists Know about Winter Squash

Like other orange vegetables, winter squash is an excellent source of beta-carotene, which is believed to have antioxidant and anti-inflammatory properties. It's also a very good source of vitamin C, potassium, dietary fiber, and manganese, and a good source of folate, vitamin B_1, copper, vitamin B_6, niacin, and pantothenic acid.

Tunisian Winter Squash Puree

Makes about 2 cups/6 side-dish servings, 8 to 10 appetizer servings

■ **VEGETARIAN** ■ **VEGAN** ■ **LOW-CALORIE** ■ **LOW-FAT**
■ HIGH-PROTEIN ■ **GLUTEN-FREE*** ■ HIGH IN OMEGA-3S

This is one of many North African spicy cooked vegetable purees typically served as starters. Other vegetables that are prepared in a similar fashion include carrots and zucchini. In North Africa the squash is boiled, but I think that roasting it intensifies the flavors, and the resulting puree is less watery. The authentic dish is seasoned with harissa, a fiery hot-pepper paste used widely in Tunisia and Algeria. If you can't get hold of harissa easily, the heat in this dish will come from the cayenne. Serve the puree as an hors d'oeuvre, side dish, or salad.

2 pounds winter squash, such as kabocha or butternut

2 tablespoons plus 1 teaspoon fresh lemon
or lime juice

2 tablespoons plus 1 teaspoon extra virgin olive oil

1–2 garlic cloves, peeled

Salt

1 teaspoon ground caraway seeds

¾ teaspoon ground coriander

1 teaspoon harissa, or ¼–½ teaspoon cayenne

Imported black olives

Small romaine lettuce leaves

Warm flat bread, optional

*If you omit the flat bread

1. Preheat the oven to 425°F. Line a baking sheet with foil and brush lightly with oil. Halve the squash, scoop out the seeds and stringy membranes, brush the cut sides with some oil and place cut side down on the baking sheet. Bake for 40 minutes, or until soft enough to pierce easily with a knife. Remove from the heat and allow to cool, then peel and mash with a fork, or puree in a food processor. Stir in 2 tablespoons of the lemon or lime juice and 2 tablespoons of the oil.

2. Mash the garlic and ¼ teaspoon salt to a paste with a mortar and pestle. Stir into the squash puree, along with the caraway, coriander, harissa (if using), and salt to taste. Mound on a platter or in a wide bowl. Mix together the remaining 1 teaspoon lemon juice and 1 teaspoon oil and drizzle over the puree. Decorate with the olives. Serve with the romaine leaves for scooping, and warm flat bread, if desired.

Per serving (based 6 servings): 109 calories, 1 g protein, 15 g carbohydrates, 3 g fiber, 6 g fat, 1 g sat fat, 0 mg cholesterol, 29 mg sodium

ADVANCE PREPARATION: This is best freshly made. It keeps for about 3 days in the refrigerator, though it becomes more pungent.

Winter Squash Fries

Makes 4 servings

■ **VEGETARIAN** ■ **VEGAN** ■ LOW-CALORIE ■ LOW-FAT
■ HIGH-PROTEIN ■ **GLUTEN-FREE** ■ HIGH IN OMEGA-3S

This is my new favorite way to cook squash. I like it much better than French fries. If you're cooking it for 4 people, you'll have to do it in batches. You can keep each batch warm on a baking sheet in the oven while you cook the next.

3–4 tablespoons extra virgin olive oil

1 pound winter squash, cut into ½-inch dice (about
3½ cups) or into ½-inch-wide sticks (like
French fries)

Salt and ground black pepper

Preheat the oven to 250°F. Working in batches, for each batch heat 1 to 2 tablespoons olive oil (depending on the size of your pan) in a heavy cast iron or nonstick skillet over medium-high heat. Add the squash in a single layer. Turn the heat down to medium. Cook for 5 minutes, or until the squash is nicely browned on one side. Using tongs, turn the pieces of squash over and cook for 5 to 10 minutes longer, or until the squash is nicely browned on the other side and tender when pierced by a knife or skewer. Season with salt and black pepper, toss in the pan for another minute or so, and remove from the heat. Transfer to a baking sheet and keep the first batch warm in a low oven while you cook the remaining squash.

Per serving: 150 calories, 1 g protein, 14 g carbohydrates, 2 g fiber, 11 g fat, 2 g sat fat, 0 mg cholesterol, 41 mg sodium

ADVANCE PREPARATION: This is best served right away.

FOR MORE WINTER SQUASH RECIPES SEE:

Andean Bean Stew with Winter Squash and Quinoa (page 284)

Couscous with Winter Vegetables and Beans (page 276)

North African Bean and Squash Soup (page 84)

Pureed White Bean and Winter Squash Soup (page 81)

Risotto with Roasted Winter Squash (page 232)

Winter Squash Gratin (page 269)

Sweet Potatoes

Sweet potatoes are an essential winter staple for me. I bake them and keep them in the refrigerator, where they continue to sweeten. I eat them for lunch, usually with cottage cheese or with a salty cheese like feta, and I feed them to my son when he needs a snack. I'm talking about the deep orange sweet potatoes that are often mistakenly identified as yams. My favorites are garnets (dark-red skin with orange flesh) and jewels (orange skin with deep orange flesh). Both types have moist, sweet flesh that oozes syrup as they bake.

What Nutritionists Know about Sweet Potatoes

Sweet as they are, sweet potatoes are relatively low in calories—105 in a $3\frac{1}{2}$-ounce serving. They're high in fiber, and an excellent source of vitamin A in the form of beta-carotene. They're also high in vitamin C and manganese, and a good source of copper, vitamin B_6, potassium, and iron.

Baked Sweet Potatoes

Makes 4 servings

■ **VEGETARIAN** ■ **VEGAN** ■ **LOW-CALORIE** ■ **LOW-FAT**
■ HIGH-PROTEIN ■ **GLUTEN-FREE** ■ HIGH IN OMEGA-3S

Think of baked sweet potatoes not only as a side dish, but also as a lunch or snack. Don't try to save time and use a microwave for this. Your sweet potatoes won't be nearly as sweet if you cook them that way; they need the time in the hot oven for their enzymes to convert starch into maltose, the sugar (about one-third as sweet as table sugar) that makes sweet potatoes sweet. They will also get sweeter over time in the refrigerator

4 medium sweet potatoes, scrubbed

1. Preheat the oven to 425°F. Pierce the sweet potatoes in several places with a sharp knife. Place the potatoes on a foil-lined baking sheet. Bake for 45 minutes to 1 hour, depending on the size of the potatoes, until thoroughly soft and beginning to ooze. Remove from the heat.

2. If not serving hot, place the sweet potatoes on a plate and allow to cool. Cover with plastic wrap and refrigerate. Serve cold (cut into thick slices and remove the skin) or at room temperature, or reheat for 20 to 30 minutes in a 350°F oven.

Per serving: 100 calories, 2 g protein, 23 g carbohydrates, 4 g fiber, 0 g fat, 0 g sat fat, 0 mg cholesterol, 70 mg sodium

ADVANCE PREPARATION: Baked sweet potatoes will hold in the refrigerator for about 5 days.

VARIATION: BAKED SWEET POTATOES WITH LIME

Make the recipe through Step 1. Transfer to a baking dish that will hold the potatoes snugly. Allow the baked potato to cool completely. Cut in half lengthwise and place in a baking dish, cut side up. Douse with the freshly squeezed juice of 1 to 2 limes, to taste. Cover and refrigerate overnight. Serve at room temperature or reheat for 20 to 30 minutes in a 350°F oven.

Sweet Potato Puree with Apples

Makes 6 servings

■ **VEGETARIAN** ▪ VEGAN ■ **LOW-CALORIE** ■ **LOW-FAT** ▪ HIGH-PROTEIN ■ **GLUTEN-FREE** ▪ HIGH IN OMEGA-3S

I make this sweet, tangy puree every year for Thanksgiving and don't know why I don't make it in between. It's my favorite dish on the menu, and everybody loves it, not only because of its intense good flavor, but also for its heavenly, silky texture. Once you've tried it you'll retire those candied yams for good.

2 pounds sweet potatoes, scrubbed

2 tart apples, such as Granny Smith or Braeburn

Juice of 1 lime

¼ cup plain low-fat yogurt

1–2 tablespoons unsalted butter, melted

1 tablespoon mild flavored honey, such as clover

Pinch of salt

1. Preheat the oven to 425°F. Pierce the sweet potatoes and apples in several places with a sharp knife.

Line a baking sheet with foil and place the potatoes and apples on top. Bake for 40 minutes, or until the apples are soft and oozing, and remove the apples. Continue to bake the sweet potatoes until thoroughly soft and beginning to ooze, 5 to 15 minutes, depending on the size. Remove from the heat and allow to cool until you can handle them.

2. Reduce the heat to 350°F. Remove the skins from the potatoes. Peel and core the apples, scraping all the flesh from the skins. Chop the potatoes and apples coarsely and place in a food processor fitted with the steel blade. Puree until smooth. Add the lime juice, yogurt, butter, honey, and salt. Blend well. Transfer to a lightly buttered 2- or 3-quart baking dish.

3. Heat the puree in the 350°F oven for 20 to 30 minutes, until steaming. Serve hot.

Per serving: 169 calories, 3 g protein, 36 g carbohydrates. 5 g fiber, 2 g fat, 1 g sat fat, 6 mg cholesterol, 114 mg sodium

ADVANCE PREPARATION: This can be made through Step 2 a day ahead and kept covered in the refrigerator. Reheating will take 30 to 40 minutes.

Tomatoes

Fresh vine-ripened tomatoes are one of the best things about summer. That they're good for you is a bonus. More than any other vegetable, tomatoes are not worth the salt that you will undoubtedly need to season them if they have not ripened on the vine in a garden near you. As my father used to say about corn, "it's a short season," and the tomatoes you buy weekly at the farmers' market will be worth every precious penny you spend on them.

What Nutritionists Know about Tomatoes

Tomatoes are an excellent source of vitamins C, E, beta-carotene, and lycopene, a carotenoid pigment found in tomatoes and other red fruits and vegetables. Lycopene is thought to have potent antioxidant properties. The European Commission is so interested in lycopene that it is backing a 5-year science project called Lycocard, a multidisciplinary consortium of scientists, technologists, and patient organizations that is studying the role of lycopene in the prevention of cardiovascular disease, cancer, and osteoporosis, diseases that can result in part from oxidative stress.

Summer Tomato Gratin

Makes 4 servings

■ **VEGETARIAN** ■ **VEGAN** ■ **LOW-CALORIE** ■ **LOW-FAT**
■ HIGH-PROTEIN ■ GLUTEN-FREE ■ HIGH IN OMEGA-3S

When you bake tomatoes for a very long time, as you do here, they become incredibly sweet, their juice almost syrupy. The topping crisps up like a crumble topping. Indeed, this dish is so sweet and comforting, it's almost like a dessert. It's definitely a treat.

2 pounds ripe but firm tomatoes, sliced

Salt and ground black pepper

½ teaspoon sugar

½ cup fresh or dry bread crumbs, preferably whole wheat

2 tablespoons chopped flat-leaf parsley

2 tablespoons extra virgin olive oil

1. Preheat the oven to 375°F. Oil a 2-quart gratin dish or baking dish. Layer the tomatoes in the dish, seasoning each layer with salt, black pepper, and a sprinkle of the sugar.

2. Toss together the bread crumbs, parsley, and olive oil. Spread over the tomatoes in an even layer. Place the tomatoes in the oven and bake for 1 to 1½ hours, or until the juices are thick and syrupy and the top is golden. Don't worry if some of the tomatoes are charred on the edges. Remove from the oven and allow to cool for at least 15 minutes before serving.

Per serving: 157 calories, 4 g protein, 19 g carbohydrates, 3 g fiber, 8 g fat, 1 g sat fat, 0 mg cholesterol, 148 mg sodium

ADVANCE PREPARATION: You can make this several hours ahead, as it's excellent served at room temperature.

Tomatoes Stuffed with Bulgur and Herbs

Makes 6 servings

■ **VEGETARIAN** ■ **VEGAN*** ■ **LOW-CALORIE** ■ **LOW-FAT****
■ HIGH-PROTEIN ■ GLUTEN-FREE ■ HIGH IN OMEGA-3S

Whereas some recipes for stuffed vegetables take a lot of time, these tomatoes are simple. They make a great summer dish, served either warm or at room temperature. I like to use bulgur for stuffed vegetables because it's so light and it softens quickly.

½ cup medium or coarse bulgur

Salt

6 ripe but firm medium tomatoes

½ cup chopped mixed fresh herbs, such as flat-leaf parsley, dill, mint, chives, chervil, and basil

¼ cup pine nuts, lightly toasted

¾ teaspoon ground cinnamon

2 tablespoons extra virgin olive oil

Ground black pepper

1-2 garlic cloves

1 cup Drained Yogurt (page 25) or thick Greek yogurt

1 tablespoon chopped fresh mint

*If you omit yogurt topping

**If you use low-fat yogurt

1. Place the bulgur in a bowl and add ¼ teaspoon salt. Mix together. Bring 1 cup water to a boil and pour over the bulgur. Allow to sit for 30 minutes, or until the bulgur is soft and fluffy. Strain through a sieve and press out excess water. Set aside.

2. Preheat the oven to 350°F. Slice off the tops of the tomatoes, about ¾ inch down from the stem (or far enough down so that it will be easy for you to hollow them out). Set the tops aside. Using a teaspoon or a grapefruit spoon, carefully scoop out the seeds. Place the scooped-out seeds in a sieve set over a bowl. Rub the seed pods against the sieve to extract the juice. Discard the seeds. Carefully scoop out the pulp from the tomatoes, taking care not to cut through the skins. Finely chop the pulp.

3. Mix together the bulgur, herbs, pine nuts, cinnamon, tomato pulp, ¼ cup of the strained juice, and 1 tablespoon of the oil. Season to taste with salt and black pepper. Season the hollowed-out tomatoes with salt and pepper. Fill each tomato with the bulgur filling (you may have some filling left over). Place in a baking dish that is small enough to fit the tomatoes snugly. Drizzle ½ teaspoon of the olive oil over each one and place the tomato tops on top. Pour about ½ inch of water into the pan and cover with foil. Bake for 45 minutes. Remove from the oven and uncover.

4. Mash the garlic with a pinch of salt to a paste with a mortar and pestle. Stir into the yogurt, along with the mint. Serve the stuffed tomatoes, warm or at room temperature, with a dollop of the yogurt.

Per serving: 167 calories, 6 g protein, 17 g carbohydrates, 4 g fiber, 10 g fat, 2 g sat fat, 2 mg cholesterol, 46 mg sodium

ADVANCE PREPARATION: You can make these several hours ahead as they are good served at room temperature.

Fried Green Tomatoes

Makes 4 servings

■ **VEGETARIAN** ■ **VEGAN** ■ LOW-CALORIE ■ LOW-FAT
■ HIGH-PROTEIN ■ **GLUTEN-FREE** ■ HIGH IN OMEGA-3S

Classic Southern fried green tomatoes are cooked in bacon drippings in a cast iron skillet. My version is more Mediterranean— and I'm sure that at the end of the tomato season Mediterranean cooks do something similar. I use a heavy nonstick skillet, which requires less oil than cast iron, but either will work.

1 pound firm green tomatoes

½ cup yellow cornmeal

Salt and ground black pepper

3-4 tablespoons extra virgin olive oil or canola oil

1. Slice the tomatoes about ½ inch thick. Season the cornmeal with salt and black pepper, and dredge the tomatoes in it. You can do this in a large bowl, in a flatter baking dish, or in a brown paper bag, whatever is easiest for you.

2. Heat a heavy cast iron or nonstick skillet over medium-high heat. Add enough oil to coat the bottom by about ⅛ inch. Fry the tomatoes for 2 to 3 minutes per side, or until golden. Drain on paper towel, a paper bag, or a rack, and keep warm in a low oven until all of the tomatoes are fried. Serve hot or warm.

Per serving: 194 calories, 3 g protein, 22 g carbohydrates, 2 g fiber, 11 g fat, 2 g sat fat, 0 mg cholesterol, 51 mg sodium

ADVANCE PREPARATION: You can keep these warm in a low oven for a little while, but they're best served right away.

VARIATION: FRIED GREEN TOMATO SANDWICH
If you like tomato sandwiches (a weakness of mine), you'll love these. Spread slices of country bread or whole grain bread (toasted if desired) with mayonnaise, Russian dressing, or pesto, and top with fried green tomatoes. Add basil leaves, sliced onion, lettuce, and watercress or arugula if desired. Top with another slice of bread, also spread with mayonnaise, Russian dressing, or pesto.

Chapter 7

RICE AND OTHER GRAINS

O f all the food groups, grains is the one that I suspect we as a nation know the least about. Rice may be the exception, but even this grain comes in many different varieties, each one with its own characteristics that make it suitable for certain dishes. We need to take advantage of grains, like so many people in the rest of the world have done for centuries.

I began learning about grains when I became a vegetarian, and although I am no longer a strict vegetarian, I have never lost my taste for them. In fact, I find most grains somewhat addictive (though it's difficult to overeat this wholesome food) because of their chewy textures as well as their flavors. Some, like bulgur, quinoa, and brown rice, are nutty, while grains like wild rice, barley, and farro (a strain of wheat) have earthy flavors. They are all delicious and satisfying on their own, but they're versatile too. They can be the foundation for a hearty risotto-type dish, a gratin, and a main-dish salad, or they can be added to a soup or served with a stew or a stir-fry. I've noticed, too, that kids, even some picky eaters, eat grains.

There is still quite a bit of debate in the nutritional community about the role carbohydrates should play in our diet. One thing that is becoming clear, though, is that a diet with moderate carbohydrate restriction trumps low-fat or extreme low-carb diets. The type of carbohydrate consumed is significant: Starches such as whole grains, which have a high fiber content and are slowly digested, have a much smaller impact on our insulin levels than pure sugars or refined starches, and they add nutritional value to our diets. It should be noted also that more refined grains like hulled (white) rice are usually eaten, in the countries where they are staples, along with lots of high-fiber produce.

Grains fill us up, which is significant if you are trying to reduce your intake of red meats and other foods high in saturated fat in favor of plant foods. Whole grains are also convenient. Once cooked, they keep in the refrigerator for 3 to 4 days (reheat in a 225°F oven for 20 minutes or in a pan on top of the stove, or in the microwave) and freeze well (store them in resealable plastic freezer bags). Even those that take a while to cook are easy to cook in quantity, so you can keep them on hand in the freezer, ready to thaw and use.

Rice

I've got several types of rice in my pantry: lots of basmati, both white and brown; regular medium-grain brown rice; red rice from Bhutan; and Chinese black "forbidden" rice, which is really purple. There's starchy Spanish rice and Italian Arborio rice for risotto (see pages 221–234 for a selection of risottos), and jasmine rice from Thailand. It's a good thing that rice has a long storage life and, indeed, in some cultures older rice, such as basmati, is prized. But rice, like flour, will attract grain moths if it sits around for too long, so I try to get to my rice before they do.

My rice bible is *Seductions of Rice* (Artisan, 1998) by Jeffrey Alford and Naomi Duguid, renowned food writers, photographers, and world travelers. My information about the nutritional aspects of rice and about cooking the various types comes largely from this book, which is a beautiful, well researched survey of rice traditions around the world. Rice is, after all, the staple food for much of the world's population.

I am not in the same camp with those who shun white rice as a high-carb food (I am generally not in the anti-carb camp as I consider variety and a balanced diet the most important requirement for eating well). Although it has less fiber than brown rice, it has other nutritional qualities; according to Alford and Duguid, "rice has the highest protein digestibility and energy digestibility among all the staple foods." And in most rice cultures, rice is supplemented with vegetables and legumes, small amounts of meat and fish, and oil. It is a thoroughly sustaining food. Many nutritionists and health writers prefer brown rice because the high fiber content slows down the carbohydrate-absorption rate. But I, like most rice-eating cultures, combine rice with high-fiber vegetables and legumes, making this a nonissue.

I was especially interested in a point Alford and Duguid make about the nutritional quality of brown rice versus white rice: "Many people believe that brown rice is 'healthier' than white (milled) rice. It is true that brown rice has more calcium and iron as well as higher protein levels and significantly more of the B vitamins [and] more fiber than white rice. But brown rice is less digestible than white. The aleurone layer and embryo, still present in brown rice, contain phytate phosphorus, which seems to interfere with the absorption of calcium, zinc, and iron…" Its B vitamins, they go on to say, are easily absorbed. However, B vitamins are present in many other foods, as is fiber, so if you prefer white rice, just make sure you're also eating lots of vegetables and/or beans along with it. Don't get me wrong—I like brown rice a lot, just not to the exclusion of other types of rice.

Basic Steamed Long-Grain Rice

See note on yield, right

■ **VEGETARIAN*** ■ **VEGAN*** ■ LOW-CALORIE ■ **LOW-FAT**
■ HIGH-PROTEIN ■ **GLUTEN-FREE** ■ HIGH IN OMEGA-3S

Rice can be cooked many ways, but here's the technique that I find to be most reliable: Combine the rice with water, bring to a boil, reduce the heat, cover tightly, and simmer over very low heat for 15 minutes. Once the water has evaporated from the pot, place a towel between the lid of the pot and the rice and let it sit for 10 minutes, to absorb more moisture and steam. The amount of liquid you choose to use will affect the texture of your rice. A ratio of 2 parts liquid to 1 part rice produces soft, tender rice. Chewier rice will result with anywhere from 1 to 1½ parts liquid to 1 part rice. I usually use a 2:1 ratio for a long-grain rice like basmati. Basmati is traditionally soaked for 30 minutes and up to 2 hours before it is cooked. The grains are brittle, and soaking them gives them the chance to absorb a little water so that they won't break during cooking. (I have to admit I frequently skip this step and my rice turns out fine.) Cooked rice will keep for 3 to 4 days in the refrigerator and can be reheated in a microwave or in a 325°F oven in a covered baking dish.

1 cup long-grain white rice or white basmati rice

½ teaspoon salt

Water, Vegetable Stock (page 67), or chicken stock

*If made with Vegetable Stock or water

1. Place the rice in a bowl in the sink and rinse and drain several times with water, until the water runs clear. If using basmati, cover with fresh water, and soak for 30 minutes if you have the time. Drain the rice and measure out 1½ to 2 cups water or stock, depending on how tender you like your rice (see above).

2. Combine the water, rice, and salt in a heavy 2- or 3-quart saucepan. Bring to a boil, reduce the heat to low, and cover with a tight-fitting lid. Simmer for 12 to 15 minutes, or until all of the liquid has been absorbed. Turn off the heat.

3. Uncover the rice and place a clean kitchen towel over the top of the pan (it should not be touching the rice). Replace the lid and allow to sit for 10 minutes, undisturbed. Serve.

> **Note on Yield:** *Each type of rice yields a different amount when cooked. Basmati expands to 3 times its original volume, so 1 cup of raw rice would feed 4 people if served as a side dish. However, if rice is at the center of your plate, 1 cup of raw rice, cooked, would feed 2 people, perhaps with a little left over. Arborio and regular long-grain and brown rice expand to 2 times their original volume.*

Based on 2 servings (rice as the center of the plate): 338 calories, 7 g protein, 74 g carbohydrates, 1 g fiber, 1 g fat, 0 g sat fat, 0 mg cholesterol, 586 mg sodium

ADVANCE PREPARATION: Rice can be cooked ahead and reheated. Once you have followed the recipe through Step 3, spread the rice in a lightly oiled 2-quart baking dish and allow to cool completely, uncovered. To reheat, cover with foil and place in a 325°F oven for 20 minutes.

VARIATIONS: BASIC RICE PILAF To make a typical Middle Eastern pilaf, proceed with Step 1 as instructed. Heat 1 to 2 tablespoons butter or oil in a heavy 2- or 3-quart saucepan over medium heat. Add ¼ to ½ cup finely chopped onion, if desired, and cook, stirring, until it begins to soften, about 3 minutes. Add the rice and cook, stirring, for 2 to 3 minutes, until the rice is sizzling and the grains are separate. Add the water or stock and the salt and bring to a boil. Reduce the heat, cover, and simmer for 12 to 15 minutes, or until all the liquid has been absorbed. Proceed with Step 3.

Basic Steamed Brown Rice

Makes about 2½ cups/4 servings

■ **VEGETARIAN** ■ **VEGAN** ■ **LOW-CALORIE** ■ **LOW-FAT**
■ HIGH-PROTEIN ■ **GLUTEN-FREE** ■ HIGH IN OMEGA-3S

I don't use brown rice interchangeably with white rice, because it tastes and feels like a different grain. I like its chewy texture, its nutty flavor, and its heartiness.

½–¾ teaspoon salt

1 cup brown rice (long-, medium-, or short-grain)

1. Bring 2½ cups water to a boil in a saucepan over high heat. Add the salt and brown rice. Return to a boil. Reduce the heat, cover, and simmer for 35 to 45 minutes, or until the water has been absorbed.

2. Remove from the heat and let sit, covered and undisturbed, for 10 minutes.

> **Per serving:** 171 calories, 4 g protein, 36 g carbohydrates, 2 g fiber, 1 g fat, 0 g sat fat, 0 mg cholesterol, 294 mg sodium

ADVANCE PREPARATION: Brown rice keeps well in the refrigerator for 3 to 4 days and can be frozen. Reheat in the oven (325°F for 20 minutes), in a saucepan on top of the stove, or in the microwave.

Basic Cooked Wild Rice

Makes 4 to 6 servings

■ **VEGETARIAN*** ■ **VEGAN*** ■ **LOW-CALORIE** ■ **LOW-FAT**
■ HIGH-PROTEIN ■ **GLUTEN-FREE** ■ HIGH IN OMEGA-3S

Wild rice is a grass that is now cultivated in many places, from the lakes of northern Minnesota to California. It has an earthy/nutty flavor and makes a wonderful pilaf or salad. It used to be a fancy specialty grain, very expensive because it was indeed wild, and was only harvested by Native Americans in Minnesota. Now it's on supermarket shelves everywhere. When wild rice has been simmered until tender, the outer husk will break and the ends of the grain will begin to fan out, or splay. This is a good way to tell that the rice is ready.

3½ cups Vegetable Stock (page 67), water, or chicken stock

Salt to taste

1 cup wild rice

*If made with Vegetable Stock or water

Bring the stock or water to a boil in a saucepan over high heat. Add the salt and wild rice. Return to a boil. Reduce the heat, cover, and simmer for 40 to 45 minutes, or until the rice is tender and has begun to splay. Drain and return the rice to the pot. Cover until ready to serve.

> **Per serving (based on 4 servings):** 160 calories, 6 g protein, 34 g carbohydrates, 2 g fiber, 0.5 g fat, 0 g sat fat, 0 mg cholesterol, 679 mg sodium

ADVANCE PREPARATION: Wild rice keeps well in the refrigerator for 3 to 4 days and can be frozen. Reheat in the oven at 325°F for 20 minutes, in a saucepan on top of the stove, or in the microwave.

Thai Combination Fried Rice

Makes 2 to 4 servings

■ **VEGETARIAN*** ■ VEGAN ■ LOW-CALORIE ■ **LOW-FAT**
■ HIGH-PROTEIN ■ GLUTEN-FREE ■ HIGH IN OMEGA-3S

This is loosely based on Thailand's ubiquitous fried rice dish, kao pad. Usually some kind of animal protein accompanies the rice—squid, crabmeat, ham, chicken, whatever the cook has on hand. Tofu does the trick as well. I've made the version below almost vegetarian (it does contain fish sauce), as the most important ingredients are the rice itself, the garlic, and the fish sauce. If you are vegetarian, substitute soy sauce for the fish sauce. Have all of your ingredients prepared and close to the stove. Cooking goes very quickly.

2 tablespoons canola or vegetable oil

1 large carrot, grated

4 ounces tofu, patted dry and cut into ½-inch dice

8 garlic cloves, minced

4 eggs, beaten and seasoned with salt and pepper

5 cups cooked rice, preferably Thai jasmine rice

2–3 tablespoons Thai or Vietnamese fish sauce

2–3 teaspoons Thai or Indonesian chili sauce

1 tomato, chopped

1 bunch scallions, chopped

½ cup chopped cilantro

Thinly sliced cucumber

Lime wedges

Scallions

Fish sauce with hot chiles (*nam pla prik*)

If you omit all fish sauce

1. Heat a large wok or large, heavy nonstick skillet over medium-high heat until a drop of water evaporates upon contact. Add the oil, swirl, and add the carrot and tofu. Cook, stirring, until lightly colored, about 2 minutes. Add the garlic, cook, stirring, until golden, about 30 seconds. Pour in the beaten egg. Cook, stirring, until scrambled.

2. Add the rice (if you feel you need to add more oil, add another tablespoon) and cook for about 2 minutes, scooping the rice up, then pressing it into the pan and scooping it up again. Add the fish sauce, chile sauce, tomato, and scallions, stir together for 30 seconds, and serve, garnishing each plate with the cilantro and cucumbers, and passing the lime wedges, scallions, and fish sauce with chiles.

Per serving (based on 2 servings): 927 calories, 35 g protein, 130 g carbohydrates, 7 g fiber, 30 g fat, 5 g sat fat, 423 mg cholesterol, 759 mg sodium

ADVANCE PREPARATION: Cooked rice will keep for 3 to 4 days in the refrigerator. The dish is a last-minute stir-fry.

Steamed Jasmine Rice with Grilled Eggplant Salad

Makes 4 servings

■ **VEGETARIAN*** ■ **VEGAN*** ■ **LOW-CALORIE** ■ LOW-FAT
■ HIGH-PROTEIN ■ GLUTEN-FREE ■ HIGH IN OMEGA-3S

Jasmine rice is an aromatic, soft, long-grain rice that is widely used in Thailand. The Thai dishes that are served with it are highly seasoned, so the rice is traditionally cooked without salt. The grilled eggplant salad here is adapted from a recipe in Jeffrey Alford and Naomi Duguid's wonderful book, Seductions of Rice *(Artisan, New York). I like to use my panini grill for grilling eggplant.*

1 cup Thai jasmine rice

Salt (optional)

1 ½ pounds long, thin Japanese eggplants, or
   1 large globe eggplant, sliced crosswise about
   ¼ inch thick (slice on the diagonal if using long,
   thin eggplants)

2 tablespoons canola oil

¼ cup chopped cilantro

¼ cup finely chopped fresh mint

1 large plum tomato, diced

5 tablespoons fresh lime juice

2 tablespoons Thai fish sauce or soy sauce

¼ teaspoon sugar

½–1 serrano or bird chile pepper, finely minced
   (wear plastic gloves when handling)

*If you omit the fish sauce

1. Place the rice in a bowl, cover with water, and swish the rice around. Drain and repeat this step until the water runs clear, 2 or 3 more times. Drain, place the rice in a heavy saucepan, and add enough water to cover the rice by a little more than ½ inch (measure by placing the tip of your index finger on the surface of the rice; the water should come to just below the first joint). Add salt, if desired, and bring to a boil. Allow the water to boil hard for about 15 seconds, then reduce the heat, cover, and cook over very low heat for 15 minutes. Do not lift the lid during this time.

2. Turn off the heat, uncover the rice, and place a clean kitchen towel over the top of the pan (it should not be touching the rice). Replace the lid and allow to sit for 10 minutes, undisturbed. Remove the lid and towel, and gently turn the rice with a paddle to bring the rice up from the bottom of the pot. Replace the towel, return the lid, and let stand while you prepare the eggplant.

3. Heat a panini grill to high, or prepare a hot grill. Brush the eggplant with the oil and grill for 3 to 4 minutes in the panini grill, 5 to 8 minutes per side on a regular grill, or until lightly browned and tender all the way through. As each batch is done, transfer to a bowl. When all of the eggplant has been grilled, cover the bowl tightly and allow the eggplant to steam and eventually to cool.

4. Coarsely chop the eggplant and toss with the cilantro, mint, and tomato. Mix together the lime juice, fish sauce, sugar, and chile pepper. Toss with the eggplant mixture. Allow to sit for 30 minutes to 1 hour, then taste and adjust the seasoning.

5. Place the rice on a platter or on individual plates, top with the eggplant mixture, and serve.

Per serving: 194 calories, 4 g protein, 31 g carbohydrates, 6 g fiber, 7 g fat, 0.5 g sat fat, 0 mg cholesterol, 700 mg sodium

ADVANCE PREPARATION: The eggplant salad will keep for a day in the refrigerator. The cooked rice will keep for 3 to 4 days.

Wild Rice and Brown Rice Salad with Walnut Vinaigrette and Asparagus

Makes 6 servings

■ **VEGETARIAN*** ■ **VEGAN*** ■ LOW-CALORIE ■ LOW-FAT
■ HIGH-PROTEIN ■ **GLUTEN-FREE** ■ **HIGH IN OMEGA-3S**

A main-dish salad is a perfect destination for grains. Tossed with a vinaigrette, a selection of vegetables and herbs, perhaps some walnuts to add crunch and flavor, and you've got all you need for the center of your plate. I love the contrast of textures and colors in this salad. The wild rice is earthy, the brown rice nutty, and both are chewy in different ways. Walnuts and walnut oil not only add perfect complementary flavor and crunch, but also contribute omega-3 fatty acids to the mix.

For the salad:

5 cups Vegetable Stock (page 67), water, or chicken stock

Salt

1 cup wild rice

$\frac{1}{2}$ cup short-grain brown rice

$\frac{1}{2}$ pound asparagus, trimmed, cut into 1-inch pieces

For the dressing:

2 tablespoons fresh lemon juice

1 tablespoon sherry vinegar or champagne vinegar

Salt

1 teaspoon Dijon mustard

1 small garlic clove, finely minced or pureed in a mortar and pestle

$\frac{1}{4}$ cup walnut oil

$\frac{1}{4}$ cup extra virgin olive oil

$\frac{1}{4}$ cup chopped flat-leaf parsley

2 tablespoons chopped fresh herbs such as chives, dill, tarragon, marjoram

$\frac{1}{3}$ cup walnuts

Ground black pepper

*If made with Vegetable Stock or water

1. To make the salad: Bring $3\frac{1}{2}$ cups of the stock or water to a boil in a saucepan over high heat. Add salt to taste and the wild rice. Return to a boil. Reduce the heat, cover, and simmer for 40 to 45 minutes, or until the rice is tender and has begun to splay. Drain and transfer the rice to a large bowl.

2. Meanwhile, combine the brown rice, the remaining $1\frac{1}{2}$ cups stock or water, and salt to taste in another saucepan and bring to a boil. Reduce the heat, cover, and simmer for 35 to 40 minutes, or until the rice is tender. Remove from the heat. If any liquid remains in the pan, drain. Add to the wild rice.

While the rice cooks, steam the asparagus for 3 to 4 minutes, until just tender, and rinse with cold water. Drain on paper towels.

3. To make the dressing: Whisk together the lemon juice, vinegar, salt, mustard, and garlic. Whisk in the oils. Taste and adjust the seasonings. Toss at once with the warm rice.

4. Add the asparagus to the rice, along with the parsley, herbs, walnuts, and black pepper. Toss together, taste, adjust the seasonings, and serve.

Per serving: 388 calories, 7 g protein, 41 g carbohydrates, 4 g fiber, 24 g fat, 3 g sat fat, 0 mg cholesterol, 349 mg sodium

ADVANCE PREPARATION: You can make this up to a day ahead, but don't add the asparagus, parsley, and herbs until shortly before serving, because their colors will fade.

Basic Cooked Barley

Makes 3 cups/4 to 6 servings

■ **VEGETARIAN*** ■ **VEGAN*** ■ LOW-CALORIE ■ **LOW-FAT**
■ HIGH-PROTEIN ■ GLUTEN-FREE ■ HIGH IN OMEGA-3S

Barley is a hearty, chewy grain that looks somewhat like a beige version of brown rice. It has a chewy texture and earthy flavor, and goes very well with mushrooms. It does contain gluten, so if you are gluten intolerant, you should also avoid barley.

3 cups water or chicken stock

1 cup pearl or whole barley

½–¾ teaspoon salt

*If you omit the chicken stock

Bring the water or stock to a boil in a saucepan over high heat. Add the barley and salt. Return to a boil. Reduce the heat, cover, and simmer for 40 to 45 minutes, or until the barley is tender. Pour off any liquid remaining in the pan, cover, and allow the grains to sit for 10 to 15 minutes before serving.

Per serving (based on 4 servings): 176 calories, 5 g protein, 39 g carbohydrates, 8 g fiber, 1 g fat, 0 g sat fat, 0 mg cholesterol, 301 mg sodium

Note: *For a nuttier flavor, toast the barley first, stirring it in a heavy saucepan over medium heat until it begins to smell like popcorn. Add the simmering water or stock and the salt, and proceed with the recipe.*

Barley Orzotto with Cauliflower and Red Wine

Makes 6 servings

■ **VEGETARIAN*** ■ VEGAN ■ LOW-CALORIE ■ LOW-FAT
■ HIGH-PROTEIN ■ GLUTEN-FREE ■ HIGH IN OMEGA-3S

The Italians make risotto-like dishes with other grains besides rice. When they use barley the dish is called orzotto. It has a chewier, more robust texture than risotto made with rice, it's not as creamy, and it has considerably more fiber. I like to use red wine for this, both for its flavor and because I like the way it tints the cauliflower.

7–8 cups Vegetable Stock (page 67) or chicken stock

Salt

2 tablespoons extra virgin olive oil

1 small or ½ medium onion, minced

2 large garlic cloves, minced

1 medium cauliflower, separated into small florets, the florets broken into smaller pieces or sliced ½ inch thick

1½ cups barley

1 cup robust red wine, such as a Côtes du Rhône

3 tablespoons chopped flat-leaf parsley

½ cup (2 ounces) grated Parmesan

Ground black pepper

*If made with Vegetable Stock

1. Season the stock well with salt and bring to a simmer in a saucepan.

2. Heat the oil in a large, heavy nonstick skillet or a wide, heavy saucepan over medium heat. Add the onion. Cook, stirring, until the onion begins to soften, about 3 minutes. Add the garlic, cauliflower, barley, and a generous pinch of salt. Cook, stirring,

for 2 to 3 minutes, until the grains of barley separate and begin to crackle.

3. Add the wine and cook, stirring, until there is no wine visible in the pan. Stir in enough of the simmering stock to just cover the barley. The stock should bubble slowly. Cook, stirring often, until it is just about absorbed. Add more stock and continue to cook in this fashion, adding more stock when the barley is almost dry, until the barley is tender but still chewy, about 40 minutes. Taste and add salt if necessary.

4. Add 1 ladleful of stock to the barley. Stir in the parsley and Parmesan and immediately remove from the heat. Add black pepper, taste, and adjust the salt. Serve at once.

Per serving: 489 calories, 13 g protein, 79 g carbohydrates, 16 g fiber, 10 g fat, 2.5 g sat fat, 6 mg cholesterol, 777 mg sodium

ADVANCE PREPARATION: You can begin this dish several hours ahead and cook the barley for 15 to 20 minutes as instructed above. Spread in a thin layer in the pan, and resume cooking about 20 minutes before you wish to serve.

Barley and Mushroom Salad with English Peas

Makes 4 to 6 servings

■ **VEGETARIAN*** ■ VEGAN ■ LOW-CALORIE ■ LOW-FAT
■ HIGH-PROTEIN ■ GLUTEN-FREE ■ HIGH IN OMEGA-3S

We all love barley and mushroom soup, so why not change it up and use the popular combination in a salad? Toasting the barley in a dry pan before adding water increases the depth of flavor. English peas brighten the mixture and add some crunch. You can make the vinaigrette and prepare the remaining ingredients for the salad while the barley is cooking.

1 cup pearl barley

3 cups chicken stock, Vegetable Stock (page 67), or water

¾ teaspoon kosher salt

6 ounces white or cremini mushrooms, thinly sliced

Walnut Vinaigrette (page 178)

¼ cup chopped flat-leaf parsley, or a mixture of parsley and other herbs such as chives, dill, tarragon, or marjoram

2–4 leaves fresh sage, very thinly slivered

1 cup shelled English peas, uncooked, or steamed for 5 minutes

1 cup shredded radicchio

1 ounce Parmesan, shaved (about ¼ cup)

*If made with Vegetable Stock

1. Heat a saucepan over medium-high heat. Add the barley. Stir until the barley begins to smell toasty, about 5 minutes. Add the stock or water and salt and bring to a boil. Reduce the heat to low, cover, and simmer for 40 minutes, or until the barley is tender. If all the liquid has not been absorbed, drain.

2. Place the mushrooms in a salad bowl and toss with 2 tablespoons of the dressing.

3. When the barley is ready, add to the salad bowl and toss. Add the remaining dressing, the parsley or mixed herbs, sage, peas, and radicchio and toss. Serve warm or at room temperature, garnishing each serving with some Parmesan.

> **Per serving (based on 4 servings):** 446 calories, 15 g protein, 55 g carbohydrates, 10 g fiber, 19 g fat, 4 g sat fat, 12 mg cholesterol, 806 mg sodium

ADVANCE PREPARATION: You can make this up to a day ahead, but only add half of the mushrooms and don't add the herbs, peas, or radicchio. Toss these ingredients with the salad shortly before serving.

Barley Pilaf with Green Beans, Mushrooms, and Pesto

Makes 6 servings

■ **VEGETARIAN*** ■ VEGAN ■ LOW-CALORIE ■ **LOW-FAT** ■ HIGH-PROTEIN ■ **GLUTEN-FREE** ■ HIGH IN OMEGA-3S

Mushrooms and barley and also mushrooms and green beans are both classic combinations that make a really great threesome as well in this easy pilaf. There is lots of texture here, with the chewy, nutty-tasting barley, the soft, savory mushrooms, and the just-tender green beans.

1 quart chicken stock or Vegetable Stock (page 67)

½ pound green beans, broken in half

1½ cups barley

2 tablespoons olive oil

½ medium onion or 2 shallots, finely chopped (about ½ cup)

½ pound mushrooms, trimmed and sliced

¼ cup dry white wine, such as pinot grigio or fumet blanc

Salt and ground black pepper

¼ cup Basil Pesto (recipe follows)

Freshly grated Parmesan

*If made with Vegetable Stock

1. Fill a bowl with ice and water. Bring the stock to a boil and add the green beans. Cook for 5 minutes, remove the green beans with a skimmer, and transfer to the bowl of ice water. Drain and set aside. Add the barley to the boiling stock, reduce the heat to low, cover, and simmer for 40 to 45 minutes, or until the barley is tender. Drain the barley through a strainer to remove excess liquid.

2. Heat the oil over medium heat in a large, heavy nonstick skillet or a wide, heavy saucepan and add the onion or shallots. Cook, stirring, until beginning to soften, about 3 minutes. Add the mushrooms. and cook, stirring, until they begin to soften, about 3 minutes. Add the wine and cook, stirring, until the wine is no longer visible in the pan. Season with salt and black pepper and continue to cook the mushrooms until tender, about 5 minutes.

3. Stir in the green beans and the cooked barley and toss together to heat through. Stir in the pesto and Parmesan, remove from the heat, and serve.

> **Per serving:** 349 calories, 12 g protein, 51 g carbohydrates, 10 g fiber, 11 g fat, 2 g sat fat, 6 mg cholesterol, 307 mg sodium

ADVANCE PREPARATION: The cooked barley and the blanched beans will keep for 3 or 4 days in the refrigerator. The entire dish will keep for 2 or 3 days in the refrigerator. Reheat gently on top of the stove.

Simple Basil Pesto

2 cups fresh basil leaves

1–2 large garlic cloves, peeled

¼ rounded teaspoon sea salt

⅓ cup extra virgin olive oil

2 tablespoons grated Pecorino Romano cheese

¼ cup (1 ounce) grated Parmesan cheese

Ground black pepper

1. Place the basil leaves in a food processor and pulse until finely chopped. Scrape down the sides of the bowl.

2. Mash the garlic and salt to a paste with a mortar and pestle. Scrape the garlic paste into the food processor with the basil. Turn on the machine and process until the ingredients are mixed and adhering to the sides of the bowl. Scrape down the bowl. Turn on the machine and slowly drizzle in the olive oil. Continue to process until the mixture is smooth and homogenous. Add the cheeses and black pepper and pulse until everything is well blended. Taste and adjust the salt.

ADVANCE PREPARATION: Pesto will keep for a couple of weeks in the refrigerator. To store it, scrape it into a clean glass jar, cover with about ¼ inch of olive oil, and refrigerate. Every time you use some of the pesto, replenish the olive oil. Pesto also freezes well, but without the cheese.

Quinoa

Quinoa is a relative newcomer to the American pantry. The tiny ancient Peruvian grain is the seed of a leafy green vegetable, but we use it like a grain. The delicate, silky grain, with its mild, nutty flavor, is as versatile as rice. It's a particular boon to vegans and vegetarians because its protein quality is superior to that of most other grains, with all the essential amino acids. In particular, quinoa is high in lysine, an amino acid important for tissue growth and repair that is not commonly found in plant foods. Quinoa is a good source of manganese, magnesium, phosphorus, and copper, and has more iron than any other grain.

There are two varieties of quinoa available. The most common quinoa is a pale beige color. Many whole-foods stores also stock royal quinoa, a red (really rust-colored) variety that is grown only in one valley in Bolivia and is claimed to be superior. It's very pretty, but also expensive, and you'll do fine with the regular strain.

Quinoa is very easy to cook. It's important to rinse the grains well, because they are naturally coated with a bitter substance that protects them against birds and other predators. Most packaged quinoa has already been cleaned, but it doesn't hurt to soak and rinse it just in case. Quinoa cooks up in 15 minutes, and it's easy to tell when it's done because the grains display a little white thread that curls around them when they're cooked through. The first time I served quinoa to my son, who was then 10, I was worried (even though he isn't picky) that he would mind the look of the threads in his food, but he gobbled it up and asked for more.

Basic Steamed Quinoa

Makes about 4 cups/6 to 8 servings

■ **VEGETARIAN*** ■ **VEGAN*** ■ **LOW-CALORIE** ■ **LOW-FAT**
■ **HIGH-PROTEIN** ■ **GLUTEN-FREE** ■ HIGH IN OMEGA-3S

Most recipes for quinoa instruct you to cook it like rice, in 2 parts water for 1 part grain. This works, but I find the grains are fluffier if I cook them in 3 parts water and drain the excess water once the quinoa is tender. The tiny seeds swell to about 4 times their original size, so 1 cup uncooked quinoa yields about 4 cups, enough for 6 to 8 servings.

1 cup quinoa

3 cups chicken stock, Vegetable Stock (page 67), or water

½ teaspoon salt

If made with Vegetable Stock or water

1. Place the quinoa in a bowl and cover with cold water. Let sit for 5 minutes. Drain through a sieve and rinse until the water runs clear.

2. Bring the stock or water to a boil in a medium saucepan over high heat. Add the salt and quinoa. Return to a boil. Reduce the heat to low, cover, and simmer for 15 minutes, or until the quinoa is tender and translucent, and each grain displays a little thread. Drain and return to the pan. Cover the pan with a clean dish towel, replace the lid, and allow to sit undisturbed for 10 minutes. Fluff and serve.

Per serving (based on 6 servings): 147 calories, 7 g protein, 22 g carbohydrates, 2 g fiber, 3 g fat, 1 g sat fat, 4 mg cholesterol, 367 mg sodium

ADVANCE PREPARATION: Cooked quinoa will keep for 3 to 4 days in the refrigerator and can be reheated in a microwave or in the oven.

Note: *For a richer flavor, toast the quinoa first. Heat a heavy saucepan over medium-high heat and add the rinsed quinoa. Stir in the hot pan until all the water has evaporated and the quinoa is beginning to smell toasty, about 5 minutes. Add the water or stock and salt, bring to a boil, and proceed with the recipe.*

Quinoa and Tomato Gratin

Makes 4 to 6 servings

■ **VEGETARIAN** ■ VEGAN ■ LOW-CALORIE ■ LOW-FAT
■ **HIGH-PROTEIN** ■ **GLUTEN-FREE** ■ HIGH IN OMEGA-3S

Grains can be dressed up or down. This easy, comforting summer gratin is somewhere in the middle. Serve it as a main dish or a side.

2 tablespoons extra virgin olive oil

1 medium onion, chopped

2 garlic cloves, minced

¾ cup quinoa, cooked (page 185)

1 tablespoon chopped fresh basil

Salt and ground black pepper

2 large eggs

½ cup 1% milk

½ cup (2 ounces) grated Gruyère cheese

1 pound ripe but firm tomatoes, sliced

3 tablespoons grated Parmesan

1. Preheat the oven to 375°F. Oil a 2-quart gratin dish or baking dish.

2. Heat a skillet or a wide saucepan over medium-high heat. Add 1 tablespoon of the oil. Add the onion and cook, stirring often, until tender, about 5 minutes. Add the garlic and stir with the onion until fragrant, about 1 minute. Stir in the cooked quinoa and basil and season with salt and black pepper. Remove from the heat.

3. Beat the eggs and milk together in a large bowl and add ½ teaspoon salt. Stir in the quinoa mixture and the Gruyère. Season with black pepper and stir again. Scrape into the gratin dish. Layer the tomatoes over the top and season with salt and black pepper. Sprinkle on the Parmesan and drizzle on the remaining 1 tablespoon oil. Place in the oven and bake until nicely browned on top, about 25 minutes. Remove from the heat, allow to sit for about 5 minutes, and serve.

Per serving (based on 4 servings): 334 calories, 16 g protein, 30 g carbohydrates, 4 g fiber, 17 g fat, 5 g sat fat, 125 mg cholesterol, 196 mg sodium

ADVANCE PREPARATION: The cooked quinoa will keep for 3 to 4 days in the refrigerator. The recipe can be made through Step 3 several hours or even a day ahead.

Quinoa Pilaf with Chickpeas and Pomegranate

Makes 4 to 6 main-dish and 6 to 8 side-dish servings

■ **VEGETARIAN*** ■ **VEGAN**** ■ **LOW-CALORIE** ■ **LOW-FAT**
■ **HIGH-PROTEIN** ■ **GLUTEN-FREE** ■ HIGH IN OMEGA-3S

The Turkish pilaf that inspired this pilaf is made with rice or bulgur, but quinoa adapts well to other culinary traditions. The pomegranate-studded pilaf is high in protein and can be served as a main dish or a side.

1 cup quinoa

3 cups water, Vegetable Stock (page 67), or chicken stock

Salt

1 teaspoon cumin seeds

¾ teaspoon coriander seeds

2 tablespoons extra virgin olive oil

½ medium onion, chopped

2 garlic cloves, minced

1 cup cooked or canned chickpeas, rinsed

¼–½ cup pomegranate seeds (as needed)

1 small garlic clove, pureed in a mortar and pestle (optional)

1 cup Drained Yogurt (page 25), optional

*If made with Vegetable Stock or water

**If you omit the chicken stock and yogurt

1. Place the quinoa in a bowl and cover with cold water. Let sit for 5 minutes. Drain through a sieve and rinse until the water runs clear.

2. Bring the water or stock to a boil in a medium saucepan over high heat. Add ½ teaspoon salt and the quinoa. Return to a boil. Reduce the heat to low, cover, and simmer for 15 minutes, or until the quinoa is tender and translucent, and each grain displays a little thread. Drain and return to the pan. Cover the pan with a clean kitchen towel, replace the lid, and allow to sit undisturbed for 10 minutes.

3. Heat a large, heavy skillet over medium-high heat. Add the cumin seeds and coriander seeds. Toast, stirring or shaking the pan, until they begin to be fragrant. Transfer to a spice mill and allow to cool for a few minutes. Then pulse to crush or coarsely grind. Set aside.

4. Return the skillet to medium heat and add 1 tablespoon of the oil. Add the onion and cook, stirring often, until tender, about 5 minutes. Add the garlic and a generous pinch of salt, stir together for about 30 seconds, and stir in the ground spices. Add the remaining 1 tablespoon oil and stir in the quinoa, chickpeas, and 3 tablespoons of the pomegranate seeds. Stir to heat through several minutes. Taste and adjust the salt. Transfer to a platter or wide bowl and decorate with the remaining pomegranate seeds. (Alternatively, you could mold the pilaf into ½-cup ramekins or timbales and unmold onto the plate, then decorate with pomegranate seeds.)

5. If desired, stir the pureed garlic into the drained yogurt. Serve the pilaf topped with the yogurt.

Per serving (based on 6 servings): 149 calories, 5 g protein, 20 g carbohydrates, 3 g fiber, 5 g fat, 1 g sat fat, 0 mg cholesterol, 73 mg sodium

ADVANCE PREPARATION: This can be made a day ahead and reheated.

Note: *Some people like to drizzle a few drops of lemon juice or pomegranate molasses over the pilaf.*

Royal Quinoa Salad with Tofu and Ginger Vinaigrette

Makes 6 servings

■ **VEGETARIAN** ■ VEGAN ■ **LOW-CALORIE** ■ **LOW-FAT**
■ **HIGH-PROTEIN** ■ GLUTEN-FREE ■ HIGH IN OMEGA-3S

Royal quinoa is a reddish, high-protein strain of quinoa grown only in one area of Bolivia. It's particularly nutty-tasting, especially if you toast it in the pan before cooking. This combination makes a high-protein vegetarian main dish.

For the salad:

1 cup royal quinoa, rinsed

½ –¾ teaspoon salt

½ pound tofu, sliced ½ inch thick or cubed

1 tablespoon canola oil

Soy sauce

6 ounces snow peas or sugar snap peas, or 2 broccoli crowns, steamed or blanched for 3 to 5 minutes

¼ cup chopped cilantro

¼ cup chopped or thinly sliced spring onions or scallions

For the dressing:

2 tablespoons fresh lime juice

2 tablespoons Asian sesame oil or walnut oil

2 tablespoons canola oil

2 tablespoons buttermilk

½ teaspoon soy sauce

1 teaspoon minced fresh ginger

1 small garlic clove, minced

Radicchio or lettuce leaves (optional)

1. To make the salad: Heat a heavy saucepan over medium-high heat. Add the rinsed quinoa. Stir until all the water has evaporated and the quinoa is beginning to smell toasty, about 5 minutes. Add 3 cups water and ½ to ¾ teaspoon salt (to taste), and bring to a boil. Reduce the heat, cover, and simmer for 15 minutes, or until the quinoa is tender and displays little white spirals. Drain through a sieve and return to the pan. Cover the pan with a clean kitchen towel, replace the lid, and allow to sit undisturbed for 10 minutes. Uncover and transfer the quinoa to a large bowl.

2. Pat the tofu dry with paper towels, pressing on it to extract excess water. Cut into ½-inch dice. Heat the oil in a heavy nonstick skillet over medium-high heat and add the tofu. Cook, stirring or shaking the pan, until the tofu is golden, about 5 minutes. Add soy sauce to taste and toss together. Remove from the heat and add to the bowl with the quinoa. Stir in the snow peas, cilantro, and spring onions.

3. To make the dressing: Whisk together the lime juice, ginger, garlic, soy sauce, sesame or walnut oil, canola oil, buttermilk, soy sauce, ginger, and garlic. Toss with the quinoa mixture. Line plates with radicchio or lettuce leaves, if desired. Fill the leaves with the salad, and serve.

Per serving: 279 calories, 11 g protein, 24 g carbohydrates, 4 g fiber, 17 g fat, 2 g sat fat, 0 mg cholesterol, 464 mg sodium

ADVANCE PREPARATION: You can prepare this salad hours ahead of serving.

Bulgur

Bulgur is a delicate, nutty-tasting grain made from durum wheat that has been precooked, dried, and coarsely ground. If you buy your bulgur in a Middle Eastern market, you'll notice that there are four grades: Fine bulgur (#1) is very fine. It is used in *kefteh* (patties made with ground meat or cooked vegetables and fine bulgur) and tabbouleh. Medium bulgur (#2) has a medium grain. I sometimes use it in bulgur patties, even though it isn't traditional, as well as in pilafs and salads. Coarse bulgur (#3 and #4) is good for pilafs, as plain bulgur served as a side dish, and in salads.

Because bulgur has been precooked, fine or medium bulgur can be reconstituted simply by covering with hot water. For 1 cup fine or medium bulgur, pour on 2 cups hot or boiling water, add salt to taste, and stir. Allow to sit for 20 to 25 minutes, or until most of the water is absorbed. Drain through a sieve and squeeze out the water.

For 1 cup coarse bulgur, bring 2 cups water in a saucepan to a boil. Add the bulgur and salt to taste, reduce the heat, cover, and simmer for 20 minutes, or until the water is absorbed. Remove from the heat and allow to sit undisturbed for 10 minutes. Reconstituted bulgur keeps well in the refrigerator for 3 to 4 days. It can also be frozen. Reheat in the oven at 325°F for 20 minutes, in a saucepan on top of the stove, or in the microwave.

Bulgur and Walnut Kefteh

Makes about 24/6 to 8 appetizer servings

■ **VEGETARIAN** ■ **VEGAN** ■ **LOW-CALORIE** ■ **LOW-FAT**
■ HIGH-PROTEIN ■ GLUTEN-FREE ■ HIGH IN OMEGA-3S

Kefteh (also known as kufteh and köfte) is usually made with a mixture of ground meat and bulgur, but there are vegetarian versions as well. The patties are a great destination for this grain. In this pungent version, the bulgur is combined with finely chopped walnuts, parsley, and fresh mint; the walnuts add pleasant crunchy texture and the herbs contribute wonderful flavor. They make a nice appetizer.

- ³⁄₄ cup fine bulgur
- 2 garlic cloves, halved
- Salt
- ¹⁄₂ cup walnuts, lightly toasted and finely chopped
- 2 tablespoons extra virgin olive oil
- ¹⁄₄ cup finely chopped flat-leaf parsley
- 2 tablespoons finely chopped fresh mint
- Ground black pepper
- ³⁄₄ teaspoon ground cinnamon
- 2 tablespoons fresh lemon juice
- Small romaine lettuce leaves (or larger ones, cut into 2-inch or 3-inch pieces)

1. Place the bulgur and ¹⁄₄ to ¹⁄₂ teaspoon salt (to taste) in a bowl. Mix together and pour on boiling water to cover by ¹⁄₂ inch. Let sit for 30 minutes to an hour, then drain through a sieve and press out excess water.

2. Mash the garlic and a generous pinch of salt to a paste with a mortar and pestle. Stir into the bulgur. Add the walnuts, oil, parsley, mint, black pepper, cinnamon, and 1 tablespoon plus 1 teaspoon of the lemon juice. Moisten your hands and knead the mixture for a couple of minutes, then allow to sit for 15 to 30 minutes.

3. With moistened hands, form the bulgur mixture into bite-size balls, and press an indentation into the middle of each ball. Place on a lettuce leaf, sprinkle with the remaining 2 teaspoons lemon juice, and serve. Guests can use the lettuce leaves as a sort of wrap for the kefteh.

Per serving (based on 6 servings): 172 calories, 4 g protein, 16 g carbohydrates, 4 g fiber, 11 g fat, 1 g sat fat, 0 mg cholesterol, 30 mg sodium

ADVANCE PREPARATION: You can make this a day ahead and keep it in the refrigerator.

Red Lentil and Bulgur Kibbeh

Makes about 30/6 to 8 appetizer servings

■ **VEGETARIAN** ■ **VEGAN** ■ **LOW-CALORIE** ■ **LOW-FAT**
■ HIGH-PROTEIN ■ GLUTEN-FREE ■ HIGH IN OMEGA-3S

There are several vegetarian versions of kibbeh in which the bulgur is mixed with a vegetable puree of some sort and formed into patties. In this popular rendition the bulgur is mixed with red lentils. I first came across the recipe on the back of a packet of red lentils that I bought in a Middle Eastern market (from which I adapted this recipe). Serve the kibbeh as an appetizer or a side dish.

½ cup red lentils, rinsed

Salt

½ cup fine or medium bulgur

3 tablespoons extra virgin olive oil

½ large or medium onion, finely minced

1 teaspoon cumin seeds, lightly toasted and ground

½ bunch flat-leaf parsley, finely chopped

¼– ½ teaspoon Aleppo pepper (optional)

Scallions, ends trimmed

Small romaine lettuce leaves

Lemon wedges

1. Combine the lentils and 2 cups water in a large saucepan. Bring to a boil. Skim off any foam, reduce the heat, add salt to taste, and simmer for 30 minutes, or until the lentils are soft and most but not all of the water is absorbed.

2. Place the bulgur in a bowl, mix with salt, and pour in the lentils with their liquid. Stir together, then cover and let sit for 30 minutes to an hour, until the bulgur is tender and has absorbed all the liquid.

3. Meanwhile, heat 2 tablespoons of the oil in a skillet over medium-low heat and add the onion. Cook gently, stirring often, for 10 to 15 minutes, or until golden and very tender. Add the cumin and stir for about 30 seconds. Remove from the heat and stir into the lentils and bulgur.

4. Moisten your hands and knead the mixture in the bowl for 3 to 5 minutes. Moisten your hands again when the mixture begins to stick. If the mixture seems very dry and crumbly, add 1 tablespoon of water. Stir in the remaining 1 tablespoon of oil and ¼ cup of the minced parsley. For spicier kibbeh, add the Aleppo pepper. Taste and adjust the seasoning with salt.

5. Moisten your hands and shape the mixture into walnut-size balls (about 1 inch). You'll have to moisten your hands again whenever the mixture begins to stick. Place on a platter and sprinkle with the remaining parsley. Garnish with the scallions, romaine, and lemon wedges, and serve.

Per serving (based on 6 servings): 168 calories, 6 g protein, 20 g carbohydrates, 5 g fiber, 8 g fat, 1 g sat fat, 0 mg cholesterol, 32 mg sodium

ADVANCE PREPARATION: You can make these a day ahead and keep them in the refrigerator. Serve chilled or at room temperature.

Bulgur Pilaf with Chickpeas and Herbs

Makes 4 to 6 servings

■ **VEGETARIAN** ■ **VEGAN** ■ **LOW-CALORIE*** ■ **LOW-FAT**
■ **HIGH-PROTEIN** ■ GLUTEN-FREE ■ HIGH IN OMEGA-3S

When I make this dish, I cook the chickpeas, then use the hot cooking liquid for reconstituting the bulgur. If you want to make a quicker version, you can use water to reconstitute the bulgur and make the dish using canned chickpeas. The pilaf is satisfying and high in protein. You could serve it at the center of your plate, accompanied by vegetables and/or a salad, or serve it as a side dish. It couldn't be a simpler dish to make.

> 1 cup dried chickpeas, soaked for 6 hours or overnight in 1 quart water
>
> Salt
>
> 1 cup coarse bulgur
>
> 2 tablespoons extra virgin olive oil
>
> 1 bunch scallions, finely chopped
>
> 2 large garlic cloves, minced
>
> ¼ cup finely chopped flat-leaf parsley, or a combination of parsley and dill
>
> 2 tablespoons finely chopped fresh mint
>
> Juice of 1 lemon
>
> Ground black pepper

*If served as a main dish

1. Drain the soaked chickpeas and place in a pot with 1 quart water. Bring to a boil, reduce the heat, and simmer for 1 hour. Add 1 teaspoon salt to taste and continue to simmer for 30 minutes to 1 hour, or until the chickpeas are tender.

2. Place the bulgur in a 2-quart bowl. Place a sieve over the bowl and drain the chickpeas so that the hot broth covers the bulgur. Set the chickpeas aside. Cover the bowl and allow the bulgur to sit until fluffy, 20 to 30 minutes. Drain over a sieve, and press on the bulgur with your hands to squeeze out excess liquid.

3. Heat 1 tablespoon of the oil in a large, heavy skillet over medium heat. Add the scallions. Cook, stirring, until tender, 2 to 3 minutes. Stir in the garlic and continue to cook until fragrant, 30 seconds to 1 minute. Stir in the bulgur and chickpeas. Add the herbs and the remaining 1 tablespoon of oil and toss together. Remove from the heat, add the lemon juice and black pepper. Taste and adjust the salt. Add more lemon juice if desired. Serve hot or room temperature.

Per serving (based on 4 servings): 360 calories, 14 g protein, 58 g carbohydrates, 15 g fiber, 10 g fat, 1 g sat fat, 0 mg cholesterol, 60 mg sodium

ADVANCE PREPARATION: You can make the pilaf hours ahead, but do not add the herbs. Reheat in a microwave or in a nonstick skillet over medium heat, then stir in the herbs and serve.

VARIATION: BARLEY PILAF WITH CHICKPEAS AND HERBS Substitute 1 cup barley, cooked following the

directions on page 180, for the bulgur. Drain the chickpeas at the end of Step 1, omit Step 2, and proceed with Step 3.

Bulgur and Winter Squash Kefteh

Makes 4 servings

■ **VEGETARIAN** ■ **VEGAN** ■ **LOW-CALORIE** ■ **LOW-FAT**
■ HIGH-PROTEIN ■ GLUTEN-FREE ■ HIGH IN OMEGA-3S

This mixture can be formed into patties, but it is just as wonderful and a lot easier to spread it in a baking dish and serve by the spoonful.

½ cup fine or medium (#1 or #2) bulgur

Salt

1 pound winter squash, peeled and cut in chunks

3 tablespoons extra virgin olive oil

½ medium onion, finely minced

1 teaspoon cumin seeds, lightly toasted and ground

¼ cup finely chopped flat-leaf parsley

2 tablespoons finely chopped fresh mint

Ground black pepper

Small romaine lettuce leaves, for garnish

1. Combine the bulgur with ¼ teaspoon salt in a bowl. Cover with hot water. Let sit for 30 minutes, until the bulgur is tender and has absorbed all of the liquid.

2. Meanwhile, steam the squash over 1 to 2 inches of boiling water for 15 to 20 minutes until thoroughly tender. Remove from the heat and allow to drain for 5 to 10 minutes, then mash with a fork and stir into the bulgur.

3. Heat 2 tablespoons of the olive oil over medium-low heat and add the onion. Cook gently for 10 to 15 minutes, until golden and very tender. Stir often. Add the cumin and a pinch of salt and stir together for about 30 seconds. Stir the onions and squash into the bulgur.

4. Knead the mixture in the bowl with the back of a spoon or with a pestle for a few minutes. Stir in the remaining 1 tablespoon of olive oil, the parsley, and the mint. Taste and adjust the salt. Season with black pepper. Spoon into a lightly oiled baking dish. Serve at room temperature, or heat through in a 325°F oven until warm.

Per serving: 207 calories, 4 g protein, 26 g carbohydrates, 6 g fiber, 11 g fat, 2 g sat fat, 0 mg cholesterol, 47 mg sodium

ADVANCE PREPARATION: You can make this a day ahead and keep in the refrigerator.

Wheat Berries and Farro

Wheat berries and farro are different strains of whole grain wheat (despite what some food writers have written about farro and spelt, they are the same strain of wheat). Whole wheat berries come from the same hard North American wheat that our flour is milled from. The grains are round, quite hard, and chewy when cooked. Farro or spelt (*épautre* in French), from a softer European wheat, has the same earthy taste, but the grains are slightly softer. They don't take quite as long to cook, and they are more suitable to risotto-type dishes (*farrotos*), though they will not release starch the way short-grain Italian rice does (farottos aren't creamy like risottos). If either grain is more than a year old, they will be even harder and take a longer time to cook. I love farro, but it is often expensive and less readily available, so I often use wheat berries instead, especially for salads and pilafs. I cook both types of wheat berries in abundant water, after soaking for 1 hour or longer. When the grains have softened, I drain off the excess water. Wheat berries and farro are an excellent source of manganese and a good source of niacin, copper, phosphorus, protein, and fiber.

Basic Cooked Wheat Berries or Farro

Makes 3 cups/4 to 6 servings

■ **VEGETARIAN*** ■ **VEGAN*** ■ **LOW-CALORIE** ■ **LOW-FAT**
■ HIGH-PROTEIN ■ GLUTEN-FREE ■ HIGH IN OMEGA-3S

1 cup wheat berries or farro

1 quart chicken stock, Vegetable Stock (page 67), or water

1 teaspoon salt

*If made with Vegetable Stock or water

Combine the wheat berries or farro and stock or water in a saucepan and soak for 1 hour. Add the salt and bring to a boil. Reduce the heat, cover, and simmer for 45 minutes to 1 hour, or until the grains are tender and just beginning to splay. Turn off the heat and allow the wheat berries to sit in the hot water for 15 minutes. Drain.

Per serving (based on 4 servings): 246 calories, 12 g protein, 42 g carbohydrates, 6 g fiber, 3 g fat, 1 g sat fat, 7 mg cholesterol, 634 mg sodium

ADVANCE PREPARATION: Cooked wheat berries and farro keep well in the refrigerator for 3 to 4 days and can be frozen. Reheat in the oven at 325°F for 20 minutes, in a pan on top of the stove, or in the microwave.

Farro Salad with Beets, Beet Greens, and Feta

Makes 8 servings

■ **VEGETARIAN** ■ **VEGAN*** ■ **LOW-CALORIE**** ☐ LOW-FAT
☐ HIGH-PROTEIN ☐ GLUTEN-FREE ■ **HIGH IN OMEGA-3S**

Farro is a sweet, nutty-tasting grain that's sturdy enough to stand up to other lusty ingredients like beet greens. The farro contrasts nicely with salty feta or goat cheese. The grain will absorb the red from red beets, so this salad is sort of pink. Make sure to cook the farro until tender, or the salad will be too chewy.

2 medium or 3 small beets (any color), with greens, the beets roasted (page 125), peeled, and diced, the greens stemmed and washed in 2 changes of water

1 cup farro, soaked for 1 hour in water to cover, and drained

Salt

2 tablespoons sherry vinegar

1 teaspoon balsamic vinegar

1 small garlic clove, minced or pureed in a mortar and pestle

1 teaspoon Dijon mustard

½ cup extra virgin olive oil (may substitute 1–2 tablespoons walnut oil for 1–2 tablespoons olive oil)

½ cup (2 ounces) crumbled feta or goat cheese, plus additional for garnish, optional

½ cup broken walnut pieces

¼ cup chopped fresh herbs, such as flat-leaf parsley, tarragon, marjoram, chives, or mint

*If you omit the cheese
**If served as a main dish

1. Bring 2 quarts water to a boil in a medium saucepan over high heat. Fill a bowl with ice water. When the water comes to a boil, add salt to taste and the beet greens. Blanch for 2 minutes, then with a slotted spoon, scoop out the greens and transfer to the ice water. Allow to cool for a few minutes, then squeeze out excess water. Chop coarsely and set aside.

2. Return the water to a boil and add the farro. Reduce the heat, cover, and simmer for 45 minutes to 1 hour, stirring occasionally, until the farro is tender. Remove from the heat and allow the grains to swell in the cooking water for about 15 minutes, then drain.

3. While the farro is cooking, make the vinaigrette. Whisk together the sherry and balsamic vinegars, salt, garlic, and mustard. Whisk in the oil. Add to the drained farro. Add the beets, along with the beet greens, feta or goat cheese, walnuts, and herbs. Toss together and serve warm or at room temperature, with a little more cheese sprinkled over the top, if desired.

> **Per serving:** 291 calories, 6 g protein, 20 g carbohydrates, 3 g fiber, 21 g fat, 4 g sat fat, 8 mg cholesterol, 170 mg sodium

ADVANCE PREPARATION: The farro, roasted beets, and cooked beet greens will keep for 3 to 4 days in the refrigerator. You can assemble this salad hours or even a day ahead; it will become redder with time.

Wheat Berry and Tomato Salad

Makes 6 servings

■ **VEGETARIAN** ■ VEGAN ■ **LOW-CALORIE** ■ LOW-FAT
■ HIGH-PROTEIN ■ GLUTEN-FREE ■ HIGH IN OMEGA-3S

Whole wheat berries lend themselves to both summer and winter dishes. Much of the flavor in this salad comes from the tangy juice of chopped tomatoes, which is almost like a marinade for the chewy wheat. The salad is all about texture, with crunchy celery and/or cucumber, and soft feta cheese contrasting with the wheat.

1 cup wheat berries or farro

Salt

2 ripe medium tomatoes (½ to ¾ pound)

Ground black pepper

1 tablespoon sherry vinegar

1 teaspoon balsamic vinegar

1 cup diced celery or cucumber, or a combination

3 tablespoons fresh lemon juice

3 tablespoons extra virgin olive oil

½ cup (2 ounces) crumbled feta cheese

1 to 2 tablespoons chopped fresh mint

3 tablespoons chopped flat-leaf parsley

1. Combine the wheat berries or farro and 1 quart water in a large saucepan and soak for at least 1 hour. Add ½ to ¾ teaspoon salt and bring to a boil over high heat. Reduce the heat, cover, and simmer for 45 minutes to 1 hour, or until the grains are tender. Turn off the heat and allow the wheat berries to sit in the hot water for 15 minutes. Drain.

2. While the wheat berries are cooking, dice the tomatoes and place in a bowl (you should have 1½ to 2 cups). Sprinkle with salt and black pepper and add the sherry and balsamic vinegars. Toss together and let sit for 1 hour.

3. After you drain the wheat berries, toss with the tomatoes and juices. If possible, allow to marinate for 1 hour. Add the celery or cucumber, lemon juice, oil, feta, mint, and parsley and toss. Refrigerate until ready to serve, or serve at once.

Per serving: 210 calories, 6 g protein, 25 g carbohydrates, 5 g fiber, 10 g fat, 3 g sat fat, 11 mg cholesterol, 181 mg sodium

ADVANCE PREPARATION: This salad keeps well for several hours in the refrigerator.

Polenta

For those who miss mashed potatoes but have long ago forsworn the carbohydrates and fats that come with them (if you've enjoyed them in a restaurant, or at home for that matter, it's because they're packed with butter and cream); and for those who cannot eat wheat, and so have said good-bye to pasta, polenta may be your magic bullet. This delicious porridge—for that is what polenta is, made by cooking cornmeal in salted water until the mixture is stiff—is as comforting as mashed potatoes.

An excellent source of iron, magnesium, phosphorus, zinc, and vitamin B_6, polenta comes in different grinds. It can be coarsely ground or finely ground, and this will affect the softness of the finished dish. The more finely ground, the softer and creamier your polenta will be. I've used plain stone-ground cornmeal, which is more floury than traditional polenta, and I like the soft, creamy version that it yields, which is like loose mashed potatoes.

Easy Oven-Baked Polenta

Makes 4 servings

■ **VEGETARIAN** ■ **VEGAN*** ■ **LOW-CALORIE** ■ **LOW-FAT**
■ HIGH-PROTEIN ■ **GLUTEN-FREE** ■ HIGH IN OMEGA-3S

The traditional way to make polenta is on top of the stove. You slowly drizzle the cornmeal into salted boiling water, stirring all the while, and continue to stir—some say continually but others are less rigid about it—until you have a smooth, stiff mixture that your spoon will stand up in. I use a less labor-intensive method. I combine the cornmeal and the liquid, put it in the oven and forget about it for 50 minutes. Then I stir in a tablespoon of butter and put it back in the oven for 10 to 20 minutes, depending on how thick I want it, and that's it. The method comes from the package of my favorite brand of polenta, Golden Pheasant.

1 cup polenta

1 teaspoon salt

1 tablespoon unsalted butter or olive oil

*If you substitute olive oil for the butter

1. Preheat the oven to 350° F. Combine the polenta, salt, and 1 quart water in a 2-quart baking dish. Stir together and place in the oven. Bake for 50 minutes. Remove from the oven and stir in the butter, using a fork or a spatula to stir the polenta well. Return to the oven for 10 minutes. Remove from the oven and stir again. Carefully taste the polenta. If the grains are not completely soft, return to the oven for 10 minutes.

2. Serve right away for soft polenta, or let sit for 5 minutes for a stiffer polenta. Spoon onto a plate, make a depression in the middle, and serve with the topping of your choice, or serve plain as a side dish.

3. Alternatively, allow to cool and stiffen in the baking dish—or scrape into a lightly oiled or buttered bread pan, cover, and chill in the refrigerator—for grilling or use in another recipe.

Per serving: 155 calories, 3 g protein, 27 g carbohydrates, 2 g fiber, 3 g fat, 2 g sat fat, 8 mg cholesterol, 583 mg sodium

ADVANCE PREPARATION: If you are serving the polenta hot with a topping, it's best to serve it when it comes out of the oven, though it can sit for 5 minutes.

VARIATION: POLENTA WITH PARMESAN When you remove the polenta from the oven, stir in $1/3$ cup freshly grated Parmesan. Serve at once. I like to grind a little black pepper over the top.

Microwave Polenta

Makes 3 servings

■ **VEGETARIAN** ■ **VEGAN*** ■ **LOW-CALORIE** ■ **LOW-FAT**
■ HIGH-PROTEIN ■ GLUTEN-FREE ■ HIGH IN OMEGA-3S

If you want polenta in a hurry—which you might if your kids like polenta as much as my son does—you can prepare it in the microwave. Just be sure to use a large enough bowl, and be very careful when handling the bowl. Allow the steam to escape before you stir, as the mixture will be extremely hot.

$3/4$ cup polenta

$3/4$ teaspoon salt

1 tablespoon unsalted butter or olive oil

*If you omit unsalted butter

Combine the polenta, salt, and 3 cups water in a $2^1/_2$- to 3-quart microwaveable bowl and stir together. Cover the bowl with a plate, and place in the microwave. Microwave on high for 8 minutes. Remove from the microwave carefully, wearing oven mitts as the bowl will be quite hot. Carefully remove the plate and allow the steam to escape. Stir in the butter and mix well with a fork. Cover the bowl again with the plate and return to the microwave. Microwave on high for 3 minutes. Again, remove from the microwave carefully, and allow the steam to escape. Stir the polenta, cover, and return to the microwave for

3 more minutes. Carefully remove from the microwave and uncover, stir, and serve. Or pour into a lightly buttered bread pan and allow to cool, then slice and grill or sear in a lightly oiled pan.

Per serving: 207 calories, 5 g protein, 31 g carbohydrates, 3 g fiber, 7 g fat, 3 g sat fat, 14 mg cholesterol, 949 mg sodium

Grilled Polenta

Makes 6 to 8 servings

■ **VEGETARIAN** ■ **VEGAN*** ■ **LOW-CALORIE** ■ **LOW-FAT**
■ HIGH-PROTEIN ■ **GLUTEN-FREE** ■ HIGH IN OMEGA-3S

Grilled polenta makes a great side dish, and it's a perfect solution for vegetarians at a barbecue. The squares of polenta are best if they're thick, so the basic polenta recipe is increased by half, and the polenta is cooked for a longer time.

$1^1/_2$ cups polenta

$1^1/_2$ teaspoons salt

$1^1/_2$ tablespoons unsalted butter or olive oil

Extra virgin olive oil

*If you omit unsalted butter

1. Preheat the oven to 350°F. Combine the polenta, salt, and $1^1/_2$ quarts water in a 2-quart baking dish and stir together. Place the baking dish on top of a baking sheet (so that if the water sloshes when you put it in the oven it will just go onto the sheet) and place in the oven. Bake for 1 hour. Remove from the oven, stir in the butter, and return to the oven for 20 minutes. Remove from the oven and stir again. Return to the oven for 10 to 20 minutes, or until stiff. Remove from the oven and allow to cool in the pan, or immediately scrape the polenta into a lightly oiled bread pan (for bread pan-size slices). Refrigerate for 1 hour or more.

2. Preheat a grill to medium or heat an electric griddle on medium. Cut the polenta into squares, or slice the polenta if you have chilled it in a loaf pan, and brush both sides with some olive oil. Place on the grill or griddle. When grill marks appear or when nicely browned, usually 2 to 3 minutes, turn and brown on the other side. Serve hot.

Per serving (based on 6 servings): 162 calories, 3 g protein, 27 g carbohydrates, 2 g fiber, 4 g fat, 2 g sat fat, 8 mg cholesterol, 582 mg sodium

ADVANCE PREPARATION: The cooked polenta will keep for 3 to 4 days in the refrigerator.

VARIATION: PAN-SEARED POLENTA SQUARES You don't get the attractive grill marks or the charcoal flavor here, but this is another nice way to serve polenta. Heat 1 tablespoon olive oil in a heavy nonstick skillet over medium-high heat, and sear the polenta squares on both sides until lightly colored. The surface should be slightly crisp.

Polenta with Parmesan and Tomato Sauce

Makes 4 servings

■ **VEGETARIAN** ■ VEGAN ■ **LOW-CALORIE** ■ LOW-FAT
■ HIGH-PROTEIN ■ **GLUTEN-FREE** ■ HIGH IN OMEGA-3S

This is my favorite way to serve polenta, and it's the simplest too. My son loves it, and says "it's like pasta but it isn't," because of the tomato sauce and Parmesan.

1 cup polenta

1 teaspoon salt

1 tablespoon unsalted butter

⅓ cup grated Parmesan plus additional for sprinkling

1½ cups Summer Tomato Sauce (page 19) or Basic Pantry Marinara Sauce (page 20)

1. Preheat the oven to 350° F. Combine the polenta, salt, and 1 quart water in a 2-quart baking dish. Stir together and place in the oven. Bake for 50 minutes. Remove from the oven, stir in the butter, and return to the oven for 10 minutes. Remove from the oven and stir. Return to the oven for 10 minutes. Meanwhile, warm the tomato sauce in a saucepan.

2. When the polenta is done, remove from the oven and stir in the Parmesan, if using. Spoon onto plates, make a depression in the middle with the back of a spoon, and spoon ¼ to ⅓ cup of the tomato sauce into the depression. Sprinkle with additional Parmesan and serve.

Note: *You can also cook the polenta in the microwave (page 199).*

Per serving: 256 calories, 7 g protein, 39 g carbohydrates, 5 g fiber, 9 g fat, 3 g sat fat, 11 mg cholesterol, 1,002 mg sodium

ADVANCE PREPARATION: Both the cooked polenta and the tomato sauce will keep for 3 to 4 days in the refrigerator. The gratin can be assembled a day ahead and kept in the refrigerator.

VARIATION: POLENTA AND TOMATO SAUCE GRATIN
This is how to make this dish with leftover or chilled polenta. Preheat the oven to 375°F. Oil a 2-quart gratin dish. Cut the polenta into squares or rectangles and arrange the polenta in the dish, overlapping the pieces slightly. Spread the tomato sauce over the polenta slices and sprinkle on the additional Parmesan. Drizzle a little olive oil over the top. Bake for 15 to 20 minutes, until sizzling. Remove from the heat and serve.

Polenta with Mushrooms, Favas, and Tomatoes

Makes 4 to 6 servings

■ **VEGETARIAN** ■ VEGAN ■ **LOW-CALORIE** ■ LOW-FAT
■ HIGH-PROTEIN ■ **GLUTEN-FREE** ■ HIGH IN OMEGA-3S

I can never resist adding fresh fava beans to a dish during their short season. If you can't find fresh fava beans or just don't feel like taking the time to skin them, you could substitute fresh or frozen peas or edamame, or you can leave them out; the mushroom and tomato mixture is excellent on its own.

Easy Oven-Baked Polenta (page 198)

1 pound fava beans, shelled

1 tablespoon extra virgin olive oil

2–4 garlic cloves, or fresh green garlic, thinly sliced

8 ounces mushrooms, either regular or wild, or a combination, cleaned, trimmed, and cut or torn into thick slices

1 teaspoon fresh thyme leaves

Salt

¼ cup dry white or red wine

1 can (14 ounces) diced tomatoes, with juice

Ground black pepper

Slivered fresh basil

¼ cup (1 ounce) grated Parmesan

1. Make the polenta as directed and while it is baking, make the topping.

2. Bring a medium pot of water to a boil. Drop the fava beans into the water and boil small favas for 1 minute, large favas for 2, then transfer at once to a bowl of ice water. Drain. Remove the skins, using your thumbnail to open up the skin at the spot where the bean attached to the pod, then gently squeezing out the bean.

3. Heat the oil in a large, heavy skillet over medium heat. Add the garlic and stir until fragrant, about 30 seconds. Stir in the mushrooms, thyme, and ½ teaspoon salt. Cook, stirring often, until the mushrooms are moist and beginning to soften, about 5 minutes. Add the wine, increase the heat to high, and cook, stirring, until the liquid in the pan has reduced and glazed the mushrooms. Stir in the tomatoes, add salt and black pepper to taste, and bring to a simmer. Cook, uncovered, stirring often, until the tomatoes have cooked down (but there's still some liquid in the pan) and the mixture is fragrant, about 10 minutes. Add the fava beans and simmer for 5 to 10 minutes. Taste, adjust the seasonings, and remove from the heat.

4. When the polenta is ready, cut it into squares or rectangles and place on plates. Top with the fava bean mixture. Sprinkle with the basil and Parmesan. Serve at once.

Note: *You can also cook the polenta in the microwave (page 199).*

Per serving (based on 4 servings): 649 calories, 38 g protein, 97 g carbohydrates, 26 g fiber, 12 g fat, 4 g sat fat, 12 mg cholesterol, 1,211 mg sodium

ADVANCE PREPARATION: Both the cooked polenta and the cooked mushrooms and tomatoes will keep for 3 to 4 days in the refrigerator. The gratin can be assembled a day ahead and kept in the refrigerator.

VARIATION: To make this dish with chilled polenta: Either grill or sear the polenta (page 199) and serve the mushroom mixture on the side, or make a gratin.

VARIATION: POLENTA GRATIN WITH MUSHROOMS AND TOMATOES Preheat the oven to 375°F. Oil a 2-quart gratin dish and arrange the cut polenta in the dish, overlapping the pieces slightly. Top with the mushrooms and tomatoes. Sprinkle the Parmesan over the top and place in the oven for 15 to 20 minutes, or until the mixture is bubbling and the cheese has melted.

Couscous

Couscous is a staple that I like to keep on hand in my pantry. It's convenient and goes well with everything. Some people consider this grain product a type of pasta, but it really isn't, although most couscous is made from the same type of durum wheat semolina that is used for pasta. Couscous is made from crushed, not ground semolina, thus is less refined than pasta. It should never be boiled (pay no attention to the instructions on most boxes), just reconstituted and steamed. The steaming step is important to complete the cooking of the couscous. Steamed couscous should be fluffy and soft.

I'm now seeing whole wheat couscous side by side with regular couscous on grocery store shelves. This is good news, as whole wheat couscous has a much higher fiber content, as well as very good amounts of manganese, tryptophan, and magnesium. You will find more couscous recipes in the beans section starting on page 274 and Fish Couscous on page 319.

Couscous is a great vehicle for all sorts of seasonal vegetables and beans. In Northern Africa it's served with brothy stews called tagines. I particularly like spicy, hearty Tunisian-style tagines. In Tunisia a small amount of mutton or lamb might be added for flavor, but I find the spicing and the aromatics sufficiently robust, and legumes supply plenty of protein, which is complemented by the protein in the couscous. These hearty dishes make great dinner party fare, especially if there are vegetarians or vegans at your table.

FOR MORE ARTICHOKE RECIPES SEE:

Couscous with Beans and Cauliflower
(page 287)

Couscous with Black-Eyed Peas and Greens
(page 289)

Couscous with Winter Vegetables and Beans
(page 276)

Fish Couscous (page 319)

Morning Couscous with Oranges and Dates (page 10)

Reconstituted, Steamed Couscous

Makes 6 generous servings

■ VEGETARIAN ■ **VEGAN*** ■ LOW-CALORIE ■ **LOW-FAT**
■ HIGH-PROTEIN ■ GLUTEN-FREE ■ HIGH IN OMEGA-3S

2 cups couscous

1 teaspoon salt

1. Place the couscous and salt in a bowl and mix together. If serving with a stew, combine $\frac{1}{2}$ to 1 cup of the broth from the stew with enough warm water to cover the couscous by about $\frac{1}{2}$ inch. Let sit for 20 minutes, or until the water is absorbed. Stir every 5 minutes with a wooden spoon or rub the couscous between your moistened thumbs and fingers, to prevent the couscous from clumping. The couscous will now be fairly soft. Fluff it with a fork

or with your hands. Add 1 to 2 tablespoons of olive oil and rub the couscous between your fingers to distribute the oil.

2. If serving with a stew, bring the stew to a simmer. Line a colander, sieve, or the top part of a couscousier (a special pot for making couscous) with a single layer of cheesecloth and place the couscous in it. Set it over the stew, making sure that the bottom of the colander or sieve does not touch the liquid (remove some of the liquid if it does). If your sieve or colander does not fit snugly on top of the pot and there is a space between the rim of the pot and the rim of the col-

ander or sieve, fill the space by wrapping with a towel so that steam doesn't escape. Steam for 20 to 30 minutes. The couscous should be fluffy, the grains dry and separate, not at all al dente, and not at all mushy. If you are not serving the couscous with a stew, steam above a couple of inches of boiling water.

OTHER STEAMING METHODS:

To steam in the oven, place the reconstituted couscous in a lightly oiled baking dish, cover tightly with foil, and place in a 350°F oven for 30 minutes. To steam in a microwave, transfer to a microwaveable

bowl, cover tightly with a plate, and microwave for 2 minutes. Let sit for 1 minute, then carefully remove the plate and fluff with a fork. For an even fluffier couscous, repeat one more time.

Per serving: 217 calories, 7 g protein, 45 g carbohydrates, 3 g fiber, 0 g fat, 0 g sat fat, 0 mg cholesterol, 393 mg sodium

ADVANCE PREPARATION: The couscous can be reconstituted up to a day ahead, then steamed shortly before serving.

Chapter 8
PASTA AND RISOTTO

The pasta dishes that I publish in my column are among the most popular, despite the fact that there are still those who shun carbohydrates, and an increasing number of people, or so it seems, have a genuine intolerance for wheat. But I will always be a big fan of pasta. It can be a vehicle for whatever vibrant vegetables the market has to offer, it's easy to prepare, and everybody in the family loves it. As people used to say about potatoes when I was a child—"It's not the potato, it's what you put on it," so it goes for pasta.

In my house, pasta is the fall-back dinner that I can make any time. I freeze the tomato sauce I make from my garden tomatoes during the summer and thaw it as needed; and when I run out of that I make sauce with canned tomatoes. In the summer I don't even bother to cook my tomatoes; I just chop them up, season them with garlic, salt, olive oil, and basil, and toss this "salsa cruda" with hot pasta. I might also include other vegetables like arugula (page 209) or green beans in the mix, or pump up the protein by adding a can of chickpeas (page 210). Or I may not accompany my pasta with any tomato sauce at all; it isn't the only option. Greens, winter squash, mushrooms, and spring vegetables like asparagus go hand in hand with pasta, no sauce required.

On Italian menus, risottos accompany pastas and soups in the "primi" or first-course section. On my table they're the main event. Risotto is my dinner party go-to dish, especially when the dinner is an impromptu one. I can always rely on this dish to impress guests and satisfy my family. So I make sure to keep chicken or vegetable stock on hand in my freezer, and I keep my pantry stocked with Arborio or Carnaroli rice, the starchy short-grain Italian rice that is used for risotto.

The vegetables that I stir into a risotto define the dish, the way pasta is defined by its sauce or vegetable accompaniment. I don't hesitate to impulse-buy at the farmers' market because I can always use any surplus in a risotto. If the fava beans and asparagus look wonderful, for example, I'll buy a couple of pounds and know that if I don't use them for anything else, that's where they'll end up. Even simple vegetables like carrots and leeks seem downright elegant when showcased in a creamy risotto (page 228).

These risottos taste rich, but that has nothing to do with butter or cream. It's the starch in the rice that gets released into the broth as you stir it during its slow simmer that makes the dish seem creamy. Adding lots of butter at the end, the way chefs do in restaurants, is overkill. A last ladleful of well-seasoned stock and an ounce or two of grated Parmesan are all you need to enrich a properly made risotto.

Gluten-Free Pasta

If you cannot tolerate gluten, you may have said good-bye to pasta a long time ago. If you miss it terribly, try some of the gluten-free pastas that are currently on the market. The main trick when working with gluten-free pasta is to follow the cooking directions to the letter. If you cook them for too long, they fall apart; not long enough and they're rubbery.

Here are some of the brands that I've had success with:

Andean Dream Quinoa Pasta: Available at Whole Foods, this is made from a mixture of organic rice flour and organic quinoa flour from royal quinoa, a strain of quinoa grown in Bolivia that is exceptionally high in protein. The spaghetti takes a good 15 minutes to cook, but the macaroni only takes 6 to 7 minutes and it makes a good choice in dishes like pasta e fagiole (page 218), because it won't become soggy.

Brown Rice Pasta: I use the Trader Joe's brand but have found most other brands to be similar. The brown rice fusilli takes about 9 min-

utes to cook and resembles regular pasta in mouth feel and flavor.

Papadini Pasta: Developed by an organization called EATIT WORLD (**E**cological **A**pplications of **T**echnology for **I**nternational **T**rade) and available online from eatitworld.com, this pasta is made from flours ground from legumes such as green lentils and mung beans. The fettuccine-like noodles cook in 2 minutes and have a vegetable flavor that lends itself to Malaysian noodle dishes and goes well with tomato sauce (pages 19 and 21).

Fusilli or Orecchiette with Cherry Tomatoes and Arugula

Makes 4 servings

■ **VEGETARIAN** ■ VEGAN ■ **LOW-CALORIE** ■ **LOW-FAT**
■ HIGH-PROTEIN ■ GLUTEN-FREE ■ HIGH IN OMEGA-3S

I think this recipe has more fans than any other recipe I've written for my column. It's based on a popular pasta from the southern Italian region of Apulia. The arugula contributes a wonderful peppery/herbal flavor (all the more if you can find pungent wild arugula) and all those nutrients associated with leafy greens (folate, iron, vitamins A and K, beta-carotene, manganese, calcium).

1 pint cherry tomatoes, quartered

1 garlic clove, minced

Salt (I like to use French coarse sea salt
    or fleur de sel for this)

1 teaspoon balsamic vinegar (optional)

1 cup chopped fresh arugula

1 tablespoon slivered or chopped fresh basil

2 tablespoons extra virgin olive oil

¾ pound fusilli or orecchiette

¼ cup (1 ounce) grated ricotta salata or Parmesan

1. Combine the cherry tomatoes, garlic, salt, balsamic vinegar, arugula, basil, and oil in a wide bowl. Let sit for 15 to 30 minutes (or longer). Taste and adjust the seasonings.

A Generous Amount of Salt

You can skip this if you don't eat salt. I do eat salt, and although I'm not one to overdo it, I do feel that it's important to season food, and it's especially important to add enough salt to the cooking water when you're cooking pasta. What do I mean when I say "salt generously" or "add a generous amount of salt" to the boiling water in which you are going to cook the pasta (or blanch vegetables)? The actual amount depends on the size of your pot. But the water should taste like the ocean. The cooked noodles will be seasoned with the salt in the cooking water, but they will not absorb all of it; you'll only be consuming a fraction of what you added to the water (if you don't believe me, taste the water after you cook the pasta; it will still taste salty). Likewise, when you blanch vegetables in salted water, the salt seasons the vegetables but they don't absorb all the salt. When I cook pasta in an 8-quart pasta pot, I usually add a rounded tablespoon or two of salt. But the best way to gauge the amount is to add salt, then taste the water.

2. Meanwhile, bring a large pot of water to a rolling boil over high heat. Salt generously and add the pasta. Cook al dente, until the pasta is firm to the bite, following the timing directions on the package but checking 1 to 2 minutes before the suggested cooking time. Drain, toss with the tomato and arugula mixture, sprinkle on the cheese, and serve.

Per serving: 413 calories, 14 g protein, 66 g carbohydrates, 4 g fiber, 11 g fat, 2 g sat fat, 4 mg cholesterol, 118 mg sodium

ADVANCE PREPARATION: You can make the sauce a few hours before you cook the pasta.

Summer Pasta with Tomatoes and Chickpeas

Makes 4 servings

■ **VEGETARIAN** ■ VEGAN ■ **LOW-CALORIE** ■ **LOW-FAT**
■ **HIGH-PROTEIN** ■ GLUTEN-FREE ■ HIGH IN OMEGA-3S

In the summer, I serve most of my pasta dishes with uncooked tomato sauces. I make a one-dish meal by adding fresh in-season vegetables or a can of chickpeas to the mix. If you prefer a cooked tomato sauce, make the dish with Summer Tomato Sauce (page 19) or Basic Pantry Marinara Sauce (page 20).

   1 pound ripe tomatoes, peeled if desired and finely chopped

   1 garlic clove, minced

   Salt and ground black pepper

   1 teaspoon balsamic vinegar (optional)

   1 tablespoon slivered or chopped fresh basil

   1 tablespoon extra virgin olive oil

   1 can (15 ounces) chickpeas, rinsed and drained

   ¾ pound fusilli or farfalle

   ¼ cup (1 ounce) crumbled feta cheese or grated Parmesan

1. Combine the tomatoes, garlic, salt, black pepper, vinegar, basil, and oil in a wide bowl. Let sit for 15 to 30 minutes (or longer). Stir in the chickpeas. Taste and adjust the seasonings.

2. Meanwhile, bring a large pot of water to a rolling boil over high heat. Salt generously and add the pasta. Cook al dente, until the pasta is firm to the bite, following the directions on the package but checking 1 to 2 minutes before the suggested cooking time. Drain, toss with the tomatoes and chickpeas, sprinkle on the cheese, and serve.

VARIATION: Add ¼ to ½ pound broccoli florets or green beans. Before adding the pasta to the boiling water, blanch the broccoli for 3 minutes, green beans for 4 to 5 minutes. Transfer to a bowl of ice water, then drain. Return the water to a boil and proceed with the recipe. Toss the vegetables with the pasta along with the tomatoes and chickpeas.

Per serving: 442 calories, 16 g protein, 78 g carbohydrates, 7 g fiber, 8 g fat, 2 g sat fat, 6 mg cholesterol, 205 mg sodium

ADVANCE PREPARATION: You can make the sauce a few hours before you cook the pasta.

Pasta with Tuna and Olives

Makes 4 servings

■ VEGETARIAN ■ VEGAN ■ LOW-CALORIE ■ **LOW-FAT**
■ HIGH-PROTEIN ■ GLUTEN-FREE ■ **HIGH IN OMEGA-3S**

If you want to make a complete meal of this, add a green vegetable to the mix (see the variation in the preceding recipe). I use fusilli because I like the way the tuna gets lodged in the twists of the corkscrews, but other types of pasta, such as penne, farfalle, or spaghetti, work well too.

1 can (5 ounces) water-packed light (not albacore) tuna, drained (see sidebar, page 54)

2 tablespoons extra virgin olive oil

1 garlic clove, minced

2 tablespoons chopped flat-leaf parsley or slivered fresh basil

1 cup Summer Tomato Sauce (page 19) or Basic Pantry Marinara Sauce (page 20)

Salt and ground black pepper

$1/4$–$1/2$ teaspoon red-pepper flakes

$1/2$ cup pitted imported black olives, such as kalamatas, halved or quartered lengthwise

$3/4$ pound fusilli, penne, farfalle, or spaghetti

Parmesan shavings (optional)

1. Bring a large pot of water to a rolling boil over high heat. Break up the tuna and mix with the oil, garlic, and parsley in a large pasta bowl.

2. Heat the tomato sauce in a small saucepan and add salt and black pepper to taste, the red-pepper flakes, and the olives.

3. When the water for the pasta comes to a boil, salt generously and add the pasta. Cook al dente, until firm to the bite, following the timing directions on the package but checking 1 to 2 minutes before the suggested cooking time. Measure out $1/2$ cup of the cooking water. Mix $1/4$ cup with the tuna and set the remaining $1/4$ cup aside.

4. When the pasta is al dente, drain and transfer to the bowl with the tuna. Add the tomato sauce with the olives and toss everything together. Add some of the reserved cooking water if the mixture seems dry, and serve. Pass the Parmesan at the table.

Per serving: 487 calories, 21 g protein, 70 g carbohydrates, 5 g fiber, 14 g fat, 2 g sat fat, 10 mg cholesterol, 420 mg sodium

ADVANCE PREPARATION: The recipe can be prepared through Step 2 several hours before you cook the pasta. The tomato sauce will keep for 3 to 4 days in the refrigerator. It freezes well.

Pasta with Dried Mushrooms and Tomato Sauce

Makes 4 servings

■ **VEGETARIAN** ■ **VEGAN*** ■ LOW-CALORIE ■ **LOW-FAT**
■ HIGH-PROTEIN ■ GLUTEN-FREE ■ HIGH IN OMEGA-3S

Whenever I want to add a meaty dimension to a dish, I consider mushrooms. Fresh mushrooms have a texture and a savory quality that we associate with meat, a flavor dimension known to some cooks as umami. Dried mushrooms are more concentrated and add a bolder, more complex dimension to the flavor of any dish, even this simple vegetarian pasta sauce.

Porcinis, like other mushrooms, are an excellent source of riboflavin and niacin, and a good source of selenium and potassium. They also contain a powerful antioxidant called L-ergothioneine.

1 ounce (about 1 cup) dried porcini mushrooms

1 tablespoon extra virgin olive oil

¼ cup finely chopped onion or shallot

Salt

2-3 garlic cloves, minced

1 can (28 ounces) diced tomatoes, coarsely pureed
    with juice in a food processor

1 teaspoon fresh thyme leaves, chopped,
    or ½ teaspoon dried thyme

Ground black pepper

¾ pound fusilli or other pasta of your choice

Grated Parmesan for serving (optional)

*If you omit the Parmesan

1. Place the mushrooms in a heatproof bowl or a glass measuring cup and cover with 2 cups hot or boiling water. Soak for 15 to 30 minutes, until thoroughly soft. Line a sieve with cheesecloth and set it over a bowl. Drain the mushrooms and squeeze them over the sieve, then rinse in several changes of water and chop coarsely. Measure out ½ cup of the mushroom soaking liquid and set aside. Reserve the rest of the soaking liquid.

2. Bring a large pot of water to a rolling boil over high heat. Heat the olive oil in a wide, heavy non-stick skillet over medium heat. Add the onion or shallot. Cook, stirring, until tender, 3 to 5 minutes. Add a generous pinch of salt and the garlic and stir together until fragrant, 30 seconds to 1 minute. Add the mushrooms and stir together for 1 to 2 minutes, or until fragrant and coated with oil. Add the tomatoes, the reserved ½ cup soaking liquid, the thyme, and salt (about ½ teaspoon). Stir and increase the heat. When the tomatoes begin to bubble, reduce the heat to medium and cook, stirring often, until thick and fragrant, 15 to 20 minutes. Add black pepper, taste, and adjust the seasonings. Keep warm.

3. When the pasta water comes to a boil, salt generously and add the pasta. Cook al dente, until the pasta is firm to the bite, following the timing directions on the package but checking 1 to 2 minutes before the suggested cooking time. Scoop out ½ cup of the pasta cooking water and stir it into the mushroom sauce. Drain the pasta and toss with the sauce in the skillet if possible. If you wish to thin out the sauce or moisten the pasta further, add an additional ¼ to ½ cup of the reserved mushroom soaking liquid. Serve hot, passing the Parmesan at the table.

Per serving: 512 calories, 24 g protein, 91 g carbohydrates, 11 g fiber, 6 g fat, 1 g sat fat, 0 mg cholesterol, 361 mg sodium

ADVANCE PREPARATION: The sauce will keep about 3 to 4 days in the refrigerator and can be frozen. You can make the recipe through Step 2 and hold the sauce on the top of the stove for a few hours.

Pasta with Spicy Tomato Sauce

Makes 6 servings

■ **VEGETARIAN** ■ VEGAN ■ **LOW-CALORIE** ■ **LOW-FAT**
■ HIGH-PROTEIN ■ GLUTEN-FREE ■ HIGH IN OMEGA-3S

The sauce for this pantry pasta is a vegetarian take on arrabbiata and amatriciana sauces, two spicy tomato sauces from Southern Italy that include pancetta or guanciale. The authentic versions would call for grated Pecorino Romano cheese, but I've already broken with tradition here, so you can use all Pecorino or all Parmesan or a combination of both.

- 1 can (28 ounces) diced tomatoes
- 1–2 tablespoons extra virgin olive oil
- 2 garlic cloves, minced
- 1 small dried red chile pepper, crumbled, or ¼ teaspoon red-pepper flakes
- Salt
- 1 teaspoon dried oregano
- 1 pound penne, bucatini, or spaghetti
- ½ cup (2 ounces) grated Pecorino Romano or Parmesan, or a combination

1. Bring a large pot of water to a rolling boil over high heat.

2. Pulse the tomatoes (with juice) in a food processor, or pass through the medium blade of a food mill before you begin. Heat the oil in a large, heavy nonstick skillet or wide saucepan over medium heat. Add the garlic and chile pepper or red-pepper flakes. Cook, stirring, for 30 seconds to 1 minute, or until the garlic is translucent and begins to be fragrant. Add the tomatoes, salt, and oregano. Stir and increase the heat. When the tomatoes begin to bubble, reduce the heat to medium and cook, stirring often, until thick and fragrant, 15 to 25 minutes. Taste and adjust the seasonings. Keep warm while you cook the pasta.

3. When the pasta water comes to a boil, salt generously and add the pasta. Cook al dente, until the pasta is firm to the bite, following the timing directions on the package but checking 1 to 2 minutes before the suggested cooking time. When the pasta is done, drain and transfer to the pan with the sauce and toss together over medium heat until the pasta is well coated with the sauce. Add half of the cheese, toss together, and serve. Pass the remaining cheese at the table.

Per serving: 365 calories, 14 g protein, 64 g carbohydrates, 4 g fiber, 6 g fat, 2.5 g sat fat, 6 mg cholesterol, 386 mg sodium

ADVANCE PREPARATION: The tomato sauce will keep for about 3 to 4 days in the refrigerator and can be frozen.

Pasta with Swiss Chard and Tomato Sauce

Makes 4 servings

■ **VEGETARIAN** ■ VEGAN ■ LOW-CALORIE ■ LOW-FAT
■ HIGH-PROTEIN ■ GLUTEN-FREE ■ HIGH IN OMEGA-3S

Pasta is always a good vehicle for greens. In this savory sauce, which tastes complex but is really very simple, I've combined Swiss chard, including the crunchy stems, blanched and seasoned with garlic and olive oil, and marinara sauce.

  1 bunch Swiss chard

  Salt

  ¾ pound fusilli or penne

  2 tablespoons extra virgin olive oil

  2 garlic cloves, minced

  1 cup Summer Tomato Sauce (page 19) or Basic
    Pantry Marinara Sauce (page 20)

  Ground black pepper

  Red-pepper flakes

  ½ cup (2 ounces) grated Parmesan

1. Bring a large pot of water to a boil over high heat. Fill a bowl with ice water. Tear the leaves from the stems of the Swiss chard and wash thoroughly in several changes of water. Clean the stems, trim off the ends, and cut into ¼-inch dice.

2. When the water comes to a boil, salt generously and add the Swiss chard leaves. Boil for 1 to 2 minutes, until tender but still bright green, then remove from the water with a slotted spoon or skimmer and transfer to the ice water. Drain and squeeze out the excess water. Chop coarsely and set aside.

3. Return the water to a rolling boil and add the pasta. Meanwhile, heat the oil over medium heat in a large, heavy nonstick skillet and add the diced

chard stems. Cook, stirring often, for 3 to 5 minutes, or until just tender. Add the garlic. Cook, stirring, until fragrant, 30 seconds to 1 minute. Stir in the chard leaves and salt and black pepper to taste. Cook, stirring, for about 30 seconds, then stir in the tomato sauce and black pepper or red-pepper flakes. Taste and adjust the seasonings.

4. Cook the pasta al dente, until firm to the bite, following the timing directions on the package but checking 1 to 2 minutes before the suggested cooking time. Scoop out ¼ to ½ cup of the cooking water, add to the chard mixture, and stir together. Drain the pasta and toss with the chard mixture. Serve topped with the Parmesan.

Per serving: 454 calories, 17 g protein, 68 g carbohydrates, 4 g fiber, 13 g fat, 4 g sat fat, 12 mg cholesterol, 359 mg sodium

ADVANCE PREPARATION: The blanched Swiss chard and the tomato sauce will keep for 3 to 4 days in the refrigerator.

Fettuccine with Pan-Cooked Mushrooms

Makes 4 servings

■ **VEGETARIAN** ■ VEGAN ■ **LOW-CALORIE** ■ LOW-FAT
■ HIGH-PROTEIN ■ GLUTEN-FREE ■ HIGH IN OMEGA-3S

You can make this dish with regular white or brown cremini mushrooms, or use a mix of regular and wild mushrooms. The mushroom sauce is easy to make and will be just fine if you use mushrooms that have been in your refrigerator for a few days; they may not be fresh enough for a salad, but they'll cook up nicely here.

  1 pound white or cremini mushrooms, or a mixture
    of white or cremini mushrooms and wild
    mushrooms (such as oyster mushrooms,
    maitakes, chanterelles, girolles), rinsed briefly
    and wiped dry, ends trimmed

2 tablespoons extra virgin olive oil

1 shallot, minced

2 garlic cloves, minced

1–2 teaspoons chopped fresh thyme or rosemary, or a combination

Salt and ground black pepper

¼ cup dry white wine, such as sauvignon blanc

¾ pound fettuccine

1–2 tablespoons chopped flat-leaf parsley

¼ cup (1 ounce) grated Parmesan for serving

1. Bring a large pot of water to a boil over high heat. Cut the mushrooms into thick slices. Heat a large, heavy skillet over medium-high heat and add 1 tablespoon of the oil. When the oil is hot (you can feel the heat when you hold your hand above the pan), add the mushrooms and cook, stirring or tossing in the pan, for 2 to 3 minutes, or until they begin to soften and sweat. Add the remaining 1 tablespoon oil, reduce the heat to medium, and add the shallot, garlic, and thyme or rosemary. Stir together, add salt and black pepper to taste, and cook, stirring often, for 1 to 2 minutes, or until the shallot and garlic have softened and the mixture is fragrant. Add the wine and cook, stirring often and scraping the bottom of the pan, until the wine has evaporated, 1 to 2 minutes. Taste and adjust the seasonings. Keep warm while you cook the pasta.

2. When the pasta water comes to a boil, salt generously and add the fettuccine. Cook al dente, until the pasta is firm to the bite, following the timing directions on the package but checking 1 to 2 minutes before the suggested cooking time. Scoop out ½ cup of the pasta cooking water, stir it into the mushrooms, and heat through. Drain the pasta and toss in the pan with the mushrooms. Add the parsley and serve, passing the Parmesan to sprinkle on top.

Per serving: 435 calories, 16 g protein, 69 g carbohydrates, 3 g fiber, 10 g fat, 2 g sat fat, 4 mg cholesterol, 126 mg sodium

ADVANCE PREPARATION: You can make the mushroom topping through Step 1 several hours ahead and reheat. If it dries out, add a little water, stock, or wine to the pan when you reheat.

Fusilli with Cauliflower, Tomato Sauce, and Olives

Makes 4 servings

■ **VEGETARIAN** ■ VEGAN ■ LOW-CALORIE ■ LOW-FAT ■ HIGH-PROTEIN ■ GLUTEN-FREE ■ HIGH IN OMEGA-3S

From Italy to Greece to North Africa, you'll find the triumvirate of cauliflower, tomatoes, and olives in all sorts of dishes. It could be because cauliflower is on the bland side and Mediterranean black olives have such a pronounced flavor, but whatever the reason, the two go beautifully together.

½ medium head cauliflower, broken into florets

Salt

1–2 tablespoons extra virgin olive oil

2 garlic cloves, minced

¼–½ teaspoon red-pepper flakes

1 can (14 ounces) diced tomatoes

Pinch of sugar

1 teaspoon fresh thyme leaves or ½ teaspoon dried thyme

Ground black pepper

12 kalamata olives, pitted and halved lengthwise

¾ pound fusilli

½ cup (2 ounces) crumbled feta cheese, ricotta salata, Parmesan, or a mix of grated Parmesan and Pecorino Romano

1. Bring a large pot of water to a boil over high heat. Fill a bowl with ice water. When the water comes to a

boil, salt generously and add the cauliflower. Boil the cauliflower for 5 to 8 minutes, or until tender, and transfer to the ice water. Drain and blot dry. Quarter the cauliflower florets and set aside.

2. Meanwhile, heat 1 tablespoon of the oil in a large, heavy nonstick skillet or in a 3-quart saucepan over medium heat. Add the garlic and red-pepper flakes. Cook, stirring, until fragrant, 30 seconds to 1 minute. Add the tomatoes (with juice), sugar, thyme, black pepper, and salt, and bring to a simmer. Reduce the heat to medium-low and simmer, stirring often, until cooked down and fragrant, 15 to 20 minutes. Stir in the cauliflower and olives and heat through for 1 to 2 minutes. Taste and adjust the seasonings.

3. Return the water to a rolling boil. Add the fusilli and cook al dente, until the pasta is firm to the bite, following the timing directions on the package but checking 1 to 2 minutes before the suggested cooking time. Scoop out $^{1}/_{4}$ to $^{1}/_{2}$ cup of the pasta cooking water and add to the tomato and cauliflower mixture. Drain the pasta and toss with the cauliflower-tomato mixture and, if desired, another 1 tablespoon olive oil. Sprinkle the cheese over the top and serve at once.

Per serving: 457 calories, 16 g protein, 72 g carbohydrates, 6 g fiber, 12 g fat, 4 g sat fat, 17 mg cholesterol, 691 mg sodium

ADVANCE PREPARATION: The recipe can be made through Step 2 several hours or a day ahead. Refrigerate if making the day before.

Macaroni with Tomato Sauce and Goat Cheese

Makes 4 to 6 servings

■ **VEGETARIAN** ■ VEGAN ■ **LOW-CALORIE** ■ LOW-FAT
■ HIGH-PROTEIN ■ GLUTEN-FREE ■ HIGH IN OMEGA-3S

My refrigerator is an extension of my pantry. Parmesan and goat cheese are two items I try to always have on hand in it, so I can make dishes like this grown-up macaroni and cheese without a special trip to the market. In this version, creamy tomato sauce stands in for béchamel.

2 tablespoons extra virgin olive oil

2 garlic cloves, minced

1 can (28 ounces) plus 1 can (14 ounces) diced tomatoes

Pinch of sugar

Salt

2 basil sprigs

Ground black pepper

4 ounces soft, mild goat cheese

$^{1}/_{4}$ cup (1 ounce) grated Parmesan

$^{1}/_{2}$ pound penne rigate

Ground black pepper

$^{1}/_{2}$ cup bread crumbs

1. Bring a large pot of water to a boil over high heat. Meanwhile, pulse the tomatoes (with juice) in a food processor, or pass through the medium blade of a food mill, before you begin. Heat 1 tablespoon of the oil in a large nonstick skillet or saucepan over medium heat. Add the garlic. Cook, stirring, for 30 seconds to 1 minute, or until it begins to be fragrant. Add the tomatoes (with juice), the sugar, salt, and basil. Stir and increase the heat. When the tomatoes begin to bubble,

reduce the heat to medium and cook, stirring often, until thick and fragrant, 15 to 20 minutes, or longer if the sauce still seems watery. Remove the basil sprigs and wipe any sauce adhering to them back into the pan. Add black pepper, stir in the goat cheese and Parmesan and combine well. Taste and adjust the seasonings.

2. Preheat the oven to 350°F. Oil a 2-quart baking dish or gratin with olive oil.

3. When the water for the pasta comes to a boil, salt generously and add the pasta. Cook al dente, until the pasta is firm to the bite, following the timing directions on the package but checking 1 to 2 minutes before the suggested cooking time. It should still be a little underdone as it will finish cooking in the oven. Drain and transfer to a large bowl. Add the tomato–goat cheese sauce and stir together until the pasta is thoroughly coated. Transfer to the baking dish.

4. Toss the bread crumbs with the remaining 1 tablespoon of oil and sprinkle over the top of the macaroni. Bake in the preheated oven until the casserole is bubbling and the bread crumbs are lightly browned, about 30 minutes. Let stand for 5 to 10 minutes before serving.

Per serving (based on 4 servings): 499 calories, 20 g protein, 60 g carbohydrates, 4 g fiber, 19 g fat, 8 g sat fat, 29 mg cholesterol, 857 mg sodium

ADVANCE PREPARATION: You can make the tomato sauce, without adding the cheese, up to 3 days ahead and keep it in the refrigerator. Reheat and stir in the cheese just before tossing with the pasta. The assembled macaroni will keep for several hours outside of the refrigerator and can be covered and refrigerated for up to 3 days before baking.

Baked Orzo with Tomatoes, Roasted Pepper, and Zucchini

Makes 6 servings

■ **VEGETARIAN** ▪ VEGAN ■ **LOW-CALORIE** ▪ LOW-FAT
▪ HIGH-PROTEIN ▪ GLUTEN-FREE ▪ HIGH IN OMEGA-3S

If you like comforting dishes like macaroni and cheese, you'll like this. Orzo, a type of pasta that looks like rice, is popular in Greece, where it is baked in casseroles. You can add other vegetables if you like; it can be a festival of leftovers or a clean-out-the-refrigerator dish.

Salt

½ pound (about 1⅛ cups) orzo

1 large red bell pepper, roasted (page 24) and diced

3 tablespoons extra virgin olive oil

2 medium zucchini, sliced about ¼ inch thick

1–2 garlic cloves, minced

1 pound ripe tomatoes, peeled, seeded, and diced, or 1 can (14 ounces) diced tomatoes

½ cup (2 ounces) grated Parmesan or crumbled goat cheese

Ground black pepper

1. Bring a large pot of water to a rolling boil over high heat. Salt generously and add the orzo. Cook for 8 minutes, or until it is cooked through but still firm to the bite. Drain and transfer to a large bowl. Toss with the diced roasted pepper and 1 tablespoon of the oil.

2. Preheat the oven to 375°F. Oil a 2-quart baking dish. Heat 1 tablespoon of the oil in a large skillet over medium-high heat. Add the zucchini and cook, stirring and turning the slices or tossing them in the pan, until just cooked through and lightly colored, about 5 minutes. Scrape into the bowl with the orzo.

3. Return the pan to the heat. Add the remaining 1 tablespoon of oil and the garlic. Cook just until

fragrant, 20 to 30 seconds. Add the tomatoes and salt to taste. Cook, stirring occasionally, until the tomatoes have cooked down slightly and are fragrant, about 10 minutes. Taste and adjust the seasoning. Scrape into the bowl with the orzo, add the Parmesan or goat cheese, and mix everything together. Add black pepper to taste and adjust the salt. Transfer to the baking dish.

4. Bake for 30 to 40 minutes, or until the top is just beginning to color. Serve hot or warm.

Per serving: 268 calories, 10 g protein, 37 g carbohydrates, 4 g fiber, 10 g fat, 2 g sat fat, 6 mg cholesterol, 143 mg sodium

ADVANCE PREPARATION: You can assemble this several hours, even a day, before baking.

Pasta e Fagiole

Makes 4 to 6 servings

■ **VEGETARIAN** ■ **VEGAN*** ■ LOW-CALORIE ■ LOW-FAT
■ HIGH-PROTEIN ■ GLUTEN-FREE ■ HIGH IN OMEGA-3S

Pasta e fagiole is Italian for pasta and beans. It's a classic, simple peasant dish that I never tire of, comfort food incarnate. Italian cooks consider pasta e fagiole a soup, and in an Italian restaurant you'd get a soupier version of the recipe that follows.

1 tablespoon extra virgin olive oil

1 medium or large onion, chopped

Salt

2 teaspoons chopped fresh or ½ teaspoon crumbled dried rosemary

2–4 garlic cloves, minced

1 heaping tablespoon tomato paste

1 can (28 ounces) diced tomatoes

Ground black pepper

½ pound dried white or borlotti beans, rinsed and picked over, soaked for 6 hours or overnight in 1 quart water

Bouquet garni made with 1 bay leaf, 1 Parmesan rind, 1 small dried red chile pepper, and a couple of sprigs each of thyme and flat-leaf parsley (page 67)

½ pound macaroni

½ cup (2 ounces) grated Parmesan for serving

*If you omit the Parmesan

1. Heat the oil in a large, heavy soup pot or Dutch oven over medium heat. Add the onion. Cook, stirring, until just tender, about 5 minutes. Add ½ teaspoon salt, the rosemary, and garlic. Cook, stirring, for 1 minute, or until the garlic is fragrant. Add the tomato paste and cook, stirring, for 1 to 2 minutes. Add the tomatoes (with juice), some salt and black pepper, and cook, partially covered, stirring often, for 15 minutes, or until the tomatoes have cooked down and the mixture is very fragrant.

2. Drain the beans. Add the beans, bouquet garni, and 2 quarts water to the soup pot. Bring to a boil over high heat, reduce the heat to low, cover, and simmer for 1 hour. Add salt to taste, cover, and simmer for 1 hour, or until the beans are tender. Remove the bouquet garni.

3. Add the pasta to the beans. It will take a little longer to cook than the instructions on the package indicate, as the liquid is not going to be at a rolling boil. When the pasta is cooked al dente, taste and adjust the seasonings. Serve, passing the Parmesan in a bowl.

Per serving (based on 4 servings): 549 calories, 28 g protein, 88 g carbohydrates, 13 g fiber, 9 g fat, 3 g sat fat, 12 mg cholesterol, 734 mg sodium

ADVANCE PREPARATION: You can make the dish through Step 2 up to 1 to 2 days ahead. Refrigerate, then return to a simmer, stirring often, before continuing. The mixture will have thickened, so add water if necessary.

Buckwheat Pasta with Kale

Makes 4 to 6 servings

■ **VEGETARIAN** ■ VEGAN ■ LOW-CALORIE ■ LOW-FAT
■ HIGH-PROTEIN ■ GLUTEN-FREE ■ HIGH IN OMEGA-3S

This is a healthier, pared-down version of a rich, hearty dish from Lombardy that is made with buckwheat pasta (pizzoccheri), cabbage, potatoes, and abundant butter and cheese. You can substitute Japanese soba for the pizzoccheri, and if you can find neither, use whole wheat fettuccine. If you don't want to use butter in this dish, you can omit it and use a total of 2 tablespoons olive oil instead.

1 tablespoon unsalted butter

1 tablespoon extra virgin olive oil

2 large leeks, white and light-green parts only, halved lengthwise, then sliced crosswise and well washed

4 fresh sage leaves, thinly slivered

Salt

¾ pound kale, stemmed, washed thoroughly, and cut crosswise into strips

¾ pound buckwheat pasta (pizzoccheri or soba) or whole wheat fettuccine

½ cup (2 ounces) shaved Parmesan

2 ounces Fontina or Gruyère cheese, cut into ¼-inch dice (about ½ cup)

1. Bring a large pot of water to a boil over high heat. Meanwhile, heat the butter and oil in a large, heavy nonstick skillet over medium-low heat. Add the leeks and sage and cook, stirring often, until the leeks begin to soften, about 3 minutes. Add ½ teaspoon salt and continue to cook, stirring often, until the leeks are tender, about 5 minutes. Remove from the heat.

2. When the water comes to a boil, salt generously and add the kale. Boil for 4 minutes, or until tender but still bright. Using a slotted spoon or a skimmer, transfer the kale to the pan with the leeks and stir together. Keep warm over low heat.

3. Return the water to a rolling boil and add the pasta. Cook al dente. (Soba will cook quickly, usually in under

5 minutes. Pizzoccheri and whole wheat fettuccine will take longer.) Scoop out ½ cup of the pasta cooking water to the pan with the kale and leeks. Drain the pasta and toss in the pan or in a warm pasta bowl with the leeks and kale, and the cheeses. Serve at once.

Per serving (based on 4 servings): 554 calories, 22 g protein, 80 g carbohydrates, 3 g fiber, 17 g fat, 8 g sat fat, 37 mg cholesterol, 412 mg sodium

ADVANCE PREPARATION: You can make the dish through Step 2 several hours ahead. Remove from the heat, then reheat when you cook the pasta.

Fusilli or Orecchiette with Broccoli Rabe

Makes 4 servings

■ **VEGETARIAN** ■ VEGAN ■ LOW-CALORIE ■ LOW-FAT ■ HIGH-PROTEIN ■ GLUTEN-FREE ■ HIGH IN OMEGA-3S

This is based on a classic dish from Apulia, in Southern Italy, where it is always made with orecchiette, pasta shaped like "little ears." The chopped broccoli rabe settles into the indentations in the orecchiette, also into the spirals of fusilli, so either pasta is a good choice. I love the bitter flavor of the broccoli rabe.

Broccoli rabe is a member of the Brassica family of vegetables, famous for antioxidant-rich phytonutrients, along with a substantial wallop of calcium, potassium, folate, and vitamins C, K, and beta-carotene.

1 bunch (about 1 pound) broccoli rabe, washed in 2 changes of water

Salt

2 tablespoons extra virgin olive oil

2 garlic cloves, minced

¼–½ teaspoon red-pepper flakes

¾ pound fusilli or orecchiette

½ cup (2 ounces) grated Parmesan, or a combination of Pecorino and Parmesan

1. Bring a large pot of water to a boil over high heat. Fill a bowl with ice water. Trim off the bottoms of the broccoli rabe stems and cut the remaining part of the stems into ½-inch pieces. When the water comes to a boil, salt generously and add the broccoli rabe. Cook for 4 minutes, or until tender, and transfer using a spider or a slotted spoon to the ice water. Set aside for a few minutes and drain. Squeeze out water and finely chop. Return the water in the pot to a boil.

2. Meanwhile, heat 1 tablespoon of the oil in a large nonstick skillet over medium heat. Add the garlic and red-pepper flakes. Cook until the garlic smells fragrant, 30 seconds to 1 minute. Add the broccoli rabe. Toss together for 1 minute, season to taste with salt, and remove from the heat but keep warm.

3. When the water in the pot comes to a boil, add the pasta. Cook al dente, until the pasta is firm to the bite, following the timing directions on the package but checking 1 to 2 minutes before the suggested cooking time. Scoop out ½ cup of the pasta water and stir into the greens. Drain the pasta and toss with the greens, the remaining 1 tablespoon of oil, and the cheese. Serve at once.

Per serving: 414 calories, 14 g protein, 66 g carbohydrates, 4 g fiber, 11 g fat, 2 g sat fat, 4 mg cholesterol, 118 mg sodium

ADVANCE PREPARATION: The broccoli rabe can be prepared through Step 2 up to a day ahead of time and refrigerated. Reheat in a skillet and proceed with the recipe.

Basic Risotto

Makes 4 to 6 servings

■ **VEGETARIAN*** ■ VEGAN ■ **LOW-CALORIE** ■ LOW-FAT
■ HIGH-PROTEIN ■ **GLUTEN-FREE** ■ HIGH IN OMEGA-3S

All risottos are made basically the same way, and this is more or less the template. You can make a very satisfying basic risotto with nothing but the ingredients that follow. If you've never made risotto, start with this one, which is utterly simple and classic. If you can make this, you can make any risotto.

> About 7 cups Vegetable Stock (page 67) or chicken stock, as needed
>
> Salt
>
> 2 tablespoons extra virgin olive oil
>
> 1/2 cup minced onion
>
> 1 1/2 cups Arborio or Carnaroli rice
>
> 1–2 garlic cloves, minced (optional)
>
> 1/2 cup dry white wine, such as pinot grigio or sauvignon blanc
>
> Ground black pepper
>
> 1/2 cup (2 ounces) grated Parmesan

*If made with Vegetable Stock

1. Bring the stock to a simmer in a saucepan, with a ladle nearby or in the saucepan. Make sure the stock is well seasoned.

2. Heat the oil in a large, heavy skillet or wide saucepan over medium heat. Add the onion and a generous pinch of salt. Cook gently until just tender, about 3 minutes. Do not brown.

3. Add the rice and garlic (if using) and stir until the grains separate and begin to crackle. Add the wine and stir until it has evaporated and been absorbed by the rice, which shouldn't take much longer than a minute or two. Begin adding the simmering stock, a couple of ladlefuls (about 1/2 cup) at a time. The stock should just cover the rice, and should be bubbling, not too slowly but not too quickly. Cook, stirring often, until it is just about absorbed, a few minutes. Add 1 to 2 more ladlefuls of the stock and continue to cook in this fashion, stirring in more stock when the rice is almost dry. You do not have to stir constantly, but stir often and vigorously. When the rice is tender all the way through but still chewy, 20 to 25 minutes, it is done. Taste and adjust the seasoning with salt and black pepper.

4. Add another ladleful of stock to the rice. Stir in the Parmesan and remove from the heat. The mixture should be creamy (add more stock if it isn't). Serve right away in wide soup bowls or on plates, spreading the risotto in a thin layer rather than a mound.

Per serving (based on 4 servings): 428 calories, 10 g protein, 69 g carbohydrates, 3 g fiber, 11 g fat, 3 g sat fat, 9 mg cholesterol, 769 mg sodium

ADVANCE PREPARATION: You can partially cook this several hours ahead and finish it just before serving. The rice should still be hard when you remove it from the heat after about 15 minutes, and there should not be any liquid in the pan. Spread it in an even layer in the pan and keep it away from the heat until you resume cooking. If the pan is not wide enough for you to spread the rice in a thin layer, transfer it to a baking sheet. About 15 minutes before serving, return the remaining stock to a simmer and reheat the rice. Resume cooking as instructed.

Arborio and Carnaroli Rice

Italians use medium-grain, high-starch rice to make risotto. The rice is categorized according to grain size (length to width ratio) into *commune, semifino, fino,* and *superfino.* Arborio and Carnaroli are both in the superfine category, and although Arborio is the most commonly recognized outside of Italy, many chefs prefer Carnaroli rice because it has a higher starch content and firmer texture, so it keeps its shape better during the making of risotto. Another superfine type of rice that is highly regarded for risotto, especially by chefs in the Veneto, is *Vialone Nano,* which yields a creamy risotto. I go with the rice that is most readily available, and that tends to be Arborio, which I buy at Trader Joe's.

Risotto with Spring Onion, Saffron, and Green Garlic

Makes 4 servings

■ **VEGETARIAN*** ■ VEGAN ■ LOW-CALORIE ■ LOW-FAT
■ HIGH-PROTEIN ■ **GLUTEN-FREE** ■ HIGH IN OMEGA-3S

If you shop at farmers' markets, then you've probably seen green garlic. It appears in early spring in California, late spring in colder climates. The cloves are just beginning to set within the bulbs, which resemble leeks or spring onions in appearance. Green garlic has a sweet, mild flavor and is much less pungent than mature garlic.

About 7 cups Garlic Broth (page 67), Vegetable Stock (page 67), or chicken stock, as needed

Salt

2 tablespoons unsalted butter or extra virgin olive oil, or 1 tablespoon each

1/2 cup finely chopped spring onion or leek

2/3 cup finely chopped green garlic (2 bulbs)

1 1/2 cups Arborio or Carnaroli rice

Generous pinch of saffron threads

1/2 cup dry white wine, such as pinot grigio or sauvignon blanc

Ground black pepper

1/2 cup (2 ounces) grated Parmesan

*If made with Vegetable Stock or Garlic Broth

1. Bring the stock to a simmer in a saucepan, with a ladle nearby or in the saucepan. Make sure the stock is well seasoned.

2. Heat the butter and/or oil in a large, heavy skillet or wide saucepan over medium heat. Add the spring onion or leek, garlic, and a generous pinch of salt. Cook gently until just tender, about 3 minutes. Do not brown.

3. Add the rice and stir until the grains separate and begin to crackle. Rub the saffron between your thumb and fingers and stir into the rice. Add the wine and stir until it has evaporated and been absorbed by the rice, which shouldn't take much longer than 1 to 2 minutes. Begin adding the simmering stock, a couple of ladlefuls (about 1/2 cup) at a time. The stock should just cover the rice, and should be bubbling, not too slowly but not too quickly. Cook, stirring often, until it is just about absorbed, a few minutes. Add 1 to 2 more ladlefuls of the stock and continue to cook in this fashion, stirring in more stock when the rice is almost dry. You do not have to stir constantly, but stir often and vigorously. When

the rice is tender all the way through but still chewy, 20 to 25 minutes, it is done. Taste and adjust the seasoning.

4. Add another ladleful of stock to the rice. Stir in the black pepper and Parmesan and remove from the heat. The mixture should be creamy (add more stock if it isn't). Serve right away in wide soup bowls or on plates, spreading the risotto in a thin layer rather than a mound.

Per serving: 526 calories, 12 g protein, 75 g carbohydrates, 3 g fiber, 15 g fat, 6 g sat fat, 28 mg cholesterol, 833 mg sodium

ADVANCE PREPARATION: See Basic Risotto (page 221).

Baby Artichoke Risotto

Makes 4 servings

■ **VEGETARIAN*** ■ **VEGAN**** ■ LOW-CALORIE ■ LOW-FAT
■ HIGH-PROTEIN ■ **GLUTEN-FREE** ■ HIGH IN OMEGA-3S

This is a great dish to add to your artichoke repertoire. If you don't want to take the time to trim fresh baby artichokes, frozen will do fine here. The tiny amount of lemon zest and juice really bump up the flavor, so don't leave them out. Cheese is optional.

10 baby artichokes (fresh or frozen)

1 lemon plus 1–2 teaspoons fresh lemon juice

About 7 cups Vegetable Stock (page 67) or chicken stock, as needed

Salt

2 tablespoons extra virgin olive oil

½ cup minced onion or spring onion

2 garlic cloves, minced

1 ½ cups Arborio or Carnaroli rice

1 teaspoon fresh thyme leaves or ½ teaspoon dried thyme

½ cup dry white wine, such as pinot grigio or sauvignon blanc

1 bay leaf

Ground black pepper

2 tablespoons minced flat-leaf parsley

1 teaspoon grated lemon zest

½ cup (2 ounces) grated Parmesan or a combination of Parmesan and Pecorino Romano (optional)

*If you omit Vegetable Stock

**If made with Vegetable Stock and you omit the Parmesan

1. Trim the artichokes if using fresh, following the directions on page 120. Rub them with a cut lemon as you go along, and slice ¼ to ⅓ inch thick. Place them in a bowl of water acidulated with the juice of ½ lemon. If using frozen artichokes, thaw and drain well. Bring the stock to a simmer in a saucepan, with a ladle nearby or in the saucepan. Make sure the stock is well seasoned.

2. Drain the artichoke hearts and pat dry. Heat the oil in a large, heavy skillet or wide saucepan over medium heat. Add the onion and a generous pinch of salt. Cook gently until tender, 3 to 5 minutes. Add the artichoke hearts and garlic. Cook, stirring, for 2 to 3 minutes, or until the artichoke hearts are beginning to color.

3. Add the rice and thyme and stir until the grains separate and begin to crackle. Add the wine and bay leaf and stir until the wine has evaporated and been absorbed by the rice, which shouldn't take much longer than 1 to 2 minutes. Begin adding the simmering stock, a couple of ladlefuls (about ½ cup) at a time. The stock should just cover the rice and should be bubbling, not too slowly but not too quickly. Cook, stirring often, until it is just about absorbed,

a few minutes. Add 1 to 2 more ladlefuls of the stock and continue to cook in this fashion, adding more stock when the rice is almost dry and stirring often, for 20 to 25 minutes. When the rice is tender all the way through but still chewy, it is done. Add black pepper, taste, and adjust the seasoning. Discard the bay leaf.

4. Mix the parsley and lemon zest together, and add to the risotto, along with 1 to 2 ladlefuls of stock. Remove from the heat, add 1 to 2 teaspoons of lemon juice, and stir in the cheese (if using). Serve right away, in wide soup bowls or on plates, spreading the risotto in a thin layer rather than a mound.

Per serving: 400 calories, 7 g protein, 71 g carbohydrates, 5 g fiber, 8 g fat, 1 g sat fat, 0 mg cholesterol, 629 mg sodium

ADVANCE PREPARATION: You can partially cook this several hours ahead and finish it just before serving. The rice should still be hard when you remove it from the heat after about 15 minutes, and there should not be any liquid in the pan. Spread it in an even layer in the pan and keep it away from the heat until you resume cooking. If the pan is not wide enough for you to spread the rice in a thin layer, then transfer it to a baking sheet. About 15 minutes before serving, return the remaining stock to a simmer and reheat the rice. Resume cooking as instructed.

Risotto with Asparagus, Fresh Fava Beans, and Saffron

Makes 4 to 6 servings

■ **VEGETARIAN*** ■ VEGAN ■ LOW-CALORIE ■ LOW-FAT ■ HIGH-PROTEIN ■ **GLUTEN-FREE** ■ HIGH IN OMEGA-3S

Fava beans are at the top of my list when it comes to favorite spring vegetables. Like English peas, their season is a short one. Once shelled, the tough skin that surrounds each bean must be removed in order to get to the tender, high-protein, high-fiber treasure within. The 15 minutes that it will take you to perform that task will be well spent.

2 pounds fava beans, shelled

About 7 cups Vegetable Stock (page 67) or chicken stock, as needed

Salt

1 pound asparagus (woody stalks snapped off and reserved), cut into 1-inch pieces

2 tablespoons extra virgin olive oil

1/2 cup minced onion or spring onion

2 garlic cloves, minced

1 1/2 cups Arborio or Carnaroli rice

Pinch of saffron threads

1/2 cup dry white wine, such as pinot grigio or sauvignon blanc

1 tablespoon finely chopped flat-leaf parsley

1/2 cup (2 ounces) grated Parmesan

Ground black pepper

2 tablespoons chopped chives (optional)

*If made with Vegetable Stock

1. Bring a pot of water to a boil over high heat. Fill a bowl with ice water. Drop the fava beans into the boiling water and boil small favas for 1 minute, large favas

for 2 minutes, then transfer at once to the ice water. Drain. (Keep the bowl of ice water for the asparagus in the next step.) Remove the skins, using your thumbnail to open up the skin at the spot where the bean attached to the pod, then gently squeezing out the bean. (This goes more quickly than you'd think.)

2. Bring the stock to a boil in a saucepan over high heat. Add the asparagus and blanch for 3 minutes. Remove the asparagus with a slotted spoon or skimmer, refresh in the bowl of ice water, drain, and set aside. Reduce the heat under the stock, add the asparagus stalks and simmer for 15 minutes, then discard. Keep the stock at a simmer, with a ladle nearby or in the pot. Make sure the stock is well seasoned.

3. Heat the oil in a large, heavy skillet or wide saucepan over medium heat. Add the onion and a generous pinch of salt. Cook, stirring, until tender, about 3 minutes. Add the garlic and rice. Cook, stirring, until the grains of rice separate and begin to crackle, 1 to 2 minutes. Rub the saffron between your thumb and fingers and stir into the rice.

4. Add the wine and stir until it has evaporated and been absorbed by the rice, which shouldn't take much longer than 1 to 2 minutes. Begin adding the simmering stock, a couple of ladlefuls (about $1/2$ cup) at a time. The stock should just cover the rice and should be bubbling, not too slowly but not too quickly. Cook, stirring often, until it is just about absorbed, a few minutes. Add 1 to 2 ladlefuls more of stock and continue to cook in this fashion, adding more stock when the rice is almost dry and stirring often, for 15 minutes. Stir in the asparagus and fava beans and another ladleful or two of stock. Continue adding stock and stirring the rice for 10 to 15 minutes, or until the rice is tender all the way through but still chewy and the vegetables are tender.

5. Add 1 ladleful of stock to the rice, and stir in the parsley, Parmesan, black pepper, and chives. Remove from the heat. The mixture should be creamy (add more stock if it is not). Taste and adjust the seasonings. Serve right away, in wide soup bowls or on plates, spreading the risotto in a thin layer rather than a mound.

Per serving (based on 4 servings): 572 calories, 22 g protein, 93 g carbohydrates, 12 g fiber, 12 g fat, 3 g sat fat, 9 mg cholesterol, 853 mg sodium

ADVANCE PREPARATION: You can begin this several hours ahead and finish it just before serving. Cook halfway through Step 4, about 15 minutes. The rice should still be hard when you remove it from the heat. Spread in an even layer in the pan and arrange the asparagus and fava beans over the top. Resume cooking as instructed 15 minutes before serving. The fava beans can be shelled, blanched, and peeled 1 to 2 days ahead and refrigerated.

Fresh Herb and Garlic Risotto

Makes 4 to 6 servings

■ **VEGETARIAN*** ■ VEGAN ■ LOW-CALORIE ■ LOW-FAT
■ HIGH-PROTEIN ■ **GLUTEN-FREE** ■ HIGH IN OMEGA-3S

This beautiful risotto is given a huge, flavorful blast of fresh herbs at the very end of cooking. Serve it as a main dish or a side. Use a combination of sweet-tasting herbs such as tarragon, chives, chervil, and parsley, and vivid tasting salad greens like wild arugula.

About 7 cups Vegetable Stock (page 67) or chicken stock, as needed

Salt

2 cups finely chopped fresh herbs, such as flat-leaf parsley, tarragon, chives, chervil, dill, basil, chives, arugula

4 garlic cloves, minced

2 tablespoons extra virgin olive oil

$^2/_3$ cup finely chopped onion or leek

1 $^1/_2$ cups Arborio or Carnaroli rice

$^1/_2$ cup dry white wine, such as pinot grigio or sauvignon blanc

Ground black pepper

1 teaspoon grated lemon zest

1 tablespoon fresh lemon juice

$^1/_2$ cup (2 ounces) grated Parmesan

*If made with Vegetable Stock

1. Bring the stock to a simmer in a saucepan, with a ladle nearby or in the saucepan. Make sure the stock is well seasoned. Combine the herbs and 1 of the minced garlic cloves in a bowl and set aside.

2. Heat the oil in a large, heavy skillet or wide saucepan over medium heat. Add the onion or leek and a generous pinch of salt. Cook gently until just tender, about 3 minutes. Do not brown. Add the rice and the

remaining 3 cloves of garlic, and stir until the grains of rice separate and begin to crackle, 1 to 2 minutes.

3. Add the wine and stir until it has evaporated and been absorbed by the rice, which shouldn't take much longer than 1 to 2 minutes. Begin adding the simmering stock, a couple of ladlefuls (about $^1/_2$ cup) at a time. The stock should just cover the rice, and should be bubbling, not too slowly but not too quickly. Cook, stirring often, until it is just about absorbed, a few minutes. When most of the stock has been absorbed, add another ladleful or two of the stock and continue to cook in this fashion, adding more stock when the rice is almost dry and stirring often. When the rice is just tender all the way through but still chewy, in 20 to 25 minutes, it is done. Taste and adjust the seasoning.

4. Add 1 ladleful of stock to the rice. Stir in the herbs, black pepper, lemon zest, lemon juice, and Parmesan. Remove from the heat. The mixture should be creamy (add more stock if it is not). Serve right away, in wide soup bowls or on plates, spreading the risotto in a thin layer rather than a mound.

Per serving (based on 4 servings): 465 calories, 13 g protein, 73 g carbohydrates, 5 g fiber, 12 g fat, 3 g sat fat, 12 mg cholesterol, 850 mg sodium

ADVANCE PREPARATION: You can begin this several hours ahead and finish it just before serving. Cook halfway through Step 3, about 15 minutes. The rice should still be hard when you remove it from the heat, and there should not be any liquid in the pan. Spread it in an even layer in the pan and keep it away from the heat until you resume cooking. If the pan is not wide enough for you to spread the rice in a thin layer, transfer it to a baking sheet. About 15 minutes before serving, return the remaining stock to a simmer and reheat the rice. Resume cooking as instructed.

Risi e Bisi

Makes 4 to 6 servings

■ **VEGETARIAN*** ■ VEGAN ■ LOW-CALORIE ■ LOW-FAT
■ HIGH-PROTEIN ■ **GLUTEN-FREE** ■ HIGH IN OMEGA-3S

Risi e Bisi—rice and peas—is a springtime risotto that should only be contemplated during that small window in spring when fresh English peas come on the market. I urge you to splurge on them so you can make this classic dish.

About 7 cups Vegetable Stock (page 67) or chicken stock, as needed

2 tablespoons extra virgin olive oil

½ cup minced onion or spring onion

Salt

1½ cups Arborio or Carnaroli rice

1 garlic clove, minced

½ cup dry white wine, such as pinot grigio or sauvignon blanc

2 pounds fresh English peas, shelled (about 1½ cups)

2 tablespoons chopped flat-leaf parsley

½ cup (2 ounces) grated Parmesan

Ground black pepper

*If made with Vegetable Stock

1. Bring the stock to a simmer in a saucepan, with a ladle nearby or in the saucepan. Make sure the stock is well seasoned.

2. Heat the oil in a large, heavy skillet or wide saucepan over medium heat. Add the onion and a generous pinch of salt. Cook gently until tender and translucent, 3 to 5 minutes.

3. Add the rice and garlic and stir until the grains of rice separate and begin to crackle, 1 to 2 minutes. Add the wine and stir until it has evaporated and been absorbed by the rice, which shouldn't take much longer than 1 to 2 minutes. Begin adding the simmering stock, a couple of ladlefuls (about ½ cup) at a time. The stock should just cover the rice and should be bubbling, not too slowly but not too quickly. Cook, stirring often, until it is just about absorbed, a few minutes. Add 1 to 2 ladlefuls of the stock and continue to cook in this fashion, adding more stock when the rice is almost dry and stirring often, for 10 minutes. Add the peas and continue adding stock and stirring for 15 minutes. The peas should be tender and the rice tender all the way through but still chewy. Taste and adjust the seasoning.

4. Add 1 to 2 ladlefuls of stock to the rice. Stir in parsley, Parmesan, and black pepper. Remove from the heat. The mixture should be creamy (add more stock if it is not). Stir once and serve right away in wide soup bowls or on plates, spreading the risotto in a thin layer rather than a mound.

Per serving (based on 4 servings): 492 calories, 15 g protein, 7 g carbohydrates, 6 g fiber, 12 g fat, 3 g sat fat, 12 mg cholesterol, 837 mg sodium

ADVANCE PREPARATION: You can partially cook this several hours ahead and finish it just before serving. The rice should still be hard when you remove it from the heat after about 15 minutes, and there should not be any liquid in the pan. Spread it in an even layer in the pan and keep it away from the heat until you resume cooking. If the pan is not wide enough for you to spread the rice in a thin layer, then transfer it to a baking sheet. When you resume cooking, bring the stock back to a simmer and reheat the rice. Pick up Step 3 at the point where you add the peas and continue cooking as instructed.

Risotto with Spring Carrots and Leeks

Makes 4 to 6 servings

■ **VEGETARIAN*** ■ VEGAN ■ LOW-CALORIE ■ LOW-FAT
■ HIGH-PROTEIN ■ **GLUTEN-FREE** ■ HIGH IN OMEGA-3S

You could make this risotto year-round, but it's especially delicious in the spring, when new, tender, sweet carrots and leeks come into the farmers' markets.

About 7 cups Vegetable Stock (page 67) or
   chicken stock, as needed

2 tablespoons extra virgin olive oil

¾ pound tender spring carrots, thinly sliced on the
   diagonal (see note)

2 large leeks, white and light-green parts only, halved
   lengthwise, well washed, and chopped

Salt

1½ cups Arborio or Carnaroli rice

2 teaspoons fresh thyme leaves

2 garlic cloves, minced

½ cup dry white wine, such as pinot grigio or
   sauvignon blanc

2–3 tablespoons chopped flat-leaf parsley, or a
   combination of parsley, tarragon, and marjoram
   or chives

Ground black pepper

¼–½ cup (1–2 ounces) grated Parmesan

1–2 teaspoons fresh lemon juice

*If made with Vegetable Stock

1. Bring the stock to a simmer in a saucepan, with a ladle nearby or in the saucepan. Make sure the stock is well seasoned.

2. Heat the oil in a large, heavy skillet or wide saucepan over medium heat. Add the carrots, leeks, and ½ teaspoon salt. Cook, stirring, until the vegetables begin to soften, about 3 minutes. Add the rice, thyme, and garlic. Cook, stirring, until the grains of rice separate and begin to crackle, 1 to 2 minutes.

3. Add the wine and stir until it has evaporated and been absorbed by the rice, which shouldn't take much longer than 1 to 2 minutes. Begin adding the simmering stock, a couple of ladlefuls (about ½ cup) at a time. The stock should just cover the rice, and should be bubbling, not too slowly but not too quickly. Cook, stirring often, until it is just about absorbed, a few minutes. Add 1 to 2 more ladlefuls of the stock and continue to cook in this fashion, adding more stock when the rice is almost dry, until the rice is cooked through but still chewy, 20 to 25 minutes. Stir in the chopped herbs, add black pepper, taste, and adjust the seasonings.

4. When the rice is cooked al dente, remove the pan from the heat and stir in 1 ladleful of stock, the Parmesan, and lemon juice. The mixture should be creamy (add more stock if it is not). Serve right away, in wide soup bowls or on plates, spreading the risotto in a thin layer rather than a mound.

Per serving (based on 4 servings): 470 calories, 10 g protein, 83 g carbohydrates, 6 g fiber, 9 g fat, 2 g sat fat, 4 mg cholesterol, 747 mg sodium

ADVANCE PREPARATION: You can partially cook this several hours ahead and finish it just before serving. The rice should still be hard when you remove it from the heat after about 15 minutes, and there should not be any liquid in the pan. Spread it in an even layer in the pan and keep it away from the heat until you resume cooking. If the pan is not wide enough for you to spread the rice in a thin layer, then transfer it to a baking sheet. About 15 minutes before serving, return the remaining stock to a simmer and reheat the rice. Resume cooking as instructed.

Note: *If your carrots are fat at one end, cut the fat part in half lengthwise, then slice, so that the pieces will be more uniform.*

Red Bell Pepper Risotto with Saffron

Makes 4 to 6 servings

■ **VEGETARIAN*** ■ VEGAN ■ LOW-CALORIE ■ LOW-FAT
■ HIGH-PROTEIN ■ **GLUTEN-FREE** ■ HIGH IN OMEGA-3S

As this stunning risotto simmers, it takes on a red hue from the bell peppers. Saffron adds depth of flavor and contributes to the risotto's beautiful color, but if you want to leave it out you'll still have a delicious and beautiful risotto.

About 7 cups Vegetable Stock (page 67) or chicken stock, as needed

Salt

2 tablespoons extra virgin olive oil

½ cup finely chopped onion or shallot

2 garlic cloves, minced

2 large red bell peppers, finely diced

1½ cups Arborio or Carnaroli rice

½ cup dry white wine, such as pinot grigio or sauvignon blanc

Pinch of saffron threads (optional)

Ground black pepper

½ cup (2 ounces) grated Parmesan

2 tablespoons chopped flat-leaf parsley, or a combination of parsley and thyme

*If made with Vegetable Stock

1. Bring the stock to a simmer in a saucepan, with a ladle nearby or in the saucepan. Make sure the stock is well seasoned.

2. Heat the oil in a large, heavy skillet or wide saucepan over medium heat. Add the onion or shallot.

Cook gently until it begins to soften, about 3 minutes. Add the garlic, bell peppers, and ½ teaspoon salt. Cook, stirring, until they are limp and fragrant, 8 to 10 minutes. Add the rice and stir until the grains are separate and begin to crackle, 1 to 2 minutes.

3. Add the wine and stir until it has evaporated and been absorbed by the rice, which shouldn't take much longer than 1 to 2 minutes. Begin adding the simmering stock, a couple of ladlefuls (about ½ cup) at a time. The stock should just cover the rice, and should be bubbling, not too slowly but not too quickly. Cook, stirring often, until it is just about absorbed, a few minutes. If using saffron, rub the threads between your fingers and add to the rice, along with 1 to 2 more ladlefuls of the stock. Continue to cook in this fashion, stirring often and adding more stock when the rice is almost dry, until the rice is cooked through but still chewy, 20 to 25 minutes. Taste and adjust the seasoning.

4. When the rice is cooked through, add black pepper to taste, and stir in 1 ladleful of stock, the Parmesan, and herbs. Remove from the heat. Taste and adjust the seasonings. The mixture should be creamy (add more stock if it is not). Serve right away in wide soup bowls or on plates, spreading the risotto in a thin layer rather than a mound.

> **Per serving (based on 4 servings):** 474 calories, 13 g protein, 74 g carbohydrates, 5 g fiber, 12 g fat, 3.5 g sat fat, 12 mg cholesterol, 836 mg sodium

ADVANCE PREPARATION: You can partially cook this several hours ahead and finish it just before serving. The rice should still be hard when you remove it from the heat after about 15 minutes, and there should not be any liquid in the pan. Reheat and proceed with the recipe shortly before serving.

Summer Squash Risotto

Makes 4 to 6 servings

■ **VEGETARIAN*** ■ VEGAN ■ LOW-CALORIE ■ LOW-FAT
■ HIGH-PROTEIN ■ **GLUTEN-FREE** ■ HIGH IN OMEGA-3S

Summer squash becomes very soft as you cook this, resulting in a creamy risotto. For color and texture I remove half of the cooked squash from the pan before I add the rice, then stir it back into the risotto at the end.

> About 7 cups Vegetable Stock (page 67) or chicken stock, as needed
>
> Salt
>
> 2 tablespoons extra virgin olive oil
>
> ½ cup finely chopped onion
>
> 1–2 garlic cloves, minced
>
> 1–1¼ pounds mixed yellow and green summer squash, cut into small dice
>
> Salt and ground black pepper
>
> 1½ cups Arborio or Carnaroli rice
>
> ½ cup dry white wine
>
> 2 tablespoons chopped flat-leaf parsley, or a combination of parsley and marjoram
>
> ¼–½ cup (1–2 ounces) grated Parmesan

*If made with Vegetable Stock

1. Bring the stock to a simmer in a saucepan, with a ladle nearby or in the saucepan. Make sure the stock is well seasoned.

2. Heat the oil in a large, heavy skillet or wide saucepan over medium heat. Add the onion and cook gently until tender, about 5 minutes. Add the garlic and stir for about 1 minute, or until the garlic smells fragrant, and stir in the squash. Cook, stirring, until the squash begins to be translucent, about 5 minutes. Add ½ teaspoon salt and black pepper to taste, and continue to cook, stirring

often, until the squash has released water and the water has evaporated, about 8 minutes. Remove half of the squash from the pan and set aside.

3. Add the rice, and stir until the grains separate and begin to crackle, 1 to 2 minutes. Add the wine and stir until it has evaporated and been absorbed by the rice, which shouldn't take much longer than 1 to 2 minutes. Begin adding the simmering stock, a couple of ladlefuls (about $^1/_2$ cup) at a time. The stock should just cover the rice and should be bubbling, not too slowly but not too quickly. Cook, stirring often, until it is just about absorbed, a few minutes. Add 1 to 2 more ladlefuls of the stock and continue to cook in this fashion, stirring in more stock when the rice is almost dry. When the rice is tender all the way through but still chewy, 20 to 25 minutes, it is done.

4. Add 1 to 2 more ladlefuls of stock to the rice, and stir in the squash that you removed from the pan, along with the parsley and Parmesan. Remove from the heat. The mixture should be creamy (add a little more stock if it isn't). Add black pepper, taste, and adjust the salt. Serve right away in wide soup bowls or on plates, spreading the risotto in a thin layer rather than a mound.

Per serving (based on 4 servings): 440 calories, 11 g protein, 74 g carbohydrates, 5 g fiber, 10 g fat, 2 g sat fat, 6 mg cholesterol, 728 mg sodium

ADVANCE PREPARATION: You can partially cook this several hours ahead and finish it just before serving. The rice should still be hard when you remove it from the heat after about 15 minutes, and there should not be any liquid in the pan. Spread it in an even layer in the pan and keep it away from the heat until you resume cooking. If the pan is not wide enough for you to spread the rice in a thin layer, then transfer it to a baking sheet. Resume cooking as instructed 20 minutes before serving.

Pink Risotto with Beet Greens and Roasted Beets

Makes 4 to 6 servings

■ **VEGETARIAN*** ■ VEGAN ■ LOW-CALORIE ■ LOW-FAT
■ HIGH-PROTEIN ■ **GLUTEN-FREE** ■ HIGH IN OMEGA-3S

Because both the beets and their greens bleed into the rice as this risotto simmers, the final richly flavored risotto is decidedly pink. Maybe it will be the key to getting your picky daughter to eat vegetables!

About 7 cups Vegetable Stock (page 67) or chicken stock, as needed

Salt

1 bunch beet greens, stemmed and washed

2 tablespoons extra virgin olive oil

$^1/_2$ cup finely chopped onion

$1^1/_2$ cups Arborio or Carnaroli rice

2 garlic cloves, minced

$^1/_2$ cup red, rosé, or dry white wine

$^3/_4$ pound beets (1 bunch small), roasted (page 125)

Ground black pepper

$^1/_4$-$^1/_2$ cup (1-2 ounces) grated Parmesan

2 tablespoons finely chopped flat-leaf parsley

*If made with Vegetable Stock

1. Bring the stock to a simmer in a saucepan, with a ladle nearby or in the saucepan. Season well with salt and turn the heat to low. Stack the beet greens and cut crosswise into 1-inch-wide strips.

2. Heat the oil in a large, heavy skillet or wide saucepan over medium heat. Add the onion. Cook, stirring, until the onion begins to soften, about 3 minutes. Add the rice and garlic. Cook, stirring, until the grains separate and begin to crackle, 1 to 2 minutes.

3. Add the wine and stir until it has evaporated and been absorbed by the rice, which shouldn't take much longer than 1 to 2 minutes. Begin adding the simmering stock, a couple of ladlefuls (about ¹/₂ cup) at a time. The stock should just cover the rice, and should be bubbling, not too slowly but not too quickly. Cook, stirring often, until it is just about absorbed, a few minutes. Add 1 to 2 more ladlefuls of the stock and continue to cook in this fashion, stirring often and adding more stock when the rice is almost dry, for 10 minutes.

4. Stir in the greens and beets. Continue to add more stock, enough to barely cover the rice, and stir often, for 10 to 15 minutes, or until the rice is cooked through but still chewy. Taste and adjust the seasonings.

5. When the rice is cooked through, add black pepper to taste, and stir in 1 ladleful of stock, the Parmesan, and parsley. Remove from the heat. The mixture should be creamy (if it isn't, add a little more stock). Serve right away in wide soup bowls or on plates, spreading the risotto in a thin layer rather than a mound.

Note: *I often blanch greens when I get them home from the market so that they won't wilt or rot in the refrigerator if I don't get around to cooking them right away. If you do this, and want to use them for this risotto, chop the blanched greens and set aside. Add them to the risotto during the last few minutes of cooking, just to heat them through and incorporate into the dish.*

Per serving (based on 4 servings): 459 calories, 11 g protein, 78 g carbohydrates, 6 g fiber, 10 g fat, 2 g sat fat, 6 mg cholesterol, 823 mg sodium

ADVANCE PREPARATION: The roasted beets will keep for 5 days in the refrigerator. You can begin the risotto ahead and finish it just before serving.

Cooking it just through Step 3. Spreading the rice in an even layer in the pan or on a baking sheet. About 15 minutes before serving, return the stock to a simmer and reheat the rice. Proceed with Step 4.

Risotto with Roasted Winter Squash

Makes 4 to 6 servings

■ **VEGETARIAN*** ■ VEGAN ■ LOW-CALORIE ■ LOW-FAT ■ HIGH-PROTEIN ■ **GLUTEN-FREE** ■ HIGH IN OMEGA-3S

Roasting squash lightly caramelizes it, making a naturally sweet vegetable even sweeter. I stir a small portion of the roasted squash into this luxurious risotto at the beginning, and the rest at the end of cooking. The squash that is added at the beginning falls apart as the risotto cooks, enriching the mixture and adding color.

1 pound winter squash (about ¹/₂ of a good-size butternut, for example), such as butternut, banana or hubbard, peeled, seeded, and cut into ¹/₂-inch dice

2 tablespoons extra virgin olive oil

About 7 cups Vegetable Stock (page 67) or chicken stock, as needed

1 small or ¹/₂ medium onion

2 large garlic cloves, minced

Salt

1 ¹/₂ cups Arborio or Carnaroli rice

¹/₂ cup dry white wine, such as pinot grigio or sauvignon blanc

1 teaspoon chopped fresh sage

¹/₄-¹/₂ cup (1-2 ounces) grated Parmesan

3-4 tablespoons chopped flat-leaf parsley

Ground black pepper

*If made with Vegetable Stock

1. Preheat the oven to 425°F. Cover a baking sheet with foil. Toss the squash with 1 tablespoon of the oil and spread on the baking sheet in an even layer. Place in the oven and roast for 30 to 40 minutes, stirring every 10 minutes, until tender and caramelized. Remove from the heat.

2. Bring the stock to a simmer in a saucepan, with a ladle nearby or in the saucepan.

3. Heat the remaining 1 tablespoon oil in a large, heavy skillet or wide saucepan over medium heat. Add the onion. Cook, stirring, until the onion begins to soften, about 3 minutes. Add the garlic, 1/2 teaspoon salt, and one-third of the squash. Cook, stirring, until the onion is tender and the garlic fragrant, 1 to 2 minutes. Add the rice. Cook, stirring, until the grains of rice are separate and beginning to crackle, 1 to 2 minutes.

4. Add the wine and stir until it has evaporated and been absorbed by the rice, 1 or 2 minutes. Stir in 1 to 2 ladlefuls of the simmering stock, enough to just cover the rice and squash. The stock should bubble slowly. Cook, stirring often, until it is just about absorbed. Add the sage and 1 ladleful of the stock, and continue to cook in this fashion, adding more stock when the rice is almost dry, until the rice is tender all the way through but still chewy, 20 to 25 minutes. Taste and adjust the seasonings.

5. Add the remaining roasted squash and 1/2 cup of stock to the rice. Stir in the Parmesan and parsley, and remove from the heat. Add black pepper, taste, and adjust the salt. The mixture should be creamy (add more stock if it is not). Serve right away in wide soup bowls or on plates, spreading the risotto in a thin layer rather than a mound.

Per serving (based on 4 servings): 461 calories, 10 g protein, 80 g carbohydrates, 5 g fiber, 10 g fat, 2 g sat fat, 6 mg cholesterol, 730 mg sodium

ADVANCE PREPARATION: You can partially cook this several hours ahead and finish it just before serving. The rice should still be hard when you remove it from the heat after about 15 minutes, and there should not be any liquid in the pan. Spread the rice out in the pan or on a baking sheet. Reheat and proceed with the recipe shortly before serving.

Corn Risotto with Sage

Makes 4 to 6 servings

■ **VEGETARIAN*** ■ VEGAN ■ LOW-CALORIE ■ LOW-FAT
■ HIGH-PROTEIN ■ **GLUTEN-FREE** ■ HIGH IN OMEGA-3S

Every once in a while, I buy corn at the farmers' market, and then for some reason I don't get around to eating it right away and I find it a few days later in the refrigerator. The corn is still sweet, though not as vibrant as it was when I bought it, and those nearly forgotten kernels often go into risotto. I love the textures in this risotto, the slightly crunchy corn kernels with the chewy rice.

7 cups Vegetable Stock (page 67) or chicken stock, as needed

Salt

2 ears corn

2 tablespoons extra virgin olive oil (or 1 tablespoon each unsalted butter and extra virgin olive oil)

1/2 cup minced onion

1 1/2 cups Arborio or Carnaroli rice

1/2 cup dry white wine, such as pinot grigio or sauvignon blanc

1 tablespoon slivered fresh sage leaves

Ground black pepper

1/4-1/2 cup (1-2 ounces) grated Parmesan

*If made with Vegetable Stock

1. Bring the stock to a simmer in a saucepan, with a ladle nearby or in the saucepan. Cut the kernels off the corncobs, and set aside. Add the cobs to the stock. Cover and simmer for 20 minutes. Remove the cobs from the stock. Taste the stock and make sure that it is well seasoned.

2. Heat the oil (or butter and oil) in a large, heavy skillet or wide saucepan over medium heat. Add the onion and a generous pinch of salt, and cook gently until it is just tender, about 3 minutes. Do not brown.

3. Add the rice. Cook, stirring, until the grains are separate and beginning to crackle, 1 to 2 minutes. Add the wine and stir until it has evaporated and been absorbed by the rice, which shouldn't take much longer than 1 to 2 minutes. Begin adding the simmering stock, a couple of ladlefuls (about ½ cup) at a time. The stock should just cover the rice and should be bubbling, not too slowly but not too quickly. Cook, stirring often, until it is just about absorbed, a few minutes. Add 1 to 2 more ladlefuls of the stock and continue to cook in this fashion, adding more stock and stirring when the rice is almost dry. You do not have to stir constantly, but stir often. After 10 minutes, stir in the corn kernels and continue to add stock and stir the rice until the rice is tender all the way through but still chewy, 10 to 15 minutes. Stir in the sage and pepper to taste and cook for 1 to 2 minutes. Taste and adjust the seasoning.

4. Add 1 ladleful of stock to the rice. Stir in the Parmesan and remove from the heat. The mixture should be creamy (add more stock if it is not). Serve right away in wide soup bowls or on plates, spreading the risotto in a thin layer rather than a mound.

Per serving (based on 4 servings): 461 calories, 11 g protein, 78 g carbohydrates, 4 g fiber, 11 g fat, 2 g sat fat, 6 mg cholesterol, 785 mg sodium

ADVANCE PREPARATION: You can partially cook this several hours ahead and finish it just before serving. The rice should still be hard when you remove it from the heat after about 15 minutes, and there should not be any liquid in the pan. Spread it in an even layer in the pan and keep it away from the heat until you resume cooking. If the pan is not wide enough for you to spread the rice in a thin layer, then transfer it to a baking sheet. Return the remaining stock to a simmer and reheat the rice 15 minutes before serving. Resume cooking as instructed.

Chapter 9
VEGETARIAN MAIN COURSES

I grew up in a meat-eating family. We ate very well, but "What's for dinner?" usually had a one-word answer: chicken, beef, lamb, or fish. When you remove meat from the center of your dinner plate, many different types of food can step in to claim its place. The dishes often have names that evoke the way the foods are prepared, and that in turn evoke a particular cuisine: Couscous with Beans and Cauliflower (page 287); Black Bean Enchiladas (page 279); Artichoke Heart Frittata (page 247); Spicy Stir-Fried Tofu with Bok Choy or Baby Broccoli (page 256).

Omelets, frittatas, and gratins are frequently found on my dinner table. They're terrific vehicles for vegetables and herbs of all kinds and can transform leftovers into an altogether different dish.

One of my favorite quick dinners is unadorned scrambled eggs, velvety and comforting. A pan of sautéed bell and chile peppers becomes a main dish when eggs are scrambled with them (Pipérade, page 248).

Most of the dishes in this chapter are substantial enough to stand alone as one-dish meals (some served with grains or noodles). Although they contain no meat, you don't have to be vegetarian to enjoy a savory bean stew, comforting vegetable gratin, a frittata packed with vegetables, or a spicy stir-fry. You could accompany them with a salad and/or a side dish but you don't have to. That's not to say that they wouldn't also be welcome as part of a multicourse meal, but I developed them all with a weekday dinner in mind.

Eggs

I don't know why many health-conscious eaters are still afraid of eggs. Eggs are a healthy food, a perfect food in fact. They are delicious, with lots of high-quality protein but not a lot of calories, and contain abundant nutrients, including vitamins A, B$_{12}$, and E, riboflavin, folate, selenium, iron, and phosphorus. And even though they're not plants, eggs also contain the phytochemicals lutein and zeaxanthin (both very important for good eye health), and choline, a nutrient that, paradoxically, helps the body prevent the accumulation of cholesterol in the liver. If you're trying to increase your omega-3 intake, you can now find omega-enriched eggs. But eggs have been getting a bad rap since the 1960s, when we first became aware that there was a connection between high cholesterol and heart disease; then the low-fat mania of the '90s finished them off in the eyes of the diet-conscious. More recently, though, we've learned that saturated fat, the kind found in today's intensively produced red meat and full-fat dairy products, has greater impact on blood cholesterol than dietary cholesterol does. Unless you're vegan, eggs—all of the egg, not just the white—should be a welcome food.

Scrambled Eggs à la Provençale

Makes 4 servings

■ VEGETARIAN ▪ VEGAN ■ LOW-CALORIE ▪ LOW-FAT
■ HIGH-PROTEIN ■ GLUTEN-FREE ▪ HIGH IN OMEGA-3S

If you have a little leftover tomato sauce or marinara sauce on hand, make these salmon-colored eggs for an impromptu late-night supper or brunch. The sauce adds a dimension of flavor and contributes a velvety texture to the dish.

  8 large or extra-large eggs

  Salt and ground black pepper

  ¼ cup Summer Tomato Sauce (page 19) or Basic Pantry Marinara Sauce (page 20)

  1 tablespoon extra virgin olive oil

  1 tablespoon slivered fresh basil or chopped chives

1. Beat the eggs in a bowl. Add the salt, black pepper, and tomato sauce and whisk together.

2. Heat a heavy saucepan or nonstick skillet over low heat and add the oil. When it is hot (but not too hot—this is gentle cooking), add the egg mixture, scraping in every last bit with a silicone spatula. Cook slowly over low heat, stirring gently and scraping the eggs from the bottom of the pan with the spatula or a wooden spoon, until the eggs are just set. Stir in the basil or chives. Serve hot, with toast.

Per serving: 184 calories, 13 g protein, 2 g carbohydrates, 0.5 g fiber, 14 g fat, 4 g sat fat, 423 mg cholesterol, 185 mg sodium

Fresh Herb Omelet

Makes 2 rolled omelets, serving 2

■ VEGETARIAN ▪ VEGAN ■ LOW-CALORIE ▪ LOW-FAT
■ HIGH-PROTEIN ■ GLUTEN-FREE ▪ HIGH IN OMEGA-3S

In France this is called a fines herbes omelet, and usually contains finely minced parsley and chives, and sometimes tarragon or chervil as well. The herbs should be sweet ones rather than bitter or sharp (such as oregano or sage); basil, mint, and dill would all work. This is a classic French rolled omelet, served hot, right out of the pan, an utterly satisfying quick meal. The classic French version is made with butter; if you wish, do it the Mediterranean way with olive oil. No matter which cooking fat you choose, use a heavy nonstick pan.

4 large or extra-large eggs

4 teaspoons 1% milk

Salt and ground black pepper

3 tablespoons minced mixed fresh herbs, such as flat-leaf parsley, dill, chives, tarragon, chervil, basil, or mint (use no more than 3)

4 teaspoons unsalted butter or extra virgin olive oil

1. Break 2 eggs into a bowl and beat with a fork or a whisk until frothy. Add 2 teaspoons of the milk and salt (I use about $\frac{1}{8}$ teaspoon) and black pepper to taste. Add half of the herbs and whisk well.

2. Heat an 8-inch nonstick omelet pan over medium-high heat. Add 2 teaspoons of the butter or olive oil. When the pan feels hot when you hold your hand above it, pour in the eggs, scraping every last bit into the pan. Swirl the pan to distribute the eggs evenly over the surface. Shake the pan gently, tilting it slightly with one hand and using a spatula held in your other hand to lift up the edges of the omelet, allowing the eggs to run underneath during the first few minutes of cooking. As soon as the eggs are set on the bottom, jerk the pan quickly away then back toward you so that the omelet folds over onto itself. Tilt the pan and roll out onto a plate. Repeat with the milk, herbs, and butter or oil to make a second omelet.

Per serving: 217 calories, 13 g protein, 2 g carbohydrates, 0 g fiber, 18 g fat, 8 g sat fat, 444 mg cholesterol, 221 mg sodium

The Forgotten Omelet

When I lived in France I often received letters from vegetarians inquiring about how to eat in French restaurants, where the menus are mainly focused on animal proteins. My answer was always to choose from the starters and to request an omelet. Any French chef is more than willing to make one; indeed, one French chef told me that during his apprenticeship, the chefs always judged him on the quality of his omelet.

An omelet is one of the most satisfying meals I can think of, yet here in the United States we hardly ever think of making one for dinner. You need very little to make a good omelet: eggs of course, a spoonful of milk (though that isn't essential), salt and pepper, butter or olive oil, and a good pan, preferably nonstick. If you want to make a meal of it, add any number of vegetables: greens (blanched, chopped, sautéed in a little olive oil with garlic), cooked asparagus or broccoli, fresh herbs, cooked summer squash or mushrooms, tomatoes. Or use leftovers to fill your omelet—the last of the ratatouille, the spoonful of eggplant Parmesan, or potato gratin lingering in your refrigerator.

Restaurants often use three eggs to make an omelet, which is excessive; do you ever eat 3 boiled or poached eggs at a sitting? For home, a 2-egg omelet is just fine. If you wish, substitute olive oil for the butter as they do in the Mediterranean. When I'm making omelets for myself, or myself and one other person, I make 1 or 2 quick, classic rolled or folded French omelets. When they involve more than 4 eggs, I make flat omelets, which we know by their Italian name, frittata.

Whatever their fillings, omelets or frittatas are almost always made using the same technique. Now that we have such effective heavy nonstick pans to work with, it's easy to make either type without relying on excessive butter or oil to lubricate the pan. It's important, no matter what type of pan you use, that the pan be quite hot when the eggs go into it so they begin to cook immediately, forming a cooked layer on the bottom—otherwise you'll have scrambled eggs that don't hold together.

Asparagus and Parmesan Omelet

Makes 2 rolled omelets, serving 2

■ **VEGETARIAN** ■ VEGAN ■ **LOW-CALORIE** ■ LOW-FAT
■ **HIGH-PROTEIN** ■ **GLUTEN-FREE** ■ HIGH IN OMEGA-3S

Make these omelets with delicate, thin asparagus stalks. If you're cooking for more than two people, stir the filling into the beaten eggs for a frittata.

5 thin or medium asparagus spears, trimmed

4 large or extra-large eggs

4 teaspoons 1% milk

Salt and ground black pepper

4 teaspoons grated Parmesan

1 tablespoon chopped fresh flat-leaf parsley, dill, chives, or tarragon, or a combination

4 teaspoons extra virgin olive oil

1. Steam the asparagus over boiling water until tender, about 5 minutes. Refresh with cold water, and pat dry. Cut into ½-inch slices and set aside.

2. Break 2 eggs into a bowl and beat with a fork or a whisk until frothy. Add 2 teaspoons milk and salt (I use ⅛ teaspoon) and black pepper to taste. Whisk in 2 teaspoons of the Parmesan and half of the herbs and mix well.

3. Heat an 8-inch nonstick omelet pan over medium-high heat. Add 2 teaspoons of the oil. When the oil feels hot when you hold your hand above it, drizzle a drop of the eggs in. If they sizzle upon contact, the pan is ready. Pour in the eggs, scraping every last bit into the pan. Swirl the pan to distribute the eggs evenly over the surface. Shake the pan gently, tilting it slightly with one hand and using a spatula held in your other hand to lift up the edges of the omelet, allowing the eggs to run underneath during the first few minutes of cooking. As soon as the eggs are set on the bottom, sprinkle half of the asparagus down the middle of the eggs. Jerk the pan quickly away then toward you so that the omelet folds over onto itself. If you don't like your omelet runny in the middle (I do), jerk the pan again so that the omelet folds over once more. Cook for up to 1 minute longer, or to desired doneness. Tilt the pan and roll out onto a plate. Repeat with the remaining eggs, milk, Parmesan, herbs, oil, and asparagus to make a second omelet.

Per serving: 251 calories, 15 g protein, 3 g carbohydrates, 1 g fiber, 20 g fat, 5 g sat fat, 426 mg cholesterol, 270 mg sodium

Rolled Omelets

When I was teaching myself to cook, I went through several dozen eggs before I mastered the technique for making a classic 2-egg omelet. I hope the directions in these recipes will help you avoid my mistakes.

The technique for rolling or folding the omelet is all in the wrist action with the pan: You need to push the pan away from you and jerk it back quickly, so that the omelet moves up the far edge of the pan and then folds back onto itself when you jerk the pan back. And the pan must be hot enough so that the eggs are cooked on the bottom and not sticking to the pan.

Fresh Herb and Scallion Frittata

Makes one 10-inch frittata/4 servings

■ **VEGETARIAN** ■ VEGAN ■ **LOW-CALORIE** ■ LOW-FAT
■ **HIGH-PROTEIN** ■ **GLUTEN-FREE** ■ HIGH IN OMEGA-3S

If you want to make the fresh herb omelet for the family in one go, it's more convenient, if not quite as elegant, to make it as a flat omelet (frittata). This one includes a bunch of sautéed scallions.

2 teaspoons plus 1 tablespoon unsalted butter or extra virgin olive oil

1 bunch scallions, white and light-green parts only, trimmed and sliced

8 large or extra-large eggs

6 tablespoons minced mixed fresh herbs, such as flat-leaf parsley, dill, chives, tarragon, chervil, basil, or mint (use no more than 3)

1/2 teaspoon salt

Ground black pepper

2 tablespoons plus 2 teaspoons 1% milk

1. Heat 2 teaspoons of the butter or oil in a small skillet or saucepan over medium heat. Add the scallions. Cook, stirring, until tender, 3 to 5 minutes. Remove from the heat.

2. Beat the eggs in a bowl. Add the herbs, salt, black pepper, milk, and scallions and beat together.

3. Heat the remaining 1 tablespoon butter or oil over medium-high heat in a 10-inch heavy nonstick skillet. Hold your hand above it; it should feel hot. Drop a bit of egg into the pan. If it sizzles and cooks at once, the pan is ready. Pour in the egg mixture. Swirl the pan to distribute the eggs and filling evenly over the surface. Shake the pan gently, tilting it slightly with one hand and using a spatula held in your other hand to lift up the edges of the frittata, allowing the eggs to run underneath during the first few minutes of cooking. Reduce the heat to low and cover the pan. Cook for 8 to 10 minutes, shaking the pan every once in a while, until the frittata is just about set. Meanwhile, preheat the broiler.

4. If the frittata is not quite set on the top, place it under the broiler, about 3 inches from the heat, for 1 to 2 minutes, watching closely, until set on the top. It's fine if it's just beginning to color. Do not allow the eggs to brown too much or they'll taste bitter. Remove from the heat, allow the frittata to sit in the pan for 5 minutes or longer, then carefully slide out onto a platter, or cut into wedges in the pan. Serve warm, at room temperature, or chilled.

Per serving: 159 calories, 14 g protein, 4 g carbohydrates, 1 g fiber, 10 g fat, 3 g sat fat, 424 mg cholesterol, 443 mg sodium

ADVANCE PREPARATION: The frittata can be prepared several hours or even a day ahead, covered and refrigerated until shortly before serving. It does not reheat well.

Asparagus and Herb Frittata

Makes one 10-inch frittata/4 to 6 servings

■ **VEGETARIAN** ■ VEGAN ■ **LOW-CALORIE** ■ LOW-FAT
■ **HIGH-PROTEIN** ■ **GLUTEN-FREE** ■ HIGH IN OMEGA-3S

The frittata version of the asparagus and herb omelet is always a crowd pleaser. You can serve it as a main dish, or cut it into diamond shapes and serve it as a beautiful appetizer.

¾ pound asparagus, trimmed

8 extra-large eggs

2 tablespoons 1% milk

½ teaspoon salt

Ground black pepper

¼ cup finely chopped flat-leaf parsley, dill, chives, or tarragon, or a combination

¼ cup (1 ounce) grated Parmesan

1 tablespoon extra virgin olive oil

1. Steam the asparagus over boiling water until tender, about 5 minutes. Refresh under cold running water, drain and pat dry. Cut into ½-inch slices and set aside.

2. Beat the eggs in a large bowl. Beat in the milk, salt, black pepper, and herbs. Stir in the asparagus and Parmesan.

3. Heat the olive oil in a 10-inch heavy nonstick skillet over medium-high heat. When the oil feels hot when you hold your hand above it, drizzle a drop of the eggs in. If they sizzle upon contact, the pan is ready. Pour in the egg mixture. Swirl the pan to distribute the eggs and filling evenly over the surface. Shake the pan gently, tilting it slightly with one hand and using a spatula held in your other hand to lift up the edges of the frittata, allowing the eggs to run underneath during the first few minutes of cooking. Reduce the heat to low and cover the pan. Cook for 8 to 10 minutes, shaking the pan occasionally, until the frittata is just about set. Meanwhile, preheat the broiler.

4. If the frittata is not quite set on the top, place it under the broiler, about 3 inches from the heat, for 1 to 2 minutes, watching closely, until set on the top. It's fine if it's just beginning to color, but do not allow the eggs to brown too much or they'll taste bitter. Remove from the heat, allow the frittata to sit in the pan for 5 minutes or longer, then carefully slide onto a platter, or cut into wedges in the pan. Serve warm, at room temperature, or chilled.

Per serving (based on 4 servings): 285 calories, 18 g protein, 6 g carbohydrates, 2 g fiber, 15 g fat, 4 g sat fat, 485 mg cholesterol, 514 mg sodium

ADVANCE PREPARATION: The asparagus can be prepared a day ahead and kept in the refrigerator. The frittata can be prepared several hours or even a day ahead, covered and refrigerated until shortly before serving. It does not reheat well but is very nice served at room temperature.

Broccoli and Potato Frittata

Makes one 10-inch frittata/4 to 6 servings

■ **VEGETARIAN** ■ VEGAN ■ **LOW-CALORIE** ■ LOW-FAT
■ **HIGH-PROTEIN** ■ **GLUTEN-FREE** ■ HIGH IN OMEGA-3S

Smoked trout adds a new dimension to the asparagus and herb frittata. The trout is a rich source of omega-3s.

½ pound potatoes, scrubbed, cut into ½-inch dice

½ pound broccoli crowns

8 large eggs

½ teaspoon salt

Ground black pepper

3 tablespoons 1% milk

3 tablespoons chopped chives

1 tablespoon extra virgin olive oil

1. Steam the potatoes over boiling water until tender, about 10 minutes. Steam the broccoli for 5 minutes. Drain and refresh under cold water. Dry on paper towels.

2. Beat the eggs in a large bowl. Stir in the salt, black pepper, milk, potatoes, chives, and broccoli.

3. Heat the oil in a 10-inch heavy nonstick skillet over medium-high heat. When the oil feels hot when you hold your hand above it, drizzle a drop of the eggs in. If they sizzle upon contact, the pan is ready. Pour in the egg mixture. Swirl the pan to distribute the eggs and filling evenly over the surface. Shake the pan gently, tilting it slightly with one hand and using a spatula held in your other hand to lift up the edges of the frittata, allowing the eggs to run underneath during the first few minutes of cooking. Reduce the heat to low and cover the pan. Cook for 8 to 10 minutes, shaking the pan occasionally, until the frittata is just about set. Meanwhile, preheat the broiler.

4. If the frittata is not quite set on the top, place it under the broiler, about 3 inches from the heat, for 1 to 2 minutes, watching closely, until set on the top. Remove from the heat, allow the frittata to sit in the pan for 5 minutes or longer, then carefully slide onto a platter, or cut into wedges in the pan. Serve warm, at room temperature, or cold.

Per serving (based on 4 servings): 238 calories, 16 g protein, 14 g carbohydrates, 2 g fiber, 14 g fat, 4 g sat fat, 424 mg cholesterol, 451 mg sodium

ADVANCE PREPARATION: The asparagus can be prepared a day ahead and kept in the refrigerator. The frittata can be prepared several hours or even a day ahead, covered and refrigerated until shortly before serving. It does not reheat well but is very nice served at room temperature.

Frittata with Greens

Makes one 10-inch frittata/4 to 6 servings

■ **VEGETARIAN** ■ VEGAN ■ **LOW-CALORIE** ■ LOW-FAT
■ **HIGH-PROTEIN** ■ **GLUTEN-FREE** ■ HIGH IN OMEGA-3S

In Nice this omelet is called a truccha, *made most often with Swiss chard. Niçoise cooks aren't bashful about the garlic, usually adding it uncooked to the eggs. I soften the flavor by cooking the garlic first. The frittata can be quickly thrown together if you make a point of washing and cooking the greens—blanching them in salted boiling water, refreshing in cold water, then draining and squeezing out excess water—when you get them home from the market. Once blanched, store in a covered bowl in the refrigerator for 3 to 4 days. The dish works best with the more tender greens like chard, beet greens, and spinach.*

> 1 pound Swiss chard (any color), beet greens, or spinach (see note, opposite page)
>
> Salt
>
> 2 tablespoons extra virgin olive oil
>
> 2 garlic cloves, minced
>
> Ground black pepper
>
> 8 large or extra-large eggs
>
> 2 tablespoons 1% milk

1. Bring a large pot of water to a boil over high heat while you stem and wash the greens in two changes of water. Fill a bowl with ice water. When the water comes to a boil, salt generously and add the greens. Blanch spinach for just 30 seconds, chard and beet greens for 1 minute, or until tender. Transfer to the ice water. Let sit for a few minutes, then drain, squeeze dry, and chop.

2. Heat 1 tablespoon of the oil in a 10-inch nonstick skillet over medium heat. Add the garlic. Cook, stirring, until fragrant, 30 seconds to 1 minute. Stir in the greens. Cook, stirring, for about 1 minute, or until coated with oil. Season to taste with salt and black pepper and remove from the heat.

3. Beat the eggs in a bowl. Stir in $^1/_2$ teaspoon salt, ground black pepper to taste, the milk, and greens.

4. Clean and dry your pan and return to the stove. Heat over medium-high heat and add the remaining 1 tablespoon of oil. When the oil feels hot when you hold your hand above it, drizzle a drop of the eggs in. If they sizzle upon contact, the pan is ready. Pour in the egg mixture, scraping every last bit out of the bowl with a rubber spatula. Swirl the pan to distribute the eggs and filling evenly over the surface. Shake the pan gently, tilting it slightly with one hand and using a spatula held in your other hand to lift up the edges of the frittata, allowing the eggs to run underneath during the first few minutes of cooking. Reduce the heat to low and cover the pan. Cook for 8 to 10 minutes, shaking the pan occasionally, until the frittata is just about set. Meanwhile, preheat the broiler.

5. If the frittata is not quite set on the top, place under the broiler, about 3 inches from the heat, watching closely, for 1 to 2 minutes, or until set. It's fine if it's just beginning to color. Do not allow the eggs to brown too much or they'll taste bitter.

6. Remove the frittata from the heat. Allow it to sit in the pan for 5 minutes or longer, then carefully slide the frittata onto a platter, or cut into wedges in the pan and serve.

Per serving (based on 4 servings): 233 calories, 15 g protein, 6 g carbohydrates, 2 g fiber, 17 g fat, 4 g sat fat, 423 mg cholesterol, 421 mg sodium

ADVANCE PREPARATION: The greens can be prepared through Step 1 or Step 2 several hours or even 1 to 2 days ahead. The frittata can be made a few hours or even a day ahead and served at room temperature. It does not reheat well but is very nice served at room temperature.

Note: If you use bagged baby spinach for this, rather than blanching in a pot of boiling water, place the spinach in a bowl and cover with boiling water. Let sit for 1 minute, then transfer to a bowl of cold water, drain, squeeze dry, and proceed with the recipe.

Frittata with Red Peppers and Peas

Makes one 10-inch frittata/6 main-dish servings, 12 appetizer servings

■ **VEGETARIAN** ■ VEGAN ■ **LOW-CALORIE** ■ LOW-FAT
■ **HIGH-PROTEIN** ■ **GLUTEN-FREE** ■ HIGH IN OMEGA-3S

In my ever increasing pantheon of frittatas, there are some that I make again and again, especially for buffets. This is one of them. It always looks nice on a plate, bejeweled with bright red and green. The frittata is one of the best destinations I can think of for frozen peas, reason enough to have a bag on hand in your freezer and a red bell pepper in the refrigerator at all times.

2 tablespoons extra virgin olive oil

2 bunches scallions, thinly sliced

1 large red bell pepper, diced

1–2 large garlic cloves, minced

Salt and ground black pepper

10 large or extra-large eggs

3 tablespoons 1% milk

1 cup frozen peas, thawed (you can do this by covering with boiling water for 10 minutes, then draining)

2 tablespoons minced flat-leaf parsley

1. Heat 1 tablespoon of the oil in a 12-inch nonstick skillet over medium heat. Add the scallions and red bell pepper. Cook, stirring often, until the scallions are tender and the bell pepper begins to soften, about 3 minutes. Add the garlic, salt (about ½ teaspoon), and a few twists of the pepper mill. Continue to cook until the bell pepper is tender, 3 to 5 minutes. Stir often. Remove from the heat and scrape into a bowl. Rinse and dry the pan.

2. Beat the eggs in a large bowl. Stir in ½ teaspoon salt, black pepper, the milk, peas, parsley, and the cooked scallions and red bell pepper.

3. Heat the remaining 1 tablespoon olive oil over medium-high heat in the skillet. When the oil feels hot when you hold your hand above it, drizzle a drop of the eggs in. If they sizzle upon contact, the pan is ready. Pour in the egg mixture. Swirl the pan to distribute the eggs and filling evenly over the surface. Shake the pan gently, tilting it slightly with one hand and using a spatula held in your other hand to lift up the edges of the frittata, allowing the eggs to run underneath during the first few minutes of cooking.

4. Reduce the heat to low, cover, and cook for 10 minutes. From time to time—every 2 to 3 minutes—remove the lid and loosen the bottom of the frittata

with a wooden or silicone spatula, tilting the pan, so that the bottom doesn't burn. The bottom will, however, turn a deep golden brown. The eggs should be just about set; cook a few minutes longer if they're not. Meanwhile, preheat the broiler.

5. Finish the frittata under the broiler for 1 to 3 minutes, watching very carefully to make sure that the top doesn't burn (it's okay if it colors a little bit and puffs under the broiler). Remove from the heat, shake the pan to make sure the frittata isn't sticking, and allow it to cool for at least 5 minutes and for up to 15. Loosen the edges with a wooden or silicone spatula. Carefully slide the frittata from the pan onto a large round platter, or serve from the pan. Cut into wedges or into smaller bite-size diamonds. Serve warm, at room temperature, or chilled.

Per serving (based on 6 servings): 205 calories, 13 g protein, 9 g carbohydrates, 3 g fiber, 13 g fat, 3 g sat fat, 353 mg cholesterol, 179 mg sodium

ADVANCE PREPARATION: The filling can be made 1 to 2 days before making the frittata and held in a covered bowl in the refrigerator. The frittata can be made several hours ahead of serving, or a day ahead if serving chilled. It does not reheat well but is very nice served at room temperature.

Spicy Tunisian Carrot Frittata

Makes one 10-inch frittata/6 servings

■ **VEGETARIAN** ■ VEGAN ■ **LOW-CALORIE** ■ LOW-FAT
■ **HIGH-PROTEIN** ■ **GLUTEN-FREE** ■ HIGH IN OMEGA-3S

The frittatas made in Tunisia are usually spicy and packed with vegetables. They're sometimes baked in an earthenware dish in the oven; sometimes on top of the stove. This one, adapted from a recipe by Clifford A. Wright, is made on top of the stove like an Italian frittata, but the spices are unmistakably Tunisian.

1 pound carrots, sliced

1 tablespoon caraway seeds, ground

1–2 tablespoons harissa

4 large garlic cloves, minced

Salt

8 large or extra-large eggs

$\frac{1}{2}$ teaspoon ground black pepper

$\frac{1}{4}$ cup finely chopped flat-leaf parsley

1 tablespoon extra virgin olive oil

1. Either boil the carrots in salted water or steam until thoroughly tender, about 15 minutes. Drain and mash with a fork, or puree in a food processor. Add the caraway, harissa, and garlic, and blend together. Season to taste with salt.

2. Beat the eggs in a large bowl. Beat in $\frac{1}{2}$ teaspoon salt and black pepper to taste, and add the carrot mixture and parsley. Mix together well. Heat the oil in a 10-inch heavy nonstick skillet over medium-high heat. When the oil feels hot when you hold your hand above it, drizzle a drop of the eggs in. If they sizzle upon contact, the pan is ready. Pour in the egg mixture. Swirl the pan to distribute the eggs and filling evenly over the surface. Shake the pan gently, tilting it slightly with one hand and using a spatula held in your other

hand to lift up the edges of the frittata, allowing the eggs to run underneath during the first few minutes of cooking.

3. Cover the pan, reduce the heat to low, and cook for 10 minutes, gently shaking the pan occasionally, until the frittata is almost set. Every 2 to 3 minutes, remove the lid and loosen the bottom of the omelet with a spatula, tilting the pan, so that the bottom doesn't burn. Meanwhile, preheat the broiler.

4. Place the frittata under the broiler for 1 to 3 minutes, watching very carefully to make sure the top doesn't burn (it will color slightly, and it will puff under the broiler). Remove from the heat, shake

the pan to make sure the frittata isn't sticking, and allow to cool for at least 5 minutes and up to 15. Loosen the edges with a wooden or silicone spatula. Carefully slide the frittata from the pan onto a large round platter, or serve from the pan, warm or at room temperature.

Note: *You can find harissa, a Tunisian spice paste, in Mediterranean markets.*

Per serving: 165 calories, 10 g protein, 10 g carbohydrates, 3 g fiber, 10 g fat, 2 g sat fat, 283 mg cholesterol, 193 mg sodium

ADVANCE PREPARATION: The frittata can be made a day ahead and refrigerated, tightly wrapped. It does not reheat well but is very nice served at room temperature.

Spinach and Fresh Herb Frittata with Walnuts and Yogurt

Makes one 10-inch frittata/6 servings

■ **VEGETARIAN** ■ VEGAN ■ **LOW-CALORIE** ■ LOW-FAT
■ **HIGH-PROTEIN** ■ **GLUTEN-FREE** ■ HIGH IN OMEGA-3S

This Iranian frittata (coucou is the word for frittata in Iran) is packed with herbs; it's like a little garden. I usually include a large bunch of flat-leaf parsley, plus some dill and mint or tarragon. Finely chopped walnuts add crunch, and yogurt contributes to a billowy texture. Authentic coucous are made with no shortage of butter, but I prefer to use olive oil.

- 2 bags (6 ounces each) baby spinach or 2 bunches, stemmed and washed

- 8 large or extra-large eggs

- ½ cup plain low-fat Greek yogurt

- ¼ cup finely chopped walnuts

- ¾ teaspoon salt (or more to taste)

- Ground black pepper

- 2 cups chopped fresh herbs, such as flat-leaf parsley, mint, chervil, chives, dill, cilantro, tarragon

- 1–2 garlic cloves, finely minced

- 1 tablespoon extra virgin olive oil (2 tablespoons if you don't have a nonstick pan)

1. Bring a large pot of water to a boil over high heat. Fill a bowl with ice water. When the water comes to a boil, salt generously, add the spinach, and blanch for 10 to 20 seconds. Transfer to the ice water to cool for a few minutes, then drain and squeeze out excess water. Chop finely.

2. Beat the eggs in a large bowl. Stir in the yogurt, walnuts, salt, and black pepper. Add the spinach, herbs, and garlic and mix together well. Season with salt and pepper. Cover and refrigerate for 30 minutes so that the herbs will soften and swell. Stir occasionally.

3. Heat a 10-inch nonstick skillet over medium-high heat and add the oil. When the oil feels hot when you hold your hand above it, drizzle a drop of the eggs in. If they sizzle upon contact, the pan is ready. Pour in the egg mixture, scraping every last bit out of the bowl with a spatula. Swirl the pan to distribute the eggs and filling evenly over the surface. Shake the pan gently, tilting it slightly with one hand and using a spatula held in your other hand to lift up the edges of the frittata, allowing the eggs to run underneath during the first few minutes of cooking. Reduce the heat to low and cover the pan. Cook for 10 minutes, shaking the pan occasionally, until the frittata is just about set. Meanwhile, preheat the broiler.

4. If the frittata is not quite set on the top, place it under the broiler, about 3 inches from the heat, watching closely, for 1 to 3 minutes, or until set and just beginning to color on the top. Do not allow the eggs to brown too much or they'll taste bitter.

5. Remove from the heat, allow to sit in the pan for 5 minutes or longer, then carefully slide out onto a platter or serve from the pan, warm or at room temperature.

Per serving: 190 calories, 13 g protein, 9 g carbohydrates, 4 g fiber, 13 g fat, 3 g sat fat, 283 mg cholesterol, 491 mg sodium

ADVANCE PREPARATION: You can make this 1 to 2 days ahead. It does not reheat well but is very nice served at room temperature.

Artichoke Heart Frittata

Makes one 10-inch frittata/4 to 6 servings

■ **VEGETARIAN** ■ VEGAN ■ **LOW-CALORIE** ■ LOW-FAT
■ **HIGH-PROTEIN** ■ **GLUTEN-FREE** ■ HIGH IN OMEGA-3S

You can make this easy Italian frittata with fresh baby arti-chokes to announce the arrival of spring, or more quickly at any time of year with frozen artichoke hearts.

1 pound baby artichokes, trimmed (page 120) or
    1 package (12 ounces) frozen artichoke hearts

8 large or extra-large eggs

2 tablespoons 1% milk

Salt and ground black pepper

¼ cup (1 ounce) grated Parmesan or Pecorino
    Romano

2 tablespoons extra virgin olive oil

2 garlic cloves, minced

3 tablespoons minced flat-leaf parsley, fennel
    fronds, wild fennel, or dill

1. If using fresh artichokes, steam or boil gently in a pot of generously salted water until tender, 10 to 15 minutes. Drain, refresh with cold water, and quarter the artichokes. Thaw frozen artichokes according to package directions and drain off any liquid.

2. Beat the eggs in a bowl. Whisk in the milk, a scant ½ teaspoon salt, black pepper to taste, and the cheese.

3. Heat the oil over medium-high heat in a 10-inch heavy nonstick skillet. Add the artichokes. Cook, stirring often, until golden brown, 5 to 8 minutes. Add the garlic and cook for 30 seconds to 1 minute, or until fragrant. Stir in the herbs and season with salt and black pepper. Pour in the egg mixture. Swirl the pan to distribute the eggs and filling evenly over the surface. Shake the pan gently, tilting it slightly with one hand and using a spatula held in your other hand to lift up the edges of the frittata, allowing the eggs to run underneath during the first few minutes of cooking.

4. Reduce the heat to low, cover, and cook for 10 minutes, gently shaking the pan occasionally. From time to time remove the lid and loosen the bottom of the omelet with a spatula, tilting the pan, so that the bottom turns golden but doesn't burn. Meanwhile, preheat the broiler.

5. Finish cooking the omelet under the broiler for 1 to 3 minutes, watching very carefully to make sure the top doesn't burn, until set (it can color slightly, and it may puff under the broiler). Allow to cool in the pan for at least 5 minutes, then slide onto a platter or serve from the pan. Serve hot, warm, or at room temperature.

> **Per serving (based on 4 servings):** 284 calories, 18 g protein, 9 g carbohydrates, 5 g fiber, 20 g fat, 5 g sat fat, 430 mg cholesterol, 346 mg sodium

ADVANCE PREPARATION: You can prepare the artichokes a day ahead. The frittata is good served at room temperature, so you can make it hours before serving. It will keep well in the refrigerator overnight. It does not reheat well but is very nice served at room temperature.

Pipérade

Makes 6 servings

■ **VEGETARIAN** ▢ VEGAN ■ **LOW-CALORIE** ▢ LOW-FAT
■ **HIGH-PROTEIN** ■ **GLUTEN-FREE** ▢ HIGH IN OMEGA-3S

The classic Basque dish called pipérade also includes Bayonne ham. I've left that out here, including only the savory peperonata (a stew made with lots of peppers cooked with tomato, onion, and garlic), into which eggs are stirred and scrambled.

    2 tablespoons extra virgin olive oil

    1 medium onion, chopped

    2 large garlic cloves, minced

    2 large red and/or bell peppers, thinly sliced

1 large or 2 small green bell peppers, thinly sliced

1 jalapeño or serrano chile pepper, minced

Salt

1 can (14 ounces) diced tomatoes, drained of some but not all of its juice

1 teaspoon fresh thyme leaves or ½ teaspoon dried

Ground black pepper

8 large or extra-large eggs

1. Heat the oil in a large nonstick skillet or wide, heavy saucepan over medium heat. Add the onion. Cook, stirring, until tender, about 5 minutes. Add the garlic, bell peppers, and chile pepper. Cook, stirring often, for 5 minutes, until the peppers begin to soften. Add ½ teaspoon salt. Continue to cook for 5 minutes, or until the peppers are tender.

2. Add the tomatoes, thyme, and salt and black pepper to taste. Bring to a simmer and cook, stirring occasionally, until the tomatoes have cooked down somewhat, about 10 minutes. Cover, reduce the heat to low, and simmer for 15 to 20 minutes or longer, stirring occasionally, until the mixture is thick.

3. Whisk the eggs in a bowl until well mixed, season with salt and black pepper, and stir into the pepper mixture. Cook, stirring over low heat, until the eggs are just set but still creamy. Serve hot.

> **Per serving:** 184 calories, 10 g protein, 10 g carbohydrates, 2 g fiber, 12 g fat, 3 g sat fat, 282 mg cholesterol, 298 mg sodium

ADVANCE PREPARATION: The stewed peppers (through Step 2) will keep for about 5 days in the refrigerator.

North African Chakchouka

Makes 6 servings

■ **VEGETARIAN** ■ VEGAN ■ **LOW-CALORIE** ■ LOW-FAT
■ **HIGH-PROTEIN** ■ **GLUTEN-FREE** ■ HIGH IN OMEGA-3S

Chakchouka (there are many ways to spell it) is a classic pepper dish from Tunisia and Algeria. Like its French cousin pipérade, the word refers to the cooked peppers. In this case the mix is a spicy one, including Anaheim peppers, jalapeño or serrano chile peppers, and harissa. The eggs are poached on top.

2 tablespoons extra virgin olive oil

1 medium onion, chopped

2 large garlic cloves, minced

2 large red bell peppers, or a combination of red and yellow bell peppers, thinly sliced

2 large green peppers, thinly sliced

2 Anaheim chile peppers, thinly sliced (wear plastic gloves when handling)

1 jalapeño or serrano chile pepper, minced (wear plastic gloves when handling), optional

Salt

$\frac{1}{2}$ teaspoon coriander seeds, lightly toasted and ground

$\frac{1}{4}$ teaspoon caraway seeds, ground

$\frac{1}{8}$ teaspoon cayenne

$1\frac{1}{2}$ pounds tomatoes, peeled, seeded, and chopped, or 1 can (28 ounces) diced tomatoes, drained of some but not all of its juice

1–2 teaspoons harissa

1 teaspoon fresh thyme leaves or $\frac{1}{2}$ teaspoon dried thyme

Ground black pepper

2 tablespoons chopped flat-leaf parsley plus additional for garnish

6 large or extra-large eggs

1. Heat the oil in a large nonstick skillet or wide heavy saucepan over medium heat. Add the onion. Cook, stirring, until tender, about 5 minutes. Add the garlic, bell peppers, and chile peppers. Cook, stirring often, for 5 minutes, or until the peppers begin to soften. Add $\frac{1}{2}$ teaspoon salt, the coriander, caraway, and cayenne. Continue to cook for 5 minutes, or until the peppers are tender.

2. Add the tomatoes, harissa, thyme, and black pepper. Bring to a simmer, and cook, stirring occasionally, until the tomatoes have cooked down somewhat, about 10 minutes. Cover, reduce the heat to low, and simmer for 15 to 20 minutes or longer, stirring occasionally, until the mixture is thick and fragrant. Taste and adjust the seasonings.

3. When the stew has cooked down to a thick, fragrant mixture, stir in the parsley. Taste and adjust the seasonings. With the back of your spoon, make 6 depressions in the vegetables. Break an egg into each depression. Cover and cook for 6 to 8 minutes, or until the egg whites are set. Sprinkle the eggs with salt, black pepper, and parsley, and serve.

Per serving: 177 calories, 9 g protein, 14 g carbohydrates, 4 g fiber, 10 g fat, 2 g sat fat, 212 mg cholesterol, 129 mg sodium

ADVANCE PREPARATION: The pepper and tomato mixture can be made up to 3 days ahead. Bring back to a simmer and proceed with the recipe.

Buckwheat Crêpes

Makes about 1 dozen 8-inch crêpes

■ **VEGETARIAN** ■ VEGAN ■ LOW-CALORIE ■ LOW-FAT
■ HIGH-PROTEIN ■ GLUTEN-FREE ■ HIGH IN OMEGA-3S

When I lived in Paris, a large buckwheat crêpe with an egg cooked on top was a favorite for lunch. A young woman had a stand in the Place St.-Sulpice, down the street from my apartment (alas, the stand disappeared a few years after I arrived), and she would carefully spread the batter on a hot griddle, guiding it over the griddle with a dough scraper and leaning down very close, because she was myopic, as she worked. My favorite French street food, buckwheat crêpes are easy to make. If you have them on hand in the freezer, you can pull one out and top it with some blanched spinach and a fried or poached egg for a quick and delicious lunch or supper.

1 cup 2% milk

3 large or extra-large eggs

½ teaspoon salt

⅔ cup buckwheat flour

½ cup unbleached all-purpose flour

3 tablespoons canola oil

1. Place the milk, eggs, salt, and ⅓ cup water in a blender. Blend at low speed. Add the buckwheat flour, all-purpose flour, and oil. Blend at high speed for 1 minute. Transfer to a bowl, cover, and refrigerate for 1 to 2 hours.

2. Place a seasoned 7-inch or 8-inch crêpe pan over medium heat. Brush with melted butter or

oil, and when the pan is hot remove from the heat and ladle in about 3 tablespoons batter. Tilt or swirl the pan to distribute the batter evenly, and return to the heat. Cook for about 1 minute, or until you can easily loosen the edges with a spatula. Turn and cook on the other side for 30 seconds. Turn onto a plate. Continue until all the batter is used up.

Per crêpe: 96 calories, 4 g protein, 8 g carbohydrates, 1 g fiber, 5 g fat, 1 g sat fat, 55 mg cholesterol, 123 mg sodium

ADVANCE PREPARATION: These freeze well and will keep for several weeks. Stack them between pieces of wax paper or parchment and wrap airtight before freezing. You can make and refrigerate them up to a day ahead of serving.

Buckwheat Crêpes with Spinach and Egg

Makes 2 servings

■ **VEGETARIAN** ■ VEGAN ■ **LOW-CALORIE** ■ LOW-FAT
■ **HIGH-PROTEIN** ■ GLUTEN-FREE ■ HIGH IN OMEGA-3S

In France, for this dish, it's common to make the crêpe on a large, hot griddle and crack the egg right onto it; but that doesn't work well in a home crêpe pan. It's easier to have the crêpe already made and top it with the fried egg.

6 ounces baby spinach or 1 bunch spinach, stemmed and washed

Salt and ground black pepper

2 buckwheat crêpes (see opposite page)

2 large or extra-large eggs, poached or fried

2 tablespoons grated Gruyère cheese

1. Bring a large pot of generously salted water to a boil. Add the spinach. Blanch for 20 seconds and transfer to a bowl of ice water. Drain and squeeze dry. Chop and season with salt and pepper.

2. Heat the crêpes in a dry skillet over medium heat (or use the skillet you used to cook your eggs). Top with a spoonful of spinach. Top the spinach with the egg, setting the egg to one side so you can fold the crêpe over. Sprinkle the cheese over the top, fold the crêpe over, and transfer to a plate with a spatula. Serve hot.

Per serving: 231 calories, 14 g protein, 18 g carbohydrates, 5 g fiber, 13 g fat, 4 g sat fat, 273 mg cholesterol, 423 mg sodium

ADVANCE PREPARATION: You can have the spinach blanched and the eggs poached hours before you assemble these.

OTHER TOPPINGS FOR BUCKWHEAT CRÊPES: Choose from any of the vegetable dishes in Chapter 6. Sprinkle with cheese if desired.

Huevos Rancheros

Makes 4 servings

■ **VEGETARIAN** ▪ VEGAN ■ **LOW-CALORIE** ▪ LOW-FAT
■ **HIGH-PROTEIN** ■ **GLUTEN-FREE** ▪ HIGH IN OMEGA-3S

A classic—fried eggs on warm corn tortillas topped with cooked tomato salsa—though I probably make it a little differently than they do in your neighborhood Tex-Mex restaurant. This makes an easy supper as well as a great Mexican breakfast.

8 corn tortillas

2 pounds ripe tomatoes, peeled and coarsely chopped

2-3 serrano or jalapeño chile peppers, seeded if desired, and chopped (wear plastic gloves when handling)

2 garlic cloves, peeled

½ small onion, chopped

2 tablespoons canola oil

Salt

4-8 large or extra-large eggs

Chopped cilantro

Queso fresco

1. Preheat the oven to 350°F. Wrap the tortillas in foil and heat in the oven for 10 to 15 minutes.

2. Place the tomatoes, chile peppers, garlic, and onion in a blender. Blend, retaining a bit of texture.

3. Heat 1 tablespoon of the oil in a large, heavy nonstick skillet over high heat until a drop of the tomato mixture sizzles when it hits the pan. Add the mixture and cook, stirring, for 5 to 10 minutes, or until the sauce thickens, darkens, and leaves a trough when you run a spoon down the middle of the pan. It should be beginning to stick to the pan. Season to taste with salt and remove from the heat. Keep warm.

4. Warm 4 plates for a few minutes in the oven. Fry the eggs in a heavy skillet over medium-high heat. You won't need much oil if you have another non-stick skillet; otherwise, use the remaining 1 table-spoon of oil. Cook them sunny-side up, until the whites are solid and the yolks are set but still runny. Season with salt and pepper, and remove from the heat. Place 2 warm tortillas on each plate, overlapping if you are only serving 1 egg. Top with 1 or 2 fried eggs. Spoon the warm salsa over the whites of the eggs and the tortillas, leaving the yolks exposed if possible. Garnish with cilantro and queso fresco, and serve.

Per serving: 319 calories, 13 g protein, 39 g carbohydrates, 7 g fiber, 14 g fat, 2 g sat fat, 212 mg cholesterol, 129 mg sodium

ADVANCE PREPARATION: The cooked salsa will keep for a couple of days in the refrigerator. You may want to thin it out with a little water.

VARIATION: HUEVOS MOTULEÑOS In this Yucate-can variation, black beans are added to the mix. Heat 2 cups Simmered Black Beans (page 278) in a saucepan. Spoon the beans over the tortillas, then top with the eggs and salsa. Sprinkle a little queso fresco over the top.

Tofu

Few foods are more polarizing than tofu, and for most it's a love/hate thing. I am firmly in the love camp; I especially relish its texture, particularly firm tofu's, and the way it absorbs flavors. When I was a strict vegetarian, it was my main source of protein and it's still my favorite soy food, one I eat quite regularly.

Nutritionists appear to be at odds over the health benefits of soy; some are great advocates of soy foods, others are not. According to well-known nutritionist Marion Nestle, PhD, MPH, professor in the department of nutrition, food studies, and public health at New York University, and author of the book *What to Eat*, the numerous studies that have been and continue to be published on the subject are contradictory, and the science behind the claims at both ends of the spectrum is less than compelling.

Tofu may or may not be a magic bullet, but it certainly has a lot going for it nutritionally. Light and easily digestible, it's is a very good source of protein, magnesium, iron, calcium, omega-3 fatty acids, selenium, and copper. Furthermore, it contains isoflavones, which are structurally similar to estrogen and could be of benefit to postmenopausal women. But I've never eaten any food solely because it's healthy (nor is that why millions of Japanese, Chinese, and Koreans eat this delicate white curd made from soy milk, much the way ricotta cheese is made from dairy milk). I eat it because I like it.

For the most part, I use tofu the way it is used traditionally—in Asian cuisines. I cook it with Asian seasonings—ginger and garlic, soy sauce and chile—in stir-fries and soups, noodle dishes and fried rice dishes. I don't try to turn tofu into fake meat products like burgers and sausages. But I do like to do some novel things with tofu, like marinating and grilling or searing it (page 254), or scrambling it with Mexican ingredients and using it as a filling for delicious tacos (page 266), or baking it into a sweet, dairy-free spread that's nice for toast (page 16).

Seek out organic tofu. Most soybeans are grown from genetically modified seeds and treated with copious amounts of chemical pesticides and fertilizers, but these soybeans cannot be used to make organic tofu.

Grilled or Pan-Fried Marinated Tofu

Makes 4 servings

■ **VEGETARIAN** ■ **VEGAN** ■ **LOW-CALORIE** ■ LOW-FAT
■ **HIGH-PROTEIN** ■ GLUTEN-FREE ■ HIGH IN OMEGA-3S

Tofu absorbs flavors like a sponge. The marinade doesn't penetrate too much beneath the surface, but it gives the tofu a meaty flavor nonetheless. This is one of my favorite ways to eat tofu. Always be sure to keep some marinating in the refrigerator, then grill or pan-fry at will.

1 tablespoon Asian sesame oil

¼ cup soy sauce

2 tablespoons mirin (sweet Japanese rice wine)

1 tablespoon rice vinegar

1 tablespoon minced or grated fresh ginger

1 teaspoon sugar

For the tofu:

1 pound firm tofu

1 tablespoon canola oil or peanut oil

Soy sauce for serving

1. To make the marinade: Combine the sesame oil, soy sauce, mirin, vinegar, ginger, and sugar in a 2-quart bowl. Whisk together well.

2. Drain the tofu and pat dry with paper towels. Slice into $\frac{1}{2}$-inch-thick slabs and blot each slab with paper towels. Add to the bowl with the marinade and gently toss to coat. Cover and refrigerate for 15 minutes to 1 hour, or for up to 1 day.

3. To pan-fry the tofu: Heat the oil in a large, heavy nonstick skillet over medium-high heat. When the oil is hot, add the tofu in 1 layer (you may have to do this in batches). Cook on 1 side for 1 to 2 minutes, or until lightly colored. Using tongs, turn the tofu and cook for 1 to 2 minutes, or until lightly colored on the other side. Remove from the pan and serve, with additional marinade or with soy sauce.

4. To grill the tofu: Prepare a medium-hot grill. Brush the grill with the oil and cook the tofu until grill marks appear, $1\frac{1}{2}$ to 2 minutes per side. Remove from the heat and serve, with any remaining marinade or with additional soy sauce.

Per serving: 259 calories, 19 g protein, 11 g carbohydrates, 3 g fiber, 17 g fat, 2 g sat fat, 0 mg cholesterol, 1,332 mg sodium

ADVANCE PREPARATION: Pan-fried or grilled tofu can be kept for 5 days in the refrigerator and served hot or cold. It makes a good snack.

Note: *For a spicy dish, add 1 teaspoon Asian chile sauce, such as sambal oelek, to the marinade.*

Spicy Stir-Fried Tofu with Bok Choy or Baby Broccoli

Makes 4 servings

■ **VEGETARIAN** ■ **VEGAN** ■ **LOW-CALORIE** ■ LOW-FAT
■ **HIGH-PROTEIN** ■ GLUTEN-FREE ■ HIGH IN OMEGA-3S

Because tofu has such a mild flavor, it's well matched with spicy sauces like this one. If you serve this with rice, noodles, or other grains, it makes a great vegan main dish.

2 tablespoons canola oil or peanut oil

1 pound firm tofu, sliced ½-inch thick into
   1-inch x 2-inch dominoes

1 red bell pepper, cut into thin strips

2 garlic cloves, minced

1 tablespoon minced fresh ginger

4 scallions, chopped, dark green parts kept separate

1 pound bok choy or baby broccoli, stems sliced,
   leaves or florets left whole

2 tablespoons soy sauce

1 teaspoon Asian chile sauce, such as sambal oelek

1. Heat a large skillet or wok over high heat until a drop of water evaporates on contact. Add 1 tablespoon of the oil, increase the heat to medium-high,

Stir-Fries

Many stir-fries have fairly long ingredient lists. The most efficient way—the only way in fact—to make these dishes is to measure out everything before you begin. The time you spend in the preparation of the ingredients will be more than compensated by the speed with which the dishes are cooked. Have everything chopped and measured. Combine any ingredients that will be added to the dish at the same time; for example, if you are instructed to add 2 teaspoons soy sauce and 1 teaspoon hoisin sauce after you have stir-fried other ingredients, stir them together in a small bowl before you begin. If the garlic and ginger are to be added at the same time, once they are minced, put them together in a small dish. Have everything close to the stove and have your serving dish close by as well. Don't even begin to heat the pan until you have assembled everything and set the table.

and add the tofu. Cook, stirring, for 2 to 3 minutes, or until lightly colored. Transfer to a plate.

2. Add the remaining 1 tablespoon of oil to the pan and add the bell pepper. Cook, stirring, for 3 minutes. Add the garlic, ginger, and the light parts of the scallions. Cook, stirring, for about 15 seconds and add the bok choy or baby broccoli. Cook, stirring, for about 1 minute, or until coated with oil and beginning to wilt. Add ¼ cup water. Cook, stirring, until the water evaporates, about 2 minutes. Add the tofu, soy sauce, and chile sauce. Cook, stirring, for a couple of minutes, or until the ingredients are well seasoned. Remove from the heat, sprinkle on the dark green part of the scallions, and serve.

Per serving: 266 calories, 21 g protein, 12 g carbohydrates, 5 g fiber, 18 g fat, 2 g sat fat, 0 mg cholesterol, 799 mg sodium

ADVANCE PREPARATION: This is a last-minute dish but you can have all of the ingredients prepped well in advance of cooking it.

Bok choy and baby broccoli are both members of the Brassica family and are loaded with antioxidant-rich phytochemicals called indoles, as well as calcium, potassium, and beta-carotene.

Spinach, Tofu, and Sesame Stir-Fry

Makes 3 servings

■ **VEGETARIAN** ■ **VEGAN** ■ **LOW-CALORIE** ■ LOW-FAT
■ **HIGH-PROTEIN** ■ GLUTEN-FREE ■ HIGH IN OMEGA-3S

You can serve this simple stir-fry with grains or noodles, or for a great lunch, use it as a filling for a whole wheat pita pocket.

1 tablespoon canola oil

½ pound firm tofu, cut into small dice

1 large garlic clove, minced

1 teaspoon grated or minced fresh ginger

¼ teaspoon red-pepper flakes

Soy sauce

1 bag (6 ounces) baby spinach, rinsed, or 1 bunch, stemmed, washed, and chopped

2 tablespoons sesame seeds, toasted

2 cups cooked rice

1 teaspoon Asian sesame oil

1. Heat the canola oil in a large nonstick skillet or a wok over medium-high heat. Add the tofu. Cook, stirring, until the tofu is lightly colored, 3 to 5 minutes.

Add the garlic, red-pepper flakes, and ginger. Cook, stirring, until fragrant, about 30 seconds. Add soy sauce to taste. Add the spinach and cook, stirring, until the spinach wilts, about 1 minute. Stir in the sesame seeds and add more soy sauce to taste. Remove from the heat.

2. Using tongs, transfer the spinach and tofu mixture to a serving bowl, leaving the liquid behind in the pan or wok. If you wish, use the liquid left behind in the pan or wok to moisten the rice. Drizzle the tofu mixture with the sesame oil and add more soy sauce as desired. Serve over the rice.

Per serving: 367 calories, 17 g protein, 41 carbohydrates, 5 g fiber, 16 g fat, 2 g sat fat, 0 mg cholesterol, 248 mg sodium

ADVANCE PREPARATION: This is a last-minute preparation, but you can have your ingredients prepared well in advance.

VARIATION: SPINACH TOFU SPRING ROLLS Once cooked, finely chop the tofu and spinach and use as a filling for spring rolls or wontons. Use about 1 rounded teaspoon per wonton, and for spring rolls, use soft rice-flour wrappers. Soak the wrappers in hot water for about 30 seconds, until just softened. Place 1 tablespoon of filling in the middle of the softened wrapper, fold the sides over the filling, then roll up tightly. The soft spring rolls require no further cooking. Wontons can be simmered in broth or fried in oil (I prefer simmering).

Stir-Fried Tofu with Snow Peas and Soba Noodles

Makes 4 servings

■ **VEGETARIAN** ■ **VEGAN** ■ LOW-CALORIE ■ LOW-FAT
■ **HIGH-PROTEIN** ■ GLUTEN-FREE ■ HIGH IN OMEGA-3S

This dish has Szechuan overtones, with the peanut butter and the hot red-pepper oil, which you can find in the Asian section of your supermarket. Make sure not to overcook the snow peas, which will become stringy if cooked for too long.

Snow peas are a great source of fiber, and a good source of vitamin K, calcium, vitamin C, and the eye-protective carotenoids, lutein and zeaxanthin.

½ pound soba noodles

3 tablespoons Asian sesame oil

1 tablespoon peanut butter

2 tablespoons white wine vinegar or seasoned rice vinegar

1 tablespoon plus 2 teaspoons soy sauce

1–2 teaspoons Asian chili oil

Pinch of cayenne

2 garlic cloves, minced

1 tablespoon finely minced fresh ginger

½ cup Vegetable Stock (page 67)

2 tablespoons canola oil

½ pound firm tofu, sliced ½ inch thick into 1-inch x 2-inch dominoes

½ pound snow peas, strings removed

1 bunch scallions, thinly sliced, white and light-green parts only

4 large radishes, halved and thinly sliced

3 tablespoons chopped cilantro

1. Cook the soba noodles, following the directions on page 312. Drain, toss with 1 teaspoon of the sesame oil, and set aside.

2. Heat the peanut butter for 10 seconds in a microwave to make it easier to mix. Combine with the vinegar, 1 tablespoon of the soy sauce, chili oil, cayenne, and half of the garlic and ginger, and whisk together. Whisk in the stock and the remaining 2 teaspoons of sesame oil. Set aside.

3. Heat a large skillet or wok over high heat until a drop of water evaporates on contact. Add the oil, reduce the heat to medium-high, and add the tofu. Cook, stirring, for 2 to 3 minutes, or until beginning to color. Add the snow peas. Cook, stirring, for 1 to 2 minutes. Add the scallions and the remaining garlic and ginger. Cook, stirring, for 20 seconds. Add the remaining 2 teaspoons of soy sauce and toss together. Add the noodles and the sauce. Toss together until the noodles are hot, and remove from the heat. Add the radishes and cilantro, stir, and serve.

Per serving: 466 calories, 23 g protein, 59 g carbohydrates, 6 g fiber, 19 g fat, 2 g sat fat, 0 mg cholesterol, 1,078 mg sodium

ADVANCE PREPARATION: You can cook the noodles up to 3 days ahead. The ingredients for the sauce can be combined several hours before you make the stir-fry.

Sweet and Sour Cabbage with Tofu and Grains

Makes 4 generous servings

■ **VEGETARIAN** ■ **VEGAN** ■ **LOW-CALORIE** ■ LOW-FAT
■ **HIGH-PROTEIN** ■ GLUTEN-FREE ■ HIGH IN OMEGA-3S

You can use either regular green cabbage or Napa cabbage for this slightly spicy sweet-and-sour stir-fry. I like to serve the dish with bulgur (rice would be more typically Asian), but you could also serve it with rice, noodles, or any other grain.

2 tablespoons rice vinegar or sherry vinegar

1 tablespoon sugar

¾ pound firm tofu, sliced ½ inch thick into
   1-inch x 2-inch dominoes

2 tablespoons peanut oil or canola oil

1 tablespoon soy sauce

1 small onion, sliced

1 bunch scallions, thinly sliced, dark green parts
   kept separate

2 garlic cloves, minced

1 tablespoon minced fresh ginger

Pinch of cayenne

1 medium cabbage, quartered, cored, and sliced
   crosswise

2 teaspoons sesame seeds, toasted (optional)

Cooked bulgur, rice, noodles, or other grains

1. Combine the vinegar and sugar in a small bowl. Stir to dissolve the sugar, and set aside. Blot the tofu dry with paper towels.

2. Heat a large skillet or wok over high heat until a drop of water evaporates on contact. Add 1 tablespoon of the oil, reduce the heat to medium-high, and add the tofu. Cook, stirring, for 2 to 3 minutes, or until lightly colored. Add the soy sauce, toss together for about 30 seconds, and remove from the heat. Set aside in a bowl.

3. Heat the remaining 1 tablespoon of oil in the pan over medium-high heat. Add the onion. Cook, stirring, for about 3 minutes, or until crisp-tender. Add the light parts of the scallions, the garlic, and ginger. Stir together for about 30 seconds, or until fragrant. Add the cayenne and cabbage. Cook, stirring, until the cabbage begins to wilt, about 2 minutes. Stir in the vinegar mixture and cook, stirring, until the cabbage is crisp-tender, 3 to 5 minutes.

4. Return the tofu to the pan and toss with the cabbage. Add more soy sauce to taste and stir together. Sprinkle on the dark scallion greens and sesame seeds (if using) and remove from the heat. Serve with the grains or noodles.

Per serving: 372 calories, 21 g protein, 44 g carbohydrates, 13 g fiber, 14 g fat, 2 g sat fat, 0 mg cholesterol, 414 mg sodium

ADVANCE PREPARATION: This is a last-minute dish, but you can have everything prepped and ready to go hours before you cook.

Rainbow Tofu (Stir-Fried Tofu and Peppers)

Makes 4 servings

■ **VEGETARIAN** ■ **VEGAN** ■ **LOW-CALORIE** ■ LOW-FAT
■ HIGH-PROTEIN ■ GLUTEN-FREE ■ HIGH IN OMEGA-3S

This beautiful stir-fry is inspired by a traditional Chinese dish called Rainbow Beef. The vegetarian version works well, and it's easier to make. If you prefer a very firm tofu, take the extra time to weight it as directed in Step 1, though I rarely bother.

½ pound firm tofu

2 tablespoons soy sauce

1½ teaspoons packed light brown sugar

2 tablespoons vegetable, peanut, or canola oil

2 teaspoons hoisin sauce

1 teaspoon Asian sesame oil

2 red bell peppers, cut into 1-inch squares

1 green bell pepper, cut into 1-inch squares

2 large garlic cloves, minced

1 tablespoon minced fresh ginger

¼–½ teaspoon red-pepper flakes

2 scallions, cut on the diagonal into 1-inch lengths, dark green parts kept separate

Cooked rice or noodles

1. Optional step, for firmer tofu: Blot the tofu dry, wrap in a clean kitchen towel, and place a cutting board on top. Let sit for about 15 minutes. Whether weighted or not, slice the tofu about ½ inch thick into 1-inch by 2-inch dominoes.

2. Mix together 1 tablespoon of the soy sauce, 1 teaspoon of the brown sugar, and 1 tablespoon of the oil in a bowl. Toss with the tofu and stir to make sure all of the pieces are coated. Let sit for 5 to 10 minutes while you prepare the other ingredients.

3. Stir together the hoisin sauce, sesame oil, and remaining 1 tablespoon soy sauce and ½ teaspoon brown sugar in a small bowl. Set aside.

4. Heat a large skillet or wok over high heat until a drop of water evaporates on contact. Add the remaining 1 tablespoon oil, reduce the heat to medium-high, and add the bell peppers. Cook, stirring, for 2 minutes, or until the peppers begin to soften. Add the garlic and ginger. Cook, stirring, for 20 seconds, or until the garlic and ginger begin to smell fragrant. Add the tofu, red-pepper flakes, and white and light green parts of the scallions. Cook, stirring, for 2 minutes. Give the sauce a stir and add to the pan. Cover and cook for 3 minutes. Uncover, stir in the dark green parts of the scallions, taste, and adjust the seasonings. Serve with the rice or noodles.

Per serving: 305 calories, 13 g protein, 36 g carbohydrates, 4 g fiber, 14 g fat, 2 g sat fat, 0 mg cholesterol, 732 mg sodium

ADVANCE PREPARATION: Everything can be prepped hours ahead. The cooking is last-minute.

Stir-Fried Tofu and Eggplant with Asian Basil

Makes 4 servings

■ **VEGETARIAN*** ■ **VEGAN*** ■ **LOW-CALORIE** ▪ LOW-FAT
■ **HIGH-PROTEIN** ▪ GLUTEN-FREE ▪ HIGH IN OMEGA-3S

My friend John Lyons designs kitchen gardens and has taught me everything I know about growing vegetables. He's always bestowing me with surprises from his own garden, and one day he brought me a big bag of Asian basil and some beautiful Japanese eggplants. This Thai-influenced dish is what became of them.

1 pound eggplant, preferably long Japanese eggplants, diced

1 pound firm tofu

3 large garlic cloves, peeled

¼ teaspoon salt

1 tablespoon minced fresh ginger

2 serrano chile peppers, seeded if desired and minced (wear plastic gloves when handling)

1 tablespoon fish sauce or soy sauce

2 teaspoons soy sauce

1 teaspoon sugar

Ground black pepper

3 tablespoons peanut oil or vegetable oil, as needed

1 cup Asian basil leaves, coarsely chopped

2 cups cooked rice

*If you omit the fish sauce

1. Salt the eggplant generously and leave in a colander to sweat for 15 to 30 minutes, while you prepare the remaining ingredients. Rinse and drain on a clean kitchen towel.

2. Meanwhile, blot the tofu dry, wrap in a clean kitchen towel and place a cutting board on top. Let sit for 15 to 30 minutes, then cut into ¾-inch dice.

3. Place the garlic and salt in a mortar and mash to a paste with a pestle. Add the ginger and chile peppers, and continue to mash to a paste with the garlic. Mix together the fish sauce, soy sauce, sugar, and black pepper in a small bowl, and set aside.

4. Heat a large, heavy nonstick skillet or wok over high heat until a drop of water evaporates on contact. Add 1 tablespoon of the oil, reduce the heat to medium-high, and add the garlic paste. Cook, stirring, for 15 seconds. Add the tofu. Cook, stirring, for about 3 minutes, or until the tofu has colored lightly. Transfer from the pan to a bowl or plate.

5. Heat the remaining 2 tablespoons of oil and add the eggplant. Cook, stirring, until the eggplant is lightly browned and almost cooked through, about 10 minutes. Stir the tofu mixture back into the pan and add the fish sauce mixture. Add $1/4$ cup water, cover, reduce the heat to medium, and steam the mixture for 5 minutes. Uncover and stir in the basil leaves. Cook, stirring, for 30 seconds to 1 minute. Remove from the heat, and serve with the rice.

Per serving: 399 calories, 22 g protein, 37 g carbohydrates, 7 g fiber, 21 g fat, 3 g sat fat, 0 mg cholesterol, 623 mg sodium

ADVANCE PREPARATION: I have made this dish, refrigerated it for a few hours, then reheated and served it with warm rice. The leftovers, which will keep for a couple of days in the refrigerator, make a great filling for lettuce wraps or spring rolls.

Stir-Fried Tofu and Greens

Makes 4 servings

■ **VEGETARIAN** ■ **VEGAN** ■ **LOW-CALORIE** ■ LOW-FAT
■ **HIGH-PROTEIN** ■ GLUTEN-FREE ■ HIGH IN OMEGA-3S

This is a simple combination of tofu and greens seasoned with ginger, garlic, and hoisin sauce. It's a perfect destination for those 1-pound bags of washed, stemmed, mixed sturdy greens (usually a mixture of kale, collards, and mustard greens) that you can get in the supermarket. I like to serve this dish with noodles, but rice is also good with it.

> $3/4$ to 1 pound firm tofu
>
> Salt
>
> 2 large bunches greens (about $1^{1}/_{2}$ pounds), such as Swiss chard, beet greens, turnip greens, or kale, stemmed and washed well in several changes of water, or 1 bag (1 pound) stemmed, cleaned cooking greens
>
> 2 tablespoons soy sauce
>
> 1 tablespoon hoisin sauce
>
> $1/4$ cup water
>
> 2 tablespoons vegetable, canola, or peanut oil
>
> 2 large garlic cloves, minced
>
> 1 tablespoon minced or grated fresh ginger
>
> Cooked rice noodles

1. Blot the tofu dry, wrap in a clean kitchen towel, and place a cutting board on top. Let sit for about 30 minutes. Slice about $1/2$ inch thick into 1-inch by 2-inch dominoes.

2. Bring a large pot of water to a boil over high heat. Fill a bowl with ice water. When the water comes to a boil, salt generously and add the greens. Cook the greens for 2 minutes, or until just tender, and transfer with a slotted spoon or deep-fry skimmer to the ice water. Drain and gently squeeze out the water (you don't have to squeeze them completely dry). Chop coarsely.

3. Combine 1 tablespoon of the soy sauce with the hoisin sauce and stock or water in a small bowl or measuring cup. Set aside. Heat a large, heavy skillet or wok over high heat until a drop of water evaporates on contact. Add 1 tablespoon of the oil, swirl to coat the pan, and reduce the heat to medium-high. Add the tofu and cook, stirring, for 2 to 3 minutes, or until lightly colored.

4. Add the remaining 1 tablespoon of oil and the garlic and ginger. Cook, stirring, until fragrant and beginning to color, about 20 to 30 seconds. Stir in the remaining 1 tablespoon of soy sauce, then add the greens, and cook, stirring, for 30 seconds to 1 minute. Add the soy sauce and hoisin mixture. Stir together for about 1 minute, and serve with the noodles.

Per serving: 334 calories, 19 g protein, 36 g carbohydrates, 6 g fiber, 15 g fat, 2 g sat fat, 1 mg cholesterol, 1,171 mg sodium

ADVANCE PREPARATION: The cooked greens will keep for 3 to 4 days in a covered bowl in the refrigerator.

Tofu and Rainbow Chard Hotpot

Makes 6 servings

■ **VEGETARIAN** ■ **VEGAN** ■ **LOW-CALORIE** ■ LOW-FAT
■ **HIGH-PROTEIN** ■ GLUTEN-FREE ■ HIGH IN OMEGA-3S

Rainbow chard yields a broth with a pinkish hue, which is picked up by the tofu. This dish is like a combination stir-fry/stew, with lots of broth to spoon over rice.

1 ounce dried shiitake mushrooms

1 large or 2 small bunches rainbow chard (about 1½ pounds)

2 tablespoons soy sauce

1 teaspoon sugar

2 tablespoons dry sherry or rice wine

2–3 teaspoons Asian chile sauce, such as sambal oelek

2 tablespoons canola oil or peanut oil

1 pound firm tofu, cut into ¾-inch cubes or dominoes (½ inch thick x 1 inch x 2 inches)

1 medium onion, sliced

2–3 large garlic cloves, minced

1 tablespoon minced fresh ginger

Rice or noodles for serving

1. Put the mushrooms in a heatproof bowl or a large glass measuring cup and cover with 3 cups boiling water. Allow to sit for 15 to 30 minutes. Set a cheesecloth-lined sieve over a bowl and drain the mushrooms. Squeeze the mushrooms over the sieve and reserve the soaking liquid. Rinse the mushrooms in several changes of water. Cut away and discard the stems, and slice the caps about ¼ inch thick. Set aside. Add 1 tablespoon of the soy sauce to the mushroom soaking liquid and set aside.

2. Stem the chard and wash the leaves in 2 changes of water. Rinse the stems, trim the ends, and dice the thick bottom ends. Set aside. Stack the leaves and cut into 1-inch-wide ribbons. Set aside.

3. Combine the sugar, sherry or rice wine, chile sauce, and remaining 1 tablespoon of soy sauce in a small bowl or measuring cup.

4. Heat a large skillet or wok over high heat until a drop of water evaporates on contact. Add 1 tablespoon of the oil, reduce the heat to medium-high, and add the tofu. Cook, stirring, for 2 to 3 minutes, or until lightly colored. Transfer to a bowl and reduce the heat to medium. Add the remaining 1 tablespoon of oil to the pan and add the onion. Cook, stirring often, until

tender, about 5 minutes. Add the garlic and ginger. Cook, stirring, for 30 seconds to 1 minute, or until fragrant. Add the chard stems and mushrooms. Cook, stirring, for 3 minutes, or until the chard stems are crisp-tender. Return the tofu to the pan, stir in the sherry-soy mixture, and cook, stirring, for about 30 seconds. Add the mushroom soaking liquid and bring to a simmer. Simmer for 10 minutes, uncovered. Turn up the heat so that the mixture is bubbling hard, and add the chard leaves. Cook, stirring often, until the chard is tender but still bright and the liquid has reduced somewhat, about 5 minutes. Taste and adjust the seasoning, adding soy sauce or salt as desired. Serve in wide bowls over rice or noodles.

Per serving: 209 calories, 15 g protein, 15 g carbohydrates, 4 g fiber, 12 g fat, 1 g sat fat, 1 mg cholesterol, 707 mg sodium

ADVANCE PREPARATION: Although you make this initially like a stir-fry, it is a brothy dish that can either be made at the last minute, or made up to a few hours ahead and reheated.

Soft Tacos with Scrambled Tofu and Tomatoes

Makes 4 servings

■ **VEGETARIAN** ■ **VEGAN** ■ **LOW-CALORIE** ■ LOW-FAT
■ **HIGH-PROTEIN** ■ **GLUTEN-FREE** ■ HIGH IN OMEGA-3S

Soft tofu makes a wonderful stand-in for scrambled eggs. These savory tacos make are as good for dinner or lunch as they are for breakfast.

> 1 can (14 ounces) tomatoes, drained
>
> 2 large garlic cloves, coarsely chopped
>
> 1 serrano or jalapeño chile pepper, seeded if desired and chopped (wear plastic gloves when handling)
>
> 1 tablespoon canola oil

> 1 small or 1/2 medium onion, chopped
>
> 1 teaspoon cumin seeds, lightly toasted and ground
>
> Salt
>
> 12 ounces medium-firm or firm silken tofu
>
> Soy sauce
>
> 1/4 cup chopped cilantro
>
> 8 corn tortillas
>
> Salsa Fresca (page 22) or bottled salsa

1. Combine the tomatoes, garlic, and chile pepper in a blender and blend until smooth.

2. Heat the oil in a large nonstick skillet over medium heat. Add the onion and cook, stirring, for minutes, or until tender. Increase the heat to medium-high and add the cumin. Stir together and when the pan is quite hot pour in the tomato mixture. It should sizzle. Cook, stirring, for 5 minutes, or until the sauce is thick, dark, and fragrant, and leaves a channel when you run your spoon down the center of the pan. Add salt to taste.

3. Add the tofu to the pan and mash it into the sauce, using the back of your spoon. Add soy sauce and cook for 5 minutes longer, stirring and mashing the tofu. Stir in the cilantro. Taste and adjust the seasonings.

4. Heat the tortillas. Either wrap them in foil and warm in a 350°F oven for 10 to 15 minutes, or heat through one at a time in a dry skillet. Place 2 tortillas on each plate. Top with the tofu mixture and serve, passing salsa to serve on the side.

Per serving: 328 calories, 19 g protein, 38 g carbohydrates, 7 g fiber, 13 g fat, 1 g sat fat, 0 mg cholesterol, 630 mg sodium

ADVANCE PREPARATION: Unlike scrambled eggs, scrambled tofu keeps well for a couple of days. You can reheat it, and I even like to eat this cold as a quick lunch.

Vegetable Gratins

There are many ways to put vegetables at the center of your plate, and gratins are among the most appealing. A vegetable gratin is simply a vegetable casserole, baked in the oven (preferably in an earthenware baking dish) until the top and sides are browned, or gratinéed. The French verb *gratter* (pronounced grah-tay) means to scrape (that's where our word for grater comes from), and if a gratin is properly baked, you will want to scrape the delicious browned bits away from the sides of the dish and eat them. The simplest French gratins are made by napping cooked vegetables with a rich béchamel sauce and baking until browned. These gratins are more substantial; they include eggs and a small amount of cheese, usually Gruyère, and make good vegetarian main dishes. You can serve them hot or at room temperature, so they make very convenient dishes for entertaining or for doing ahead.

Summer Squash Gratin

Makes 6 servings

■ **VEGETARIAN** ■ VEGAN ■ **LOW-CALORIE** ■ LOW-FAT
■ **HIGH-PROTEIN** ■ **GLUTEN-FREE** ■ HIGH IN OMEGA-3S

In summer, when you're getting more squash than you can handle in your CSA box, or you can't resist the mountains of multi-colored squash at the farmers' market, you can use a lot of it in this is a typical Provençal gratin, bound with rice and eggs.

  2 tablespoons extra virgin olive oil

  ½ medium onion, chopped

  2 large garlic cloves, minced

  1½ pounds summer squash, cut into ½-inch dice

  1 red bell pepper, diced (optional)

  Salt and ground black pepper

  2 tablespoons chopped flat-leaf parsley

  2 large or extra-large eggs

  ½ cup 1% milk

  ½ cup Arborio or Carnaroli rice, cooked (see sidebar, next page)

  1 teaspoon coarsely chopped fresh thyme leaves

  ½ cup (2 ounces) grated Gruyère cheese

  ¼ cup (1 ounce) grated Parmesan

1. Preheat the oven to 375°F. Oil a 2-quart baking dish with olive oil.

2. Heat the olive oil in a large, heavy skillet over medium heat and add the onion. Cook, stirring often, until tender, 5 to 8 minutes. Add the garlic, summer squash, bell pepper (if using), and ¹⁄₂ to ³⁄₄ teaspoon salt. Increase the heat to medium-high and cook, stirring, until the squash is translucent and the bell pepper tender, about 10 minutes. Add black pepper, taste and adjust the salt. Stir in the parsley and remove from the heat.

3. Beat together the eggs, milk, and salt (I use ¹⁄₂ teaspoon) and black pepper, in a medium bowl. Stir in the cooked rice, thyme, the sautéed squash and the cheeses. Scrape into the baking dish.

4. Bake for 35 to 40 minutes, until nicely browned on the top and edges. Remove from the oven and allow to stand for at least 10 minutes before serving, or allow to cool. The gratin is good hot, warm, or at room temperature.

Per serving: 221 calories, 11 g protein, 21 g carbohydrates, 2 g fiber, 11 g fat, 4 g sat fat, 86 mg cholesterol, 165 mg sodium

ADVANCE PREPARATION: The filling will keep for 3 days in the refrigerator. The gratin can be made a day ahead and reheated, and leftovers will be good for 4 to 5 days.

Cooking Short-Grain Rice for a Gratin

You can cook the rice here as you would cook pasta, in a large pot of boiling water. Bring 2 quarts water to a boil in a saucepan, salt generously, and add the rice. Boil for 15 minutes, until the rice is tender, then drain through a sieve and set aside.

Swiss Chard and Red Bell Pepper Gratin

Makes 6 servings

■ **VEGETARIAN** ■ VEGAN ■ **LOW-CALORIE** ■ LOW-FAT
■ **HIGH-PROTEIN** ■ **GLUTEN-FREE*** ■ HIGH IN OMEGA-3S

The seasons for red bell peppers and Swiss chard overlap, with the chard beginning to come in while peppers are still piled high in farmers' market stalls. The two look beautiful side by side in the market and on the plate.

1 generous bunch Swiss chard or 2 smaller bunches (about 1 ¹⁄₂ pounds)

3 tablespoons extra virgin olive oil

1 medium onion, chopped

1 red bell pepper, diced

Salt

2 large garlic cloves, minced

Ground black pepper

3 large or extra-large eggs

¹⁄₂ cup 1% milk

³⁄₄ cup (3 ounces) grated Gruyère cheese

¹⁄₂ cup Arborio or Carnaroli rice, cooked (see sidebar)

1 teaspoon fresh thyme leaves or ¹⁄₂ teaspoon dried thyme

2 tablespoons fresh or dry bread crumbs (optional)

*If you omit the bread crumbs

1. Bring a large pot of water to a boil over high heat. Fill a bowl with ice water. Strip the leaves from the stems of the Swiss chard. Set the stems aside. Wash the leaves in several rinses of water. When the water comes to a boil, salt generously and add the chard leaves. Blanch for about 1 minute, or just until tender. Using a skimmer or slotted spoon, transfer

immediately to the ice water. Let sit for a few minutes, then drain, squeeze out excess water, and chop medium-fine.

2. Preheat the oven to 375° F. Brush a 2-quart baking or gratin dish with some olive oil.

3. Trim both ends off the chard stems, then dice. Heat 2 tablespoons of the oil in a large, heavy non-stick skillet over medium heat. Add the onion. Cook, stirring, until tender, about 5 minutes. Add the chard stalks, bell pepper, and $^1/_2$ teaspoon salt, and cook, stirring often, for 5 to 8 minutes, or until the vegetables are just tender. Add the garlic, stir together for 30 seconds to 1 minute, until the garlic is fragrant. Stir in the chard leaves. Stir together for 30 seconds to 1 minute, just to blend the mixture and coat the chard with oil. Season with salt and black pepper, and remove from the heat.

4. Beat the eggs and milk together in a large bowl. Add the chard mixture, cheese, cooked rice, and thyme. Stir together. Season with salt and black pepper, if desired. Transfer to the baking dish. Sprinkle the bread crumbs (if using), over the top and drizzle on the remaining 1 tablespoon oil. If you're not using bread crumbs, still drizzle with the oil.

5. Bake for 35 to 40 minutes, or until firm and browned on the top. Remove from the heat and cool for at least 10 minutes before serving. You can serve this warm or at room temperature.

Per serving: 256 calories, 12 g protein, 21 g carbohydrates, 3 g fiber, 15 g fat, 4 g sat fat, 122 mg cholesterol, 357 mg sodium

ADVANCE PREPARATION: The blanched greens will keep for 3 to 4 days in the refrigerator in a covered bowl. The recipe can be prepared through Step 3 up to 2 days ahead. The finished recipe will keep for 3 to 4 days in the refrigerator.

Winter Squash Gratin

Makes 4 to 6 servings

■ **VEGETARIAN** ■ VEGAN ■ **LOW-CALORIE** ■ LOW-FAT
■ **HIGH-PROTEIN** ■ **GLUTEN-FREE** ■ HIGH IN OMEGA-3S

Winter squash can seem daunting, especially those big kabochas in the farmers' market. They're irresistible, but once you get one home you might be hard-pressed to know what to do with it. I roast my winter squash first, then it often ends up as a filling for a gratin. You can either puree the squash or dice it before mixing with the egg, milk, and cheese. Fresh sage is a particularly nice match for winter squash.

2 pounds winter squash (butternut, hubbard, kabocha)

2 tablespoons extra virgin olive oil

1 medium onion, chopped

2 garlic cloves, minced

2 tablespoons minced flat-leaf parsley

1 teaspoon minced fresh sage

Salt and ground black pepper

3 large or extra-large eggs

$^1/_2$ cup 1% milk

$^1/_2$ cup (2 ounces) grated Gruyère cheese,

$^1/_4$ cup (1 ounce) grated Parmesan

1. Preheat the oven to 400°F. Cover a baking sheet with foil and brush lightly with some olive oil. If using a big, hard squash like kabocha or hubbard, put it in the oven for 30 minutes, or until it has softened enough for you to cut it easily. Cut a 2-pound piece, cut away the seeds and membranes, and lay it on the foil. If using butternut squash, halve the squash, scoop out the seeds and stringy membranes, brush the cut sides with olive oil, and lay cut side down on the foil-covered baking sheet. Bake for 40 minutes, or until soft enough to pierce easily with a knife. Remove from the heat and

allow to cool, then peel and either mash with a fork, puree in a food processor or finely dice. You should have about 2 cups of pureed or diced squash.

2. Reduce the heat to 375°F. Oil a 2-quart gratin or baking dish. Heat the 2 tablespoons olive oil in a heavy skillet over medium heat. Add the onion. Cook, stirring, until tender, about 5 minutes. Add the garlic and cook, stirring, until fragrant, 30 seconds to 1 minute. Stir in the parsley, sage, and squash, and remove from the heat. Season to taste with salt and black pepper.

3. Beat the eggs in a large bowl and whisk in the milk. Add ½ teaspoon salt and black pepper to taste. Stir in the squash mixture and the Gruyère. Season with salt and black pepper. Scrape into the prepared baking dish and sprinkle the Parmesan over the top.

4. Bake for 30 to 40 minutes, or until lightly browned on the top and sizzling. Serve hot, warm, or at room temperature.

> **Per serving (based on 4 servings):** 316 calories, 15 g protein, 28 g carbohydrates, 4 g fiber, 18 g fat, 6 g sat fat, 181 mg cholesterol, 266 mg sodium

ADVANCE PREPARATION: You can make this up to a day ahead and reheat in a low oven.

Provençal Kale and Cabbage Gratin

Makes 6 servings

■ **VEGETARIAN** ■ VEGAN ■ **LOW-CALORIE** ■ LOW-FAT
■ **HIGH-PROTEIN** ■ **GLUTEN-FREE*** ■ HIGH IN OMEGA-3S

Provençal gratins, bound with rice and egg, make sturdy main dishes that are as good to eat cold or at room temperature as when they are hot out of the oven. This is a particularly pretty one, flecked with light strips of cabbage and dark strips of kale. You might even get your kids to eat greens if you make this gratin for them. It makes a perfect vegetarian main dish.

3 tablespoons extra virgin olive oil

1 medium onion, finely chopped

Salt

2 large garlic cloves, minced

6 leaves fresh sage, chopped

1 teaspoon fresh thyme leaves

1 pound kale (preferably cavolo nero), stemmed, washed thoroughly, and slivered

1 pound cabbage (preferably savoy cabbage), quartered, cored, and slivered

Ground black pepper

2 large or extra-large eggs

½ cup short-grain white rice, preferably Arborio or Carnaroli, or brown rice, cooked (see note, page 268)

¾ cup (3 ounces) grated Gruyère cheese

3 tablespoons bread crumbs (optional)

*If you omit the bread crumbs

1. Preheat the oven to 375°F. Oil a 2-quart baking dish. Heat 2 tablespoons of the oil in a large, heavy nonstick skillet over medium heat. Add the onion. Cook, stirring often, until tender and translucent, about 5 minutes. Stir in a generous pinch of

salt, the garlic, sage, and thyme. Cook for 1 minute, or until fragrant, then stir in the kale. Stir often, and when most of the kale has wilted, add the cabbage and salt to taste. Add $^{1}/_{2}$ cup water and bring to a simmer. Cook, stirring often, for 10 minutes, or until the water has evaporated and the kale and cabbage are wilted and fragrant but still have some texture and color. Add black pepper, taste, and adjust the salt.

2. Beat the eggs in a bowl and stir in the cooked vegetables, cooked rice, and cheese. Stir together well and scrape into the baking dish. Sprinkle the bread crumbs (if using) over the top and drizzle on the remaining 1 tablespoon of oil. If you're not using the bread crumbs, still drizzle with the oil. Bake for 40 to 45 minutes, or until firm and browned on the top. Allow to sit for 10 to 15 minutes before serving. Serve hot or warm.

Per serving: 264 calories, 11 g protein, 26 g carbohydrates, 4 g fiber, 14 g fat, 4 g sat fat, 86 mg cholesterol, 140 mg sodium

ADVANCE PREPARATION: This can be made a day ahead and reheated. Or prepare the vegetables through Step 1 a day ahead and assemble the gratin the next day. It will keep for 4 to 5 days in the refrigerator.

Corn and Vegetable Gratin with Cumin

Makes 6 servings

■ **VEGETARIAN** ■ VEGAN ■ **LOW-CALORIE** ■ LOW-FAT
■ **HIGH-PROTEIN** ■ **GLUTEN-FREE** ■ HIGH IN OMEGA-3S

This pretty gratin tastes rich but actually contains very little fat. I blend the kernels from one of the ears of corn with the eggs and milk for a sweet, thick custard that holds it all together. Cumin seeds accent the mixture and give it a Southwestern character.

> 1 tablespoon extra virgin olive oil
>
> 1 medium onion, finely chopped
>
> 1 medium red bell pepper, diced
>
> Salt
>
> 1 large garlic clove, minced
>
> $^{1}/_{2}$ pound zucchini, thinly sliced or diced
>
> Ground black pepper
>
> Kernels from 2 ears corn (about 2 cups)
>
> 3 large eggs
>
> $^{1}/_{2}$ cup 1% milk
>
> 1 teaspoon cumin seeds, lightly toasted and crushed or ground
>
> $^{1}/_{2}$ cup (2 ounces) grated Gruyère cheese

1. Preheat the oven to 375°F. Oil a 2-quart gratin or baking dish. Heat the 1 tablespoon olive oil in a large, nonstick skillet over medium heat. Add the onion. Cook, stirring often, until it begins to soften, about 3 minutes. Add the bell pepper and a generous pinch of salt. Cook, stirring often, until the onion and bell pepper are tender, about 5 minutes. Add the garlic and zucchini, stir together, and add

another generous pinch of salt and some black pepper. Cook, stirring often, until the zucchini is just beginning to look bright green and some of the slices are translucent, about 3 to 4 minutes. Add half of the corn kernels, stir together for 1 to 2 minutes, and remove from the heat. Scrape into a large bowl.

2. Place the eggs, milk, ½ teaspoon salt, and remaining corn kernels in a blender. Blend until smooth. Pour into the bowl with the vegetables. Add the cumin and cheese and stir everything together. Scrape into the gratin dish.

3. Bake for 35 to 40 minutes, or until the top is browned and the gratin is firm to the touch. Serve hot or warm.

Per serving: 170 calories, 9 g protein, 15g carbohydrates, 3 g fiber, 9 g fat, 3 g sat fat, 117 mg cholesterol, 114 mg sodium

ADVANCE PREPARATION: The vegetable filling can be prepared through Step 1 a day ahead and kept in the refrigerator.

Beans

Beans are an economical, delicious, and comforting way to feed your family well. They're an excellent source of protein, very low in fat, and exceptionally high in fiber. They're also a very good source of calcium, iron, folate, and potassium. Perhaps it's because beans are so economical that the custom of eating them on New Year's Day for prosperity exists in so many cultures.

Humble though beans may be, I often serve them at dinner parties in one form or another, and guests are always happy about it. They're also a reliable bet for kids; everybody seems to love a good pot of beans.

One thing that stops people from cooking beans is that they are considered time-consuming, a food that requires advance planning. While you can't just come home from work and decide to have a good pot of black beans for dinner, but you certainly could make any of the lentil dishes in this chapter, or the Warm Black-Eyed Peas Salad on page 285, because those beans cook quickly. As for the time-consuming element, beans require hardly any work, but some require long unsupervised simmering. If you're home, you can do something else while they cook. Since most bean dishes taste even better the next day, you could make many of the dishes in this chapter on a Sunday or a weeknight and have dinner for the week.

There is one trick to succeeding with beans, and that is not to boil them hard. If you do that, the beans will break apart before they are cooked through. To get intact beans with a soft, pillowy texture, bring them to a boil slowly, and when they reach the boiling point, reduce the heat and simmer them slowly until they are done. Also, make sure your beans have not been stored for too long. Look at the date on the package, or if you buy them in bulk, date the bag or jar you store them in. As beans age, they become hard and brittle. Some will simply never soften, even after long hours of simmering.

I've often heard this is an old wives' tale: That you shouldn't salt beans until the end of cooking or they won't soften properly. Both of these have been disproved, but out of habit I usually don't salt during the first hour of cooking; I make sure to salt, though, during the second half of the cooking time so that the beans have time to absorb the seasoning.

FOR MORE BEAN RECIPES, SEE:

Catalan Chickpea Stew

Makes 6 servings

■ **VEGETARIAN** ■ **VEGAN** ■ LOW-CALORIE ■ **LOW-FAT**
■ **HIGH-PROTEIN** ■ **GLUTEN-FREE** ■ HIGH IN OMEGA-3S

This slightly picante stew, based on a recipe from Catalonia in northeastern Spain, benefits from being made a day or two ahead. If you eat meat you can spice it up with a small amount of sausage if you wish.

1 pound chickpeas, soaked for 6 hours or overnight in 2 quarts water

1 bay leaf

Salt

1 tablespoon extra virgin olive oil

1 medium onion, chopped

1 medium green or red bell pepper, chopped

2 large garlic cloves, minced

1 can (28 ounces) diced tomatoes

$\frac{1}{2}$ teaspoon dried thyme

Ground black pepper

1 dried cayenne chile pepper or $\frac{1}{4}$–$\frac{1}{2}$ teaspoon red-pepper flakes

1. Drain the chickpeas and combine with enough water to cover by 2 inches in a large soup pot or Dutch oven. Add the bay leaf and bring to a gentle boil. Reduce the heat and skim off any foam. Cover and simmer for 1 hour. Add salt to taste and simmer for 1 hour, or until tender. Drain through a sieve set over a bowl and reserve 2 cups of the cooking liquid. Discard the bay leaf. Set the chickpeas aside.

2. Heat the oil in a large heavy pot over medium heat and add the onion. Cook over medium heat, stirring, until it begins to soften, about 3 minutes. Add the bell pepper. Cook, stirring often, until the onion and bell pepper are tender, 5 to 10 minutes. Add the garlic, stir together for 1 to 2 minutes, or until fragrant. Stir in the tomatoes (with the juice), thyme, and salt and black pepper to taste. Cook, stirring often, for about 10 minutes, or until the tomatoes have cooked down slightly. Add the chickpeas, cayenne pepper or red-pepper flakes, and the reserved chickpea cooking liquid. Return to a simmer and stir. Reduce the heat to very low, cover, and cook gently for 30 minutes to 1 hour, or until the beans are very tender and the broth is fragrant. Taste, adjust the seasonings, and serve.

Per serving: 329 calories, 17 g protein, 55 g carbohydrates, 16 g fiber, 7 g fat, 0.5 g sat fat, 0 mg cholesterol, 211 mg sodium

ADVANCE PREPARATION: This will keep for 3 to 4 days in the refrigerator and benefits from being made a day ahead and reheated.

Couscous with Winter Vegetables and Beans

Makes 8 generous servings

■ **VEGETARIAN** ■ **VEGAN** ■ **LOW-CALORIE** ■ **LOW-FAT**
■ HIGH-PROTEIN ■ GLUTEN-FREE ■ HIGH IN OMEGA-3S

You can make this nourishing, warming winter couscous with any number of beans—borlottis, pintos, chickpeas, Jacob's cattle. Don't be put off by the long ingredient list—most of them are spices. The dish is quite simple to make and can be made ahead; in fact it benefits from it.

1 tablespoon extra virgin olive oil

1 large onion, chopped

2 leeks, white and light-green parts only, thickly sliced and well-washed

4 large garlic cloves, minced

Salt

2 teaspoons cumin seeds, lightly toasted and ground

1 teaspoon coriander seeds, lightly toasted and ground

1 teaspoon caraway seeds, lightly toasted and ground

½ teaspoon cayenne

2 cups dried white beans, soaked for 6 hours or overnight in 2 quarts water

Bouquet garni made of 8 sprigs each of parsley and cilantro (page 67)

1–2 tablespoons harissa plus additional for serving

2 tablespoons tomato paste

1½ pounds winter squash, peeled, seeded, and cut into large dice (about 4 cups)

1 pound turnips, cut into wedges, or carrots, thickly sliced (or ½ pound each)

1 pound greens, stemmed and washed thoroughly, blanched in salted boiling water, and coarsely chopped

½ cup chopped flat-leaf parsley or cilantro, or a combination

2⅔ cups couscous, preferably whole wheat

1. Heat the oil in a large, heavy soup pot or Dutch oven over medium heat. Add the onion and leeks. Cook, stirring, until tender, about 5 minutes. Add the garlic, ½ teaspoon salt, the cumin, coriander, caraway, and cayenne and cook, stirring, for about 1 minute. Add the beans and their soaking liquid, 1 quart water, and the bouquet garni. Bring to a gentle boil. Add salt to taste, reduce the heat, cover, and simmer for 1 hour.

2. Add the harissa, tomato paste, squash, and turnips and/or carrots. Return to a simmer and cook for 45 minutes, or until the squash is beginning to fall apart and the beans are tender. Stir in the greens and parsley and/or cilantro. Simmer for 10 minutes. Taste and adjust the salt. The stew should be spicy and flavorful.

3. Reconstitute and steam the couscous, following the instructions on page 204. Serve the couscous in wide bowls or mound onto plates and top with the stew and a generous amount of broth. Pass more harissa at the table.

Per serving: 441 calories, 22 g protein, 86 g carbohydrates, 18 g fiber, 4 g fat, 0.5 g sat fat, 0 mg cholesterol, 434 mg sodium

ADVANCE PREPARATION: The stew can be made a day ahead and reheated. Leftovers will keep for 3 to 4 days in the refrigerator. The couscous can be reconstituted up to a day ahead, then steamed before serving.

Simmered Black Beans

Makes 6 servings

■ **VEGETARIAN** ■ **VEGAN** ■ **LOW-CALORIE** ■ **LOW-FAT**
■ **HIGH-PROTEIN** ■ **GLUTEN-FREE** ■ HIGH IN OMEGA-3S

Any successful dish made with black beans begins with a great pot of beans, sufficiently seasoned and slowly simmered with lots of onion and garlic, until they are soft pillows suspended in a thick, inky, savory broth. There's no comparison between that pot of black beans and the black beans that come in a can. With the beans in the can you not only lose out on flavor, but also on the nutrients that end up in the broth. In Mexico a sprig of epazote or a few dried avocado leaves are usually added to the pot. Those ingredients aren't as easy to find as cilantro, which is what I routinely use to season the beans. But if you do have access to epazote or avocado leaves, by all means use one or the other.

1 pound dried black beans, rinsed and picked over

1 tablespoon canola oil

1 medium onion, chopped

4 large garlic cloves, minced

1 epazote sprig or 2 dried avocado leaves
(optional)

Salt

¼ cup chopped cilantro plus additional
for garnish

1. Soak the beans in 2 quarts water for at least 6 hours. If they will be soaking for a long time in warm weather, put them in the refrigerator. Don't throw out the soaking liquid.

2. Heat the oil in a large, heavy soup pot or Dutch oven over medium heat. Add the onion. Cook, stirring, until it begins to soften, about 3 minutes. Add half of the garlic. Cook, stirring, until fragrant, about 1 minute. Add the beans and soaking liquid. They should be covered by at least 1 inch of water. Add more water as necessary, and bring to a gentle boil. Reduce the heat to low, and skim off any foam that rises. If using epazote or avocado leaves, add now. Cover and simmer for 1 hour.

3. Add salt, the cilantro, and remaining garlic. Continue to simmer for 1 hour, or until the beans are quite soft and the broth is thick and fragrant. Taste. Is there enough salt? Does it need more garlic? Add if necessary. Let sit overnight in the refrigerator for the best flavor.

Per serving: 282 calories, 15 g protein, 49 g carbohydrates, 7 g fiber, 2 g fat, 0 g sat fat, 0 mg cholesterol, 25 mg sodium

ADVANCE PREPARATION: The cooked beans will keep for about 3 to 4 days in the refrigerator and freeze well.

Refried Black Beans

Makes 6 servings

■ **VEGETARIAN** ■ **VEGAN** ■ LOW-CALORIE ■ **LOW-FAT**
■ **HIGH-PROTEIN** ■ **GLUTEN-FREE** ■ HIGH IN OMEGA-3S

These are not refried in lard like traditional frijoles. A more accurate description would be reduced black beans, as they are reduced in their broth over medium-high heat. Spread these on crisp corn tortillas for nachos or chalupas, or serve as a side dish, sprinkled with queso fresco (also known as queso ranchero).

Simmered Black Beans (opposite page)

2 tablespoons canola oil

1 tablespoon cumin seeds, lightly toasted and ground

2 teaspoons mild chili powder

1. Drain off about 1 cup of liquid from the beans, setting it aside in a separate bowl to use later for moistening the beans should they dry out. Coarsely mash half of the beans in a food processor or with a bean or potato masher. Don't puree them (you want texture). Stir the mashed beans back into the pot.

2. Heat the oil in a large, heavy nonstick skillet over medium-high heat. Add the cumin and chili powder. Cook, stirring for 30 seconds to 1 minute, until the spices begin to sizzle and cook. Add the beans. (This can be done in batches; in which case, cook the spices in batches as well.) Cook the beans, stirring and mashing often, until they thicken and begin to get crusty on the bottom. Stir up the crust each time it forms, and mix into the beans. Cook for about 20 minutes, stirring often and mashing the beans with the back of your spoon or a bean masher. The beans should be thick but not dry. They will continue to thicken and dry out when you remove them from the heat. Add the reserved liquid if they seem too dry, but save some for moistening the beans before you reheat them, if you are serving them later. Taste the refried beans and adjust the salt. They should be very aromatic. Set aside in the pan if you are serving within a few hours. Otherwise, transfer the beans to a lightly oiled baking dish, cover, and refrigerate.

Per serving: 327 calories, 15 g protein, 49 g carbohydrates, 7 g fiber, 7 g fat, 0.5 sat fat, 0 mg cholesterol, 27 mg sodium

ADVANCE PREPARATION: These will keep for 3 to 4 days in the refrigerator. To reheat, cover with foil and reheat in a 325°F oven for about 20 to 30 minutes.

Black Bean Enchiladas

Makes 6 servings

■ **VEGETARIAN** ■ VEGAN ■ LOW-CALORIE ■ LOW-FAT
■ HIGH-PROTEIN ■ **GLUTEN-FREE** ■ HIGH IN OMEGA-3S

Black bean enchiladas was my signature dish when I began my cooking career in Austin, Texas. It begins with a great pot of beans and well-seasoned tortillas. When you serve the enchiladas they may break apart, but that shouldn't stop you from loving them.

Simmered Black Beans (opposite page)

3 tablespoons canola oil

1 tablespoon plus 1 teaspoon cumin seeds, lightly toasted and ground

2-3 teaspoons mild chili powder

Salt

1 can (8 ounces) tomato sauce

1½ cups (6 ounces) grated medium or sharp white Cheddar cheese

12-14 corn tortillas

½ cup chopped walnuts (optional)

Chopped cilantro

Salsa Fresca (page 22) or bottled salsa, optional

1. Pour off half the liquid from the black beans and set aside. Puree half of the beans in some of the remaining liquid and stir back into the pot. Heat 1 tablespoon of the oil in a large nonstick skillet over medium-high heat. Add 1 tablespoon of the cumin and 1 to 2 teaspoons of the chili powder. Allow the spices to sizzle for about 30 seconds, then stir in the beans. Allow the beans to bubble and thicken for 10 to 15 minutes, stirring often, pressing down to mash them with the back of your spoon, and scraping the bottom and sides of the pan. They should be like runny refried beans. Taste, adjust the seasonings, and transfer to the bean pot. Clean and dry the skillet.

2. Preheat the oven to 350°F. Oil two 2-quart baking dishes. Heat the skillet over medium-high heat. Add 1 tablespoon of the oil and a generous pinch each of

The Power of Beans

Black beans stand out because in that shiny black coating there are at least eight different flavonoids, phytochemicals that are believed to have strong antioxidant powers. They're the same family of nutrients, called anthocyanins, found in red grapes and red wine, red cabbage, and other dark red fruits and vegetables. Black beans are an equally rich source. They also contain small amounts of omega-3 fatty acids, three times more than other legumes provide.

cumin and chili powder and a small pinch of salt. Add 3 tablespoons of the tomato sauce and stir together. One at a time, soften the tortillas in the mixture, turning as soon as the tortilla begins to buckle, about 10 seconds on each side. Use a spatula

to scrape off excess sauce. Remove from the heat and set aside in the baking dish or on a baking sheet. Add oil, spices, and tomato sauce to the pan as needed and continue to soften all the tortillas.

3. Set aside 1½ cups of the black bean sauce and ¾ cup of the cheese. If necessary, thin out the bean sauce with the black bean broth that you set aside. To assemble the enchiladas, spread a large spoonful of black bean sauce over each tortilla, then a sprinkling of cheese. Roll up and place in the baking dish seam side down, filling each baking dish with a single layer of the enchiladas (you should be able to get 6 or 7 enchiladas in each baking dish). When all the tortillas have been filled, pour on the reserved sauce and sprinkle with the reserved cheese and the walnuts (if using). Cover tightly with foil and bake for 30 to 40 minutes, or until the cheese is bubbling. Uncover, garnish with the cilantro, and serve. Use 2 spatulas as these tend to fall apart. If desired, pass the salsa at the table.

Per serving: 709 calories, 28 g protein, 96 g carbohydrates, 14 g fiber, 23 g fat, 7 g sat fat, 25 mg cholesterol, 582 mg sodium

ADVANCE PREPARATION: The beans can be made through Step 1 up to 3 days ahead. The enchiladas may be assembled and kept in the refrigerator overnight. Cover tightly with plastic and foil. Remember to remove the plastic before heating in the oven.

Soft Black Bean Tacos

Makes 8

■ **VEGETARIAN** ■ VEGAN ■ **LOW-CALORIE** ■ **LOW-FAT**
■ HIGH-PROTEIN ■ **GLUTEN-FREE** ■ HIGH IN OMEGA-3S

Soft tacos are very easy to throw together if you have some refried beans on hand and the ingredients for a fresh salsa. I heat my tortillas in a microwave, pile on the beans, top with salsa, sprinkle with a little crumbled cheese, and dinner is ready.

2 cups Refried Black Beans (page 279)

8 corn tortillas

1 cup Salsa Fresca (page 22) or bottled salsa

½ cup crumbled queso fresco or feta cheese

1. Heat the black beans in a nonstick skillet over medium heat, adding a little water (or liquid from the simmered beans), to moisten if necessary.

2. Heat the tortillas, 2 or 3 at a time, in a dry skillet over medium-high heat, or in a microwave. Top with the black beans, about 2 rounded tablespoons for each tortilla. Spoon on some salsa and sprinkle with the cheese. Fold the tortillas in half, and serve.

Per serving: 344 calories, 14 g protein, 55 g carbohydrates, 7 g fiber, 7 g fat, 1 g sat fat, 2 mg cholesterol, 88 mg sodium

ADVANCE PREPARATION: The refried black beans will keep for 3 days in the refrigerator.

Soaking Beans and Keeping the Soaking Liquid

I've been soaking my beans ever since I learned to cook them, because that's what I was told needed to be done in order for them to cook properly. But recently I've begun listening to colleagues who insist that beans do not require soaking. What I've found is that some beans cook perfectly well without soaking, though it takes a little more time. If you do soak your beans it's important to use the soaking liquid when you cook them so that you don't lose nutrients that leach out, especially with beans that have dark pigments, such as red and black beans. (I make an exception for white beans, as I don't care for the flavor of the soaking liquid.) You will not suffer from more gas if you don't throw out the liquid. That's a myth. As you eat more beans, your body will adjust to the additional fiber.

Black Bean Chili

Makes 6 to 8 servings

■ **VEGETARIAN** ■ **VEGAN*** ■ **LOW-CALORIE** ■ **LOW-FAT**
■ **HIGH-PROTEIN** ■ **GLUTEN-FREE** ■ HIGH IN OMEGA-3S

Black beans are a great choice for a vegetarian chili. This one is incredibly rich-tasting. It's medium-hot. If you prefer 3-alarm chili, make it hotter by using hot chili powder or adding more medium chili powder. This tastes best if you make the simmered black beans a day before you wish to serve the chili.

Simmered Black Beans (page 278)

2 tablespoons canola oil

1 onion, finely chopped

4 large garlic cloves, minced

3 tablespoons mild or hot chili powder

1 tablespoon cumin seeds, lightly toasted and ground

1 can (28 ounces) diced tomatoes

1 teaspoon dried oregano, preferably Mexican oregano

Salt

2 tablespoons tomato paste dissolved in 1 cup water

2 chipotle chiles in adobo sauce, seeded and chopped

½ cup chopped cilantro

4 ounces goat cheese or queso fresco, crumbled (about 1 cup)

*If you omit the cheese

1. Make the black beans as directed, preferably the day before you wish to serve.

2. Heat the oil in a nonstick skillet over medium heat. Add the onion. Cook, stirring often, until the onion is lightly colored, about 10 minutes. Add the garlic, stir together for about 1 minute, or until fragrant. Add the chili powder and cumin. Cook, stirring, for 2 to 3 minutes, or until the mixture begins to stick to the pan. Add the tomatoes (with juice), oregano, and salt to taste. Bring to a simmer and cook, stirring often, until the tomatoes have cooked down and the mixture is beginning to stick to the pan, about 10 minutes. Stir in the tomato paste dissolved in water and the chipotles and return to a simmer. Season with salt to taste and simmer, stirring often, for 15 minutes, or until the mixture is thick and fragrant.

3. Add the tomato mixture to the beans and bring to a simmer. Cook, stirring often, for 30 to 45 minutes. Taste and adjust the salt.

4. Just before serving, stir in the cilantro. Spoon into bowls and garnish each bowl with a generous spoonful of goat cheese or queso fresco.

> **Note:** *If you want a thicker chili, puree 1 to 2 cups of the beans in a blender or a food processor and stir back into the pot.*

> **Per serving (based on 6 servings):** 441 calories, 21 g protein, 58 g carbohydrates, 9 g fiber, 13 g fat, 4 g sat fat, 15 mg cholesterol, 526 mg sodium

ADVANCE PREPARATION: The simmered beans can be made 3 to 4 days ahead and the chili will keep for 3 to 4 days in the refrigerator. This freezes well.

Storing Tomato Paste

If you usually buy tomato paste in a can, you have probably thrown out a lot of moldy tomato paste that sat for too long in your refrigerator after you used the tablespoon or two called for in your recipe. Whenever you open a can from now on, measure out the tomato paste remaining in the can by the tablespoon, wrap each tablespoon of paste in plastic, place in a freezer bag, and freeze. Thaw as needed.

Chickpeas with Baby Spinach

Makes 3 servings

■ **VEGETARIAN** ■ **VEGAN** ■ **LOW-CALORIE** ■ **LOW-FAT**
■ HIGH-PROTEIN ■ **GLUTEN-FREE** ■ HIGH IN OMEGA-3S

This is mostly a pantry dish, very quick to put together. You can serve it on its own or with couscous, bulgur, pasta, or over a thick slice of toasted bread rubbed with garlic.

1 tablespoon extra virgin olive oil

1 medium onion, chopped

2 garlic cloves, minced

1 teaspoon cumin seeds, lightly toasted
    and ground

1 tablespoon tomato paste

Salt

1 can (15 ounces) chickpeas, rinsed and drained

1 cup Vegetable Stock (page 67) or water

Cayenne pepper

1 bag (6 ounces) baby spinach, or 1 12-ounce bunch
    spinach, stemmed, washed, and coarsely chopped

Ground black pepper

1. Heat the oil in a large, heavy saucepan over medium heat. Add the onion. Cook, stirring, until tender, about 5 minutes. Add the garlic, cumin, tomato paste, and ¹/₂ teaspoon salt and cook, stirring, for 1 to 2 minutes, or until fragrant and the tomato paste has turned a darker color. Add the chickpeas, the stock or water, and cayenne to taste, and bring to a simmer. Cover, reduce the heat, and simmer for 10 minutes.

2. Add the spinach a handful at a time, stirring until each addition of spinach wilts. Add salt to taste and simmer uncovered, stirring often, for 5 minutes. Add lots of black pepper, taste, and adjust the seasoning with salt and cayenne, and serve.

Per serving: 186 calories, 7 g protein, 28 g carbohydrates, 8 g fiber, 6 g fat, 1 g sat fat, 0 mg cholesterol, 368 mg sodium

ADVANCE PREPARATION: This can be made up to a day ahead and refrigerated, but when you reheat you'll want to add a little more liquid. It can sit on top of the stove for a few hours, off the heat.

Andean Bean Stew with Winter Squash and Quinoa

Makes 6 to 8 generous servings

■ **VEGETARIAN** ■ **VEGAN** ■ **LOW-CALORIE** ■ **LOW-FAT**
■ **HIGH-PROTEIN** ■ **GLUTEN-FREE** ■ HIGH IN OMEGA-3S

This savory, filling bean and vegetable stew is inspired by a Chilean dish. I've substituted quinoa for the corn called for in the authentic version. Make it a day ahead for the best flavor.

1 pound dried pinto beans, soaked for 6 hours or overnight in 2 quarts water

Salt

2 tablespoons extra virgin olive oil

1 medium onion, chopped

1 tablespoon sweet paprika

4 large garlic cloves, minced

1 can (14 ounces) diced tomatoes

1 bay leaf

1 pound winter squash, such as butternut, peeled and cut into ¾-inch cubes

½ cup quinoa, rinsed thoroughly

Ground black pepper

3 tablespoons chopped fresh basil, cilantro, or flat-leaf parsley

1. Place the beans and soaking liquid in a large pot. Add water if necessary to cover the beans by about 2 inches, and bring to a gentle boil. Skim off any foam, reduce the heat to low, cover, and simmer gently for 1 hour, or until the beans are tender but intact. Add salt to taste.

2. Heat the oil in a large, heavy nonstick skillet over medium heat. Add the onion. Cook, stirring, until the onion is tender, about 5 minutes. Add a generous pinch of salt and the paprika. Stir together for about 1 minute, and add the garlic. Cook, stirring, for 1 to 2 minutes, or until the garlic and onion are very fragrant but not brown. Add the tomatoes (and juice) and salt to taste. Cook, stirring often, until the tomatoes have cooked down slightly and are fragrant, 5 to 10 minutes. Remove from the heat and scrape the contents of the pan into the pot of beans.

3. Return the beans to a simmer. Add the bay leaf and squash, and simmer, covered, for 30 minutes, or until the squash and beans are thoroughly tender. Add the quinoa and simmer for 20 to 30 minutes, or until the quinoa is translucent and displays an opaque thread. Taste and adjust the salt. Add a generous amount of black pepper. Stir in the chopped herbs and simmer for 2 to 3 minutes. Discard the bay leaf.

Per serving (based on 6 servings): 401 calories, 20 g protein, 68 g carbohydrates, 19 g fiber, 7 g fat, 1 g sat fat, 0 mg cholesterol, 191 mg sodium

ADVANCE PREPARATION: This tastes best if made a day ahead and reheated. The stew will thicken up, so you will probably want to thin out with water and adjust the seasonings accordingly. Add the fresh herbs when you reheat. It will keep for at least 5 days in the refrigerator. It freezes well.

Warm Black-Eyed Pea Salad

Makes 6 to 8 servings

■ **VEGETARIAN** ■ **VEGAN** ■ **LOW-CALORIE** ■ LOW-FAT
■ **HIGH-PROTEIN** ■ **GLUTEN-FREE** ■ HIGH IN OMEGA-3S

I serve this somewhat addictive salad every New Year's Day, without fail. It's called a salad because of the dressing, but it's really a one-dish meal. It's just tangy enough, with Southwestern flavors (cumin, cilantro), and even though it bears no resemblance to Southern-style black-eyed peas, I like to serve it with cornbread. You can serve it warm or cold; I like it best warm.

For the black-eyed peas:

1 tablespoon extra virgin olive oil

1 medium onion, chopped

3–4 garlic cloves, minced

1 pound dried black-eyed peas, rinsed
   and picked over

1 bay leaf

1–2 teaspoons salt

For the dressing and salad:

1/4 cup red wine vinegar or sherry vinegar

1 garlic clove, minced

1 teaspoon Dijon mustard

1–2 teaspoons cumin seeds, lightly toasted
   and ground

Salt and ground black pepper

1/3 cup extra virgin olive oil

1 large red bell pepper, diced

1/2 cup chopped cilantro

1. To make the black-eyed peas: Heat the oil in a large, heavy soup pot over medium heat. Add the onion. Cook, stirring, until tender, about 5 minutes. Add half of the garlic and cook, stirring, until the garlic is fragrant, 30 seconds to a minute. Add the black-eyed peas and 2 quarts water and bring to a simmer. Skim off any foam from the surface of the water. Add the bay leaf and salt. Reduce the heat, cover, and simmer for 30 minutes. Taste and add more salt, if desired. Add the remaining garlic, cover, and simmer until the black-eyed peas are tender but intact, about 15 minutes. Taste and adjust the salt. Remove from the heat and carefully drain through a colander or sieve set over a bowl. Transfer to a large salad bowl and reserve ½ cup of the cooking liquid. Discard the bay leaf.

2. To make the dressing and the salad: Whisk together the vinegar, garlic, mustard, cumin, salt and black pepper to taste in a measuring cup or a small bowl. Whisk in the reserved bean broth, and olive oil. Taste and adjust the seasonings. Add a little more vinegar if you wish. Stir the dressing into the warm beans. Stir in the bell pepper and cilantro, and serve, or allow to cool and serve at room temperature.

Per serving (based on 6 servings): 398 calories, 17 g protein, 48 g carbohydrates, 15 g fiber, 16 g fat, 2 g sat fat, 0 mg cholesterol, 444 mg sodium

ADVANCE PREPARATION: The beans will keep for about 5 days in the refrigerator. Toss them with the vinaigrette, but wait to add the cilantro just before serving.

Red Chard, Potato, and White Bean Ragout

Makes 4 to 6 servings

■ **VEGETARIAN** ■ **VEGAN*** ■ **LOW-CALORIE** ■ **LOW-FAT**
■ **HIGH-PROTEIN** ■ **GLUTEN-FREE** ■ HIGH IN OMEGA-3S

You can use regular Swiss chard for this comforting ragout if you can't find red chard, but I love the way it looks when it's made with the red chard, because the potatoes become infused with pink. The ragout makes a hearty meal; serve it with a salad and crusty bread.

1 cup dried white beans, soaked for 6 hours or overnight in 1 quart water

Bouquet garni made with 1 bay leaf, a couple of sprigs of thyme, and a Parmesan rind (page 67)

Salt

1 generous bunch (¾ to 1 pound) red Swiss chard or rainbow chard

2 tablespoons extra virgin olive oil

1 medium onion, chopped

2–4 garlic cloves, sliced

1 pound Yukon gold potatoes, scrubbed and cut into ½-inch dice

1 teaspoon fresh thyme leaves

Ground black pepper

1–2 tablespoons chopped flat-leaf parsley (optional)

Grated Parmesan

*If you omit the Parmesan and Parmesan rind

1. Drain the beans and combine with 1 quart fresh water in a heavy soup pot or Dutch oven. Bring to a gentle boil. Skim off any foam, then add the bouquet garni. Reduce the heat, cover, and simmer for 1 hour. Add 1 teaspoon salt or to taste.

2. Meanwhile, stem and clean the chard leaves in 2 changes of water. Rinse the stems and dice. Set aside. Cut the leaves into ribbons, or coarsely chop, and set aside.

3. Heat the oil in a heavy nonstick skillet over medium heat. Add the onion and chard stems. Cook, stirring often, until tender, about 5 minutes. Add a pinch of salt and the garlic and cook, stirring, until the garlic is fragrant, about 1 minute. Add the potatoes and stir together, then transfer to the pot with the beans. Return to a simmer, cover, and simmer for 30 minutes, or until the potatoes and beans are tender. Taste and adjust the salt.

4. Add the chard leaves and thyme to the pot, cover partially, and simmer for 15 minutes. The leaves should be very tender. Stir in black pepper to taste and the parsley. Taste, adjust the seasonings, and serve, passing the Parmesan at the table.

Per serving (based on 4 servings): 371 calories, 18 g protein, 58 g carbohydrates, 11 g fiber, 8 g fat, 1.5 g sat fat, 1 mg cholesterol, 259 mg sodium

ADVANCE PREPARATION: The dish will keep for 3 to 4 days in the refrigerator. If you are making it ahead, add the chard shortly before serving, so that the color of the chard doesn't dull too much.

Couscous with Beans and Cauliflower

Makes 6 to 8 servings

■ VEGETARIAN ■ VEGAN ■ LOW-CALORIE ■ LOW-FAT
■ HIGH-PROTEIN ■ GLUTEN-FREE ■ HIGH IN OMEGA-3S

I'm always pushing cauliflower, and I look to the cuisines of the Mediterranean for recipe ideas. Tunisia, with so many vegetable couscous dishes, is a great source. A more authentic version might call for some lamb or mutton as well, but I love the pure flavor of the spices, beans, and vegetables, and I love the way the cauliflower absorbs flavor as it stews in the spicy broth.

2 tablespoons extra virgin olive oil

1 medium onion, chopped

4 large garlic cloves, minced

Salt

2 teaspoons cumin seeds, lightly toasted and ground

1 teaspoon caraway seeds, lightly toasted and ground

1 teaspoon coriander seeds, lightly toasted and ground

2 cups dried chickpeas or white beans, soaked for 6 hours or overnight in 2 quarts water

1-2 tablespoons harissa or ½-1 teaspoon cayenne, plus additional for serving

2 tablespoons tomato paste

1 large head cauliflower, cut into small florets

2-2⅔ cups couscous, preferably whole wheat

1 cup frozen peas, thawed

½ cup chopped flat-leaf parsley or cilantro, or a combination

1. Heat the oil in a large, heavy soup pot or Dutch oven over medium heat. Add the onion and cook, stirring often, until tender, about 5 minutes. Add the garlic, $\frac{1}{2}$ teaspoon salt, the cumin, caraway, and coriander, and cook, stirring, for 1 minute, or until fragrant. Add the beans and their soaking liquid, and an additional 1 quart water, and bring to a boil over high heat. Reduce the heat to low, add salt to taste, cover, and simmer for 1 hour. Add the harissa or cayenne and the tomato paste. Simmer for 30 minutes to 1 hour, or until the beans are completely tender and the broth fragrant. Set aside $\frac{1}{2}$ cup of the liquid to use to reconstitute the couscous.

2. Add the cauliflower to the simmering stew and cook, partially covered, for 20 minutes, or until the cauliflower is tender and falling apart. Taste and adjust the seasonings, adding salt, garlic, or harissa or cayenne as desired. The stew should be spicy.

3. Reconstitute and steam the couscous, following the instructions on page 204.

4. Meanwhile, stir the peas and parsley and/or cilantro into the simmering stew. Simmer for 5 minutes or longer. Taste and adjust the seasonings. Transfer the couscous to a wide serving bowl or directly to

wide soup plates. Spoon on the stew, and serve, passing harissa or cayenne at the table.

Per serving (based on 6 servings): 471 calories, 22 g protein, 81 g carbohydrates, 21 g fiber, 9 g fat, 1 g sat fat, 0 mg cholesterol, 156 mg sodium

ADVANCE PREPARATION: The dish can be prepared through Step 1 up to a day ahead and refrigerated. Return to a simmer before proceeding. The entire stew can be prepared a day ahead and refrigerated. Return to a simmer and proceed with the recipe. You may need to add a little more water to the pot.

Tunisian Spice Mix

If you like the spicy Tunisian stews that go so well with couscous, you might want to make up a batch of the spice mix that I use in most of these dishes. Lightly toast 1 part each coriander seeds and caraway seeds, and 2 parts cumin seeds. Toast them by shaking them in a small pan over medium-high heat until they begin to give off a toasty, popcornlike aroma. Immediately transfer to a bowl and allow to cool, then blend in a spice mill. Keep in a jar or a plastic bag in the freezer. Use the total number of teaspoons of the combined spices called for in a recipe.

Couscous with Black-Eyed Peas and Greens

Makes 6 to 8 servings

■ **VEGETARIAN** ■ **VEGAN** ■ LOW-CALORIE ■ **LOW-FAT**
■ **HIGH-PROTEIN** ■ **GLUTEN-FREE** ■ HIGH IN OMEGA-3S

This is a North African approach to a dish you probably associate with the American South. But black-eyed peas came to the Americas from Africa, and show up in many Greek and Middle Eastern as well as North African dishes. Black-eyed peas are a good source of calcium, folate, iron, potassium, and fiber.

2 tablespoons extra virgin olive oil

1 medium onion, chopped

4 large garlic cloves, minced

2 teaspoons cumin seeds, lightly toasted and ground

1 teaspoon caraway seeds, lightly toasted and ground

1 teaspoon coriander seeds, lightly toasted and ground

Salt

1 pound dried black-eyed peas, rinsed and picked over

1–2 tablespoons harissa, or $\frac{1}{2}$–1 teaspoon cayenne, plus additional for serving

2 tablespoons tomato paste

1$\frac{1}{2}$ pounds greens (such as Swiss chard, kale, mustard greens), stemmed, washed thoroughly in 2 changes water, and coarsely chopped

1 large bunch flat-leaf parsley or cilantro, or a combination, chopped

2$\frac{1}{2}$ cups couscous, preferably whole wheat

1. Heat the oil in a heavy soup pot or Dutch oven over medium heat. Add the onion. Cook, stirring, until tender, about 5 minutes. Add the garlic, cumin,

caraway, coriander, and ½ teaspoon salt, and stir together for about 1 minute, or until the garlic is fragrant. Add the black-eyed peas and 3 quarts water, and bring to a boil over medium-high heat. Reduce the heat to low, add salt to taste, cover, and simmer for 30 minutes. Add the harissa or cayenne and the tomato paste. Cover and simmer for 15 to 30 minutes, or until the beans are tender and fragrant. Scoop out ½ cup of the liquid to use when reconstituting the couscous, and set aside.

2. Add the greens 1 handful at a time, allowing each handful to cook down a bit before adding the next. It will seem like a lot of greens at first but they'll soon lose their volume. Simmer for 20 minutes, or until the greens are very tender. Stir in the parsley and/or cilantro and simmer for 5 minutes. Remove from the heat. Taste and adjust the seasonings, adding salt, garlic, or harissa or cayenne as desired.

3. Reconstitute and steam the couscous, following the instructions on page 204.

4. Transfer the couscous to a wide serving bowl, or directly to wide soup plates. Spoon on the stew with a generous amount of broth and serve, passing the harissa or cayenne at the table.

Per serving (based on 6 servings): 510 calories, 27 g protein, 90 g carbohydrates, 17 g fiber, 7 g fat, 1 g sat fat, 0 mg cholesterol, 290 mg sodium

ADVANCE PREPARATION: The black-eyed peas can be cooked up to 3 days ahead and the finished stew can be made 1 to 2 days ahead. You may want to add more liquid when you reheat.

White Beans with Celery

Makes 4 servings

■ **VEGETARIAN** ■ **VEGAN** ■ **LOW-CALORIE** ■ LOW-FAT
■ **HIGH-PROTEIN** ■ **GLUTEN-FREE** ■ HIGH IN OMEGA-3S

This is inspired by a Greek recipe from Diane Kochilas's The Glorious Foods of Greece *that calls for giant white beans and about 3 times as much olive oil. I love the textures in this dish. The celery retains a little crunch, which contrasts nicely with the soft beans.*

½ pound (1 heaping cup) dried white beans such as navy, great Northern, or small white beans, soaked for 6 hours or overnight in 1 quart water

Salt

¼ cup extra virgin olive oil, plus additional for drizzling, if desired

4–5 cups chopped celery, including the leaves

4 large garlic cloves, minced

1 can (8 ounces) tomato sauce or 2 tablespoons tomato paste diluted with 1 cup water

¼–½ cup finely chopped flat-leaf parsley

Juice of 1 lemons

1. Drain the beans and combine in a large saucepan with water to cover by 2 inches. Bring to a gentle boil, reduce the heat to low, add salt to taste, cover, and simmer until the beans are just tender, about 45 minutes to 1 hour. Do not let the beans boil hard or they'll fall apart before they're cooked through.

2. Heat 2 tablespoons of the oil in a large skillet over medium heat. Add the celery and a generous pinch of salt. Cook, stirring often, until it just begins to soften, about 3 minutes. Add the garlic. Stir together for 1 minute, or until the garlic is fragrant, and remove from the heat.

3. Preheat the oven to 350°F. Drain the beans in a sieve set over a bowl, reserving the broth. Transfer the beans to a large, preferably earthenware baking dish. Toss with the celery and garlic, the remaining 2 tablespoons of oil, and the tomato sauce. Add enough of the reserved broth to cover by 1 inch. Cover the dish tightly with foil and bake for 1 hour, or until the beans are soft and creamy.

4. Uncover the beans, stir in the parsley, and add salt and black pepper to taste. Add 1 to 2 tablespoons of lemon juice, or more if desired, and adjust salt and pepper. Serve hot, warm, or at room temperature, with a little more olive oil drizzled over the top, if desired.

> **Per serving:** 368 calories, 19 g protein, 38 g carbohydrates, 12 g fiber, 17 g fat, 3 g sat fat, 17 mg cholesterol, 247 mg sodium

ADVANCE PREPARATION: The beans will keep for 3 days in the refrigerator. You may want to thin them out with a little water or broth.

White Beans with Pesto

Makes 4 to 6 servings

■ **VEGETARIAN** ■ VEGAN ■ LOW-CALORIE ■ LOW-FAT
■ **HIGH-PROTEIN** ■ GLUTEN-FREE ■ HIGH IN OMEGA-3S

Pasta isn't the only vehicle for pesto. Of all the beans to try with the pungent basil paste, white beans stand out. The subtle flavor and creamy color of the beans contrast beautifully with the pesto.

1 pound dried white beans, rinsed and picked over and soaked for 6 hours or overnight in 2 quarts water

1 onion, halved

2 garlic cloves, minced

1 bay leaf

Salt

¼ cup Simple Basil Pesto (page 184)

1. Drain the beans and place in a pot with 2 quarts fresh water, the onion, garlic, and bay leaf. Bring to a boil, reduce the heat to low, cover, and simmer 1 hour. Add salt to taste and simmer for another 30 minutes to an hour, until the beans are soft and fragrant. Discard the onion and the bay leaf, and drain the beans through a colander set over a bowl.

2. Return the beans to the pot and stir in the pesto. Thin out as desired with the reserved broth from the beans. Serve hot or warm.

> **Per serving (based on 4 servings):** 457 calories, 26 g protein, 75 g carbohydrates, 29 g fiber, 7 g fat, 2 g sat fat, 3 mg cholesterol, 118 mg sodium

ADVANCE PREPARATION: The beans can be cooked up to 3 days ahead and reheated. The pesto should be stirred in just before serving.

Lentils

You always have dinner if you have lentils in your pantry. The high-fiber, protein-rich legume cooks in 20 to 40 minutes (depending on the dish), requires no soaking, and can be the focus of a starter or salad, soup or stew, side dish or Middle Eastern pasta. Lentils always taste like lentils, but they adapt well to the classic seasonings used in a variety of cuisines from France through the Mediterranean, to India and on to Mexico and North America.

The most readily available supermarket lentils are brown lentils, but there are other varieties, and they're all worth seeking out. Chefs prefer the pricier small black "beluga" lentils (in their raw state they're small and glistening black like caviar, but the resemblance stops there), and the firm green Le Puy lentils from France, because they stay intact and maintain a firmer texture when cooked. The flavors of all three are similar. Red lentils, available in Indian and Mediterranean markets, have a different flavor, more akin to dried fava beans or split peas, and a very different texture when cooked, so do not substitute these.

Unlike other beans, lentils do not contain the gas-producing compounds found in other legumes. In addition to being an excellent source of soluble fiber and a good source of protein, manganese, iron, phosphorous, copper, vitamin B_1, and potassium, lentils are an excellent source of folate and molybdenum, an important mineral that helps in the metabolism of fats, and carbohydrates, and the absorption of iron.

Middle Eastern Lentils with Pasta

Makes 6 generous servings

■ **VEGETARIAN** ■ **VEGAN** ■ **LOW-CALORIE** ■ **LOW-FAT**
■ HIGH-PROTEIN ■ GLUTEN-FREE ■ HIGH IN OMEGA-3S

Middle Eastern cooks often combine legumes and pasta. Here a subtly spiced lentil ragout takes on the role of pasta sauce.

1/2 pound brown or green lentils, rinsed and picked over

2 onions, 1 halved, 1 finely chopped

4 garlic cloves, 2 halved, 2 minced

1 bay leaf

Salt

2 tablespoons extra virgin olive oil

1 red bell pepper, cut into small dice

1 1/2 teaspoons cumin seeds, lightly toasted and ground

1 teaspoon coriander seeds, lightly toasted and ground

Pinch of cayenne or 1/4 teaspoon Aleppo pepper

Ground black pepper

12 ounces pasta, either a strand pasta like spaghetti, tagliatelle, or fettuccine, or a shape that will catch the lentil sauce, like orecchiette or farfalle

1/4 cup chopped cilantro

1. Combine the lentils, halved onion, halved garlic cloves, and bay leaf in a heavy saucepan. Add enough water to cover by 1 1/2 inches, and bring to a boil over high heat. Reduce the heat, cover, and simmer for

25 minutes. Add salt to taste (undersalt because you will be reducing the liquid) and continue to simmer for 10 to 20 minutes, or until the lentils are tender but intact. Remove from the heat. Place a sieve over a bowl and drain the lentils, reserving the broth. Discard the bay leaf.

2. Begin heating a large pot of water for the pasta. Meanwhile, heat the oil in a large, heavy nonstick skillet over medium heat and add the chopped onion. Cook, stirring, until it begins to soften, about 3 minutes. Add the bell pepper. Cook, stirring, until the vegetables are tender and the onion is beginning to color, 5 to 8 minutes. Add ½ teaspoon salt, the chopped garlic, cumin, coriander, and cayenne or Aleppo pepper. Cook, stirring, for 1 minute, or until the garlic is fragrant. Stir in the reserved broth. Increase the heat, bring to a boil, and cook until the

broth reduces slightly. Stir in the lentils. Add black pepper, taste, and adjust the salt. Keep warm while you cook the pasta.

3. When the water comes to a boil, salt generously, add the pasta, and cook al dente, until firm to the bite, following the timing directions on the package but checking 1 to 2 minutes before the suggested cooking time. Drain and toss with the lentils. Add the cilantro, and serve.

Per serving: 409 calories, 18 g protein, 70 g carbohydrates, 14 g fiber, 6 g fat, 1 g sat fat, 0 mg cholesterol, 38 mg sodium

ADVANCE PREPARATION: You can prepare the recipe through Step 2 several hours before serving. Keep at room temperature, or refrigerate and reheat gently.

Stewed Lentils with Cabbage

Makes 4 to 6 servings

■ **VEGETARIAN** ■ **VEGAN*** ■ **LOW-CALORIE** ■ **LOW-FAT**
■ **HIGH-PROTEIN** ■ **GLUTEN-FREE** ■ HIGH IN OMEGA-3S

Three hearty staples—potatoes, lentils, and cabbage—add up to a satisfying, hearty main dish that is far from plain. Brown, beluga, or green lentils will work here.

2 tablespoons extra virgin olive oil

1 medium onion, half chopped, half sliced

3 garlic cloves, minced

½ pound lentils (brown, beluga, or green), rinsed and picked over

1 dried red chile pepper

1 bay leaf

Salt

6 ounces waxy potatoes, scrubbed and sliced about ½ inch thick

1½ pounds green cabbage (½ large head), cored and cut crosswise into ¾-inch-wide ribbons

Ground black pepper

1 tablespoon chopped flat-leaf parsley

Grated Parmesan (optional)

*If you omit the cheese

1. Heat 1 tablespoon of the oil in a 3-quart saucepan or Dutch oven over medium heat. Add the chopped onion and cook, stirring often, until tender, about 5 minutes. Add two-thirds of the garlic and cook, stirring, until fragrant, 30 seconds to 1 minute. Add the lentils, 3½ cups water, the chile pepper, and bay leaf. Bring to a simmer. Reduce the heat to low, cover, and simmer for 15 minutes. Add 1 teaspoon salt and the potatoes and simmer gently for 30 minutes, or until the lentils and potatoes are tender. Taste and adjust the seasonings. Discard the bay leaf.

2. While the lentils are simmering, heat the remaining 1 tablespoon of oil in a large skillet over medium heat. Add the sliced onion. Cook, stirring often, until tender, about 5 minutes. Add ½ teaspoon salt and the remaining garlic and cook, stirring, until the garlic is fragrant, about 1 minute. Add the cabbage and increase the heat to medium-high. Cook, stirring, until the cabbage begins to wilt, 3 to 5 minutes. Add ¼ cup water, reduce the heat to medium, cover, and simmer for 10 to 15 minutes, or until the cabbage is tender and sweet, stirring occasionally. Add salt and black pepper to taste.

3. Spread the cabbage over the bottom of the pan in an even layer. Top with the lentils and potatoes and sprinkle on the parsley. Serve in wide soup bowls, sprinkled with Parmesan if desired.

Per serving (based on 4 servings): 349 calories, 18 g protein, 54 g carbohydrates, 22 g fiber, 8 g fat, 1 g sat fat, 0 mg cholesterol, 141 mg sodium

ADVANCE PREPARATION: You can make this dish up to a day ahead and reheat on top of the stove.

Lentil Dal

Makes 4 to 6 servings

■ **VEGETARIAN** ■ **VEGAN*** ■ LOW-CALORIE ■ **LOW-FAT**
■ **HIGH-PROTEIN** ■ **GLUTEN-FREE** ■ HIGH IN OMEGA-3S

In India, dal refers to a number of lentil-shaped legumes, as well as simple lentil-based dishes like this one. They're served with rice and curries, and are usually soupy, unlike this thick rendition, which resembles refried beans in consistency. If you prefer to serve this as a soup, double the amount of liquid.

½ pound (1 heaping cup) brown lentils, rinsed and picked over

1 small onion, halved

2 garlic cloves, halved

1 bay leaf

2 tablespoons canola or peanut oil

1–2 teaspoons curry powder

1 teaspoon cumin seeds, lightly toasted and ground

½ teaspoon chili powder

½ teaspoon turmeric

Salt

Plain low-fat yogurt

Chopped cilantro

*If you omit the yogurt

1. Combine the lentils, onion, garlic, bay leaf, and 1 quart water in a soup pot or a heavy saucepan. Bring to a boil over high heat, reduce the heat to low, cover, and simmer for 30 minutes. Add salt to taste (undersalt because you will be reducing the liquid) and continue to simmer for 15 minutes, or until the lentils are falling-apart tender and fragrant. Discard the onion, garlic, and bay leaf.

2. Heat the oil in a large, heavy nonstick skillet over medium-high heat. Add the curry powder, cumin, chili powder, and turmeric, and stir as they sizzle for about 30 seconds, or until very fragrant. Add the lentils with their liquid and cook, stirring and mashing with the back of a wooden spoon, until the mixture thickens like refried beans, about 10 minutes. Add salt to taste once the mixture has reduced to the desired consistency. Spoon onto plates and garnish each serving with a generous spoonful of yogurt and a sprinkling of chopped cilantro.

> **Per serving (based on 4 servings):** 269 calories, 15 g protein, 36 g carbohydrates, 17 g fiber, 7 g fat, 0.5 g sat fat, 0 mg cholesterol, 48 mg sodium

ADVANCE PREPARATION: This will keep for 2 to 3 days in the refrigerator, but you will need to thin it out with water when you reheat.

Chapter 10
FISH AND POULTRY

Although my *Recipes for Health* focus primarily on produce, pantry staples like grains and beans, and refrigerator staples like tofu, yogurt, and eggs, it's fine to include fish and meat in your diet occasionally. It doesn't always have to be at the center of the plate though, and when it is, it can be there to show off a plant-based food, like lentils or mushrooms or corn.

Fish and shellfish have a lot going for them. Low in calories and high in protein, vitamins, and minerals, certain varieties are excellent sources of omega-3s, and others like canned sardines and salmon are rich in calcium. But eating fish is a choice with caveats, and "choice" is the key word here. Some types of fish—swordfish, certain tunas (bluefin, bigeye, and yellowfin tuna), shark, Chilean sea bass, and orange roughy, among others—have been found to have high levels of environmental contaminants like mercury and PCBs, and some—Atlantic cod, flounder, sole, and halibut; Chilean sea bass, big-eye, bluefin, and yellowfin tuna—have been overfished to the point of near extinction. Some fish that are farmed, such as Atlantic salmon and imported shrimp, are farmed in ways that are unsustainable and very bad for the environment, and not so great for the fish themselves. Farmed salmon, for example, are not fed the kind of plankton-rich food that salmon in the wild eat, thus they are not as good for you as wild salmon. They are also kept in very close quarters, so they're subject to disease the way all intensively farmed animals are.

When it comes to making choices about what seafood to buy, I've found the charts that the Environmental Defense Fund has on their Web site to be very useful. They include a downloadable Pocket Seafood Selector ("Fish choices that are good for you and the ocean") that breaks down the different types of fish and shellfish into three categories—best choices, OK choices, and worst choices. There's also a similar Sushi Selector, and a table that groups fish and shellfish by how often they can safely be eaten.

Luckily, there's still a range of safe fish and shellfish to choose from, and some, like Atlantic mackerel, are not very expensive. As for the best ways to cook fish, there are many. I tend to go for methods that don't leave a lingering smell of fish in my kitchen, such as roasting in a covered baking dish or in individual foil packets, poaching in a gutsy stew, or slow steaming in the oven. I steam mollusks such as mussels and clams in wine in a wide pan or a pot and serve them with the broth, and on warm nights I love to grill fish outdoors.

Sometimes I serve fish simply, embellishing it with fresh herbs, lemon, and its own cooking juices. But I also like to combine assertive fish with robust tomato-based Mediterranean sauces, with salsas, and with nut-based sauces, all of which contribute a great deal to the overall nutritional value of your meal.

As for chicken, it's an excellent source of protein, and without the skin, the amount of saturated fat in a serving is low. I make an effort to seek out chickens that have been raised on organic feed, without hormones or antibiotics. Look for the word *organic*, or better still, seek out local producers at your farmers' market.

The Best Fish to Buy

These are the Best Choices on the Environmental Defense Fund's online Seafood Selector. (Note that the ocean or country of origin of the fish, and the way they are caught, matters.)

Abalone (farmed)

Barramundi (U.S.)

Catfish (U.S.)

*Char, Arctic (farmed)

Clams (farmed)

Clams, softshell

Cod, Pacific (Alaska, longline)

Crab, Dungeness

Crab, stone

Crawfish (U.S.)

Halibut, Pacific

Lobster, spiny (Caribbean from U.S.)

*Mackerel, Atlantic

Mahimahi (U.S. pole/troll)

Mullet (U.S.)

Mussels (farmed)

Oysters (farmed)

*Sablefish/black cod (Alaska, Canada)

Salmon (Alaska, wild)

Salmon, canned pink/sockeye

Sardines (U.S.)

Scallops, bay (farmed)

Shrimp, pink (Oregon)

Spot prawns (Canada)

Squid, longfin (U.S.)

Striped bass (farmed)

Tilapia (U.S.)

*Trout, rainbow (farmed)

*Tuna, albacore (Canada, U.S.—fresh; canned albacore is an OK choice, but high in mercury or PCBs)

Tuna, skipjack (pole/troll)

Tuna, yellowfin (U.S., pole/troll)

Wreckfish

*Also high in omega-3s and low in contaminants

Grilled Sardines

Makes 4 servings

■ VEGETARIAN ■ VEGAN ■ **LOW-CALORIE** ■ LOW-FAT
■ **HIGH-PROTEIN** ■ **GLUTEN-FREE** ■ **HIGH IN OMEGA-3S**

You may think you don't like sardines, but you've probably only had them from a can (though canned sardines can be excellent!). Fresh sardines are a very different experience. Brush them with olive oil, throw a few sprigs of rosemary onto your hot grill, and grill them. They take 2 to 3 minutes to grill, and about that long to eat.

Sardines are a rare treat, and a great nutritional package, with lots of omega-3s, selenium, vitamin B$_{12}$, niacin, and phosphorus.

24 medium or large fresh sardines, cleaned

2 tablespoons extra virgin olive oil

Salt (preferably coarse sea salt) and ground black pepper

A handful of rosemary sprigs

Lemon wedges

1. Prepare a hot grill and make sure the grill rack is oiled. Rinse the sardines and dry with paper towels. Toss with the oil and season with salt and black pepper.

2. When the grill is ready, toss the rosemary sprigs directly on the fire. Wait for the flames to die down, then place the sardines directly over the heat, in batches if necessary. Grill for 1 to 2 minutes on each side, depending on the size. Transfer from the grill to a platter using tongs or a wide metal spatula, and serve with the lemon wedges.

Per serving: 337 calories, 31 g protein, 0 g carbohydrates, 0 g fiber, 23 g fat, 5 g sat fat, 103 mg cholesterol, 1,160 mg sodium

ADVANCE PREPARATION: This is last minute, but you can have the fish rinsed and dried hours ahead. Keep in the refrigerator.

Baked Halibut with Tomato Caper Sauce

Makes 6 servings

■ VEGETARIAN ■ VEGAN ■ **LOW-CALORIE** ■ **LOW-FAT**
■ **HIGH-PROTEIN** ■ **GLUTEN-FREE** ■ HIGH IN OMEGA-3S

I serve this with a pungent tomato sauce that I learned to make in Provence. It goes well with any type of robust fish. The recipe for the sauce will yield 2½ cups, more sauce than you will need for the fish, but it's a great keeper and goes well with pasta, or as a topping for bruschetta. Look for Pacific halibut, as Atlantic halibut has been overfished.

For the tomato caper sauce:

1 tablespoon extra virgin olive oil

½ medium onion, finely chopped

4 large garlic cloves, minced or mashed to a paste with a mortar and pestle

¼ cup capers, drained, rinsed, and finely chopped or mashed along with the garlic

2 pounds ripe tomatoes, peeled, seeded, and finely chopped, or 1 can (28 ounces) diced tomatoes

Salt and ground black pepper

Pinch of sugar

1 teaspoon chopped fresh thyme leaves

For the baked halibut:

6 Pacific halibut fillets (6 ounces each)

Salt and ground black pepper

1 tablespoon extra virgin olive oil

6 lemon slices

1 tablespoon slivered fresh basil leaves

1. To make the sauce: Heat the oil in a large, heavy skillet over medium heat. Add the onion. Cook, stirring often, until tender, 3 to 5 minutes. Add the garlic and capers. Cook, stirring, for 3 to 5 minutes, or until the onion has softened thoroughly and the mixture is fragrant. Add the tomatoes (with juice), salt, black pepper, sugar, and thyme. Bring to a simmer and cook, stirring often, for 15 to 20 minutes, or until the sauce is thick and fragrant. Taste and adjust the seasonings.

2. To make the fish: Preheat the oven to 450°F. Oil a baking dish large enough for the fish to fit in a single layer. Season the fish with salt and black pepper and arrange in the baking dish. Drizzle the oil over the fillets and place a lemon slice on each one. Cover the dish tightly with foil and place in the oven. Bake for 15 minutes. Check the fish. If you can cut into it with a fork, it is done. If it doesn't give (halibut fillets tend to be thick, so it may well need more time), cover and return it to the oven for an additional 5 minutes. Remove it from the oven and check again. When the fish is done, remove the lemon slices and discard.

3. Place a spoonful of sauce on each plate and place a piece of fish partially on top. Spoon some of the liquid from the baking dish over the fish. If you wish, top the fish with another spoonful of sauce, garnish with the basil leaves, and serve.

Per serving: 268 calories, 37 g protein, 9 g carbohydrates, 3 g fiber, 9 g fat, 1 g sat fat, 54 mg cholesterol, 319 mg sodium

ADVANCE PREPARATION: The sauce will keep for about 5 days in the refrigerator.

Buying Fillet without Breaking the Bank

A 6-ounce fillet makes an adequate serving of fish. Ask your fishmonger to cut large fillets into smaller pieces, or do it yourself when you get it home. For 6 people, you only need 2 pounds plus 4 ounces of fish.

Whole Rainbow Trout Baked in Foil

Makes 4 servings

■ VEGETARIAN ■ VEGAN ■ **LOW-CALORIE** ■ LOW-FAT
■ **HIGH-PROTEIN** ■ **GLUTEN-FREE** ■ **HIGH IN OMEGA-3S**

It's easy to find farmed rainbow trout these days. They're usually sold boned and butterflied, opened up with the two halves still attached. I bake them in foil packets, then when I serve them I spoon on the savory juice that accumulates inside the packets as they bake.

4 small rainbow trout, boned

Salt and ground black pepper

8 tarragon or dill sprigs, or 4 rosemary sprigs

2 lemons, one sliced, one cut into wedges

2 teaspoons extra virgin olive oil

Chopped fresh tarragon, dill, or flat-leaf parsley for serving

1. Preheat the oven to 450°F. Cut 4 sheets of heavy-duty foil, or 8 sheets of lighter foil into squares that are 3 inches longer than your fish. If using lighter foil, make 4 double-thick squares. Oil the dull side of the foil and place a trout on each square. Season both sides of the fish with salt and black pepper and open them out flat, skin side down. Place 2 tarragon or dill sprigs, or 1 rosemary sprig, and 2 lemon slices down the middle of each, and fold the two sides together. Drizzle 1/2 teaspoon of olive oil over each fish.

2. Making sure that the trout are in the middle of each square, fold the foil up loosely around the fish and crimp the edges together tightly to make a packet. Place the packets on a baking sheet and bake for 10 to 15 minutes, checking one of the packets after 10 minutes. The flesh should be opaque and pull apart easily when tested with a fork.

3. Place each packet on a plate. Carefully cut across the top to open it, taking care not to let the steam from inside the packet burn you. Gently remove the fish from the packet and pour the juices over. Sprinkle with the chopped tarragon, dill, or parsley, and serve, passing the lemon wedges.

Per serving: 139 calories, 17 g protein, 3 g carbohydrates, 1 g fiber, 7 g fat, 2 g sat fat, 47 mg cholesterol, 65 mg sodium

ADVANCE PREPARATION: You can prepare the fish and make the foil packets several hours ahead. Keep in the refrigerator until shortly before cooking.

VARIATION: TROUT WITH GREENS Fill the trout with Swiss chard or other greens sautéed with garlic and olive oil (page 138) and serve with more on the side.

Easy Fish Stew with Mediterranean Flavors

Makes 4 servings

■ VEGETARIAN ■ VEGAN ■ **LOW-CALORIE** ■ **LOW-FAT**
■ **HIGH-PROTEIN** ■ **GLUTEN-FREE** ■ **HIGH IN OMEGA-3S**

This is a typical fisherman's stew. No need to make a fish stock; water, aromatics, and anchovies will suffice. Even if you're not a fan of anchovies, use them, as they add great depth of flavor, not to mention omega-3s; I promise the dish won't taste like anchovies.

4 large garlic cloves, halved

Salt

4 anchovy fillets (see note on page 304), soaked in water for 4 minutes, drained and rinsed

2 tablespoons extra virgin olive oil

1 large onion, chopped

1 celery rib, chopped

1 medium carrot, chopped

1 can (28 ounces) diced tomatoes

1 pound small red potatoes, scrubbed and quartered or sliced

Bouquet garni made with 1 bay leaf, 1 strip of orange zest, a couple of sprigs each of thyme and flat-leaf parsley, and 1 small dried red chile pepper, if desired (page 67)

Ground black pepper

1–1 1/2 pounds firm white-fleshed fish such as Pacific halibut, Pacific cod, or tilapia (from the U.S.), cut into 2-inch pieces

2–4 tablespoons minced flat-leaf parsley

1. Mash the garlic cloves and 1/4 teaspoon of salt to a paste with a mortar and pestle. Add the anchovy fillets and mash with the garlic. Set aside.

2. Heat the oil in a large, heavy soup pot or Dutch oven over medium heat. Add the onion, celery, carrot, and $\frac{1}{2}$ teaspoon salt. Cook, stirring, until the onion is tender, about 5 minutes. Add the pureed garlic and anchovy. Cook, stirring, until the mixture is very fragrant, about 1 minute. Add the tomatoes (with juice). Cook, stirring often, until the tomatoes have cooked down a bit and the mixture is aromatic, 10 to 15 minutes. Add the potatoes, salt to taste, the bouquet garni, and 1 quart water and bring to a simmer. Reduce the heat to low, cover partially, and simmer for 30 minutes. Taste, adjust the salt, and add black pepper to taste. Remove the bouquet garni.

3. Season the fish with salt and black pepper and stir into the soup. The soup should not be boiling. Simmer for 5 to 10 minutes (depending on the type and thickness of the fillets), or just until it flakes easily when poked. Remove from the heat, stir in the parsley, taste once more, adjust the seasonings, and serve.

Per serving: 346 calories, 30 g protein, 34 g carbohydrates, 5 g fiber, 10 g fat, 2 g sat fat, 40 mg cholesterol, 583 mg sodium

ADVANCE PREPARATION: You can make this through Step 2 up to 3 days ahead. Keep in the refrigerator, return to a simmer and proceed with the recipe.

Note: *If you can find salted anchovies, as opposed to anchovy fillets in oil, I recommend them. They have a much cleaner, more vivid flavor than the anchovies in oil. You must carefully rinse off the salt first, then detach the fillets from the bones and soak the fillets in water for 5 to 10 minutes before using.*

Spanish-Style Shrimp with Garlic (Gambas al Ajillo)

Makes 6 to 8 appetizer servings, 4 main-dish servings

■ VEGETARIAN ■ VEGAN ■ **LOW-CALORIE** ■ LOW-FAT
■ **HIGH-PROTEIN** ■ **GLUTEN-FREE** ■ HIGH IN OMEGA-3S

Garlic holds center stage with shrimp in this classic Spanish dish, which is served as a tapa in Spain, but also makes a great main dish. Authentic gambas al ajillo is made with about four times as much olive oil as this, but you still get lots of juice for dipping here. Serve with rice or crusty bread.

1 ¼ pounds medium shrimp (U.S.-farmed or Oregon pink), peeled and deveined

Sea salt or kosher salt

3 tablespoons extra virgin olive oil

½ teaspoon mild or hot paprika

6 garlic cloves, coarsely chopped or thinly sliced

1 bay leaf, broken in half

1 dried red chile pepper, seeded and crumbled

2 tablespoons minced flat-leaf parsley

1. Sprinkle the shrimp with salt, toss, and let sit for 15 minutes.

2. Heat the oil in a large, heavy nonstick skillet over medium heat. Add the paprika, garlic, bay leaf, and chile pepper. Cook, stirring, until the garlic begins to color, about 1 minute. Increase the heat to medium-high and add the shrimp. Cook, stirring, until the shrimp turn pink and are cooked through, 2 to 3 minutes. Remove from the heat, discard the bay leaf, sprinkle with the parsley, and serve.

Per serving (based on 6 appetizer servings):
172 calories, 20 g protein, 3 g carbohydrates, 0 g fiber, 9 g fat, 1 g sat fat, 144 mg cholesterol, 161 mg sodium

ADVANCE PREPARATION: Everything can be prepped and ready to go hours ahead, but the cooking here is last minute.

Farmed Shrimp

I can't emphasize enough how important it is to seek out shrimp that are raised in the United States. The intensive shrimp farming in Southeast Asia has been an environmental disaster, laying waste to the mangrove swamps that have been so important to the coastal ecology of the region, which has led to the depletion of local fish stocks, the pollution of marine environments, local agricultural land, and groundwater and drinking water.

Malaysian Stir-Fried Noodles with Shrimp

Makes 4 servings

■ VEGETARIAN ■ VEGAN ■ **LOW-CALORIE** ■ LOW-FAT
■ **HIGH-PROTEIN** ■ GLUTEN-FREE ■ HIGH IN OMEGA-3S

These spicy noodles are based on a classic Malaysian noodle dish, mee goreng, but I've reduced the number of ingredients. You can make it with regular or gluten-free noodles, such as lentil-flour Papadini noodles or wide dried rice noodles (see note).

½ pound turnip greens or mustard greens, cleaned, thick stems discarded

Salt

½ pound cabbage, cut into ¾-inch cubes

½ pound flat wide noodles, such as Chinese egg noodles, Papadini, or rice noodles

3 tablespoons peanut oil or canola oil

1½ tablespoons soy sauce

1½ teaspoons sugar

1½ teaspoons Asian chile sauce, such as sambal oelek

2 large garlic cloves, minced

1 tablespoon minced fresh ginger

1 can (14 ounces) diced tomatoes, drained

½ pound medium shrimp (U.S.-farmed or Oregon pink), shelled, halved lengthwise, and deveined

6 ounces bean sprouts (about 2 generous handfuls)

¼ cup chopped cilantro

1 lime, cut into wedges

1. Bring a large pot of water to a boil over high heat. Fill a bowl with ice water. When the water comes to a boil, salt generously and add the greens. Cook for only 30 seconds, then immediately transfer to the ice water using a slotted spoon or deep-fry skimmer.

Drain, squeeze out the excess water, and chop coarsely. Set aside. Return the water to a boil, add the cabbage, blanch for 30 seconds, and transfer to the ice water. Drain in a colander and set aside.

2. Return the water to a boil and add the noodles. Cook according to the package directions, drain, shake off the excess water, toss with 1 tablespoon of the oil, and set aside.

3. Mix together the soy sauce, sugar, chile suace, and salt to taste in a small bowl. Stir to dissolve the salt and sugar and set aside.

4. Heat a wok or large, heavy nonstick skillet over medium-high heat. Add the garlic, ginger, and remaining 2 tablespoons oil. Cook, stirring, for about 30 seconds, or until the garlic and ginger are fragrant. Add the tomatoes and increase the heat slightly. Stir until the tomatoes begin to break down and stick to the pan, about 3 minutes. Add the shrimp, blanched greens and cabbage, and cook, stirring, until the shrimp turn pink and curl, and the cabbage is crisp-tender, 4 to 5 minutes. Add the noodles and soy sauce mixture and stir together until the noodles are heated through and coated with the sauce. Add the bean sprouts and cilantro, toss together quickly, and remove from the heat. Serve, with the lime wedges on the side.

Per serving: 444 calories, 24 g protein, 57 g carbohydrates, 6 g fiber, 14 g fat, 3 g sat fat, 145 mg cholesterol, 875 mg sodium

ADVANCE PREPARATION: You can prep all the ingredients hours ahead. Keep in the refrigerator.

Note: If using dried rice noodles, soak them for 20 minutes in warm water, then cook for 1 minute or until tender in boiling water. Drain and toss with 1 tablespoon oil as directed.

Chinese Fried Rice with Shrimp and Peas

Makes 4 to 6 servings

▪ VEGETARIAN ▪ VEGAN ▪ LOW-CALORIE ▪ **LOW-FAT**
▪ **HIGH-PROTEIN** ▪ GLUTEN-FREE ▪ HIGH IN OMEGA-3S

This is a great dish to make when you have cooked rice on hand. It's a delicious vehicle for whatever vegetables may be in your refrigerator. Feel free to add other cooked vegetables and/or meat or seafood to this dish.

3 large eggs

Salt

2 tablespoons vegetable or canola oil

½ pound medium shrimp (U.S.-farmed or Oregon pink), peeled, deveined, and cut into ¾-inch pieces

2 garlic cloves, minced

2 teaspoons minced fresh ginger

1 tablespoon dry sherry

5–6 cups cooked and cooled basmati, jasmine, or long-grain rice

1 bunch scallions, thinly sliced, dark green parts kept separate

½ cup cooked fresh or thawed frozen peas

2 tablespoons soy sauce

¼ cup chopped cilantro

1. Beat 1 of the eggs in a small bowl and salt lightly. Heat 1 teaspoon of the oil in a small nonstick skillet over medium-high heat. Add the beaten egg. Swirl the pan to coat evenly like a thin pancake. When the egg is cooked through, roll up and slide onto a plate. Cut into thin strips (you can use scissors or a knife for this). Set aside.

2. Beat the remaining 2 eggs in a small bowl. Heat a wok or large, heavy nonstick skillet over medium-high heat until a drop of water evaporates on contact. Add the remaining 1 tablespoon plus 2 teaspoons oil, swirl it around, and add the shrimp. Cook, stirring and tossing with a spatula or wok scoop, until just about cooked through and pink, about 1 minute. Add the garlic and ginger and cook, stirring, for 30 seconds. Add the sherry, stir together, and when the sizzling stops, pour in the remaining beaten eggs. Cook, stirring, until the eggs are scrambled and the shrimp are cooked through. Add the rice and cook, scooping it up, then pressing it into the pan and scooping it up again, for about 2 minutes. Stir in the light parts of the scallions, the peas, and soy sauce. Stir together for about 30 seconds and transfer to a warm serving platter. Sprinkle the egg strips, dark scallion greens, and cilantro over the top. Serve hot.

Per serving (based on 4 servings): 465 calories, 24 g protein, 63 g carbohydrates, 2 g fiber, 12 g fat, 3 g sat fat, 245 mg cholesterol, 859 mg sodium

ADVANCE PREPARATION: This dish is best served right away, but you can prepare the ingredients a few hours ahead.

Oven-Steamed Salmon with Pan-Cooked Mushrooms

Makes 4 servings

■ VEGETARIAN ■ VEGAN ■ **LOW-CALORIE** ■ LOW-FAT
■ **HIGH-PROTEIN** ■ **GLUTEN-FREE** ■ **HIGH IN OMEGA-3S**

You'll never want to cook salmon any other way after you make this. It steams above a pan of water in a low oven, resulting in a very moist piece of fish. The mushrooms are wonderful on top or on the side.

1½ pounds wild Alaska or Washington salmon fillet, or two 12-ounce fillets

Salt and ground black pepper

2 tablespoons extra virgin olive oil

1 pound white or cremini mushrooms, rinsed briefly and wiped dry

2 shallots, minced

2–4 garlic cloves, minced

2 teaspoons chopped fresh thyme or rosemary (or a combination), or ½–1 teaspoon dried

¼ cup dry white wine, such as sauvignon blanc

1. Preheat the oven to 300°F. Cover a baking sheet with foil and lightly oil the foil. Place the salmon on top. Season with salt and black pepper. Bring 3 to 4 cups of water to a boil and pour into a baking pan or a roasting pan. Set the pan on the oven floor.

2. Place the salmon in the oven and bake until the

fish pulls apart when prodded with a fork, and white bubbles of protein appear on the surface, 10 to 20 minutes, depending on the size of the fillets. Remove from the heat.

3. Meanwhile, heat a large, heavy skillet over medium-high heat. Add 1 tablespoon of the oil. When the oil is hot (you can feel the heat when you hold your hand above the pan), add the mushrooms and cook, stirring or tossing in the pan, for 2 to 3 minutes, or until the mushrooms begin to soften and sweat. Add the remaining 1 tablespoon of oil, reduce the heat to medium, and add the shallots, garlic, and herbs. Stir together, add ½ teaspoon salt and black pepper to taste, and cook, stirring often, for 1 to 2 minutes, or until the shallots and garlic have softened and the mixture is fragrant. Add the wine and cook, stirring often and scraping the bottom of the pan, until the wine has just about evaporated.

4. Serve the salmon with a spoonful of mushrooms on top or on the side.

Per serving: 410 calories, 36 g protein, 6 g carbohydrates, 0 g fiber, 25 g fat, 4 g sat fat, 94 mg cholesterol, 120 mg sodium

ADVANCE PREPARATION: You can make the mushrooms several hours ahead and reheat. You can cook the salmon ahead, too, and serve it at room temperature.

Choosing Salmon

I don't cook farmed salmon anymore. It's too fatty, it has very little flavor, and it isn't farmed in a sustainable way. I have read that farmed salmon are fed grain, like cattle, and that they require heavy doses of antibiotics because of the intensity with which they are farmed, which is bad for them and for the environment. Treat salmon like the luxury that it should be—to be bought wild, at great expense, and only in season.

Oven-Steamed Salmon with Lentils and Sun-Dried Tomatoes

Makes 4 servings

■ VEGETARIAN ■ VEGAN ■ LOW-CALORIE ■ LOW-FAT
■ **HIGH-PROTEIN** ■ **GLUTEN-FREE** ■ **HIGH IN OMEGA-3S**

Lentils and salmon are a classic combination, popular in French bistros. Black beluga lentils are a nice choice because they stay intact and their color contrasts nicely with the salmon, but any type will do. In the traditional bistro version, the lentils might be cooked with bacon or a little sausage; here sun-dried tomatoes add a savory layer of flavor.

2 tablespoons extra virgin olive oil

1 medium onion, finely chopped

2 garlic cloves, minced

Salt

½ pound (1 heaping cup) lentils, preferably beluga, rinsed and picked over

2 ounces sun-dried tomatoes (dry, not oil-packed)

1 bay leaf

Ground black pepper

1½ pounds wild Alaska or Washington salmon fillet, either in 1 piece or in serving portions

Chopped fresh herbs, such as parsley, chervil, thyme

1. Heat the oil in a heavy saucepan or soup pot over medium heat. Add the onion. Cook, stirring, until tender, about 5 minutes. Add the garlic and a generous pinch of salt. Stir together for 1 minute, or until fragrant. Add the lentils, sun-dried tomatoes, bay leaf, and enough water to cover by 1 inch. Bring to a simmer, cover, and simmer for 25 minutes. Add salt and black pepper to taste and simmer for 5 to

10 minutes, or until the lentils are tender and aromatic. Taste and adjust the seasoning. Using tongs, remove and discard the bay leaf and the sun-dried tomatoes. Keep the lentils warm while you cook the salmon.

2. While the lentils are cooking, preheat the oven to 300°F. Cover a baking sheet with foil and lightly oil the foil. Place the salmon on top. Season with salt and black pepper. Bring 3 to 4 cups of water to a boil and pour into a baking pan or a roasting pan. Set the pan on the oven floor.

3. Place the salmon in the oven and bake until the fish pulls apart when prodded with a fork and white bubbles of protein appear on the surface, 10 to 20 minutes, depending on the size of the fillets. Remove from the heat.

4. Using a slotted spoon, spoon the lentils onto 4 dinner plates and place a serving of salmon on top. Sprinkle with the herbs, and serve.

Per serving: 501 calories, 49 g protein, 36 g carbohydrates, 7 g fiber, 18 g fat, 3 g sat fat, 94 mg cholesterol, 113 mg sodium

ADVANCE PREPARATION: You can make the lentils 2 to 3 days ahead and reheat.

Grilled Albacore with Romesco Sauce

Makes 6 servings

■ VEGETARIAN ■ VEGAN ■ **LOW-CALORIE** ■ **LOW-FAT**
■ **HIGH-PROTEIN** ■ **GLUTEN-FREE** ■ HIGH IN OMEGA-3S

Romesco sauce, the heady Catalan nut-thickened pepper sauce, goes well with grilled foods of all kinds. Other firm-fleshed fish, such as halibut, could also be used here.

6 6-ounce albacore tuna steaks

Salt and ground black pepper

1 to 2 tablespoons extra virgin olive oil, as needed

Romesco sauce (page 29)

Heat a ridged cast-iron grillpan over medium-high heat. Brush the tuna steaks with oil and season with salt and pepper. Grill 3 to 5 minutes per side, depending on the thickness and how well done you like your tuna. Serve at once, with a dollop of romesco sauce.

Per serving: 271 calories, 46 g protein, 3 g carbohydrates, 1 g fiber, 5.5 g fat, 1 g sat fat, 0 mg cholesterol, 46 mg sodium

ADVANCE PREPARATION: Romesco sauce keeps for at least 5 days in the refrigerator.

Meal in a Bowl with Soba, Smoked Trout, and Spinach

Makes 4 servings

■ VEGETARIAN ■ VEGAN ■ **LOW-CALORIE** ■ **LOW-FAT**
■ **HIGH-PROTEIN** ■ GLUTEN-FREE ■ **HIGH IN OMEGA-3S**

With soba noodles in comforting stock, smoked trout, and lots of spinach, this really is a meal in a bowl. Smoked trout is an ingredient that you can keep on hand in your refrigerator and pull out for surprising dishes like this one. The main-dish soup makes a comforting family meal, but it's elegant enough to serve for a dinner party.

A small amount of smoked trout contributes a great deal of flavorful protein, as well as vitamin B_{12} and B_6, niacin, phosphorus, and selenium to this meal.

6 cups kombu dashi (page 90), chicken stock, or Vegetable Stock (page 67)

Soy sauce or salt

6 ounces Japanese soba noodles, cooked (see sidebar on page 312) and tossed with 2 teaspoons Asian sesame oil or canola oil

1 bag (6 ounces) baby spinach

½ pound smoked trout fillets, cut into four 2-ounce pieces

1 bunch scallions, thinly sliced, dark green parts kept separate

1. Bring the stock to a simmer in a saucepan or soup pot over medium-high heat. Taste and adjust the seasoning, adding soy sauce or salt to taste. If the noodles have been refrigerated, warm them by placing them in a sieve and dipping the sieve into the simmering broth. Distribute the noodles among 4 deep soup bowls. Add the spinach, trout fillets, and the light parts of the scallions to the stock. Cover and turn off the heat. Allow to sit for 3 minutes.

2. Set a piece of trout on top of the noodles in each bowl. Ladle in the soup, taking care to distribute the spinach and scallions, evenly. Sprinkle the dark green part of the scallions over each serving and serve.

Per serving: 309 calories, 19 g protein, 48 g carbohydrates, 5 g fiber, 7 g fat, 2 g sat fat, 41 mg cholesterol, 1,035 mg sodium

ADVANCE PREPARATION: The noodles can be cooked ahead and kept in the refrigerator for 3 days. The stock can also be made 1 to 2 days ahead.

Cooking Japanese Soba Noodles the Japanese Way

Japanese soba noodles are finer and more delicate than American-made brands and this "add water" method for cooking them works well. Bring 4 to 5 quarts of water to a boil in a large pot. Add the noodles gradually, so that the water remains at a boil, and stir once with a long-handled spoon or pasta fork to separate. Wait for the water to return to a rolling boil and add 1 cup of cold water. Allow the water to return to a rolling boil and add another cup of cold water. Repeat once more, and when the water comes to a boil again, the noodles should be cooked through. Drain and toss with a little sesame or canola oil if not using right away. The noodles can be refrigerated in a resealable plastic bag or in a covered bowl for 3 days.

Meal in a Bowl with Salmon, Shiitakes, and Peas

Makes 4 servings

■ VEGETARIAN ■ VEGAN ■ **LOW-CALORIE** ■ LOW-FAT
■ **HIGH-PROTEIN** ■ GLUTEN-FREE ■ **HIGH IN OMEGA-3S**

This meal in a bowl, like the preceding recipe, is both comforting and beautiful. Make it in the spring, when both wild salmon and fresh peas hit the markets.

Along with their hearty flavor, dried shiitake mushrooms contribute many micronutrients to this dish. Among them is lentinan, which is reported to be a great immune system booster, and a compound called eritadenine, which may have cholesterol-lowering properties.

1 ounce (about 10) dried shiitake mushrooms

6 cups kombu dashi stock (page 90), chicken stock, or Vegetable Stock (page 67)

Soy sauce or salt

1 pound fresh green peas, shelled

6 ounces Japanese soba noodles, cooked (see opposite page) and tossed with 2 teaspoons Asian sesame oil or canola oil

12–16 ounces wild Alaska or Washington salmon fillet without skin, trimmed of fat, and cut into 4 equal pieces

1 bunch scallions, thinly sliced, dark green parts kept separate

1. Place the dried mushrooms in a large bowl. Bring the stock to a simmer in a soup pot. Pour the hot stock over the mushrooms and let sit for 30 minutes. Drain through a cheesecloth-lined sieve set over the soup pot. Squeeze the mushrooms over the sieve. Slice the mushroom caps and discard the hard stems. Set aside.

2. Return the stock in the soup pot to a simmer. Taste and adjust the seasonings, adding soy sauce or salt as desired. Add the peas and simmer 5 minutes. If the noodles have been refrigerated, warm them by placing them in a sieve and dipping the sieve into the simmering broth. Distribute the noodles among 4 deep soup bowls.

3. Add the mushrooms, salmon, and light parts of the scallions to the simmering stock. Cover and turn off the heat. Allow to sit for 5 minutes without removing the cover. The salmon should be just cooked through. Leave for another 5 minutes if it is not.

4. Place a piece of salmon on top of the noodles in each bowl. Ladle in the soup, taking care to distribute the peas, mushrooms, and scallions evenly. Sprinkle on the dark green part of the scallions and serve.

Per serving: 372 calories, 26 g protein, 52 g carbohydrates, 6 g fiber, 7 g fat, 1 g sat fat, 47 mg cholesterol, 659 mg sodium

ADVANCE PREPARATION: The noodles can be cooked ahead and kept in the refrigerator for 3 days. The stock can also be made 1 to 2 days ahead.

Grilled Pacific Halibut with Mango Salsa

Makes 4 servings

■ VEGETARIAN ■ VEGAN ■ **LOW-CALORIE** ■ LOW-FAT
■ **HIGH-PROTEIN** ■ **GLUTEN-FREE** ■ **HIGH IN OMEGA-3S**

If you're wondering how to work more fruit into your diet, you might try using it as the base for a salsa. The sweet and spicy salsa accompanying the halibut goes beautifully with firm white fish. Make sure your mango is really ripe.

Halibut isn't the only fish that goes well with this fruity salsa. Try it with other sturdy white-fleshed fish such as mahi-mahi or Pacific cod.

1 large ripe mango

¼ cup finely diced jicama

2 serrano chile peppers, minced (wear plastic gloves when handling)

1 tablespoon finely chopped cilantro

1 tablespoon finely chopped mint

2 tablespoons fresh lime juice

Salt and ground black pepper

4 Pacific halibut fillets or steaks (6 ounces each)

2 tablespoons extra virgin olive oil

2 limes, cut into wedges

1. Cut down the broad side of the mango, slightly off center, from the stem end to the tip end. The knife should slide down the side of the pit. Repeat on the

other side, cutting as close to the pit as possible. Cut the flesh from the sides of the pit, following the curve of the pit. Lay each half on your cutting surface, skin side down, and score the flesh with the tip of your knife in a crosshatch pattern, down to but not through the skin. Turn the mango half inside out. The cubes will spread out, and it will be easy to cut them away from the skin. Then cut the cubes into very small dice.

2. Toss the finely diced mango in a bowl with the jicama, chile peppers, cilantro, mint, and lime juice. Season with salt, if desired. Cover the bowl and allow to sit for 1 hour while you prepare the grill.

3. Prepare a medium-hot grill (or heat an indoor griddle or grill pan). Season the halibut with salt and black pepper, and toss with the oil in a bowl. Place the fish on the rack directly over the coals and grill for 4 to 5 minutes per side, or longer depending on thickness. The fish should be opaque all the way through and you should be able to pull it apart with a fork, but it should not be dry.

4. Remove the fish to a plate or a platter. Serve with the salsa spooned partially over the fish, partially on the side, or spoon the salsa onto plates and set the fish on top. Garnish with the lime wedges.

Per serving: 296 calories, 36 g protein, 12 g carbohydrates, 2 g fiber, 11 g fat, 2 g sat fat, 54 mg cholesterol, 131 mg sodium

ADVANCE PREPARATION: You can make the mango salsa several hours ahead and keep it in the refrigerator.

Mussels Steamed in White Wine

Makes 4 to 6 servings

■ VEGETARIAN ■ VEGAN ■ **LOW-CALORIE** ■ **LOW-FAT**
■ **HIGH-PROTEIN** ■ **GLUTEN-FREE** ■ HIGH IN OMEGA-3S

This is the classic mussel preparation. The mussels are steamed in a little white wine, with some onion or shallot and garlic thrown in for seasoning. They release their own juices when they open, providing a delicious broth that you can soak up with crusty bread, or just eat by the spoonful. The dish is utterly simple, and always satisfying. Note that this is meant to be served as a main course; that's why so many mussels are called for in the ingredients. A green salad makes a nice accompaniment.

4–4½ pounds mussels, or about 16 per person

Salt or vinegar

2 cups dry white wine, such as sauvignon blanc or pinot grigio

1 small onion or 2–3 shallots (depending on the size), minced

2–3 garlic cloves, smashed but left whole

4 flat-leaf parsley sprigs

1 small bay leaf

6 whole peppercorns

½ teaspoon dried thyme or 1 teaspoon fresh thyme leaves

1–2 tablespoons unsalted butter (optional)

3 tablespoons finely chopped flat-leaf parsley

1. Inspect each mussel carefully and discard any that have opened or have cracked shells. Pull out the beards. If they are very sandy, brush with a toothbrush. Place in a large bowl, fill the bowl with cold water and rinse in several changes of water. Place the mussels in your sink or in a bowl large enough that they can be covered with water. Add 2 tablespoons of salt or vinegar and fill with water. Let sit for 15 minutes. Drain, rinse thoroughly, and

soak one more time in salted or vinegared water for 15 minutes. Rinse thoroughly again. The mussels should be cooked soon after purging, but if you have to hold them for 1 to 2 hours, place in a bowl, cover with a damp towel, and refrigerate.

2. Combine the wine, onion or shallots, garlic, parsley sprigs, bay leaf, peppercorns, and thyme in a large pot that will accommodate all the mussels. Bring to a boil over high heat and cook for 2 minutes. Add the mussels and cover tightly. Cook for 5 minutes, or until the shells have opened, shaking the pot once or twice.

3. Spoon the mussels into wide soup bowls, discarding any that have not opened up. (If they don't open up, that means they weren't alive and should not be eaten.) Strain the broth from the pot through a cheesecloth-lined colander set over a bowl. Add the butter (if using) to the broth. When the butter has melted, spoon the broth over the mussels. Sprinkle with the parsley and serve.

> **Per serving (based on 4 servings):** 328 calories, 31 g protein, 15 g carbohydrates, 0.5 g fiber, 6 g fat, 1 g sat fat, 72 mg cholesterol, 778 mg sodium

ADVANCE PREPARATION: The mussels should be eaten immediately.

VARIATION: CURRIED MUSSELS IN WINE SAUCE
Add $\frac{1}{2}$ to 1 teaspoon curry powder to the wine.

Mussels on the Half-Shell with Salsa Fresca

Makes 4 to 6 servings

■ VEGETARIAN ■ VEGAN ■ **LOW-CALORIE** ■ LOW-FAT
■ **HIGH-PROTEIN** ■ **GLUTEN-FREE** ■ HIGH IN OMEGA-3S

This is a beautiful way to present mussels. They're steamed and tossed with fresh tomato salsa. The mussels are then set in their shells with some of the salsa. If you're making a meal of these, you'll need the full 4 pounds of mussels called for in the recipe. If you're serving them as an hors d'oeuvre, you can cut the recipe in half.

For the salsa:

2 pounds ripe tomatoes, chopped

$\frac{1}{2}$ small red onion, minced, soaked in cold water to cover for 5 minutes, drained, rinsed, and dried on paper towels

2–3 jalapeño or serrano chile peppers, seeded and minced (wear plastic gloves when handling)

4 tablespoons chopped cilantro

1 tablespoon fresh lime juice or 1 teaspoon balsamic vinegar (optional)

Salt

For the mussels:

4 pounds mussels

Salt or vinegar

1 cup dry white wine, such as sauvignon blanc or pinot grigio

2 shallots or $\frac{1}{2}$ onion, finely chopped

4 garlic cloves, smashed but left whole

Chopped cilantro for garnish

1. To make the salsa: Combine the tomatoes, onion, chile peppers, cilantro, lime juice or vinegar (if using), and salt to taste in a bowl and set aside.

2. To make the mussels: Inspect each mussel carefully and discard any that have opened or have cracked shells. Pull out the beards. If they are very sandy, brush with a toothbrush. Place in a large bowl, fill the bowl with cold water, and rinse in several changes of water. Place the mussels in your sink or in a bowl large enough so that they can be covered with water. Add 2 tablespoons of salt or vinegar and fill with water. Let sit for 15 minutes. Rinse thoroughly and repeat. Rinse thoroughly again. The mussels should be cooked soon after purging, but if you have to hold them for 1 to 2 hours, place in a bowl, cover with a damp towel, and refrigerate.

3. Combine the wine, shallots or onion, and garlic in a large pot or wok and bring to a boil over high heat. Add the mussels, cover, and cook for 5 minutes, or until the mussels open, shaking the pot or stirring halfway through to redistribute the mussels. Remove the mussels to a bowl, using tongs. Strain the cooking liquid through a cheesecloth-lined colander into another bowl. Set aside.

4. Discard any mussels that haven't opened. Remove the mussels from their shells, and set the shells aside. Rinse the mussels very briefly to wash away any lingering sand.

5. Mix the salsa with 1 cup of the strained mussel cooking liquid in a large bowl. Taste and add salt if desired. Add the mussels and toss together, cover, and refrigerate for 1 hour or longer.

6. To serve, place the mussels on half-shells and spoon on some salsa. Arrange on a platter and garnish with the cilantro.

Per serving (based on 4 servings): 324 calories, 33 g protein, 23 g carbohydrates, 3 g fiber, 6 g fat, 1 g sat fat, 72 mg cholesterol, 821 mg sodium

ADVANCE PREPARATION: The cooked mussels can be refrigerated in the marinade for up to a day.

Spicy Steamed Mussels with Tomatoes

Makes 4 to 6 servings

■ VEGETARIAN ■ VEGAN ■ **LOW-CALORIE** ■ **LOW-FAT**
■ **HIGH-PROTEIN** ■ **GLUTEN-FREE** ■ HIGH IN OMEGA-3S

This Italian take on mussels steamed in white wine is a substantial dish. Serve it with pasta for a particularly filling meal, or with crusty bread for soaking up the delicious sauce.

4-4 ½ pounds mussels, or about 16 per person

Salt or vinegar

2 tablespoons extra virgin olive oil

1 small onion or 2-3 shallots (depending on the size), minced

2-4 garlic cloves, minced

1 can (28 ounces) diced tomatoes

1 teaspoon fresh thyme leaves or ½ teaspoon dried thyme

¼-½ teaspoon red-pepper flakes

Ground black pepper

1 cup dry white wine, such as sauvignon blanc or pinot grigio

Generous pinch of saffron (optional)

3 tablespoons finely chopped flat-leaf parsley

1. Inspect each mussel carefully and discard any that have opened or have cracked shells. Pull out the beards. If they are very sandy, brush with a toothbrush. Place in a large bowl, fill the bowl with cold water and rinse in several changes of water. Place the mussels in your sink or in a bowl large enough so that they can be covered with water. Add 2 tablespoons of salt or vinegar and fill with water. Let sit for 15 minutes. Rinse thoroughly and repeat. Rinse thoroughly again. The mussels should be cooked soon after purging, but if you have to hold them for 1 to 2 hours, place in a bowl, cover with a damp towel, and refrigerate.

2. Heat the oil in a large, lidded skillet over medium heat. Add the onion or shallots and a generous pinch of salt. Cook, stirring, until tender, about 3 minutes. Add the garlic. Cook, stirring, until fragrant, about 1 minute. Add the tomatoes (with juice), thyme, red-pepper flakes, and black pepper to taste. Bring to a simmer, reduce the heat to medium-low, and simmer, stirring often, until the mixture has cooked down and is very fragrant, 20 to 25 minutes.

3. Add the white wine and saffron (if using), and bring to a boil. Add the mussels, cover, and cook for 5 minutes, or until they open. Stir the mussels halfway through to make sure they are evenly exposed to the heat. As they open, remove to a bowl with tongs (discard any that have not opened up).

4. Taste the tomato sauce and season with salt if desired. Divide the mussels among 6 wide bowls. Add the parsley to the tomato sauce, spoon over the mussels, and serve.

Per serving (based on 4 servings): 382 calories, 33 g protein, 20 g carbohydrates, 2 g fiber, 13 g fat, 2 g sat fat, 72 mg cholesterol, 1,238 mg sodium

ADVANCE PREPARATION: You can make the tomato sauce several hours ahead, but purge the mussels shortly before you cook them.

Fish Couscous

Makes 6 to 8 servings

■ VEGETARIAN ■ VEGAN ■ LOW-CALORIE ■ LOW-FAT
■ **HIGH-PROTEIN** ■ GLUTEN-FREE ■ **HIGH IN OMEGA-3S**

Fish couscous is a great dish to make for a dinner party. You can get everything done ahead of time, and cook the fish in the spicy stew while you steam the couscous shortly before you serve. Don't let the long list of ingredients deter you; this is an easy dish to make. Use a sturdy white-fleshed fish such as Pacific, halibut, or you can opt for a flakier fish, such as Alaskan cod.

2 tablespoons extra virgin olive oil

1 large onion, halved and sliced

2 leeks, white and light-green parts only, sliced and well washed (optional)

6 garlic cloves, minced

2 teaspoons cumin seeds, ground

Salt

1 can (28 ounces) diced tomatoes

2 tablespoons tomato paste dissolved in $\frac{1}{2}$ cup water

$\frac{1}{4}$–$\frac{1}{2}$ teaspoon cayenne

2 tablespoons harissa plus additional for serving

2 quarts fish stock, chicken stock, or water

$\frac{3}{4}$ pound carrots, cut crosswise into thick slices (fat ends first halved lengthwise)

$\frac{1}{2}$ pound turnips, peeled and cut into wedges or large dice

1 can chickpeas, rinsed and drained

2 $\frac{2}{3}$ cups couscous, preferably whole wheat

2 pounds fish fillets, such as Pacific halibut, Pacific cod, or tilapia (from the U.S.), cut into 2-inch pieces

Ground black pepper

1 cup chopped flat-leaf parsley or cilantro, or a combination

1. Heat the oil in a large, heavy soup pot or Dutch oven over medium heat. Add the onion and leeks (if using). Cook, stirring, until tender, about 5 minutes. Stir in the garlic, cumin, and $1/2$ teaspoon salt. Cook together, stirring, until fragrant, about 1 minute. Add the tomatoes (with juice). Cook, stirring often, until the tomatoes have cooked down and the mixture is very fragrant, about 10 minutes. Stir in the dissolved tomato paste, cayenne, harissa, stock or water, carrots, turnips, chickpeas, and salt to taste, and bring to a simmer. Cover and simmer for 30 minutes. Taste and adjust the seasonings. Scoop out 1 cup of the broth.

2. Reconstitute and steam the couscous, following the instructions on page 204.

3. Season the fish with salt and black pepper and add to the simmering stew along with the parsley and/or cilantro. Simmer very gently for 5 to 10 minutes, until the fish is opaque and flakes when poked with a fork. Taste and adjust the seasonings.

4. Transfer the couscous to a wide serving bowl or directly to wide soup plates. Top the couscous with the fish, vegetables, and plenty of broth, and serve, passing harissa at the table.

> **Per serving (based on 6 servings):** 580 calories, 51 g protein, 65 g carbohydrates, 13 g fiber, 13 g fat, 2 g sat fat, 51 mg cholesterol, 1,077 mg sodium

ADVANCE PREPARATION: The stew can be made through Step 1 a day ahead. Return to a simmer and proceed with the recipe. The couscous can be reconstituted up to a day ahead, then steamed before serving.

Tuna Seviche with Avocado

Makes 4 to 6 servings

■ VEGETARIAN ■ VEGAN ■ **LOW-CALORIE** ■ LOW-FAT
■ **HIGH-PROTEIN** ■ **GLUTEN-FREE** ■ **HIGH IN OMEGA-3S**

I make this tuna seviche as much to showcase avocados as tuna. You can serve the seviche (or the tartare variation) as a starter or a light supper. Make sure not to allow the tuna to marinate in the lime juice for too long or it will turn grey.

1 pound albacore or yellowfin tuna

$1/2$ small red onion, cut into small dice

1 garlic clove, minced

1–2 serrano or jalapeño chile peppers, seeded and minced (wear plastic gloves when handling)

1 tablespoon capers, rinsed and drained

1 ripe medium avocado, cut into small dice

Salt and ground black pepper

$1/3$ cup fresh lime juice

$1/4$ cup extra virgin olive oil

$1/4$–$1/2$ cup chopped cilantro

Leaf lettuce, baby spinach or arugula, or radicchio leaves

1. Cut the tuna into $1/2$-inch dice and refrigerate while you prepare the remaining ingredients.

2. Place the onion in a small bowl and cover with cold water. Let sit for 5 minutes, then drain, rinse, and dry on paper towels.

3. Combine the onion, garlic, chile peppers, capers, avocado, salt, black pepper, and 2 tablespoons of the lime juice in a bowl. Toss together gently. Add the tuna to the bowl.

4. Stir together the remaining lime juice and the olive oil. Pour over the tuna, and toss the mixture

together. Season to taste with salt and black pepper. Cover and refrigerate for 15 minutes, stirring gently from time to time.

5. Just before serving, add the cilantro and toss together. Taste and adjust the seasonings. Line plates with the salad greens, spoon the seviche on top, and serve.

Per serving (based on 4 servings): 333 calories, 31 g protein, 6 g carbohydrates, 3 g fiber, 19 g fat, 3 g sat fat, 0 mg cholesterol, 104 mg sodium

ADVANCE PREPARATION: You can prepare the ingredients through Step 3 several hours ahead and refrigerate. Do not toss with the lime juice until 15 minutes before serving. Use leftovers as a filling for soft tacos.

VARIATION: TUNA TARTARE Omit the chile peppers. Substitute chopped fresh dill for the cilantro

Quinoa Salad with Lime Ginger Dressing and Shrimp

Makes 4 servings

■ VEGETARIAN ■ VEGAN ■ **LOW-CALORIE** ■ LOW-FAT
■ HIGH-PROTEIN ■ **GLUTEN-FREE** ■ HIGH IN OMEGA-3S

Although quinoa is not a grain that is commonly used in Asian cuisines, it lends itself well to Asian seasonings. This salad, with its gingery lime dressing, scallions, and cilantro, and a little bit of heat, makes a good side dish or a light lunch or supper. Vegetarians can enjoy it without the shrimp.

For the dressing:

¼ cup canola oil

2 tablespoons buttermilk

2 tablespoons fresh lime juice

1 tablespoon seasoned rice vinegar

2 teaspoons Asian sesame oil or walnut oil

1 teaspoon minced fresh ginger

1 small garlic clove, minced

Salt

Pinch of cayenne

For the salad:

¾ cup quinoa, cooked (page 185)

4 scallions, white and light-green parts only, thinly sliced

1 small cucumber, halved, seeded, and thinly sliced on the diagonal

¼ cup chopped cilantro

12–16 cooked medium shrimp, peeled

1. To make the dressing: Whisk together the canola oil, buttermilk, lime juice, vinegar, sesame

or walnut oil, ginger, garlic, salt, and cayenne in a small bowl or measuring cup.

2. To make the salad: Combine the quinoa, scallions, cucumber, and cilantro in a salad bowl. Toss with the dressing and divide among salad plates. Top each portion with 3 or 4 shrimp, and serve.

Per serving: 219 calories, 6 g protein, 11 g carbohydrates, 2 g fiber, 17 g fat, 1.5 g sat fat, 28 mg cholesterol, 78 mg sodium

ADVANCE PREPARATION: The cooked quinoa will keep for 3 to 4 days in the refrigerator. You can make the dressing and prep the ingredients for the salad a few hours ahead.

Poached, Shredded Chicken Breasts

Makes about 4 cups shredded chicken

■ VEGETARIAN ■ VEGAN ■ **LOW-CALORIE** ■ **LOW-FAT** ■ **HIGH-PROTEIN** ■ **GLUTEN-FREE** ■ HIGH IN OMEGA-3S

Shredded poached chicken breasts make a low-fat, high-protein staple with endless possibilities. I learned how useful they can be years ago when I was working on my cookbook Mexican Light. *They can fill a taco or an enchilada, bulk up a soup, a pasta, pizza, wrap, or sandwich. There's quite an array of salads you can make with poached, shredded chicken breasts as well. Opt for breasts on the bone if you can find them, because the resulting poached breasts retain more moisture than boneless chicken breasts.*

Please also seek out free-range organic chicken from small producers. It may be more expensive than chicken that is raised by the thousands in closed chicken houses, but you can make that chicken stretch. Commercially raised chicken is now routinely injected with a saline solution, I might add, so if you are concerned about your sodium intake, here's another reason for you to seek out chicken raised by small producers who care about your health, the chickens they raise, and the environment.

1 onion, quartered

2 garlic cloves, smashed but left whole

1 whole chicken breast on the bone, skinned and split, or 2 boneless, skinless chicken breast halves (1.3 to 1.5 pounds total)

$\frac{1}{2}$ teaspoon dried thyme or oregano, or a combination

1–1$\frac{1}{2}$ teaspoons salt

1. Combine 2$\frac{1}{2}$ quarts water, the onion, and the garlic in a large saucepan or pot, and bring to a simmer over medium heat. Add the chicken breasts and return to a simmer. Skim off any foam that rises, then add the dried herbs. Cover partially, reduce the heat to low, and simmer for 15 to 20 minutes, until the chicken is cooked through (cut one in half and check that the meat is not pink). Add the salt. Allow the chicken to cool in the broth if there is time.

2. Remove the chicken from the broth. When cool enough to handle, shred by pulling strips of the chicken off the top of the breast, pulling with the grain. It comes apart naturally into shreds. You should have about 4 cups of shredded chicken. Strain the chicken broth and refrigerate it and the shredded chicken separately overnight. The next morning, skim off and discard the fat from the broth. Freeze the broth in small containers. You can use this light broth in recipes that call for chicken stock.

Per 1-cup serving: 166 calories, 34 g protein, 1 g carbohydrates, 0 g fiber, 2 g fat, 0.5 g sat fat, 86 mg cholesterol, 386 mg sodium

ADVANCE PREPARATION: The shredded chicken will keep for 3 days in the refrigerator.

Chicken Kebabs

Makes 4 servings

■ VEGETARIAN ■ VEGAN ■ **LOW-CALORIE** ■ **LOW-FAT** ■ **HIGH-PROTEIN** ■ **GLUTEN-FREE** ■ HIGH IN OMEGA-3S

I can't think of a better use for chicken tenders than these succulent grilled kebabs. The results are unbelievably tender and juicy (as long as you don't overcook them). Serve the kebabs with basmati rice.

1$\frac{1}{2}$ pounds chicken tenders, cut into 1-inch pieces

Salt and ground black pepper

1–2 garlic cloves, halved

1 cup plain low-fat yogurt

1 teaspoon curry powder

Seeds from 2 cardamom pods, crushed (optional)

1 tablespoon canola oil

12 cherry tomatoes

1 large red or green bell pepper, cut into 1-inch squares

For the sauce:

1–2 garlic cloves , halved

$\frac{1}{4}$ teaspoon salt

1 cup Drained Yogurt (page 25)

$\frac{1}{2}$ teaspoon cumin seeds, lightly toasted and ground

2 tablespoons finely chopped fresh mint or dill

1. Season the chicken with salt and black pepper to taste. Mash the garlic and $\frac{1}{4}$ teaspoon salt to a paste

with a mortar and pestle. Place the yogurt in a 2-quart bowl and stir in the mashed garlic, ¼ teaspoon salt, the curry powder, cardamom (if using), and oil. Transfer half of the yogurt mixture to a second bowl. Add the chicken to one bowl and the tomatoes and the peppers to the other. Toss in the marinade. Cover and refrigerate for 1 to 3 hours. Meanwhile, if using wooden skewers, soak them in water for 30 minutes or longer.

2. To make the sauce: Mash the garlic and salt to a paste with a mortar and pestle. Stir into the drained yogurt, along with the cumin and the mint or dill. Set aside.

3. Prepare a hot charcoal grill or preheat a gas grill for 15 minutes. Thread the chicken onto skewers, alternating with the peppers and tomatoes. Do not jam the pieces together tightly, but leave a little space between so that the pieces cook evenly. Place on the hot grill. Grill for 5 minutes and turn over. Grill for another 2 to 5 minutes, or until cooked through but not dry. Remove from the grill and serve, with the yogurt sauce.

Per serving: 277 calories, 46 g protein, 12 g carbohydrates, 3 g fiber, 6 g fat, 1.5 g sat fat, 105 mg cholesterol, 567 mg sodium

ADVANCE PREPARATION: The chicken must be marinated for at least an hour and won't suffer if it's marinated for several hours.

Southwestern Chicken Salad

Makes 4 to 6 servings

■ VEGETARIAN ■ VEGAN ■ **LOW-CALORIE** ■ LOW-FAT
■ **HIGH-PROTEIN** ■ **GLUTEN-FREE** ■ HIGH IN OMEGA-3S

Mexico has been a great source of inspiration for me when it comes to making dishes with poached, shredded chicken breasts. Chipotle chiles add heat and smokiness to this mixture, which you can serve as a salad, or use to fill corn tortillas for soft tacos.

For the dressing:

¼ cup extra virgin olive oil

¼ cup buttermilk

2 to 4 tablespoons chicken broth, as needed

2 tablespoons fresh lime juice

2 tablespoons white wine vinegar

Salt and ground black pepper

1 small or medium garlic clove, minced

1 scant teaspoon cumin seeds, lightly toasted and coarsely ground

For the salad:

Poached, Shredded Chicken Breasts (page 322)

Salt and ground black pepper

4 large radishes, diced, plus 2 radishes, sliced

¼ cup chopped cilantro

2-3 chipotle chiles in adobo sauce, seeded and cut into thin strips

8 romaine lettuce leaves, cut in wide strips

12 cherry tomatoes, halved

1 small avocado, sliced

1. To make the dressing: Mix together the oil, buttermilk, 2 tablespoons of the chicken broth, the lime juice, vinegar, salt, black pepper, garlic, and cumin

in a bowl. Add 2 tablespoons more chicken broth if you want a thinner consistency.

2. To make the salad: Place the chicken in a large bowl and season to taste with salt and black pepper. Toss with the diced radishes, cilantro, chile peppers, and all but 2 tablespoons of the dressing.

3. Toss the lettuce with the remaining dressing and arrange on a platter. Top with the salad. Garnish the salad with the sliced radishes, cherry tomatoes, and avocado, and serve.

Per serving (based on 4 servings): 387 calories, 36 g protein, 9 g carbohydrates, 4 g fiber, 22 g fat, 3 g sat fat, 86 mg cholesterol, 536 mg sodium

ADVANCE PREPARATION: The poached chicken breasts will keep for 3 days in the refrigerator. You can assemble the salad through Step 2, leaving out the cilantro, several hours before you serve. Toss again with the cilantro before proceeding with Step 3.

Chicken Caesar

Makes 4 to 6 servings

■ VEGETARIAN ■ VEGAN ■ LOW-CALORIE ■ LOW-FAT
■ **HIGH-PROTEIN** ■ GLUTEN-FREE ■ HIGH IN OMEGA-3S

When you order chicken Caesar in a restaurant, you usually get a Caesar salad topped with dry slices of chicken breast. Here the moist shreds are bathed in the dressing with the lettuce, and it's another story altogether. Omit the coddled egg yolk if you prefer.

For the dressing:

1 small garlic clove

1 egg, optional

Salt and ground black pepper

1 anchovy, soaked for 5 minutes in cold water, then rinsed and drained on a paper towel

1 tablespoon fresh lemon juice

1 tablespoon wine vinegar or sherry vinegar

1 teaspoon Dijon mustard

1 coddled egg yolk (see sidebar on next page), optional

6 tablespoons extra virgin olive oil

For the salad:

1 head of romaine lettuce

Poached, Shredded Chicken Breasts (page 322)

1 cup garlic croutons (see note below)

1/3 cup (about 1 1/2 ounces) grated or shaved Parmesan

Chopped fresh herbs, such as flat-leaf parsley, chives, marjoram

1. To make the dressing: If using the egg, bring a small pot of water to a boil, slowly add the egg in its shell, and cook for 3 minutes. Transfer to a bowl of ice water, then carefully crack the egg and transfer the yolk to a small bowl. Discard the egg white.

2. Mash the garlic and a little salt to a paste with a mortar and pestle. Add the anchovy and mash with the garlic. Stir in the lemon juice. Add the vinegar, mustard, egg yolk, salt, and black pepper. Whisk in the oil.

3. To make the salad: Remove the tough outer leaves of romaine and discard. Wash and dry the remaining leaves. Tear into medium pieces and place in a salad bowl with the chicken, croutons, and 1/4 cup of the Parmesan. Add the dressing and toss together. Sprinkle on the herbs and remaining Parmesan, and serve.

Note: *To make garlic croutons, lightly toast slices of French or country bread. Remove them from the toaster and immediately rub with a cut clove of garlic. Cut into small squares or break into pieces.*

Per serving (based on 4 servings): 447 calories, 39 g protein, 10 g carbohydrates, 1 g fiber, 27 g fat, 5 g sat fat, 93 mg cholesterol, 721 mg sodium

ADVANCE PREPARATION: The shredded chicken will keep for 3 days in the refrigerator. The dressing can be made several hours ahead.

Indonesian-Style Chicken Salad

Makes 4 to 6 servings

■ VEGETARIAN ■ VEGAN ■ LOW-CALORIE ■ LOW-FAT
■ **HIGH-PROTEIN** ■ **GLUTEN-FREE** ■ HIGH IN OMEGA-3S

Peanuts and peanut butter are used in many Indonesian dishes, and I've always loved the deep, rich flavor. This spicy, refreshing chicken salad makes a great summer meal.

For the salad:

Poached, Shredded Chicken Breasts (page 322)

Salt and ground black pepper (optional)

1 bunch scallions, thinly sliced green parts kept separate

1/4 cup slivered fresh mint

1/4 cup chopped cilantro

1 small red bell pepper, cut into thin strips

1 serrano chile pepper, seeded if desired and finely chopped (wear plastic gloves when handling)

1 small cucumber (preferably Persian), halved lengthwise, then sliced into thin half-moons

2 cups mung bean sprouts or sunflower sprouts

For the dressing:

1/4 cup fresh lime juice

2 teaspoons finely chopped fresh ginger

1 garlic clove, minced

1 tablespoon Thai or Vietnamese fish sauce

Pinch of cayenne

3 tablespoons crunchy or smooth natural peanut butter

1/3 cup buttermilk

1 romaine lettuce heart, leaves separated, washed and dried

1/2 cup chopped dry-roasted peanuts

1. To make the salad: Place the chicken in a large bowl and season with salt and black pepper, if desired. Add the light part of the scallions, the mint, cilantro, bell pepper, chile pepper, cucumber, and sprouts. Toss together.

2. To make the dressing: Combine the lime juice, ginger, garlic, fish sauce, and cayenne. Stir together. Warm the peanut butter for 5 to 10 seconds in the microwave to soften it, and stir into the dressing. Whisk in the buttermilk. Taste and adjust the seasonings as desired.

3. Line a platter with the lettuce leaves. Toss the chicken mixture with the dressing and arrange over the lettuce. Sprinkle the peanuts and dark scallion greens over the top, and serve.

Per serving (based on 4 servings): 414 calories, 46 g protein, 21 g carbohydrates, 6 g fiber, 17 g fat, 3 g sat fat, 86 mg cholesterol, 559 mg sodium

ADVANCE PREPARATION: The shredded chicken will keep for 3 days in the refrigerator. The dressing can be made several hours ahead.

Red Chilaquiles with Chicken

Makes 4 servings

■ VEGETARIAN ■ VEGAN ■ **LOW-CALORIE** ■ LOW-FAT
■ **HIGH-PROTEIN** ■ **GLUTEN-FREE** ■ HIGH IN OMEGA-3S

Chilaquiles is a sort of top-of-the-stove tortilla casserole. In its simplest form it consists of a freshly made salsa into which you stir fried tortillas. Sometimes eggs are stirred in as well; sometimes chicken is added. I use microwave-toasted tortillas, or if I don't have the time for that, I use baked tortilla chips. Serve this right after you've stirred in the tortillas, because when they're not fried they'll quickly become soggy.

1 can (28 ounces) diced tomatoes, drained

1 jalapeño chile pepper or 2 serrano chile peppers, seeded for a milder sauce, and chopped (wear plastic gloves when handling)

¼ cup chopped onion, soaked for 5 minutes in cold water, then drained, rinsed, and dried on paper towels

2 garlic cloves, halved

1 tablespoon canola oil

½–1 cup water, chicken stock, or Vegetable Stock (page 67), as needed

Salt

Poached, Shredded Chicken Breasts (page 322)

8 corn tortillas, toasted (see sidebar) and coarsely broken up, or 2 cups baked tortilla chips

½ cup (2 ounces) crumbled queso fresco or feta cheese

2 tablespoons chopped cilantro

1 small red or white onion, cut into thick rings, soaked for 5 minutes in cold water, then drained, rinsed, and dried on paper towels

1. Combine the tomatoes, chile peppers, chopped onion, and garlic in a blender. Blend until coarsely pureed.

2. Heat the oil in a large, heavy nonstick skillet or a wide saucepan over medium-high heat. Add a drop of the puree. It should sizzle upon contact. Add all the tomato puree and cook, stirring, for about 5 to 10 minutes, or until the sauce darkens, thickens, and begins to stick to the pan. Add the water or stock if the mixture seems dry, and season to taste with salt. Reduce the heat to low and simmer, stirring often, for about 15 minutes, or until the sauce coats the front and back of a spoon. Taste and adjust the salt.

3. Stir in the chicken and heat through. Stir in the tortilla chips or pieces, stir together for about 30 seconds, and remove from the heat. Sprinkle the cheese, cilantro, and onion rings over the top, and serve.

Per serving: 422 calories, 43 g protein, 38 g carbohydrates, 6 g fiber, 10 g fat, 2.4 g sat fat, 95 mg cholesterol, 526 mg sodium

ADVANCE PREPARATION: The shredded chicken will keep for 3 days in the refrigerator. You can make this ahead, adding the chicken just before serving.

To Toast Tortillas in the Microwave

Cut the tortillas into 4 to 6 wedges. Place on a plate in the microwave and microwave for 1 minute. Turn the wedges over and microwave for 1 minute. If still not crisp and browned, microwave in 20- to 30-second zaps until crisp and browned. Remove from the microwave immediately and cool in a bowl or basket.

Soft Tacos with Chicken and Tomato-Corn Salsa

Makes 4 servings

■ VEGETARIAN ■ VEGAN ■ **LOW-CALORIE** ■ LOW-FAT
■ **HIGH-PROTEIN** ■ **GLUTEN-FREE** ■ HIGH IN OMEGA-3S

Tomato-corn salsa is substantial, almost like a salad. These light, fresh tacos make a wonderful summer meal.

1 ear of corn, steamed for 5 minutes

1 pound ripe tomatoes, finely chopped

1-3 jalapeño or serrano chile peppers, seeded if desired and minced (wear plastic gloves when handling)

¼ cup chopped cilantro

½ small red or white onion, finely chopped, soaked for 5 minutes in cold water, then drained, rinsed, and dried on paper towels

Salt

2 tablespoons fresh lime juice

Poached, Shredded Chicken Breasts (page 322)

8 corn tortillas

½ cup (2 ounces) crumbled queso fresco or feta cheese

1. Cut the kernels off the steamed ear of corn.

2. Toss together the tomatoes, chile peppers, cilantro, onion, and corn. Season to taste with salt and add up to 1 tablespoon of the fresh lime juice. Place the shredded chicken in a bowl and season with 1 tablespoon of the lime juice and salt to taste.

3. Heat the tortillas. Either wrap them in foil and heat in a 350°F oven for 10 to 15 minutes, or heat one at a time in a dry skillet over medium-high heat until flexible. Place 2 tortillas on each plate, top with the shredded chicken and a generous spoonful of the salsa, and sprinkle some cheese on top. Serve, passing any additional salsa at the table.

Per serving: 400 calories, 44 g protein, 41 g carbohydrates, 6 g fiber, 7 g fat, 2 g sat fat, 95 mg cholesterol, 481 mg sodium

ADVANCE PREPARATION: The shredded chicken will keep for 3 days in the refrigerator. The salsa can be assembled several hours before serving but don't add salt until shortly before serving or it will become too watery.

Meal in a Bowl with Chicken, Rice Noodles, and Spinach

Makes 4 to 6 servings

■ VEGETARIAN ■ VEGAN ■ LOW-CALORIE ■ **LOW-FAT** ■ **HIGH-PROTEIN** ■ **GLUTEN-FREE** ■ HIGH IN OMEGA-3S

This easy, comforting soup is a simplified version of a Vietnamese phô or a Japanese ramen (using rice sticks instead of Japanese noodles). Note that you'll have some cooked chicken left over.

> 1 smallish chicken, 3–3½ pounds, cut up and skinned, or the equivalent of chicken pieces, skinned
>
> 1 onion, quartered
>
> 1 piece fresh ginger, about 2 inches long, peeled and sliced
>
> 4 garlic cloves, smashed but left whole

1 teaspoon black peppercorns

Salt

2 tablespoons Vietnamese or Thai fish sauce, or soy sauce

½ pound dried rice noodles

1 bag (5–6 ounces) baby spinach or 1 bunch spinach, stemmed and washed

1 cup chopped cilantro

2 limes, cut into wedges

1. If possible, do this step a day ahead: Combine the chicken and 3 quarts water in a large, heavy soup pot and bring to a simmer. Skim off any foam and add the onion, ginger, garlic, peppercorns, and 1 teaspoon salt. Reduce the heat, cover partially, and simmer for 40 minutes. Skim occasionally. Remove the chicken pieces from the broth and allow to cool. Line a colander set over a bowl with cheesecloth and strain the broth into the bowl. When the chicken is cool enough to handle, shred coarsely, discarding the skin and bones, and refrigerate in a covered container until ready to serve the soup. Refrigerate the broth for at least 3 hours or, preferably, overnight. Lift off the fat from the surface and discard.

2. About 30 minutes before you wish to serve, remove the chicken and broth from the refrigerator. Bring the broth to a simmer and add the fish sauce or soy sauce and salt to taste. Taste and adjust the seasonings. Place the rice noodles in a bowl and cover with hot water. Let sit for 20 minutes, then drain.

3. Bring a large pot of water to a boil over high heat. Add the rice noodles and cook just until tender, 30 seconds to 1 minute (longer for some brands; consult the package for times). Drain and rinse with cold water. Set aside.

4. Just before serving, add the spinach to the simmering soup. To serve the soup, distribute the noodles among 4 to 6 large bowls. Top with the shredded chicken and a handful of the cilantro. Ladle the simmering broth, with some of the spinach, into each bowl over the chicken and noodles. Serve at once, passing the limes for guests to squeeze on as they wish.

Per serving (based on 4 servings): 468 calories, 45 g protein, 59 g carbohydrates, 6 g fat, 1.4 g sat fat, 130 mg cholesterol, 528 mg sodium

ADVANCE PREPARATION: The broth can (and should) be made the day before you make the soup. It can be made up to 2 to 3 days ahead.

Turkey Burgers

Makes 4

■ VEGETARIAN ■ VEGAN ■ **LOW-CALORIE** ■ **LOW-FAT**
■ **HIGH-PROTEIN** ■ GLUTEN-FREE ■ HIGH IN OMEGA-3S

Turkey burgers are a lot leaner than hamburgers, but they can be dry and dull. I moisten these by adding some ketchup and a little bit of grated onion to the ground turkey, and this makes all the difference in the world. Make the patties thin so that they resemble burgers. Be sure to buy lean ground turkey; if the package doesn't specify this, you might as well be cooking hamburger meat.

½ medium onion

1 pound lean ground turkey

2 tablespoons ketchup

1 tablespoon Worcestershire sauce

¾ teaspoon salt

Ground black pepper

1 tablespoon canola oil, or use cooking spray

4 whole wheat hamburger buns

Accompaniments:

Sliced tomato

Sliced onion

Iceberg lettuce

Pickles

Sliced red bell pepper

Ketchup and mustard

1. Grate the onion on the fine holes of a grater. You should have about 2 tablespoons grated onion (and a lot of juice, which you can discard). Place in a bowl with the ground turkey, ketchup, Worcestershire sauce, salt, and black pepper. Mix together well using a fork. Shape into 4 patties (the mixture will be quite moist) and press the patties into ½-inch-thick rounds.

2. Heat the oil in a nonstick griddle or a large non-stick skillet over medium-high heat. When you can feel the heat when you hold your hand above it, add the patties and cook for 5 minutes on each side. If the patties are thicker than ½ inch, increase the time. Serve on buns, with the accompaniments of your choice.

Per serving: 281 calories, 32 g protein, 26 g carbohydrates, 3 g fiber, 7 g fat, 1 g sat fat, 45 mg cholesterol, 832 mg sodium

ADVANCE PREPARATION: You can make the turkey burger mix, shape it into patties, wrap in plastic, and freeze for 2 to 3 months. Thaw as needed. The raw mixture will keep for a day in the refrigerator, if it does not exceed the original use-by date on the meat's package.

Szechuan Braised Tofu with Ground Turkey and Broccoli

Makes 4 servings

■ VEGETARIAN ■ VEGAN ■ **LOW-CALORIE** ■ **LOW-FAT**
■ **HIGH-PROTEIN** ■ GLUTEN-FREE ■ HIGH IN OMEGA-3S

This is inspired by a standard Szechuan dish, Mapo Doufu, which is tofu braised with pork. Mapo Doufu is on every Szechuan restaurant menu. It used to drive me crazy when I was a vegetarian, because menus loosely translated the dish as "braised tofu." I would order it, only to find out about the pork when the dish arrived at the table. I decided to substitute ground light turkey for the pork butt, because there's less saturated fat in the turkey and it's easier to find. You need very little and you can use what's left over for Turkey Burgers (previous page). I've also added broccoli to the mixture so that you can have your protein and vegetables in one spicy dish.

1 bunch of broccoli, broken into florets, the florets sliced about ½ inch thick

Salt

¾ pound firm tofu

¾ cup water or chicken stock

2 tablespoons soy sauce

1½ tablespoons rice wine or dry sherry

1 tablespoon Chinese or Thai chile sauce

½ teaspoon sugar

2 tablespoons peanut, vegetable, or canola oil

4 large garlic cloves, minced

1 tablespoon minced fresh ginger

2 scallions, minced, dark green parts kept separate

¼ pound ground white turkey

¼–½ teaspoon ground Szechuan peppercorns

2 teaspoons cornstarch dissolved in 1½ tablespoons water or chicken stock

1 tablespoon chopped cilantro

Cooked rice

1. Bring a large pot water to a boil over high heat. Fill a bowl with ice water. When the water comes to a boil, salt generously and add the broccoli. Boil for 1 minute and transfer immediately to the ice water. Drain and set aside.

2. Blot the tofu dry with a clean dish towel or paper towels. For firmer tofu, wrap in a clean dish towel and place under a cutting board while you prepare the remaining ingredients, then cut into $1/2$-inch dice. If you don't press the tofu, cut into $1/2$-inch dice and place in a sieve while you prepare the other ingredients.

3. Stir together the water or stock, soy sauce, rice wine or sherry, chile sauce, and sugar in a small bowl or measuring cup. Stir until the sugar dissolves. Set aside.

4. Heat 1 tablespoon of the oil in a large, heavy skillet or wok over medium-high heat. When a drop of water evaporates upon contact, add the tofu and cook, stirring, for 2 to 3 minutes, or until it begins to color. Add the remaining 1 tablespoon of oil and the garlic and ginger, and cook, stirring, for 15 to 30 seconds, or until fragrant. Add the light parts of the scallions and the ground turkey, and cook, stirring, for about 3 minutes, or until there are no traces of pink and the meat is fragrant. Add the chile sauce mixture and bring to a boil. Reduce the heat to low, cover, and simmer for 10 minutes, stirring occasionally. Stir in the peppercorns and the broccoli, increase the heat to medium-high, and cook, stirring, for 1 minute. Taste and adjust the seasoning. Add the dissolved cornstarch and stir until the mixture is glazed. Remove from the heat, transfer to a serving dish, sprinkle the dark green scallion parts and the cilantro over the top, and serve with rice.

Per serving: 315 calories, 20 g protein, 33 g carbohydrates, 3 g fiber, 11 g fat, 2 g sat fat, 11 mg cholesterol, 770 mg sodium

ADVANCE PREPARATION: The blanched broccoli will keep for 2 to 3 days in the refrigerator.

Acknowledgments

First and foremost, I would like to thank Mike Mason, my editor at the *New York Times*, for allowing me to create and shape the *Recipes for Health* series. Without him, this book might never have happened. I'd also like to thank the other editors on the Health page at NYTimes.com, who post the recipes daily, make corrections when there are corrections to be made, and work behind the scenes to make the Health section the wonderful resource it is.

A huge thanks goes to photographer Andrew Scrivani, who makes all the food look so inviting, week after week on NYTimes.com, and page after page in this book.

Thanks to my editor at Rodale, Pam Krauss. What a pleasure and an honor it has been to work with you on this project. Thanks also to designer Christina Gaugler, publicist Olivia Baniuszewicz, and social media guru Sasha Smith.

As always, a big thanks to my agent, Angela Miller.

I'm particularly grateful to my devoted readers. You are the ones who inspire me to work tirelessly to give you new, healthful recipes every week.

My son Liam gets kudos for not complaining too much about never getting the same thing twice for dinner (or hardly ever), as dinner is usually the product of the day's recipe tests.

Finally, I'd like to thank my friends and colleagues Clifford A. Wright and Diane Kochilas, whose Mediterranean recipes I turn to again and again for inspiration.

Special Dietary Index

Boldfaced page references indicate photographs.

General Index

Underscored page references indicate boxed text or sidebars. **Boldfaced** page references indicate photographs.

✤ Your *Recipes for Health* column is one of the highlights of my week! —Carol N. ✤ Thank you for doing such a great job of bringing ease, health, and taste to the kitchen—your recipes are little, joyful, "That sounds amazing!" moments. —Luke P. ✤ I just wanted to let you know how much I appreciate your NYTimes recipes. I haven't tried one my husband and I have not liked. Your way of cooking—lots of dried beans, vegetables, olive oil, and cheese only to set off the main dish—is precisely the way I like to cook. Thank you. —Marie H. ✤ Thank you for such sophisticated, yet wholesome, healthy recipes. —Pat W. ✤ I have been a vegetarian since the age of 12 and often find it difficult to track down sophisticated vegetarian recipes that go beyond tofu stir-fry or homey comfort foods. So I really appreciate your *Recipes for Health* series for its focus on using vegetables creatively and elegantly. —Rae S. ✤ My boyfriend happens to be from Nice, France, and he has remarked many times on some of your Provençal dishes tasting just like—sometimes even better than—the ones his mother makes. You have brought much joy to the kitchen and dining table of our small California apartment! Thanks for sharing your incredible talents. I know these are recipes that will remain in my repertoire for a long time. —Stacey S. ✤ We love your recipes and can't imagine a day without Martha!!! —Marie B.

✦ I just want to say thank you, thank you, thank you. With a baby and cooking just for two, it's hard to make something simple but tasty . . . a lot of recipes have too many steps and the healthy ones usually just taste so-so. Yours are actually yummy! —Lee F. ✦ Just a note of appreciation for the many recipes of yours that I've captured from the NYTimes and for the cooking wisdom I've acquired from using them. If someone says, "Hey, I'm getting a bumper crop of zucchini in my garden," I say, "Let's ask Martha!" My friends and I have had many a fine meal, thanks to you, and we have all become better cooks as a result. Thanks again for sharing. —Gib A. ✦ Thank you for doing such a great job of bringing ease, health, and taste to the kitchen—your recipes are little, joyful, "That sounds amazing!" moments. —Luke P. ✦ Your *Recipes for Health* column is one of the highlights of my week! —Carol N. ✦ I regularly follow your recipes at NYTimes, and I have learned so much from them. Thank you for changing so many of our diets and minds! —Megan P. ✦ I just wanted to let you know how much I appreciate your NYTimes recipes. I haven't tried one my husband and I have not liked. Your way of cooking—lots of dried beans, vegetables, olive oil, and cheese only to set off the main dish—is precisely the way I like to cook. Thank you. —Marie H. ✦ Thank you for such sophisticated, yet wholesome, healthy recipes. —Pat W. ✦ I have been a vegetarian since